Fodor's 99

Los Angeles

The complete guide, thoroughly up-to-date

Packed with details that will make your trip

The must-see sights, off and on the beaten path

What to see, what to skip

Vacation itineraries, walking tours, day trips

Smart lodging and dining options

Essential local do's and taboos

Transportation tips

Key contacts, savvy travel advice

When to go, what to pack

Clear, accurate, easy-to-use maps

Books to read, videos to watch, background essays

Fodor's Travel Publications, Inc.
New York • Toronto • London • Sydney • Auckland
www.fodors.com

Fodor's Los Angeles

EDITOR: Amy McConnell

Editorial Contributors: Robert Andrews, David Brown, Steve Dolainski, Mark Ehrman, Jeanne Fay, Allison Joyce, Clark Norton, Megan Pincus, Lisa Oppenheimer, Heidi Sarna, Helayne Schiff, M. T. Schwartzman (Gold Guide editor), Dinah A. Spritzer, Bill Stern, Judith Babcock Wylie, Cindy Yorks

Editorial Production: Linda K. Schmidt

Maps: David Lindroth, *cartographer*; Robert Blake, *map editor*

Design: Fabrizio La Rocca, *creative director*; Guido Caroti, *associate art director*; Jolie Novak, *photo editor*

Production/Manufacturing: Mike Costa

Cover Photograph: Kit Kittle

Copyright

Special Sales

Fodor's Travel Publications are available at special discounts for bulk purchases for sales promotions or premiums. Special editions, including personalized covers, excerpts of existing guides, and corporate imprints, can be created in large quantities for special needs. For more information, contact your local bookseller or write to Special Markets, Fodor's Travel Publications, 201 East 50th Street, New York, NY 10022. Inquiries from Canada should be directed to your local Canadian bookseller or sent to Random House of Canada, Ltd., Marketing Department, 2775 Matheson Boulevard East, Mississauga, Ontario L4W 4P7. Inquiries from the United Kingdom should be sent to Fodor's Travel Publications, 20 Vauxhall Bridge Road, London SW1V 2SA, England.

PRINTED IN THE UNITED STATES OF AMERICA

10 9 8 7 6 5 4 3 2 1

CONTENTS

      Maps

ON THE ROAD WITH FODOR'S

WHEN I PLAN A VACATION, the first thing I do is cast around among my friends and colleagues to find someone who's just been where I'm going. That's because there's no substitute for a recommendation from a good friend who knows your tastes, your budget, and your circumstances, someone who's just been there. Unfortunately, such friends are few and far between. So it's nice to know that there's Fodor's *Los Angeles '99*.

In the first place, this book won't stay home when you hit the road. It will accompany you every step of the way, steering you away from wrong turns and wrong choices and never expecting a thing in return. It includes a wonderful, full-color map from Rand Mc-Nally, the world's largest commercial mapmaker. Most important of all, it's written and assiduously updated by the kind of people you *would* hit up for travel tips if you knew them. They're as choosy as your pickiest friend, except they've probably seen a lot more of Los Angeles. In these pages, they don't send you chasing down every town and sight in Los Angeles but have instead selected the best ones, the ones that are worthy of your time and money. To make it easy for you to put it all together in the time you have, they've created itineraries and neighborhood tours that you can mix and match in a snap. Just tear out the map at the perforation, and join us on the road in Los Angeles.

About Our Writers

Our success in helping to make your trip the best of all possible vacations is a credit to the hard work of our extraordinary writers.

Having lived in Los Angeles for more than 20 years and written about the city for regional and national magazines such as *Westways* and *Travel Holiday*, **Stephen Dolainski** is an expert on exploring L.A. In addition to his magazine writing, Stephen is the author of the book *Romantic Days and Nights in Los Angeles*.

Mark Ehrman has been covering the nightlife and society beat for the *Los Angeles Times* for six years. He also writes on a variety

of subjects for the *Boston Globe, Details, Playboy, Travel & Leisure,* and other publications.

Jeanne Fay, a former writer and researcher for *Buzz* magazine, swears that the West Coast is the promised land. A native New Englander, she visited Los Angeles many times as a tourist, fell in love with the city, and is now a proud L.A. resident. Drawing on her knowledge as both an insider and outsider, she shares her secrets about best beaches, hiking trails, and other outdoor activities, plus her expertise on side trips from L.A.

Allison Joyce specializes in dining reviews and recipe-related travel features in her role as features editor of *Westways* Magazine. She was formerly the managing editor of *Orange Coast,* the magazine of Orange County, and founding editor of *Orange County Woman.* Having lived in Orange County since 1980, she has compiled copious information on local breakfast joints and is currently conducting research on the best latte in the county.

A resident of Massachusetts, **Lisa Oppenheimer** has logged thousands of miles flying from coast to coast to write California travel features for *Car & Travel, Sesame Street Parents, Disney Magazine, The Robb Report,* and other national publications. A sleep-deprived mother, she relishes the plush rooms and relaxing poolside areas at L.A.'s many hotels.

Megan Pincus is both an old-timer and a newcomer to Orange County, having grown up in Irvine, then leaving in 1991, and finally returning last year. (She quickly reacquainted herself with her home territory by updating the Orange County chapter of Fodor's *Los Angeles '99*.) Megan has worked on the staff of *Orange Coast Magazine* and *Teacher* magazine, and is currently an associate editor at an educational publishing company in Brea, California.

A native New Yorker, **Bill Stern** now lives and dines in Los Angeles. Since 1981 he has been reviewing restaurants, including *The Los Angeles Times, L.A. Weekly, Buzz Weekly,* and *The L. A. Reader.* He also created the symposium "Breaking Bread: A Series of Forums on Food and Community in California, 1775–1995," which was held at the Los Angeles Central Library in 1995.

Cindy LaFavre Yorks, who has an unofficial black belt in shopping, has been covering shopping and related topics for 15 years. Her articles have appeared in national newspapers and magazines including *The Los Angeles Times, New York Daily News, The Chicago Tribune,* and *USA Weekend.*

We'd also like to thank Carol Martinez and Gail Pagala Hermano of the Los Angeles Convention & Visitors Bureau, and Leanne Lampe of the Pasadena Convention & Visitors Bureau.

Connections

We're pleased that the American Society of Travel Agents continues to endorse Fodor's as its guidebook of choice. ASTA is the world's largest and most influential travel trade association, operating in more than 170 countries, with 27,000 members pledged to adhere to a strict code of ethics reflecting the Society's motto, "Integrity in Travel." ASTA shares Fodor's devotion to providing smart, honest travel information and advice to travelers, and we've long recommended that our readers—even those who have guidebooks and traveling friends—consult ASTA member agents for the experience and professionalism they bring to your vacation planning.

On Fodor's Web site (www.fodors.com), check out the new Resource Center, an online companion to the Gold Guide chapter of this book, complete with useful hot links to related sites. In our forums, you can also get lively advice from other travelers and more great tips from Fodor's experts worldwide.

How to Use This Book

Organization

Up front is the **Gold Guide,** an easy-to-use section arranged alphabetically by topic. Under each listing you'll find tips and information that will help you accomplish what you need to in Los Angeles. You'll also find addresses and telephone numbers of organizations and companies that offer destination-related services and detailed information and publications.

The first chapter in the guide, Destination: Los Angeles helps get you in the mood for your trip. New and Noteworthy cues you in on trends and happenings, What's Where gets you oriented, Pleasures and Pastimes describes the activities and sights that make Los Angeles unique, Great Itineraries lays out a selection of complete trips, Fodor's Choice showcases our top picks, and Festivals and Seasonal Events alerts you to special events you'll want to seek out.

The Exploring chapter is divided into neighborhood sections; each recommends a walking or driving tour and lists neighborhood sights alphabetically, including sights that are off the beaten path. The remaining chapters are arranged in alphabetical order by subject (dining, lodging, nightlife and the arts, outdoor activities and sports, shopping, side trips, and Orange County).

In the Portraits chapter at the end of the book you'll find David Thomson's "Beneath Mulholland," from his acclaimed book of essays, *Mulholland Drive,* musing on L.A.'s paradoxical nature as seen through the metaphor of a famous road; and Judith Babcock Wylie's "It's Back to the Future for L.A." These are followed by suggestions for pretrip research, from recommended reading and audiotapes to movies on tape in which Los Angeles figures prominently.

Icons and Symbols

★   Our special recommendations
✕   Restaurant
🏨   Lodging establishment
⚠️   Campground
🐤   Good for kids (rubber duck)
☞   Sends you to another section of the guide for more information
✉   Address
☎   Telephone number
🕐   Opening and closing times
💲   Admission prices (those we give apply to adults; substantially reduced fees are almost always available for children, students, and senior citizens)

Numbers in white and black circles ③ ❸ that appear on the maps, in the margins, and within the tours correspond to one another.

Dining and Lodging

The restaurants and lodgings we list are the cream of the crop in each price range. Price categories are as follows:

For restaurants:

CATEGORY	COST*
$$$$	over $50
$$$	$30–$50
$$	$20–$30
$	under $20

per person for a three-course meal, excluding drinks, service, and 8¼% tax

For hotels:

CATEGORY	COST*
$$$$	over $175
$$$	$120–$175
$$	$80–$120
$	under $80

All prices are for a standard double room, excluding 14% occupancy tax.

Credit Cards

The following abbreviations are used: **AE**, American Express; **D**, Discover; **DC**, Diners Club; **MC**, MasterCard; and **V**, Visa.

Don't Forget to Write

You can use this book with the confidence that all prices and opening times are based on information supplied to us at press time; Fodor's cannot accept responsibility for any errors. Time inevitably brings changes, so always confirm information when it matters—especially if you're making a detour to visit a specific place.

Were the restaurants we recommended as described? Did our hotel picks exceed your expectations? Did you find a museum we recommended a waste of time? Keeping a travel guide fresh and up-to-date is a big job, and we welcome your feedback, positive *and* negative. If you have complaints, we'll look into them and revise our entries when the facts warrant it. If you've discovered a special place that we haven't included, we'll pass the information along to our correspondents and have them check it out. So send us your thoughts via e-mail at editors@fodors.com (specifying the name of the book on the subject line) or on paper in care of the Los Angeles editor at Fodor's, 201 East 50th Street, New York, New York 10022. In the meantime, have a wonderful trip!

Karen Cure
Editorial Director

Los Angeles

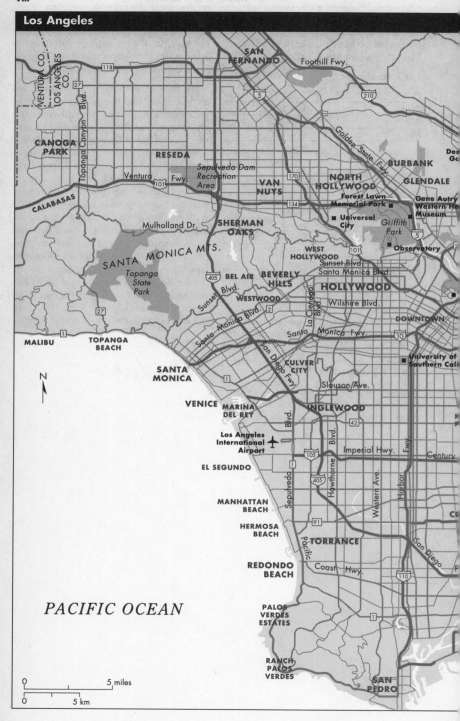

SAN FERNANDO

Foothill Fwy.

VENTURA CO.
LOS ANGELES CO.

118

5

210

CANOGA PARK

RESEDA

Golden State Fwy.

BURBANK

Des Go

GLENDALE

Sepulveda Dam Recreation Area

VAN NUYS

170

NORTH HOLLYWOOD

Gene Autry Western He Museum

Ventura Fwy.

101

134

Forest Lawn Memorial Park

CALABASAS

Mulholland Dr.

SHERMAN OAKS

Universal City

Griffith Park

5

2

Topanga Canyon Blvd.

SANTA MONICA MTS.

WEST HOLLYWOOD

Sunset Blvd.
Santa Monica Blvd.

Observatory

Topanga State Park

BEL AIR

405

Sunset Blvd.

BEVERLY HILLS

La Cienega Blvd.

HOLLYWOOD

27

WESTWOOD

2

Wilshire Blvd.

DOWNTOWN

MALIBU

TOPANGA BEACH

Santa Monica Blvd.

Santa Monica Fwy.

10

1

SANTA MONICA

San Diego Fwy.

CULVER CITY

University of Southern Cali

N

VENICE

MARINA DEL REY

Slauson Ave.

INGLEWOOD

42

Los Angeles International Airport

Sepulveda Blvd.

105

Hawthorne Blvd.

Imperial Hwy.

Western Ave.

Harbor Fwy.

Century

EL SEGUNDO

1

405

MANHATTAN BEACH

91

HERMOSA BEACH

TORRANCE

Co

REDONDO BEACH

Pacific Coast Hwy.

San Diego Fwy.

110

PACIFIC OCEAN

PALOS VERDES ESTATES

1

RANCH PALOS VERDES

SAN PEDRO

0 ___ 5 miles

0 ___ 5 km

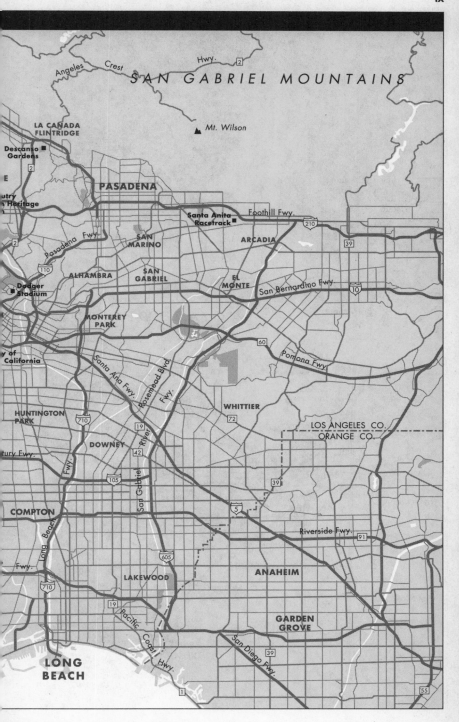

Southern California

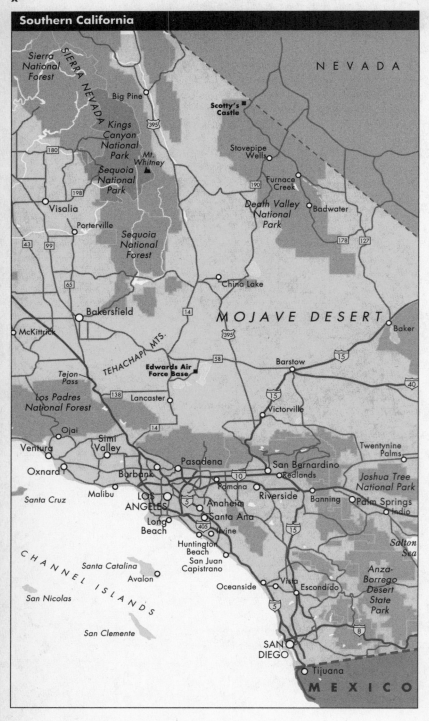

Sierra
National
Forest

SIERRA NEVADA

Big Pine

Scotty's
Castle

NEVADA

395

Kings
Canyon
National
Park

Stovepipe
Wells

180

Mt.
Whitney ▲

Sequoia
National
Park

190

Furnace
Creek

Death Valley
National
Park

Badwater

198

Visalia

Porterville

Sequoia
National
Forest

178   127

43   99

65

China Lake

Bakersfield

14

MOJAVE DESERT

McKittrick

395

Baker

TEHACHAPI MTS.

58

15

Tejon
Pass

Edwards Air
Force Base

Barstow

40

Los Padres
National Forest

138   Lancaster

15

Victorville

Ojai

14

Twentynine
Palms

Ventura

Simi
Valley

Pasadena

San Bernardino

Joshua Tree
National
Park

Oxnard

Burbank

10

Redlands

Malibu

Pomona

Riverside

Banning

Palm Springs

Santa Cruz

LOS
ANGELES

5

Anaheim

Indio

Long
Beach

405

Santa Ana

Irvine

15

Salton
Sea

CHANNEL ISLANDS

Santa Catalina

Huntington
Beach

San Juan
Capistrano

Anza-
Borrego
Desert
State
Park

San Nicolas

Avalon

Oceanside

Vista

Escondido

San Clemente

5

8

SAN
DIEGO

Tijuana

MEXICO

SMART TRAVEL TIPS A TO Z

*Basic Information on Traveling in Los Angeles,
Savvy Tips to Make Your Trip a Breeze, and
Companies and Organizations to Contact*

AIR TRAVEL

BOOKING YOUR FLIGHT

Price is just one factor to consider when booking a flight: frequency of service and even a carrier's safety record are often just as important. Major airlines offer the greatest number of departures. Smaller airlines—including regional and no-frills airlines—usually have a limited number of flights daily. On the other hand, so-called low-cost airlines usually are cheaper, and their fares impose fewer restrictions, such as advance-purchase requirements. Safety-wise, low-cost carriers as a group have a good history—about equal to that of major carriers.

When you book, **look for nonstop flights** and **remember that "direct" flights stop at least once.** Try to **avoid connecting flights,** which require a change of plane. Two airlines may jointly operate a connecting flight, so ask if your airline operates every segment.

Ask your airline if it offers electronic ticketing, which eliminates all paperwork. There's no ticket to pick up or misplace. You go directly to the gate and give the agent your confirmation number.

CARRIERS

➤ MAJOR AIRLINES: **America West**(☎ 800/235–9292). **American**(☎ 800/433–7300). **British Airways**(☎ 800/247–9297). **Continental**(☎ 800/231–0856). **Delta**(☎ 800/241–4141). **Japan Air Lines**(☎ 800/525–3663). **Northwest**(☎ 800/225–2525). **TWA** (☎ 800/892–4141).**United Airlines** (☎ 800/538–2929). **USAirways** (☎ 800/428–4322).

➤ SMALLER AIRLINES: **Alaska Airlines** (☎ 800/426–0333). **Carnival Air Lines** (☎ 800/824–7386). **Midwest**

Express (☎ 800/452–2022). **Reno Air** (☎ 800/736–6247). **Southwest** (☎ 800/435–9792).

➤ FROM THE U.K.: **American** (☎ 0345/789–789). **British Airways** (☎ 0345/222–111). **Delta** (☎ 0800/414–767). **United** (☎ 0800/888–555). **Virgin Atlantic** (☎ 01293/747–747).

CONSOLIDATORS

Consolidators buy tickets for scheduled international flights at reduced rates from the airlines, then sell them at prices that beat the best fare available directly from the airlines. Sometimes you can even get your money back if you need to return the ticket. Carefully read the fine print detailing penalties for changes and cancellations, and **confirm your consolidator reservation with the airline.**

➤ CONSOLIDATORS: **Cheap Tickets** (☎ 800/377–1000). **Up & Away Travel** (☎ 212/889–2345). **Discount Travel Network** (☎ 800/576–1600). **Unitravel** (☎ 800/325–2222). **World Travel Network** (☎ 800/409–6753).

COURIERS

When you fly as a courier, you trade your checked-luggage space for a ticket deeply subsidized by a courier service. It's all legitimate, but there are restrictions: You can usually book your flight only a week or two in advance, your length of stay may be set for a certain number of days, and you probably won't be able to book a companion on the same flight.

Courier companies in the U.S. deal only with travel from the U.S. round-trip to international destinations. Each country has its own laws governing the regulation of courier travel from their respective countries to the U.S. The best bet for non–U.S. readers of this guide is to check your local phone directories, contact your local travel agents, and search budget-travel magazines for information on courier flights to the U.S.

CUTTING COSTS

The least-expensive airfares to Los Angeles are priced for round-trip travel and usually must be purchased in advance. It's smart to **call a number of airlines, and when you are quoted a good price, book it on the spot**—the same fare may not be available the next day. Airlines generally allow you to change your return date for a fee. If you don't use your ticket, you can apply the cost toward the purchase of a new ticket, again for a small charge. However, most low-fare tickets are nonrefundable. To get the lowest airfare, **check different routings.** Compare prices of flights to and from different airports if your destination or home city has more than one gateway. Also price off-peak flights, which may be significantly less expensive.

When flying within the U.S., **plan to stay over a Saturday night** and **travel during the middle of the week** to get the lowest fare. These low fares are usually priced for round-trip travel and are nonrefundable. You can, however, change your return date for a fee ($75 on most major airlines).

Travel agents, especially those who specialize in finding the lowest fares (☞ Discounts & Deals, *below*), can be especially helpful when booking a plane ticket. When you're quoted a price, **ask your agent if the price is likely to get any lower.** Good agents know the seasonal fluctuations of airfares and can usually anticipate a sale or fare war. However, waiting can be risky: The fare could go *up* as seats become scarce, and you may wait so long that your preferred flight sells out. A wait-and-see strategy works best if your plans are flexible. If you must arrive and depart on certain dates, don't delay.

CHECK IN & BOARDING

Airlines routinely overbook planes, assuming that not everyone with a ticket will show up, but sometimes everyone does. When that happens, airlines ask for volunteers to give up

their seats. In return these volunteers usually get a certificate for a free flight and are rebooked on the next flight out. If there are not enough volunteers, the airline must choose who will be denied boarding. The first to get bumped are passengers who checked in late and those flying on discounted tickets, so **get to the gate and check in as early as possible,** especially during peak periods.

Although the trend on international flights is to drop reconfirmation requirements, many airlines still ask you to reconfirm each leg of your international itinerary. Failure to do so may result in your reservation being canceled.

Always **bring a government-issued photo ID to the airport.** You may be asked to show it before you are allowed to check in.

ENJOYING THE FLIGHT

For better service, **fly smaller or regional carriers,** which often have higher passenger-satisfaction ratings.

For more legroom, **request an emergency-aisle seat.** Don't sit in the row in front of the emergency aisle or in front of a bulkhead, where seats may not recline.

FLYING TIMES

Nonstop flights from New York to Los Angeles take about six hours and, with the three-hour time change, it is possible to leave JFK by 8 AM and be in L.A. by 11 AM. Some flights may require a midway stop, making the total excursion between 7½ to 8½ hours. Many of the flights out of Chicago are nonstop with a duration of four hours.

HOW TO COMPLAIN

If your baggage goes astray or your flight goes awry, complain right away. Most carriers require that you **file a claim immediately.**

➤ AIRLINE COMPLAINTS: U.S. Department of Transportation **Aviation Consumer Protection Division** (✉ C-75, Room 4107, Washington, DC 20590, ☎ 202/366–2220). **Federal Aviation Administration Consumer Hotline** (☎ 800/322–7873).

AIRPORTS & TRANSFERS

AIRPORTS

The major gateway to L.A. is Los Angeles International Airport, commonly called LAX. Departures are from the upper level and arrivals on the lower level. LAX is serviced by more than 85 major airlines (including all the carriers listed below) and is the third-largest airport in the world in terms of passenger traffic. Ontario International Airport, located about 35 mi east of Los Angeles, serves the San Bernardino–Riverside area. Air servers include Alaska Airlines, American, America West, Continental, Delta, Northwest, SkyWest, Southwest, TWA, United, and US Air Express. Airlines at Long Beach Airport, located at the southern tip of Los Angeles County, include American, America West, and Sunjet International. Burbank/Glendale/Pasadena Airport serves the San Fernando Valley with commuter and some longer flights. Alaska Airlines, American, America West, SkyWest, Southwest, and United Airlines are among those represented. John Wayne Airport Orange County, is served by Alaska Airlines, American, American Eagle, America West, Continental, Delta, Northwest, Reno, SkyWest, Southwest, TWA, United, United Express, and US Airways.

➤ AIRPORT INFORMATION: **Los Angeles International Airport (LAX)** (☎ 562/646–5252). **Ontario International Airport** (☎ 909/937–2700). **Long Beach Airport** (☎ 562/570–2600). **Burbank/Glendale/Pasadena Airport** (☎ 818/840–8847). **John Wayne Airport** (☎ 949/252–5006).

TRANSFERS

A taxi ride to downtown from LAX can take as little as 30 minutes, but substantially longer in traffic. Visitors should request the flat fee (about $30) to downtown or choose from the several ground transportation companies that offer set rates.

If you're driving from LAX to downtown L.A., take the San Diego Freeway (I-405) North to the Santa Monica Freeway (I-10) East to the Harbor Freeway (I-110) North until you hit downtown. To get to Beverly Hills, take the San Diego Freeway North, exit at Santa Monica Boulevard, and turn right. From Ontario Airport to downtown L.A., take the Harbor Freeway West to the San Diego Freeway North to the Harbor Freeway South; to Beverly Hills, take the Santa Monica Freeway West to the San Diego Freeway North, exit at Santa Monica Boulevard, and turn right. From Long Beach Airport to downtown L.A., take the San Diego Freeway North to Highway 710 North to the Golden State Freeway (I-5) North. To Beverly Hills, take the San Diego Freeway North to the Santa Monica Freeway East, and exit at Century Park. From the Burbank/Glendale/Pasadena Airport to downtown L.A., take the Golden State Freeway to the Harbor Freeway South. From the Burbank airport to Beverly Hills, take the Golden State Freeway South to the Ventura Freeway (Highway 134) West to the Hollywood Freeway (U.S. 101) North to the San Diego Freeway South, and exit at Santa Monica Boulevard. (To get to downtown and Beverly Hills from John Wayne Airport, see Chapter 9).

SuperShuttle's seven-passenger vans operate 24 hours a day between the airport and hotels. The trip to or from downtown hotels costs about $12. Call ahead to reserve pickup or use the SuperShuttle courtesy phone in the luggage area; the van should arrive within 15 minutes. **Shuttle One** features door-to-door service and low rates ($10 per person from LAX to hotels in the Disneyland/Anaheim area). **Airport Bus** provides regular service between LAX and the Pasadena and Anaheim areas.

Limo companies offer airport service to the L.A. Area, some charging a flat rate for the trip, others charging by the hour (minimum charges apply). Prices range from $75 for a sedan to $100-plus for stretch limousines. Many cars have bars, stereos, televisions, and cellular phones.

MTA also has limited airport service to all areas of greater L.A.; bus lines depart from bus docks at the Transit

Center attached to parking lot C. Prices vary from $1.35 to $3.10; some routes require transfers. The best line to take to downtown is Bus 42 ($1.35) or the express Bus 439 ($1.85). Both take about 70 minutes.

➤ SHUTTLES: **SuperShuttle** (☎ 310/782–6600 or 323/775–6600). **Shuttle One** (☎ 310/670–6666). **Airport Bus** (☎ 714/938–8900 or 800/772–5299). **Flyaway Service** (☎ 818/994–5554) offers transportation between LAX and the central San Fernando Valley every 30 minutes for $3.50.

From Ontario International, try SuperShuttle, **Inland Express** (☎ 909/626–6599), or **Southern California Coach** (☎ 714/978–6415). At John Wayne, **Airport Bus** (☎ 800/772–5299) is a good choice.

➤ LIMOUSINES: **Jackson Limousine** (☎ 323/734–9955). **A-1 West Coast Limousine** (☎ 323/756–5466). **Dav-El Livery** (☎ 310/550–0070).

➤ BUS: **MTA** (☎ 213/626–4455).

BIKES IN FLIGHT

Most airlines will accommodate bikes as luggage, provided they are dismantled and put into a box. Call to see if your airline sells bike boxes (about $5; bike bags are at least $100) although you can often pick them up free at bike shops. International travelers can sometimes substitute a bike for a piece of checked luggage for free; otherwise, it will cost about $100. Domestic and Canadian airlines charge a $25–$50 fee.

BUS TRAVEL

A bus ride on the **Metropolitan Transit Authority (MTA)** costs $1.35, with 25¢ for each transfer. **DASH** (Downtown Area Short Hop) minibuses travel around the downtown area, stopping every two blocks or so. There are six different routes with pickups at five-minute intervals. You pay 25¢ every time you get on. Buses generally run weekdays 6 AM–7 PM and Saturday 10 AM–5 PM; a few downtown weekend routes run on Sunday as well.

DISCOUNT PASSES

Weekly MTA buses cost $11 and are good for unlimited travel on all Metro buses and trains (biweekly and monthly passes are also sold). Passes may be purchased weekdays at Union Station (✉ 515 S. Flower St., ☎ 800/266–6883).

➤ ROUTES & SCHEDULES: **Metropolitan Transit Authority (MTA)** (☎ 213/626–4455). DASH (☎ 213/626–4455).

➤ GREYHOUND: The Los Angeles Greyhound (☎ 800/231–2222) terminal is at 1716 East 7th Street, on the corner of Alameda.

CAMERAS & COMPUTERS

EQUIPMENT PRECAUTIONS

Always **keep your film, tape, or computer disks out of the sun.** Carry an extra supply of batteries, and **be prepared to turn on your camera, camcorder, or laptop** for security personnel. Always **ask for hand inspection of film,** which becomes clouded after successive exposure to airport X-ray machines, and **keep videotapes and computer disks away from metal detectors.**

ONLINE ON THE ROAD

Ask about World Wide Web access at the business centers of major hotels, and at fax and copy centers, many of which charge an hourly rate to let you check your e-mail or surf the Web. Major fax and copy centers are often open 24 hours and on weekends. Another option is to log on at a cyber café, where tabletop computers allow you to log on while sipping coffee or listening to live jazz. Whether or not you have e-mail at home, you can **arrange to have a free, temporary e-mail address** from several services, including one available at www.hotmail.com. (The site explains how to apply for an address.)

TRAVEL PHOTOGRAPHY

➤ PHOTO HELP: Kodak Information Center (☎ 800/242–2424). *Kodak Guide to Shooting Great Travel Pictures,* available in bookstores or from Fodor's Travel Publications (☎ 800/533–6478; $16.50 plus $4 shipping).

CAR RENTAL

In Los Angeles, it's not a question of whether wheels are a hindrance or a convenience: They're a necessity.

More than 35 major companies and dozens of local rental companies serve a steady demand for cars at Los Angeles International Airport and various city locations.

Rates in L.A. begin at $29 a day and $125 a week for an economy car with air-conditioning, an automatic transmission, and unlimited mileage. This does not include tax on car rentals, which is 8¼%.

➤ MAJOR AGENCIES: **Alamo** (☎ 800/327–9633, 0800/272–2000 in the U.K.). **Avis** (☎ 800/331–1212, 800/228–4369 in Canada, 008/225–533 in Australia). **Budget** (☎ 800/527–0700, 0800/181181 in the U.K.). **Dollar** (☎ 800/800–4000; 0990/565656 in the U.K., where it is known as Eurodollar). **Hertz** (☎ 800/654–3131, 0990/996699 in the U.K., 03/9222–2523 in Australia, 03/358–6777 in New Zealand). **National InterRent** (☎ 800/227–7368; 0345/222525 in the U.K., where it is known as Europcar InterRent).

➤ LOCAL AGENCIES: **Budget, Beverly-Hills** (✉ 9815 Wilshire Blvd., Los Angeles, ☎ 310/274–9173).

CUTTING COSTS

To get the best deal, **book through a travel agent who is willing to shop around.** When pricing cars, **ask about the location of the rental lot.** Some off-airport locations offer lower rates, and their lots are only minutes from the terminal via complimentary shuttle. You also may want to **price local car-rental companies,** whose rates may be lower still, although their service and maintenance may not be as good as those of a name-brand agency. Remember to ask about required deposits, cancellation penalties, and drop-off charges if you're planning to pick up the car in one city and leave it in another.

Also **ask your travel agent about a company's customer-service record.** How has the company responded to late plane arrivals and vehicle mishaps? Are there often lines at the rental counter? If you're traveling during a holiday period, does a confirmed reservation guarantee you a car?

Be sure to **look into wholesalers,** companies that do not own fleets but rent in bulk from those that do and often offer better rates than traditional car-rental operations. Prices are best during off-peak periods.

➤ RENTAL WHOLESALERS: **Auto Europe** (☎ 207/842–2000 or 800/223–5555, FAX 800–235–6321). **Kemwel Holiday Autos** (☎ 914/835–5555 or 800/678–0678, FAX 914/835–5126).

INSURANCE

When driving a rented car you are generally responsible for any damage to or loss of the vehicle. You also are liable for any property damage or personal injury that you may cause. Before you rent, **see what coverage you already have** under the terms of your personal auto-insurance policy and credit cards.

For about $15 to $20 per day, rental companies sell protection, known as a collision- or loss-damage waiver (CDW or LDW), that eliminates your liability for damage to the car; it's always optional and should never be automatically added to your bill. Some states, including California, have capped the price of the CDW and LDW.

In most states you don't need a CDW if you have personal auto insurance or other liability insurance. However, **make sure you have enough coverage to pay for the car.** If you do not have auto insurance or an umbrella policy that covers damage to third parties, purchasing liability insurance and a CDW or LDW is highly recommended.

REQUIREMENTS

In Los Angeles you must be 21 to rent a car, and rates may be higher if you're under 25. You'll pay extra for child seats (about $3 per day), which are compulsory for children under five, and for additional drivers (about $2 per day). Non-U.S. residents will need a reservation voucher, a passport, a driver's license, and a travel policy that covers each driver, in order to pick up a car.

SURCHARGES

Before you pick up a car in one city and leave it in another, **ask about**

drop-off charges or one-way service fees, which can be substantial. Note, too, that some rental agencies charge extra if you return the car before the time specified in your contract. To avoid a hefty refueling fee, **fill the tank just before you turn in the car,** but be aware that gas stations near the rental outlet may overcharge.

CAR TRAVEL

Los Angeles is at the western terminus of I–10, a major east–west interstate highway that runs all the way east to Florida. I–15, angling down from Las Vegas, swings through the eastern communities around San Bernardino before heading on down to San Diego. I–5, which runs north–south through California, leads up to San Francisco and down to San Diego. These thoroughfares, along with a mix of local freeways, create a matrix of transportation routes that intersect at various points throughout the Los Angeles basin.

AUTO CLUBS

Members of the American Automobile Association (AAA) are entitled to free auto repair services, and can also pick up free road maps from local AAA offices.

➤ DOWNTOWN L.A.: **AAA** (✉ 2601 S. Figueroa St., ☎ 213/741–3686).

➤ HOLLYWOOD: **AAA** (✉ 5550 Wilshire Blvd., Suite 101, ☎ 323/525–0018).

➤ WEST L.A.: **AAA** (✉ 1900 S. Sepulveda Blvd., ☎ 310/914–8500).

EMERGENCY SERVICES

In most communities, **dial 911** in an emergency to reach the police, fire, or ambulance services. If your car breaks down on an interstate highway, try to pull over onto the shoulder of the road and either wait for the state police to find you or, if you have other passengers who can wait in the car, walk to the nearest emergency roadside phone and call the state police. If you carry a cellular or car telephone, *55 is the emergency number to call. When calling for help, note your location according to the small green mileage markers posted along the highway. Other highways are also patrolled but may not have

emergency phones or mileage markers. If you are a member of the AAA auto club (☞ *above*), look in a local phone book for the AAA emergency road-service number.

GASOLINE

At press time the price of gas was about $1.25 per gallon. Most gas stations are open late, and many large highways have 24-hour stations.

PARKING

Parking rules are strictly enforced in Los Angeles; illegally parked cars are ticketed and towed very quickly. Parking is generally available in garages or parking lots; prices vary from 25¢ to $2 per half hour, or a few dollars to $25 per day. In the most heavily trafficked areas, garage rates may be as high as $20 an hour, though prices tend to drop on weekends. Many restaurants offer valet parking for $2–$3 or an optional tip. Metered parking is also widely available; meter rates vary from 25¢ for 15 minutes in the most heavily trafficked areas to 25¢ for one hour. In some areas, metered parking is free on weekends or on Sundays.

ROAD CONDITIONS

Beware of weekday rush-hour traffic, which is heaviest from 7 AM to 9 AM and 3 PM to 7 PM. To encourage car sharing, some crowded expressways reserve an express lane for cars carrying more than one passenger.

ROAD MAPS

A good freeway map is a must in L.A. Basic maps can be purchased at most gas stations, convenience stores, and rest stops for about $3. Members of the Automobile Association can pick up free road maps at AAA offices (☞ *above*). If you plan to drive extensively, consider buying a *Thomas Guide,* which contains detailed maps of the entire county.

RULES OF THE ROAD

Adhere to speed limits, which are sign-posted along roads and highways. If there are no posted signs, the maximum speed is 25 mph on city streets and 65 mph on the freeways. A right turn on red after stopping is permitted unless a sign indicating otherwise is posted. All passengers must **wear seat belts at all times.** Pedestrians have the right of way.

CHILDREN & TRAVEL

CHILDREN IN LOS ANGELES

Consult Fodor's lively by-parents, for-parents *Where Should We Take the Kids? California,* available in bookstores or from Fodor's Travel Publications (☎ 800/533–6478), $17 plus $4 shipping. *L.A. Parent* (✉ Box 3204, Burbank, 91504, ☎ 818/846–0400) is a monthly magazine with events listings and resources, available free at supermarkets and museums.

➤ BABY-SITTING: **Sitters Unlimited** (☎ 800/328–1191) has franchises in and around Los Angeles.

FLYING

If your children are two or older, **ask about children's airfares.** As a general rule, infants under two not occupying a seat fly at greatly reduced fares or even for free.

In general the adult baggage allowance applies to children paying half or more of the adult fare.

Safety seats are advised for children weighing less than 40 pounds. Airlines, however, can set their own policies: U.S. carriers allow FAA-approved models but usually require that you buy a ticket, even if your child would otherwise ride free, since the seats must be strapped into regular seats. Airline rules vary, so it's important to **check your airline's policy about using safety seats during takeoff and landing.**

When making your reservation, **request children's meals or a free-standing bassinet** if you need them; the latter are available only to those seated at the bulkhead, where there's enough legroom. Remember, however, that bulkhead seats may not have their own overhead bins, and there's no storage space in front of you—a major inconvenience.

GROUP TRAVEL

When planning to take your kids on a tour, look for companies that specialize in family travel.

➤ FAMILY-FRIENDLY TOUR OPERATORS: **Families Welcome!** (✉ 92 N. Main St., Ashland, OR 97520, ☎ 541/

482–6121 or 800/326–0724, FAX 541/482–0660).

HOTELS

Most hotels in Los Angeles allow children under a certain age to stay in their parents' room at no extra charge, but others charge them as extra adults; be sure to **ask about the cutoff age for children's discounts.** Some area hotels, especially those in the vicinity of Disneyland, have children's programs.

➤ BEST CHOICES: **Loews Santa Monica Beach Hotel** (✉ 1700 Ocean Ave., Santa Monica, CA 90401, ☎ 310/458–6700 or 800/235–6397) has a supervised summer program for children. **The Westin Century Plaza Hotel and Tower** (✉ 2025 Ave. Of the Stars, Century City, CA 90067, ☎ 310/277–2000 or 800/288–3000) offers special check-in packages for little guests and takes great pains seé that families are well equipped.

CONSULATES

AUSTRALIA

Australian Consulate and Tourist Commission (✉ 2049 Century Park E., 19th Floor, Los Angeles, 90067, ☎ 310/229–4800).

CANADA

Canadian Consulate General (✉ 550 S. Hope St., 9th Floor, Los Angeles, 90071, ☎ 213/346–2700).

U.K.

British Consulate General (✉ 11766 Wilshire Blvd., Suite 400, Los Angeles, 90025, ☎ 310/477–3322).

CONSUMER PROTECTION

Whenever possible, **pay with a major credit card** so you can cancel payment or get reimbursed if there's a problem, provided that you can provide documentation. This is the best way to pay, whether you're buying travel arrangements before your trip or shopping at your destination.

If you're doing business with a particular company for the first time, **contact your local Better Business Bureau and the attorney general's offices** in your state and the company's home state, as well. Have any complaints been filed?

Finally, if you're buying a package or tour, always **consider travel insurance** that includes default coverage (☞ Insurance, *below*).

➤ LOCAL BBBs: **Council of Better Business Bureaus** (✉ 4200 Wilson Blvd., Suite 800, Arlington, VA 22203, ☎ 703/276–0100, FAX 703/525–8277).

CUSTOMS & DUTIES

When shopping, **keep receipts** for all of your purchases. Upon reentering the country, **be ready to show customs officials what you've bought.** If you feel a duty is incorrect, appeal the assessment. If you object to the way your clearance was handled, get the inspector's badge number. In either case, first ask to see a supervisor, then write to the appropriate authorities, beginning with the port director at your point of entry.

IN AUSTRALIA

Australia residents who are 18 or older may bring back $A400 worth of souvenirs and gifts (including jewelry), 250 cigarettes or 250 grams of tobacco, and 1,125 ml of alcohol (including wine, beer, and spirits). Residents under 18 may bring back $A200 worth of goods.

➤ INFORMATION: **Australian Customs Service** (Regional Director, ✉ Box 8, Sydney, NSW 2001, ☎ 02/9213–2000, FAX 02/9213–4000).

IN CANADA

Canadian residents who have been out of Canada for at least 7 days may bring in C$500 worth of goods duty-free. If you've been away less than 7 days but more than 48 hours, the duty-free allowance drops to C$200; if your trip lasts 24–48 hours, the allowance is C$50. You may not pool allowances with family members. Goods claimed under the C$500 exemption may follow you by mail; those claimed under the lesser exemptions must accompany you. Alcohol and tobacco products may be included in the 7-day and 48-hour exemptions but not in the 24-hour exemption. If you meet the age requirements of the province or territory through which you reenter Canada, you may bring in, duty-free,

1.14 liters (40 imperial ounces) of wine or liquor *or* 24 12-ounce cans or bottles of beer or ale. If you are 16 or older you may bring in, duty-free, 200 cigarettes and 50 cigars.

You may send an unlimited number of gifts worth up to C$60 each duty-free to Canada. Label the package UNSOLICITED GIFT—VALUE UNDER $60. Alcohol and tobacco are excluded.

➤ INFORMATION: **Revenue Canada** (✉ 2265 St. Laurent Blvd. S, Ottawa, Ontario K1G 4K3, ☎ 613/993–0534, 800/461–9999 in Canada).

IN NEW ZEALAND

Although greeted with a "Haere Mai" ("Welcome to New Zealand"), homeward-bound residents with goods to declare must present themselves for inspection. If you're 17 or older, you may bring back $700 worth of souvenirs and gifts. Your duty-free allowance also includes 4.5 liters of wine or beer; one 1,125-ml bottle of spirits; and either 200 cigarettes, 250 grams of tobacco, 50 cigars, or a combo of all three up to 250 grams.

➤ INFORMATION: **New Zealand Customs** (✉ Custom House, ✉ 50 Anzac Ave., Box 29, Auckland, New Zealand, ☎ 09/359–6655, ☎ 09/309–2978).

IN THE U.K.

From countries outside the EU, including the United States, you may import, duty-free, 200 cigarettes or 50 cigars; 1 liter of spirits or 2 liters of fortified or sparkling wine or liqueurs; 2 liters of still table wine; 60 milliliters of perfume; 250 milliliters of toilet water; plus £136 worth of other goods, including gifts and souvenirs.

➤ INFORMATION: **HM Customs and Excise** (✉ Dorset House, ✉ Stamford St., London SE1 9NG, ☎ 0171/202–4227).

IN THE U.S.

Non-U.S. residents ages 21 and older may import into the United States 200 cigarettes or 50 cigars or 2 kilograms of tobacco, 1 liter of alcohol, and gifts worth $100. Prohibited items include meat products, seeds, plants, and fruits.

➤ INFORMATION: **U.S. Customs Service** (Inquiries, ✉ Box 7407, Washington, DC 20044, ☎ 202/927–6724; complaints, Office of Regulations and Rulings, ✉ 1301 Constitution Ave. NW, Washington, DC 20229; registration of equipment, Resource Management, ✉ 1301 Constitution Ave. NW, Washington DC 20229, ☎ 202/927–0540).

DISABILITIES & ACCESSIBILITY

ACCESS IN LOS ANGELES

California is a national leader in making attractions and facilities accessible to travelers with disabilities. Since 1982, the state building code has required that all construction for public use include access for people with disabilities. State laws more than a decade old provide special privileges, such as license plates allowing special parking spaces, unlimited parking in time-limited spaces, and free parking in metered spaces. ID from states other than California is honored.

MAKING RESERVATIONS

When discussing accessibility with an operator or reservations agent, **ask hard questions.** Are there any stairs, inside *or* out? Are there grab bars next to the toilet *and* in the shower/tub? How wide is the doorway to the room? To the bathroom? For the most extensive facilities meeting the latest legal specifications, **opt for newer accommodations,** which are more likely to have been designed with access in mind. Older buildings or ships may have more limited facilities. Be sure to **discuss your needs before booking.**

TRANSPORTATION

➤ COMPLAINTS: **Disability Rights Section** (✉ U.S. Department of Justice, Civil Rights Division, ✉ Box 66738, Washington, DC 20035–6738, ☎ 202/514–0301 or 800/514–0301, TTY 202/514–0383 or 800/514–0383, FAX 202/307–1198) for general complaints. **Aviation Consumer Protection Division** (☞ Air Travel, *above*) for airline-related problems. **Civil Rights Office** (✉ U.S. Department of Transportation, Departmental Office of Civil Rights, S-30, ✉ 400 7th St. SW, Room 10215, Washington, DC, 20590, ☎ 202/366–4648, FAX 202/366–9371) for problems with surface transportation.

TRAVEL AGENCIES & TOUR OPERATORS

As a whole, the travel industry has become more aware of the needs of travelers with disabilities. In the U.S., the Americans with Disabilities Act requires that travel firms serve the needs of all travelers. Note, though, that some agencies and operators specialize in making travel arrangements for individuals and groups with disabilities.

➤ TRAVELERS WITH MOBILITY PROBLEMS: **Access Adventures** (✉ 206 Chestnut Ridge Rd., Rochester, NY 14624, ☎ 716/889–9096), run by a former physical-rehabilitation counselor. **CareVacations** (✉ 5019 49th Ave., Suite 102, Leduc, Alberta T9E 6T5, ☎ 403/986–6404, 800/648–1116 in Canada) has group tours and is especially helpful with cruise vacations. **Flying Wheels Travel** (✉ 143 W. Bridge St., Box 382, Owatonna, MN 55060, ☎ 507/451–5005 or 800/535–6790, FAX 507/451–1685), a travel agency specializing in customized tours and itineraries worldwide. **Hinsdale Travel Service** (✉ 201 E. Ogden Ave., Suite 100, Hinsdale, IL 60521, ☎ 630/325–1335), a travel agency that benefits from the advice of wheelchair traveler Janice Perkins.

➤ TRAVELERS WITH DEVELOPMENTAL DISABILITIES: **New Directions** (✉ 5276 Hollister Ave., Suite 207, Santa Barbara, CA 93111, ☎ 805/967–2841 or 888/967–2841, FAX 805/964–7344). **Sprout** (✉ 893 Amsterdam Ave., New York, NY 10025, ☎ 212/222–9575 or 888/222–9575, FAX 212/222–9768).

DISCOUNTS & DEALS

Be a smart shopper and **compare all your options** before making any choice. A plane ticket bought with a promotional coupon may not be cheaper than the least expensive fare from a discount ticket agency. For high-price travel purchases, such as packages or tours, keep in mind that what you get is just as important as what you save. Just because something is cheap doesn't mean it's a bargain.

CLUBS & COUPONS

Many companies sell discounts in the form of travel clubs and coupon books, but these cost money. You must use participating advertisers to get a deal, and only after you recoup the initial membership cost or book price do you begin to save. If you plan to use the club or coupons frequently, you may save considerably. Before signing up, find out what discounts you get for free.

➤ DISCOUNT CLUBS: **Entertainment Travel Editions** (✉ 2125 Butterfield Rd., Troy, MI 48084, ☎ 800/445–4137; $20–$51, depending on destination). **Great American Traveler** (✉ Box 27965, Salt Lake City, UT 84127, ☎ 801/974–3033 or 800/548–2812; $49.95 per year). **Moment's Notice Discount Travel Club** (✉ 7301 New Utrecht Ave., Brooklyn, NY 11204, ☎ 718/234–6295; $25 per year, single or family). **Privilege Card International** (✉ 237 E. Front St., Youngstown, OH 44503, ☎ 330/746–5211 or 800/236–9732; $74.95 per year). **Sears's Mature Outlook** (✉ Box 9390, Des Moines, IA 50306, ☎ 800/336–6330; $19.95 per year). **Travelers Advantage** (✉ CUC Travel Service, ✉ 3033 S. Parker Rd., Suite 1000, Aurora, CO 80014, ☎ 800/548–1116 or 800/648–4037; $59.95 per year, single or family). **Worldwide Discount Travel Club** (✉ 1674 Meridian Ave., Miami Beach, FL 33139, ☎ 305/534–2082; $50 per year family, $40 single).

CREDIT-CARD BENEFITS

When you use your credit card to make travel purchases you may get free travel-accident insurance, collision-damage insurance, and medical or legal assistance, depending on the card and the bank that issued it. American Express, MasterCard, and Visa provide one or more of these services, so **get a copy of your credit card's travel-benefits policy.** If you are a member of an auto club, always **ask hotel and car-rental reservations agents about auto-club discounts.** Some clubs offer additional discounts on tours, cruises, and admission to attractions.

DISCOUNT RESERVATIONS

To save money, **look into discount-reservations services** with toll-free numbers, which use their buying power to get a better price on hotels, airline tickets, even car rentals. When booking a room, always **call the hotel's local toll-free number** (if one is available) rather than the central reservations number—you'll often get a better price. Always ask about special packages or corporate rates.

➤ AIRLINE TICKETS: ☎ 800/FLY–4–LESS. ☎ 800/FLY–ASAP.

➤ HOTEL ROOMS: **Central Reservation Service (CRS)** (☎ 800/548–3311). **Hotel Reservations Network** (☎ 800/964–6835). **Quickbook** (☎ 800/789–9887). **Room Finders USA** (☎ 800/473–7829). **RMC Travel** (☎ 800/245–5738). **Steigenberger Reservation Service** (☎ 800/223–5652).

PACKAGE DEALS

Packages and guided tours can save you money, but don't confuse the two. When you buy a package, your travel remains independent, just as though you had planned and booked the trip yourself. Fly/drive packages, which combine airfare and car rental, are often a good deal. In cities, ask the local visitor's bureau about hotel packages. These often include tickets to major museum exhibits and other special events.

EMERGENCIES

➤ EMERGENCIES: **Dial 911** for police, ambulance, or fire.

➤ 24-HOUR EMERGENCY ROOMS: **Cedar-Sinai Medical Center** (✉ 8700 Beverly Blvd.,☎ 310/855–5000). **Queen of Angels Hollywood Presbyterian Medical Center** (✉ 1300 N. Vermont Ave.,☎ 213/413–3000).

➤ 24-HOUR PHARMACIES: **Kaiser Bellflower Pharmacy** (✉ 9400 E. Rosecrans Ave., Bellflower, ☎ 562/461–4213). Many towns have a Thrifty or Sav-On that stays open late; check local listings.

DIVERS' ALERT

Do not fly within 24 hours after scuba diving.

MEDICAL PLANS

No one plans to get sick while traveling, but it happens, so **consider signing up with a medical-assistance company.** Members get doctor referrals, emergency evacuation or repatriation, 24-hour telephone hot lines for medical consultation, cash for emergencies, and other personal and legal assistance. Coverage varies by plan, so **review the benefits of each carefully.**

➤ MEDICAL-ASSISTANCE COMPANIES: **International SOS Assistance** (✉ 8 Neshaminy Interplex, Suite 207, Trevose, PA 19053, ☎ 215/245–4707 or 800/523–6586, FAX 215/244–9617; ✉ 12 Chemin Riantbosson, 1217 Meyrin 1, Geneva, Switzerland, ☎ 4122/785–6464, FAX 4122/785–6424; ✉ 10 Anson Rd., 14-07/08 International Plaza, Singapore, 079903, ☎ 65/226–3936, FAX 65/226–3937).

GAY & LESBIAN TRAVEL

L.A. has a large and visible gay community, and West Hollywood is at the heart of it. Here you'll find many gay cafés, bars, and shops, as well as the L.A. gay community center (☞ *below*).

➤ LOCAL RESOURCES: When planning your trip, check out *Fodor's Gay Guide to the USA* (**Fodor's Travel Publications,** ☎ 800/533–6478 or in bookstores); $20. For general information in L.A., contact the **Gay and Lesbian Community Services Center** (✉ 1625 N. Schrader Blvd., Los Angeles, 90028, ☎ 323/993–7400). As in many California cities, lesbian and gay publications are available in sidewalk racks and at bars. *Edge Magazine* (☎ 323/962–6994) is an entertainment-based publication for gay men on where to go and what to do; *Frontiers* (☎ 323/848–2222), out of West Hollywood, covers news and entertainment for both men and women.

➤ GAY- AND LESBIAN-FRIENDLY TOUR OPERATORS: **R.S.V.P. Travel Productions** (✉ 2800 University Ave. SE, Minneapolis, MN 55414, ☎ 612/379–4697 or 800/328–7787, FAX 612/379–0484), for cruises and resort vacations for gays.

➤ GAY- AND LESBIAN-FRIENDLY TRAVEL AGENCIES: **Corniche Travel** (✉ 8721 Sunset Blvd., Suite 200, West Hollywood, CA 90069, ☎ 310/854–6000 or 800/429–8747, FAX 310/659–7441). **Islanders Kennedy Travel** (✉ 183 W. 10th St., New York, NY 10014, ☎ 212/242–3222 or 800/988–1181, FAX 212/929–8530). **Now Voyager** (✉ 4406 18th St., San Francisco, CA 94114, ☎ 415/626–1169 or 800/255–6951, FAX 415/626–8626). **Yellowbrick Road** (✉ 1500 W. Balmoral Ave., Chicago, IL 60640, ☎ 773/561–1800 or 800/642–2488, FAX 773/561–4497). **Skylink Women's Travel** (✉ 3577 Moorland Ave., Santa Rosa, CA 95407, ☎ 707/546–9888 or 800/225–5759, FAX 707/546–9891), serving lesbian travelers.

HOLIDAYS

Major national holidays include: New Year's Day (Jan. 1); Martin Luther King, Jr. Day (third Mon. in Jan.); President's Day (third Mon. in Feb.); Memorial Day (last Mon. in May); Independence Day (July 4); Labor Day (first Mon. in Sept.); Thanksgiving Day (fourth Thurs. in Nov.); Christmas Eve and Day (Dec. 24–25); and New Year's Eve (Dec. 31).

INSURANCE

Travel insurance is the best way to **protect yourself against financial loss.** The most useful plan is a comprehensive policy that includes coverage for trip cancellation and interruption, default, trip delay, and medical expenses (with a waiver for preexisting conditions).

Without insurance, you will lose all or most of your money if you cancel your trip, regardless of the reason. Default insurance covers you if your tour operator, airline, or cruise line goes out of business. Trip-delay covers unforeseen expenses that you may incur due to bad weather or mechanical delays. It's important to compare the fine print regarding trip-delay coverage when comparing policies.

For overseas travel, one of the most important components of travel insurance is its medical coverage. Supplemental health insurance will pick up the cost of your medical bills should you get sick or injured while traveling. Residents of the United Kingdom can buy an annual travel-insurance policy valid for most vacations taken during the year in which the coverage is purchased. If you are pregnant or have a pre-existing condition, make sure you're covered. British citizens should buy extra medical coverage when traveling overseas, according to the Association of British Insurers. Australian travelers should buy travel insurance, including extra medical coverage, whenever they go abroad, according to the Insurance Council of Australia.

Always **buy travel insurance directly from the insurance company**; if you buy it from a cruise line, airline, or tour operator that goes out of business you probably will not be covered for the agency or operator's default, a major risk. Before you make any purchase, **review your existing health and home-owner's policies** to find out whether they cover expenses incurred while traveling.

➤ TRAVEL INSURERS: In the U.S., **Access America** (✉ 6600 W. Broad St., Richmond, VA 23230, ☎ 804/285–3300 or 800/284–8300). **Travel Guard International** (✉ 1145 Clark St., Stevens Point, WI 54481, ☎ 715/345–0505 or 800/826–1300). In Canada, **Mutual of Omaha** (✉ Travel Division, ✉ 500 University Ave., Toronto, Ontario M5G 1V8, ☎ 416/598–4083, 800/268–8825 in Canada).

➤ INSURANCE INFORMATION: In the U.K., **Association of British Insurers** (✉ 51 Gresham St., London EC2V 7HQ, ☎ 0171/600–3333). In Australia, the **Insurance Council of Australia** (☎ 613/9614–1077, FAX 613/9614–7924).

LIMOUSINES

Limousines come equipped with everything from a full bar and telephone to a hot tub and a double bed. If you open any L.A.-area yellow pages, the number of limo companies will astound you. Most charge by the hour, with a three-hour minimum.

➤ LIMO COMPANIES: **Dav-El Livery** (☎ 310/550–0070 or 800/826–

5779). **First Class** (☎ 310/476–1960 or 800/400–9771). **Spectrum Limousine Service** (☎ 800/901–4546).

LODGING

APARTMENT & VILLA RENTALS

If you want a home base that's roomy enough for a family and comes with cooking facilities, **consider a furnished rental.** These can save you money, especially if you're traveling with a large group of people. Home-exchange directories list rentals (often second homes owned by prospective house swappers), and some services search for a house or apartment for you (even a mansion if that's your fancy) and handle the paperwork. Some send an illustrated catalog; others send photographs only of specific properties, sometimes at a charge. Up-front registration fees may apply.

➤ RENTAL AGENTS: **Hometours International** (✉ Box 11503, Knoxville, TN 37939, ☎ 423/690–8484 or 800/367–4668). **Property Rentals International** (✉ 1008 Mansfield Crossing Rd., Richmond, VA 23236, ☎ 804/378–6054 or 800/220–3332, FAX 804/379–2073). **Hideaways International** (✉ 767 Islington St., Portsmouth, NH 03801, ☎ 603/430–4433 or 800/843–4433, FAX 603/430–4444; membership $99) is a club for travelers who arrange rentals among themselves.

B&BS

Los Angeles has very few bed-and-breakfast inns, although there are a handful in Santa Monica and Pasadena. For information, call the visitor information center downtown (☞ Visitor Information, *below*).

HOME EXCHANGES

If you would like to exchange your home for someone else's, **join a home-exchange organization,** which will send you its updated listings of available exchanges for a year and will include your own listing in at least one of them. It's up to you to make specific arrangements.

➤ EXCHANGE CLUBS: **HomeLink International** (✉ Box 650, Key West, FL 33041, ☎ 305/294–7766 or 800/

638–3841, FAX 305/294–1148; $83
per year).

HOSTELS

No matter what your age, you can
**save on lodging costs by staying at
hostels.** In some 5,000 locations in
more than 70 countries around the
world, Hostelling International (HI),
the umbrella group for a number of
national youth hostel associations,
offers single-sex, dorm-style beds and,
at many hostels, "couples" rooms and
family accommodations. Membership
in any HI national hostel association,
open to travelers of all ages, allows
you to stay in HI-affiliated hostels at
member rates (one-year membership
is about $25 for adults; hostels run
about $10–$25 per night). Members
also have priority if the hostel is full;
they're eligible for discounts around
the world, even on rail and bus travel
in some countries.

➤ HOSTEL ORGANIZATIONS: **Hostelling
International—American Youth
Hostels** (✉ 733 15th St. NW, Suite
840, Washington, DC 20005, ☎ 202/
783–6161, FAX 202/783–6171).
Hostelling International—Canada (✉
400-205 Catherine St., Ottawa,
Ontario K2P 1C3, ☎ 613/237–7884,
FAX 613/237–7868). **Youth Hostel
Association of England and Wales** (✉
Trevelyan House, ✉ 8 St. Stephen's
Hill, St. Albans, Hertfordshire AL1
2DY, ☎ 01727/855215 or 01727/
845047, FAX 01727/844126); member-
ship in the U.S. $25, in Canada
C$26.75, in the U.K. £9.30).

MONEY

CREDIT & DEBIT CARDS

Should you use a credit card or a
debit card when traveling? Both have
benefits. A credit card allows you to
delay payment and gives you certain
rights as a consumer (☞ Consumer
Protection, *above*). A debit card, also
known as a check card, deducts funds
directly from your checking account
and helps you stay within your budget. When you want to rent a car,
though, you may still need an old-
fashioned credit card. Although you
can always *pay* for your car with a
debit card, some agencies will not
allow you to *reserve* a car with a
debit card.

Otherwise, the two types of plastic
are virtually the same. Both will get
you cash advances at ATMs worldwide if your card is properly pro-
grammed with your personal
identification number (PIN).

➤ ATM LOCATIONS: **Cirrus** (☎ 800/
424–7787). **Plus** (☎ 800/843–7587)
for locations in the U.S. and Canada,
or visit your local bank.

➤ REPORTING LOST CARDS: To report
lost or stolen credit cards, call the
following toll-free numbers: **American
Express** (☎ 800/327–2177); **Discover
Card** (☎ 800/347–2683); **Diners
Club** (☎ 800/234–6377); **Master
Card** (☎ 800/307–7309); and **Visa**
(☎ 800/847–2911).

EXCHANGING MONEY

For the most favorable rates, **change
money through banks.** Although fees
charged for ATM transactions may be
higher abroad than at home, Cirrus
and Plus exchange rates are excellent,
because they are based on wholesale
rates offered only by major banks.
You won't do as well at exchange
booths in airports or rail and bus
stations, in hotels, in restaurants, or
in stores, although you may find their
hours more convenient. To avoid lines
at airport exchange booths, **get a bit
of local currency before you leave
home.**

➤ EXCHANGE SERVICES: **Chase** *Currency To Go* (☎ 800/935–9935;
935–9935 in NY, NJ, and CT).
International Currency Express (☎
888/842–0880 on the East Coast,
888/278–6628 on the West Coast).
Thomas Cook Currency Services (☎
800/287–7362 for telephone orders
and retail locations).

TRAVELER'S CHECKS

Do you need traveler's checks? It
depends on where you're headed. If
you're going to rural areas and small
towns, go with cash; traveler's checks
are best used in cities. Lost or stolen
checks can usually be replaced within
24 hours. To ensure a speedy refund,
buy your own traveler's checks—
don't let someone else pay for them:
irregularities like this can cause delays. The person who bought the
checks should make the call to request a refund.

THE GOLD GUIDE / SMART TRAVEL TIPS

PACKING

LUGGAGE

How many carry-on bags you can bring with you is up to the airline. Most allow two, but the limit is often reduced to one on certain flights. Gate agents will take excess baggage—including bags they deem oversize—from you as you board and add it to checked luggage. To avoid this situation, make sure that everything you carry aboard will fit under your seat. Also, get to the gate early, and request a seat at the back of the plane; you'll probably board first, while the overhead bins are still empty. Since big, bulky baggage attracts the attention of gate agents and flight attendants on a busy flight, make sure your carry-on is really a carry-on. Finally, a carry-on that's long and narrow is more likely to remain unnoticed than one that's wide and squarish.

If you are flying internationally, note that baggage allowances may be determined not by piece but by weight—generally 88 pounds (40 kilograms) in first class, 66 pounds (30 kilograms) in business class, and 44 pounds (20 kilograms) in economy.

Airline liability for baggage is limited to $1,250 per person on flights within the United States. On international flights it amounts to $9.07 per pound or $20 per kilogram for checked baggage (roughly $640 per 70-pound bag) and $400 per passenger for unchecked baggage. You can buy additional coverage at check-in for about $10 per $1,000 of coverage, but it excludes a rather extensive list of items, shown on your airline ticket.

Before departure, **itemize your bags' contents** and their worth, and label the bags with your name, address, and phone number. (If you use your home address, cover it so that potential thieves can't see it readily.) Inside each bag, **pack a copy of your itinerary.** At check-in, **make sure that each bag is correctly tagged** with the destination airport's three-letter code. If your bags arrive damaged or fail to arrive at all, file a written report with the airline before leaving the airport.

PACKING LIST

The most important rule to bear in mind in packing for a southern California vacation is to prepare for temperature changes. An hour's drive can take you up or down many degrees, and there can be a marked drop in temperature from daytime to nighttime. Clothes that can be layered are your best insurance—take along a sweater or jacket but also bring some shorts and cool cottons. Always tuck in a bathing suit; most lodgings have a pool, a spa, or a sauna.

While casual dressing is a hallmark of the California lifestyle, the best restaurants sometimes require a jacket and tie in the evening, and women will be more comfortable in something dressier than the regulation sightseeing garb of cotton dresses, walking shorts, or jeans and T-shirts.

Be sure you take comfortable walking shoes. Even if you're not much of a walker at home, you're bound to find many occasions on a southern California vacation when you'll want to hoof it, and nothing ruins the pleasures of sightseeing like sore feet.

In your carry-on luggage **bring an extra pair of eyeglasses or contact lenses** and **enough of any medication you take** to last the entire trip. You may also want your doctor to write a spare prescription using the drug's generic name, since brand names may vary from country to country. **Never put prescription drugs or valuables in luggage to be checked.** To avoid customs delays, carry medications in their original packaging. And don't forget to copy down and carry addresses of offices that handle refunds of lost traveler's checks.

PASSPORTS & VISAS

When traveling internationally, **carry a passport even if you don't need one** (it's always the best form of I.D.), and make **two photocopies of the data page** (one for someone at home and another for you, carried separately from your passport). If you lose your passport, call the nearest embassy or consulate and the local police.

The best time to apply for a passport or to renew is during the fall and winter. Before any trip, be sure to check your passport's expiration date and, if necessary, renew it as soon as possible. (Some countries won't allow you to enter on a passport that's due to expire in six months or less.)

Citizens of Australia, New Zealand, and the United Kingdom who plan to stay in the United States for fewer than 90 days **do not need entry visas.** A valid passport, a return-trip ticket, and proof of financial solvency are required; you'll be asked to fill out the Visa Waiver Form, 1-94W, upon entry. Travelers who plan to stay more than 90 days can apply for the appropriate visa at the United States embassy or consulates in their home country. Canadian citizens need **valid identification but neither a passport nor a visa** to enter the United States.

PASSPORT OFFICES

➤ AUSTRALIAN CITIZENS: **Australian Passport Office** (☎ 131–232).

➤ NEW ZEALAND CITIZENS: **New Zealand Passport Office** (☎ 04/494– 0700 for information on how to apply, 0800/727–776 for information on applications already submitted).

➤ U.K. CITIZENS: **London Passport Office** (☎ 0990/21010), for fees and documentation requirements and to request an emergency passport.

VISA OFFICES

➤ AUSTRALIAN CITIZENS: **U.S. Embassy** (✉ Moonah Pl., Yaralumla, Canberra, ☎ 1–902–262–282).

➤ NEW ZEALAND CITIZENS: **U.S. Consulate General, Non-Immigrant Visa Section** (✉ General Bldg., Shortland and O'Connell Sts., 4th Floor, Auckland 1, ☎ no phone inquiries).

➤ U.K. CITIZENS: **U.S. Embassy Visa Information Line** (☎ 01891/200– 290; calls cost 49p per minute, 39p per minute cheap rate), for U.S. visa information. **U.S. Embassy Visa Branch** (✉ 5 Upper Grosvenor St., London W1A 2JB), for U.S. visa information; send a self-addressed, stamped envelope. Write the **U.S. Consulate General** (✉ Queen's House, ✉ Queen St., Belfast BTI 6EO) if you live in Northern Ireland.

SENIOR-CITIZEN TRAVEL

To qualify for age-related discounts, **mention your senior-citizen status up front** when booking hotel reservations (not when checking out) and before you're seated in restaurants (not when paying the bill). Note that discounts may be limited to certain menus, days, or hours. When renting a car, **ask about promotional car-rental discounts,** which can be cheaper than senior-citizen rates.

➤ EDUCATIONAL PROGRAMS: **Elderhostel** (✉ 75 Federal St., 3rd floor, Boston, MA 02110, ☎ 617/426– 8056).

SIGHTSEEING TOURS

Los Angeles is so spread out and has such a wealth of sightseeing possibilities that an orientation bus tour may prove useful. The cost is between $25 and $40. All tours are fully narrated by a driver-guide. Reservations must be made in advance. Many hotels can book them for you.

GENERAL TOURS

L.A. Tours and Sightseeing has a $38 tour covering various parts of the city, including downtown, Hollywood, and Beverly Hills. The company also operates tours to Disneyland, Universal Studios, Magic Mountain, beaches, and stars' homes. **Starline Tours of Hollywood** picks up passengers from area hotels as well as around the corner from Mann's Chinese Theater. Sights such as Universal Studios, Sea World, Knott's Berry Farm, stars' homes, Disneyland, and other attractions are on this popular tour company's agenda. Prices range from $26 to $68.

A more personalized look at the city can be had by planning a tour with **Casablanca Tours**, which offers a four-hour insider's look at Hollywood and Beverly Hills. Tours are in minibuses with a maximum of 14 people, and prices are equivalent to the large bus tours—$35–$68.

➤ GENERAL TOURS INFORMATION: **L.A. Tours and Sightseeing** (✉ 1717 North Highland, suite 606, ☎ 323/ 937–3361 or 800/286–8752). **Starline Tours of Hollywood** (✉ 6541 Hollywood Blvd., Hollywood 90028,

800/959–3131 or 323/463–3333). **Casablanca Tours**(✉ Roosevelt Hotel, 7000 Hollywood Blvd., Cabana 4, Hollywood 90028, ☎ 323/461–0156).

PERSONAL GUIDED TOURS

Elegant Tours for the Discriminating is a personalized sightseeing and shopping service for the Beverly Hills area. Joan Mansfield offers her extensive knowledge of Rodeo Drive to one, two, or three people at a time. Lunch is included and price varies with the itinerary. **L.A. Nighthawks** will arrange your nightlife for you. For a rather hefty price, you'll get a limousine, a guide (who ensures you're in a safe environment at all times), and immediate entry into L.A.'s hottest nightspots.

➤ PERSONAL GUIDES: **Elegant Tours for the Discriminating** (☎ 310/472–4090). **L.A. Nighthawks** (✉ Box 10224, Beverly Hills 90213, ☎ 310/392–1500).

SPECIAL-INTEREST TOURS

Grave Line Tours is a clever, off-the-beaten-track tour that digs up the dirt on notorious suicides and visits the scenes of various murders, scandals, and other crimes via a luxuriously renovated hearse. Tours take place from Tuesday through Sunday, daily at 9:30 AM, and last 2½ hours. (A 12:30 tour will be scheduled if the morning one is full, and sometimes a 3:30 PM tour leaves as well). The price is $40 per body.

Trolleywood Tours has daily tours that take you through downtown Hollywood and by the HOLLYWOOD sign, past stars' homes and through historical parts of town. Cost is $16–$37 per person, depending on the tour.

Visitors who want something dramatically different should check with Marlene Gordon of the **Next Stage.** This innovative company takes groups from 2 to 200 by foot, buses, vans, trains, and helicopters on tours "in search of the real L.A." Favorites include the "Insomniac's Tour," the "Scentimental (aroma) Journey," "L.A. Has Its Ups and Downs" (an escalator/elevator excursion), "No-

table Women in L.A.," and "Secret Gardens."

LA Today Custom Tours has a wide selection of offbeat tours, some of which tie in with seasonal and cultural events, such as theater, museum exhibits, and the Rose Bowl. Groups range from 8 to 800, and prices are from $6 to $85. The least expensive is a two-hour walking tour of downtown Los Angeles architecture that costs $6.

➤ SPECIAL-INTEREST TOURS INFORMATION: **Grave Line Tours** (✉ Box 931694, Hollywood 90093, ☎ 323/469–4149). **Trolleywood Tours** (✉ 6671 Hollywood Blvd., Hollywood 90028, ☎ 323/469–8184 or 800/782–7287). **The Next Stage** (✉ P.O. Box 1065, Pasadena 91102, ☎ 626/577–7880). **LA Today Custom Tours**(✉ 14964 Camarosa Dr., Pacific Palisades 90272, ☎ 310/454–5730).

WALKING TOURS

A very pleasant self-guided walking tour of **Santa Monica** is detailed in a brochure available at the park's Visitors Center.

The **Los Angeles Conservancy** offers low-cost walking tours of the downtown area. Each Saturday at 10 AM one of several different tours leaves from the Olive Street entrance of the Biltmore Hotel. Cost is $5 per person. Make reservations because group size is limited.

➤ WALKING TOURS INFORMATION: **Santa Monica Visitors Center** (✉ 1400 Ocean Blvd., Santa Monica ☎ 310/393–7593). The **Los Angeles Conservancy** (☎ 213/623–2489).

STUDENT TRAVEL

TRAVEL AGENCIES

To save money, **look into deals available through student-oriented travel agencies.** To qualify you'll need a bona fide student I.D. card. Members of international student groups are also eligible.

➤ STUDENT I.D.s & SERVICES: **Council on International Educational Exchange** (✉ CIEE, ✉ 205 E. 42nd St., 14th floor, New York, NY 10017, ☎ 212/822–2600 or 888/268–6245, FAX

212/822–2699), for mail orders only, in the United States. **Travel Cuts** (⊠ 187 College St., Toronto, Ontario M5T 1P7, ☎ 416/979–2406 or 800/667–2887) in Canada.

➤ STUDENT TOURS: **Contiki Holidays** (⊠ 300 Plaza Alicante, Suite 900, Garden Grove, CA 92840, ☎ 714/740–0808 or 800/266–8454, FAX 714/740–2034).

SUBWAYS

The **Metro Red Line** (☎ 213/626–4455) runs 4½ mi through downtown, from Union Station to MacArthur Park, making five stops. The fare is $1.35.

DISCOUNT PASSES

See Bus Travel, *above.*

TAXIS

You probably won't be able to hail a cab on the street in Los Angeles. Instead, you should phone one of the many taxi companies. The metered rate is $1.60 per mile, plus $1.90 to start. Beware that distances between sights in L.A. are vast, so cab fares add up quickly.

➤ TAXI COMPANIES:: Two of the more reputable companies are **Independent Cab Co.** (☎ 213/385–8294) and **United Independent Taxi** (☎ 323/653–5050).

TELEPHONES

COUNTRY CODES

The country code for the United States is 1.

INTERNATIONAL CALLS

International calls can be direct-dialed from most phones; dial 011, followed by the country code and then the local number (the front pages of many local telephone directories include a list of overseas country codes). To have an operator assist you, dial 0 and ask for the overseas operator. The country code for Australia is 61; New Zealand, 64; the United Kingdom, 44. To reach Canada, dial 1 + area code + number.

LONG-DISTANCE CALLS

Competitive long-distance carriers make calling within the United States relatively convenient and let you avoid hotel surcharges. By dialing an 800 number, you can get connected to the long-distance company of your choice.

➤ LONG-DISTANCE CARRIERS: **AT&T** (☎ 800/225–5288). **MCI** (☎ 800/888–8000). **Sprint** (☎ 800/366–2255).

PUBLIC PHONES

Instructions for pay telephones should be posted on the phone, but generally you insert your coins—35¢ for most local calls—in a slot and wait for the steady hum of a dial tone before dialing the number you wish to reach. If you dial a long-distance number, the operator will come on the line and tell you how much more money you must insert for your call to go through.

TOUR OPERATORS

Buying a prepackaged tour or independent vacation can make your trip to Los Angeles less expensive and more hassle-free. Because everything is prearranged, you'll spend less time planning.

Operators that handle several hundred thousand travelers per year can use their purchasing power to give you a good price. Their high volume may also indicate financial stability. But some small companies provide more personalized service; because they tend to specialize, they may also be more knowledgeable about a given area.

BOOKING WITH AN AGENT

Travel agents are excellent resources. In fact, large operators accept bookings made only through travel agents. But it's a good idea to **collect brochures from several agencies,** because some agents' suggestions may be influenced by relationships with tour and package firms that reward them for volume sales. If you have a special interest, **find an agent with expertise in that area**; ASTA (☞ Travel Agencies, *below*) has a database of specialists worldwide.

Make sure your travel agent knows the accommodations and other services. Ask about the hotel's location, room size, beds, and whether it has a pool, room service, or programs for children, if you care about these. Has your agent been there in person or sent others you can contact?

Do some homework on your own, too: Local tourism boards can provide information about lesser-known and small-niche operators, some of which may sell only direct.

BUYER BEWARE

Each year consumers are stranded or lose their money when tour operators—even very large ones with excellent reputations—go out of business. So **check out the operator.** Find out how long the company has been in business, and ask several travel agents about its reputation. If the package or tour you are considering is priced lower than in your wildest dreams, **be skeptical.** Try to **book with a company that has a consumer-protection program.** If the operator has such a program, you'll find information about it in the company's brochure. If the operator you are considering does not offer some kind of consumer protection, then ask for references from satisfied customers.

In the U.S., members of the National Tour Association and United States Tour Operators Association are required to set aside funds to cover your payments and travel arrangements in case the company defaults. It's also a good idea to choose a company that participates in the American Society of Travel Agent's Tour Operator Program (TOP). This gives you a forum if there are any disputes between you and your tour operator; ASTA will act as mediator.

➤ TOUR-OPERATOR RECOMMENDATIONS: **American Society of Travel Agents** (☞ Travel Agencies, *below*). **National Tour Association** (✉ NTA, ✉ 546 E. Main St., Lexington, KY 40508, ☎ 606/226–4444 or 800/755–8687). **United States Tour Operators Association** (✉ USTOA, ✉ 342 Madison Ave., Suite 1522, New York, NY 10173, ☎ 212/599–6599 or 800/468–7862, FAX 212/599–6744).

COSTS

The more your package or tour includes, the better you can predict the ultimate cost of your vacation. Make sure you know exactly what is covered, and **beware of hidden costs.** Are taxes, tips, and service charges included? Transfers and baggage handling? Entertainment and excursions? These can add up.

Prices for packages and tours are usually quoted per person, based on two sharing a room. If traveling solo, you may be required to pay the full double-occupancy rate. Some operators eliminate this surcharge if you agree to be matched with a roommate of the same sex, even if one is not found by departure time.

GROUP TOURS

Among companies that sell tours to Los Angeles, the following are nationally known, have a proven reputation, and offer plenty of options. The classifications used below represent different price categories, and you'll probably encounter these terms when talking to a travel agent or tour operator. The key difference is usually in accommodations.

➤ DELUXE: **Globus** (✉ 5301 S. Federal Circle, Littleton,CO 80123-2980, ☎ 303/797–2800 or 800/221–0090, FAX 303/347–2080). **Tauck Tours** (✉ Box 5027, 276 Post Rd. W, Westport, CT 06881-5027, ☎ 203/226–6911 or 800/468–2825, FAX 203/221–6866).

➤ FIRST CLASS: **Brendan Tours** (✉ 15137 Califa St., Van Nuys,CA 91411, ☎ 818/785–9696 or 800/421–8446, FAX 818/902–9876). **Collette Tours** (✉ 162 Middle St., Pawtucket, RI 02860, ☎ 401/728–3805 or 800/340–5158, FAX 401/728–4745). **Mayflower Tours** (✉ Box 490, 1225 Warren Ave., Downers Grove, IL 60515, ☎ 630/960–3793 or 800/323–7604, FAX 630/960–3575).

➤ BUDGET: **Cosmos** (☞ Globus, *above*).

PACKAGES

Like group tours, independent vacation packages are available from major tour operators and airlines.

➤ AIR/HOTEL/CAR: **American Airlines Vacations** (☎ 800/321–2121). **Continental Vacations** (☎ 800/634–5555).

Delta Vacations (☎ 800/872–7786). United Vacations (☎ 800/328–6877). US Airways Vacations (☎ 800/455–0123).

➤ HOTEL ONLY: SuperCities (⊠ 139 Main St., Cambridge, MA 02142, ☎ 800/333–1234).

➤ CUSTOM PACKAGES: Amtrak Vacations (☎ 800/321–8684).

➤ FROM THE U.K.: British Airways Holidays (⊠ Astral Towers, Betts Way, London Rd., Crawley, West Sussex RH10 2XA, ☎ 01293/723–121). Jetsave (⊠ Sussex House, London Rd., East Grinstead, West Sussex RH19 1LD, ☎ 01342/327–711). Key to America (⊠ 1–3 Station Rd., Ashford, Middlesex TW15 2UW, ☎ 01784/248–777). Kuoni Travel Ltd. (⊠ Kuoni House, Dorking, Surrey RH5 4AZ, ☎ 01306/740–500). Premier Holidays (⊠ Premier Travel Center, Westbrook, Milton Rd., Cambridge CB4 1YG, ☎ 01223/516–516). Trailfinders (⊠ 42–50 Earls Court Rd., London W8 6EJ, ☎ 0171/937–5400; ⊠ 58 Deansgate, Manchester M3 2FF, ☎ 0161/839–6969).

TRAIN TRAVEL

Los Angeles can be reached by Amtrak (☎ 800/872–7245). The *Coast Starlight,* a superliner, travels along the spectacular California coast. It offers service from Seattle to Portland and from Oakland to San Francisco down to Los Angeles. The *Sunset Limited* goes to Los Angeles from Florida (via Texas and New Orleans), and the *Southwest Chief* via Chicago.

Union Station (⊠ 800 N. Alameda St. ☎ 213/683–6979) in Los Angeles is one of the grande dames of railroad stations.

WITHIN LOS ANGELES

The Metrorail Blue Line (☎ 213/626–4455) runs daily 5 AM–10 PM from downtown Los Angeles (corner of Flower and 7th Streets) to Long Beach (corner of 1st Street and Long Beach Avenue), with 18 stops en route, most of them in Long Beach. The fare is $1.35 one-way.

TRANSPORTATION

It's true that a car is essential in Los Angeles. However, for certain routes, public transportation can be a handy alternative. DASH buses are inexpensive and easy to use, and new downtown weekend routes cover popular tourist destinations. The Downtown Discovery Route (DD) makes a continuous loop among downtown sites; Route E is a shopper's tour with stops in the Broadway, Jewelry, and Fashion districts, as well as at two downtown malls.

The subway is effective for trips from Union Station (downtown) to Mid-Wilshire. Buses are not as easy to use, since routes can be confusing and exact change is required.

Though long cab rides are expensive, for a $4 flat fare, up to four passengers may use a taxi to visit downtown attractions within the "One Fare Zone," which is bounded by the Harbor Freeway (I-110) to the west, Main Street to the east, Pico Boulevard to the south, and the Hollywood Freeway (U.S. 101) to the north.

TRAVEL AGENCIES

A good travel agent puts your needs first. Look for an agency that has been in business at least five years, emphasizes customer service, and has someone on staff who specializes in your destination. In addition, **make sure the agency belongs to a professional trade organization,** such as ASTA in the United States. (If your travel agency is also acting as your tour operator, *see* Buyer Beware in Tour Operators, *above*).

➤ LOCAL AGENT REFERRALS: American Society of Travel Agents (ASTA, ☎ 800/965–2782 24-hr hot line, FAX 703/684–8319). Association of Canadian Travel Agents (⊠ Suite 201, 1729 Bank St., Ottawa, Ontario K1V 7Z5, ☎ 613/521–0474, FAX 613/521–0805). Association of British Travel Agents (⊠ 55–57 Newman St., London W1P 4AH, ☎ 0171/637–2444, FAX 0171/637–0713). Australian Federation of Travel Agents (☎ 02/9264–3299). Travel Agents' Association of New Zealand (☎ 04/499–0104).

TRAVEL GEAR

Travel catalogs specialize in useful items, such as compact alarm clocks and travel irons, that can **save space when packing.**

➤ CATALOGS: **Magellan's** (☎ 800/962–4943, FAX 805/568–5406). **Orvis Travel** (☎ 800/541–3541, FAX 540/343–7053). **TravelSmith** (☎ 800/950–1600, FAX 800/950–1656).

U.S. GOVERNMENT

Government agencies can be an excellent source of inexpensive travel information. When planning your trip, **find out what government materials are available.**

VISITOR INFORMATION

For general information about Los Angeles and its environs, contact these tourism bureaus before you go. When you arrive, stop by the visitor information centers in downtown Los Angeles and Hollywood for general information.

TOURIST OFFICES

➤ CITY: **Los Angeles Convention and Visitors Bureau** (✉ 633 W. 5th St., Suite 6000, 90071, ☎ 213/624–7300 or 800/228–2452) offers the free "Destination Los Angeles," an annually updated information packet with suggestions for entertainment, lodging, dining, and a list of special events. Los Angeles also maintains a 24-hour toll-free multilingual hot line with information about community services (☎ 213/689–8822). There are two visitor information centers: **Downtown Los Angeles** (✉ 685 S. Figueroa St., ☎ 213/689–8822); **Hollywood** (✉ 6541 Hollywood Blvd.,☎ 213/689–8822).

➤ METRO AREA: **Beverly Hills** (✉ 239 S. Beverly Dr., 90212,☎ 310/248–1000 or 800/345–2210). **Catalina Island** (✉ P.O.Box 217., Avalon 90704, ☎ 310/510–1520). **Channel Islands** (✉ 8310 W. Channel Islands Blvd., Suite 6,Ventura 93035, ☎ 805/658–5730). **Glendale** (✉ 200 S. Louise St., 91205, ☎ 818/240–7870). **Hollywood** (✉ 7018 Hollywood Blvd., 90028, ☎ 323/469–8311). **Long Beach Area Convention and Visitors Bureau** (✉ 1 World Trade Center, Suite 300, 90831, ☎ 562/436–3645). **Oxnard** (✉ 200 W. 7th St., 93030, ☎ 800/269–6273). **Pasadena** (✉ 171 S. Los Robles Ave., 91101, ☎ 626/795–9311). **Santa Monica Visitors Center** (✉ 1400 Ocean Ave., 90401, ☎ 310/393–7593). **West Hollywood** (✉ 8687 Melrose Ave., Suite M26, 90069, ☎ 310/289–2525).

➤ STATE: **California Office of Tourism** (✉ 801 K St., Suite 1600, Sacramento, CA 95814, ☎ 916/322–2882 or☎ 800/862–2543) has a free visitor's guide.

In the U.K.: **California Tourist Office** (✉ ABC California, Box 35, Abingdon, Oxfordshire OX14 4TB, ☎ 0891/200–278). Calls cost 50p per minute peak rate or 45p per minute cheap rate. Brochures can be obtained by sending to the above address a check for £3 made to ABC California.

WEB SITES

Do **check out the World Wide Web** when you're planning your trip. You'll find everything from up-to-date weather forecasts to virtual tours of famous cities. Fodor's Web site, www.fodors.com, is a great place to start your on-line travels. For more information specifically on Los Angeles, visit:

The Los Angeles Times's site is a great source for up-to-the-minute local news, as well as goings-on around town: www.latimes.com. *L.A. Weekly* maintains a hip site with lively features and and insiders' guides to dining, the arts, and nightlife in the L.A. metro area: www.laweekly.com. The **city of Los Angeles,** the official site of the L.A. city government, has links to various entertainment and cultural sites: www.ci.la.ca.us

WHEN TO GO

Almost any time of the year is the right time to go to Los Angeles; the climate is mild and pleasant year-round. There is, however, a rainy season from November through March (the heaviest downpours are usually January). Summers are virtually rainless but usually see the famous Los Angeles smog at its worst, and this can cause problems for people with respiratory ailments.

CLIMATE

Seasons in Los Angeles and southern California are not as defined as in other temperate areas of the world. The Pacific Ocean is the primary moderating influence. In addition, mountains along the north and east sides of the Los Angeles coastal basin act as buffers against the extreme summer heat and winter cold of the desert and plateau regions.

Mild sea breezes and winds from the interior can mix to produce a variety of weather conditions; an unusual aspect of the Los Angeles climate is the pronounced difference in temperature, humidity, cloudiness, fog, rain, and sunshine over short distances.

➤ FORECASTS: **Weather Channel Connection** (☎ 900/932–8437), 95¢ per minute from a Touch-Tone phone.

Climate in Los Angeles

Jan.	64F	18C	May	69F	21C	Sept.	75F	24C
	44	7		53	12		60	16
Feb.	64F	18C	June	71F	22C	Oct.	73F	23C
	46	8		57	14		55	13
Mar.	66F	19C	July	75F	24C	Nov.	71F	22C
	48	9		60	16		48	9
Apr.	66F	19C	Aug.	75F	24C	Dec.	66F	19C
	51	11		62	17		46	8

THE GOLD GUIDE / SMART TRAVEL TIPS

1 Destination: Los Angeles

LOS ANGELES: A PLACE LIKE NO OTHER

WANT SOME ADVICE about Los Angeles? Don't believe everything you've heard, because chances are you've heard some exaggerated claim, good or bad. The truth lies, of course, somewhere in between. There's probably no other city on earth that's as hard to categorize. That's because L.A. is just too big to be distilled into a neat, accurate description for a travel brochure. The city of 3.5 million sprawls across 467 square mi of desert basin, mountain canyons, and coastal beaches. Outside city limits, another 6 million people live in 80 incorporated cities within Los Angeles County. Beyond that, another 5 million reside within the economic shadow of Los Angeles, in the region's four other counties. But that, as they say in the movies, is the master shot, the big picture. If we zoom in for a close-up, we discover a city immensely rich in human diversity and culture.

A lot of fuss is made of L.A.'s ethnic diversity and its status as a cultural hub of the Pacific Rim. After all, the largest population of Pacific Islanders in the nation lives in L.A., as well as the world's third-largest Hispanic population (after Mexico City and Guadalajara). People from 140 countries speaking 96 different languages call L.A. home. Signs in Spanish, Korean, Thai, Chinese, Japanese, Armenian, and Russian are as common in some areas of the city as English signs. What isn't so well known is that this kind of diversity dates back to L.A.'s beginnings: Indians, blacks, mestizos, and Spaniards were among the 44 settlers who first arrived from the Mexican provinces of Sonora and Sinaloa in September 1781.

While diversity adds rich texture to the city's makeup, it does not always create harmony. There's constant rankling about bilingual education in the schools. Bloody rioting has torn the city along racial lines more than once, most recently in 1992 when the acquittal of the police officers accused of beating motorist Rodney King provoked the nation's worst civil unrest ever. That experience left a scar of misunderstanding and mistrust that has yet to heal completely.

But another close-up angle reveals images of people pulling together to help their neighbors after the devastating 1994 Northridge earthquake and the Malibu wildfires two years later. This view of L.A. contradicts the popular media portrayal of self-indulgent Angelenos concerned only about going to the gym and buying expensive gadgets for themselves: Research conducted in 1997 indicated that Los Angeles residents actually donate money to charity at a rate above the national average.

By and large, Angelenos are also generous in spirit. People come to Los Angeles seeking a kindred spirit and the hope of finding acceptance for ideas or lifestyles shunned in less tolerant parts of the country. In the early years of this century, moviemakers, pioneers of a sort, established Hollywood as the capital of a new industry, filmmaking, which in no small way helped create the myth and mystique of L.A. as a place where dreams come true. In the 1980s the small city of West Hollywood forged its own destiny when a coalition of gay and lesbian, elderly, and immigrant residents pushed through a charter for cityhood. Today, West Hollywood is one of the country's most progressive small cities, where individual difference is celebrated and legally protected.

If there's a universal symbol of Los Angeles, it's the automobile. Cars and freeways have been a part of the L.A. image for so long that a driver's license is seen as something of a birthright here. And like it or not, freeways are the passages to the city's far-flung pleasures—at least for the time being and as long as the air remains cleaner than ever, thanks in part to tough emission controls on automobiles. Just as the automobile symbolizes the limitless possibilities in L.A., where anything goes, vanity license plates such as MUZKBIZ celebrate that spirit of freedom and self-definition that Angelenos take for granted.

So people keep coming to the city that's like no other. To the tens of thousands of resident immigrants from Mexico, Central America, and Asia, Los Angeles represents the opportunity for a productive life their own countries failed to provide. To the would-be actors and actresses who come here with stars in their eyes, this is the place where the dream of fame and fortune may come true. Each year, millions of visitors arrive in Los Angeles eager to see for themselves why people want to live here, to make sense of all they've seen and read about this sunny center of popular culture on the Pacific Rim.

We can't predict what *your* Los Angeles will turn out to be—lazy afternoons on the beach, touring Hollywood or the movie studios, taking the kids to Disneyland or Knott's Berry Farm, eating dim sum in Chinatown, practicing your Spanish at Olvera Street, or exploring the city's museums. Whatever you do, let it be a close-up shot on Los Angeles that's yours alone.

NEW AND NOTEWORTHY

Art lovers have plenty of reason to celebrate this year. The billion-dollar, Richard Meier–designed **Getty Center,** which opened in December 1997 on a hilltop above Brentwood, has proved so popular that it's hardly able to handle the traffic. Love the Center or hate it, its opening was the most important cultural event in L.A. since the 1984 Olympic Arts Festival. On a more down-to-earth scale, the **Southwest Museum** has expanded into the old May Company building, on the northeast corner of Fairfax Avenue, in a collaborative venture with the **Los Angeles County Museum of Art.** In addition to exhibiting its permanent collection of native American art and artifacts, the new satellite Southwest Museum will showcase temporary exhibits, including a 70-piece collection from the Van Gogh Museum in Amsterdam (on view from January through April 1999). The Santa Monica Museum of Art also has a new home, at the offbeat **Bergamot Station,** behind the city recycling center.

But art isn't the only news in town. The **California Science Center,** formerly known as the Museum of Science and Industry, has reinvented itself with dazzling high-

tech, interactive exhibits and and a 3-D IMAX theater. The **Long Beach Aquarium of the Pacific,** which opened its doors in June 1998, is L.A.'s first major marine-themed attraction since Marineland closed years ago.

Hollywood is on the brink of renaissance, with a subway stop scheduled to open at Hollywood Boulevard and Highland Avenue in late 1999, and several new museums and entertainment venues on the horizon. At press time, the **Museum of Hollywood History** was scheduled to open in the old Max Factor Building in late 1998, complementing the **Hollywood Entertainment Museum,** which opened in October 1996. But Hollywood will truly catch its second wind around the year 2000 or thereafter, when the Hollywood and Highland entertainment complex is completed. In addition to housing restaurants, shops, and theaters, this 3rd Street Promenade–like complex will be the permanent new home of the Academy Awards.

Sports fans will have a new place to cheer for the Lakers, the Clippers, and the Kings, when the **STAPLES Center** sports arena is completed in late 1999. The arena will be next to the Convention Center, in downtown L.A.

Disneyland heads into the Millenium with its latest version of **Tomorrowland,** a fantasy future world where you can get shrunk, ride an Astro Orbitor rocket, or tinker with the toys of tomorrow.

Wolfgang Puck's **Spago Beverly Hills** continues to bask in the limelight, proving that contemporary fusion cuisine is here to stay. In addition, a spate of new French and Italian restaurants has contributed to L.A.'s vibrant culinary climate. **Lavande, Bistro K, Mimosa, Les Deux Cafés,** and **Vincenti** are among the noteworthy newcomers.

The reopening of **L'Ermitage** marks Beverly Hills's first hotel debut in nearly a decade. The upscale hostelry, scheduled to open in spring 1998, will gear itself primarily to business travelers.

The major news on Rodeo Drive is the closing of Fred Hayman Beverly Hills, one-time kingpin of Oscar-night fashions (and also the birthplace of the Giorgio scent). In its place will be **Louis Vuitton.** The 25,000-sq-ft **flagship Tommy Hilfiger** store in Beverly Hills brings the young designer's California-casual fashions closer to L.A.

WHAT'S WHERE

To get a handle on the geography of L.A., picture yourself heading north from Los Angeles International Airport (LAX). Barring bad traffic you'd soon reach the coastal area of Santa Monica, from which two major thoroughfares run more or less due east into downtown. Sunset Boulevard winds around the upscale residential areas of Bel-Air and Beverly Hills before hitting the legendary West Hollywood commercial stretch known as the Sunset Strip. Sunset then passes through Hollywood and ends downtown near Chinatown and Dodger Stadium. The other major street, south of Sunset, is Wilshire Boulevard, which takes you from Santa Monica through Westwood, UCLA's college village, past Beverly Hills's famous shopping district, through the financial Wilshire district, and into the city center.

For a good overall view of Los Angeles, head up to the Griffith Park Observatory, just east of Hollywood proper. Standing on the terraces there (where James Dean, Natalie Wood, and Sal Mineo stood in the movie *Rebel Without a Cause*), you're well above this massive city, so the various parts should start to make sense. To the southeast are Long Beach and Orange County. To the left, a few miles southeast, is downtown, and below to the right is Hollywood (look for the whimsical Capitol Records Tower, which resembles a stack of old 45s). About 6 mi southwest of that, you'll notice ABC's twin executive towers, marking Century City, and on a clear day you can see the Pacific Ocean in the distance. Directly to your right are the Hollywood Hills, which are part of the Santa Monica Mountains. The mountains run west past the HOLLYWOOD sign through Beverly Hills, Bel-Air, and on to the coastline, rising above the ritzy shoreline community of Malibu. Over the hill behind Griffith Park lies the San Fernando Valley and, to the east of that, Glendale, Pasadena, and the San Gabriel Valley.

Beverly Hills and the Westside

Drive into Beverly Hills, Bel-Air, Brentwood, Westwood, and West L.A., and you'll discover that just looking good isn't enough—looking prosperous is the name of the game. A walk down Rodeo Drive is one way to join in on the lives of the rich and famous. But don't overlook the Westside's cultural attractions—especially the dazzling new Getty Center.

Downtown Los Angeles

Although L.A.'s more glamorous tourist areas get most of the attention, the multicultural pockets, museums, and historic buildings of downtown make it worth a couple of quarters on the DASH (Downtown Area Short Hop) transit system. Chinatown, Little Tokyo, and Olvera Street (with tiled walks, strolling mariachis, and great Mexican food) exemplify the rich cultural diversity of the city. On and around Broadway, Victorian, art deco, and beaux arts buildings (in various stages of preservation) provide snippets of L.A.'s architectural past.

Pasadena Area

A visit to Pasadena is a step back to the early 20th century, when wealthy Easterners built fabulous winter homes here. Old Town Pasadena, restored and revitalized, has one of the liveliest street scenes anywhere. The gardens and art collections at the Huntington estate in San Marino are a premier destination.

Hollywood

Hollywood has changed since the golden days of big-screen legends, but its name still conjures up images of paparazzi stealing shots of beautiful celebs making their screen debuts. Currently under revitalization, flashy Hollywood Boulevard has hidden historical treasures among souvenir shops, office buildings, and renewed facades. Still, the Walk of Fame, Mann's Chinese Theater, Hollywood Bowl, El Capitan Theater, and the Capitol Records Tower stand as reminders of this famous neighborhood's romantic past.

Orange County

Disneyland, in Anaheim, is probably the best-known attraction in this neck of the woods, but other deserving destinations see much tourist traffic as well, including Knott's Berry Farm in nearby Buena Park. Looking to join the ranks of laid-back, sun-worshiping Californians? Then head for coastal Orange County, to beach and harbor towns such as Huntington Beach, Newport Harbor, the Balboa Peninsula, and Laguna Beach.

Palos Verdes, San Pedro, and Long Beach

Far from the commotion of stars and stargazers, the peninsula of Palos Verdes and the port cities of San Pedro and Long Beach present a refreshing alternative to urban L.A. Here are aquatic parks and aquariums, verdant botanical gardens, a working harbor, a historic luxury-liner hotel, and two 19th-century adobe ranches. And you can even cap off the day with a sunset gondola cruise on the canals in Naples.

San Fernando Valley

Referred to simply as "The Valley," the San Fernando Valley is an expansive area that has metamorphosed from an expanse of orange groves and ranches into a well-populated string of towns with a mix of income levels and ethnic groups. The main sightseeing draws are Universal Studios Hollywood, studio tours of NBC and Warner Bros., and the historic Mission San Fernando Rey de Espana.

Santa Monica, Venice, Pacific Palisades, and Malibu

No matter how far up Pacific Coast Highway you drive, you're assured dramatic views, both natural and man-made. Locals flex their muscles, in-line skate, and perform along the Venice boardwalk; Santa Monica and Pacific Palisades draw vacationing families; and Malibu is where the rich-and-famous hide away in their "Colony."

PLEASURES AND PASTIMES

Beaches

L.A.'s combination of sun, sand, and 72 mi of gorgeous coastline stirs flights of fancy. It's all here: more than 30 mi of wide beaches, beach towns from the laid-back to the superchic, and plenty of sunny days to enjoy it all. Point Dume and Zuma Beach, north of Malibu, have always been popular with Angelenos for their pristine water and excellent facilities, but they're a long drive if you're not hip to L.A. distances. Easily accessible Santa Monica beaches are always a good bet—though the bay could be cleaner—and to the south, any town you're in will be the right one for a great beach experience. Manhattan Beach, Hermosa Beach, and Redondo Beach, the South Bay's prettiest beach towns, have easygoing lifestyles and plenty to do, day or night.

Dining

L.A.'s fantastic mix of cultures makes for a brilliant mix of cuisines. (If you've never tasted authentic Mexican, start right now; it's a rite of passage.) Southern California is also where the trend toward healthful eating began oh so many years ago, so there's no dearth of vegetarian and heart-healthy options. Then there's that other category, of course: celebrity chefs. L.A. elevates its star players in the food game to celeb status, and when you visit their restaurants, you'll understand why. Wolfgang Puck may have been the first, with the original Spago (and now the new Spago Beverly Hills, plus ObaChine, Granita, Chinois on Main, and Wolfgang Puck Cafés), but he's certainly not the last. The list includes Joachim Splichal, of Patina and the Pinot restaurants; Michael McCarty, of Michael's (he created California cuisine); Piero Selvaggio, of Valentino; Michel Richard, of Citrus—the list goes on and on.

Hiking

Whether you prefer your wilderness undeveloped or relatively tame, there's a place for you just a short drive from anywhere in the city. The Santa Monica Mountains begin at Griffith Park, near Hollywood, and run 50 mi out to the Malibu coastline. In addition to hikes, rangers lead nature walks and bird walks daily; most are free (though you may have to pay a nominal sum for parking). For something more challenging, you'll find marvelous trails through scenic Topanga, Solstice, Rustic, and Franklin canyons; Will Rogers State Historic Park (either a 2-mi looping trail above the humorist's 1930s estate or the 30-mi Backbone Trail that runs to Point Mugu); Malibu Creek State Park (with a small lake, waterfalls, canyons, meadows, and rock climbing); and the lower slopes of the San Gabriel Mountains above Pasadena.

Museums and Galleries

Topping this art-loving city's museum list are the new Getty Center, on a hilltop above Brentwood; the Los Angeles County Museum of Art (LACMA) in the mid-Wilshire district, the city's largest showplace; the two exciting sites of the Museum of Contemporary Art (MOCA) downtown; the Huntington Library, Art Collections, and Botanical Gardens, in San Marino; and the Norton Simon Museum, in Pasadena. More than 50 other area museums house everything from Ice Age fossils to Medieval illuminated manuscripts to contemporary artworks. Santa Monica has some of the most prestigious and avant garde art in southern California, much of it in the 20 galleries at 5-acre Bergamot Station Art Center. In fact, galleries are now part of the city's raison d'être—particularly in West Hollywood, where group gallery openings periodically take place on Saturday nights.

Few cities have the sort of whimsical roadside art you'll find here. From Hollywood's circular Capitol Records building, shaped like a stack of 45 rpm records, to West Hollywood's 600-ft-long "Blue Whale" (actually the Pacific Design Center), imagination reigns. In between, there are giant doughnuts, a few 1950s coffee shops, a Tail-o'-the Pup hot-dog stand that has appeared in several movies, a drive-in church with an outdoor pulpit, and mural after mural painted on freeway underpasses and the sides of homes from Venice to downtown L.A.

Nightlife

It's hip, it's hot, and it's one of the world's best: the club scene, that is, from hard-hitting rock, sophisticated jazz, and wailing blues joints to comedy clubs, dance clubs, and more. Look in Thursday Calendar section of the *Los Angeles Times* or the free *LA Weekly* or *LA New Times,* both published on Thursday.

The Sunset Strip and its environs in West Hollywood are famous for club- and bar-hopping, with House of Blues, Johnny Depp's Viper Room, and the Hotel Mondrian's Sky Bar among the top spots stirring up the scene—but the swingers generation now favors the Silver Lake/Los Feliz area. Though clubs on the Strip play to a young crowd, there are plenty of venues for grown-ups throughout the area, from the Troubadour on Santa Monica Boulevard to influential Luna Park on Robertson Boulevard. In the Crenshaw District, cool blues and jazz emanate from Marla's Memory Lane Supper Club, owned by comedy star Marla Gibbs herself; in Hollywood, the Cinegrill at the Clarion Hotel Hollywood Roosevelt serves top-tier jazz in a room full of movie-star memorabilia. The Catalina Bar & Grill in Hollywood books the top names in contemporary and mainstream jazz. Dance clubs, from the wild to the glamorous, spin everything from salsa to hip-hop. At the other end of the musical spectrum, swing has made a grand comeback at the Derby, a 1940s-style supper club.

Many of today's top comedians got their start playing to the crowds in local clubs. Among the best: in West Hollywood, the Improv, a showcase for top talent since 1975; Groundlings Theatre, whose comedy troupe once included *Friends'* Lisa Kudrow (you've seen other alums on *Saturday Night Live!*); and Laugh Factory, where Robin Williams, Jerry Seinfeld, Eddie Murphy, and Jay Leno have all appeared. In Pasadena, the Ice House is a favorite of Dana Carvey, and in Hermosa Beach, locals love it when Jay Leno stops by the Comedy and Magic Club to try out new material.

Shopping

Of course L.A. has malls, from the upscale designer-boutique variety to the mega-discount outlet type. But Angelenos perhaps hold dearer to their hearts the city's shopping streets and outdoor markets. These are the places where you can not only see the sky and breathe the air, but also find great shops with merchandise the malls don't carry, and pop into the best restaurants, bakeries, bookstores, and galleries for a break. A sampling: hip Main Street, upscale Montana Avenue between 9th and 17th streets, and the lively 3rd Street Promenade, in Santa Monica; elegant Rodeo Drive and all of Beverly Hills; the eclectic Farmers Market in the Fairfax district; and trendy Melrose Avenue in West Hollywood.

Studio Tours and Tapings

This is the land of entertainment, and the good news is that anyone can peek behind the scenes of Tinseltown's greatest pride. Universal Studios, the theme park of Hollywood, is ground zero for most out-of-towners: Here, a guided tram tour takes you through back lots, shows you how high-tech special effects are done, and even has a few prefab disasters on tap. If you're more interested in the actual processes of film production, opt instead for the tours at Warner Bros. or Paramount Pictures. For tips on how to see TV tapings, *see* the Stargazing Close-Up *in* Chapter 2.

Theater

On any given day you can see a Broadway-style musical, avant-garde performance art, or an innovative drama in the City of Angels. Dominating the theater scene is the Music Center downtown, with the world-class Ahmanson Theatre and the intimate Mark Taper Forum. The related James A. Doolittle Theatre in Hollywood hosts all kinds of performances. Other major players are the Geffen Playhouse in Westwood and the Wilshire Theater in Beverly Hills. From the Cast Theater in Hollywood to the Coast Playhouse in West Hollywood, literally hundreds of smaller venues present outstanding work.

GREAT ITINERARIES

If You Have 1 Day

If you've only got one day in Los Angeles, hop into your car and head straight for **Hollywood.** Amble down a stretch of the **Hollywood Walk of Fame** and check out **Mann's Chinese Theatre** and the **Hollywood Entertainment Museum.** Have lunch on the fabled **Sunset Strip** (head south from Hollywood Boulevard to Sunset Boulevard and go west). After you've walked a portion of the Strip, drive north on Laurel Canyon Boulevard to **Mulholland Drive,** which winds west through the Hollywood Hills, across the spine of Santa Monica Mountains, stopping just short of the Pacific Ocean. Stop at any of the vista points along the way for breathtaking views of the entire San Fernando Valley. Continue west on Mulholland and

then go south on the San Diego Freeway (I–405), and west on the Santa Monica Freeway (I–10) to the coast. Watch the sunset and have dinner in **Santa Monica, Venice,** or **Malibu.** Mulholland Drive may be too twisting for some drivers; an alternate route to the coast from the Fryman Canyon Overlook would be to go north on Laurel Canyon Boulevard and west on the Ventura Freeway (U.S. 101) to the San Diego Freeway.

If You Have 3 Days

Spend your first morning in **Hollywood** (☞ *above*). From the Hollywood Entertainment Museum, drive east on Hollywood Boulevard and south on Fairfax Avenue to 3rd Street, where you'll find the **Farmers Market.** Explore the market and have lunch, unless you want to eat at one of the many cafés on colorful **Melrose Avenue** back north a few blocks on Fairfax. Continue west on Melrose into **West Hollywood.** Turn right (north) on La Cienega to **Sunset Boulevard,** where you can drive or walk a portion of the **Sunset Strip.** If you still have time, continue west on Sunset into **Beverly Hills.**

Start the second day **downtown** (after the morning rush). Drive north on **Broadway** from 6th Street past the **Bradbury Building** and other historic structures. Then head over to **Olvera Street,** for a slice of L.A.'s Mexican heritage. From Olvera Street, make your way to the Santa Monica Freeway (I–10), and drive west to the coast. Have lunch and spend the rest of the day and early evening touring **Venice, Santa Monica,** and **Malibu.** Be sure to catch the Pacific sunset at either of these three coastal towns.

Set aside day three for the theme park of your choice: **Disneyland, Knott's Berry Farm,** or **Universal Studios Hollywood.**

If You Have 5 Days

Follow the three-day itinerary above. Begin day four at the **Getty Center** in Brentwood (or if you're in a less highbrow mood, the **Petersen Automotive Museum** in the Mid-Wilshire district). After lunch at the ocean view Getty Center restaurant, head north via the San Diego Freeway (I–405) to the Ventura Freeway (U.S. 101/Hwy. 134), and head east to your next stop, **Griffith Park** (exit at Victory Boulevard). Spend the rest of the afternoon here, then drive to nearby Los Feliz for dinner. Start early on your last day with a visit to the **Long Beach Aquarium of the Pacific** or the **Queen Mary** in Long Beach. At the end of the day, head north on the Long Beach Freeway (I–710) to the San Diego Freeway (I–405) north. This leads to the Harbor/Pasadena Freeway (I–110) north, which will take you to **Pasadena**, where you can have dinner and explore a little of **Old Town.**

If You Have Kids

Freeways aren't high on most kids' fun lists, so it's wise to stick to one general area per day when you visit Los Angeles with children. One good place to start is sprawling **Griffith Park** (☞ Griffith Park Closeup *in* Chapter 2). Here you'll find train, pony, and merry-go-round rides; playgrounds; and bike and horse trails. Allow several hours for the park's **Los Angeles Zoo,** where 1,200 rare animals and Adventure Island (a children's zoo) beckon young explorers. The **Autry Museum of Western Heritage** stands near the zoo. Don't miss the **Los Angeles Times Children's Discovery Gallery** inside the museum, where kids can try on cowboy gear or play pioneer.

The **Santa Monica** area is also ideal for kids, especially in warm weather. The famous **Santa Monica Pier** is home to a vintage carousel, snack bars, and **Pacific Park,** where a roller coaster and Ferris wheel soar high above the ocean (tamer rides thrill toddlers). Swim at adjoining **Santa Monica Beach** (or **Venice Beach,** south of the pier), if the waves aren't too strong. Families with young children can opt for nearby **Marina del Rey,** where small "Mother's Beach" (Marina Beach) has calm, protected waters. Then head for the **3rd Street Promenade** in downtown Santa Monica, a pedestrian-only street lined with family-friendly shops and restaurants. At night, magicians, jugglers, and other street performers entertain.

If it's not beach weather, you can substitute one or two of several varied museums grouped on the Westside along or near Wilshire Boulevard. The **George C. Page Museum of La Brea Discoveries,** with displays of Ice Age fossils found in the adjacent **La Brea Tar Pits,** is a top family choice. For a relaxed, non–rush hour taste of L.A. car culture, the **Petersen Automotive Museum** showcases rare and classic autos. Rounding out the options are the **Los Angeles County Museum of Art** and the **Ca-**

role **& Barry Kaye Museum of Miniatures,** both in the Mid-Wilshire District, and the **Museum of Tolerance,** on the Westside.

Don't overlook a day in and around downtown Los Angeles. The **Los Angeles Children's Museum** gives kids a hands-on introduction to city life. Nearby, at **El Pueblo de Los Angeles Historical Monument,** site of the city's oldest buildings, kids can sample tacos or hunt for trinkets along **Olvera Street,** a lively Mexican-flavored marketplace. For serious museum going, head southwest to **Exposition Park,** where the **California Science Center** and the **Natural History Museum of Los Angeles County** await. Both are huge, so don't overdo it.

A visit to **Universal Studios Hollywood** in Universal City can fill an entire day, especially when combined with the adjoining **CityWalk,** a pedestrian mall where you don't need a ticket to enjoy the theme-park atmosphere. But touring Hollywood isn't complete without perusing the **Hollywood Walk of Fame,** where hundreds of commemorative sidewalk stars immortalize the likes of Elvis (Presley) and Mickey (Mouse). And at **Mann's Chinese Theatre,** kids can spot dozens of celebrity foot- and handprints—along with Donald Duck's webprints. Don't forget to look up in the hills for the HOLLYWOOD sign.

While Orange County is best known for its theme parks—allow at least a day each for **Disneyland** and **Knott's Berry Farm**—it also has some of the region's best beaches. Kids can explore tide pools at **Crystal Cove State Park** and swim at **Dana Point,** to name just two choice spots. Newport Beach chips in with fishing, swimming, and the **Balboa Fun Zone,** a small amusement park. Cap the day with an evening of colorful, family-oriented "dinner theater" at **Medieval Times Dinner and Tournament** or **Wild Bill's Wild West Dinner Extravaganza,** both in Buena Park.

When to Tour Los Angeles

Contrary to popular belief, Los Angeles does have seasons, the most spectacular being winter, a time of crisp, sunny, unusually smogless days from about November to May. While this takes in the rainy season, December to April, the storms are usually brief, and afterwards the skies are brilliant. Of course, the mountains are glorious in winter, perfect for skiing. However, dining alfresco, bike riding, sailing, catching a concert under the stars—these are the domain of Los Angeles summers. Prices skyrocket and reservations are a must when tourism peaks from July through early October.

FODOR'S CHOICE

Museums

★ A tram takes visitors to the castlelike **Getty Center,** where panoramic city and ocean views vie with J. Paul Getty's vast, valuable art collection in Los Angeles's most dazzling display of cultural wealth.

★ Mark Rothko, Franz Kline, and Susan Rothenberg are among the artists represented in the handsome, red sandstone building known as the **Museum of Contemporary Art,** also known as MOCA.

★ Using state-of-the-art interactive technology, the **Museum of Tolerance** challenges visitors to confront bigotry and racism.

★ The **Natural History Museum of Los Angeles County** is the third-largest museum of its type in the United States, with more than 3.5 million specimens in its halls and galleries.

Parks and Gardens

★ Once part of the vast Spanish Rancho San Rafael that covered more than 30,000 acres, lovely **Descanso Gardens** encompasses 165 acres of native chaparral–covered slopes and lushly planted gardens.

★ **Griffith Park** encompasses 4,100 acres, making it the largest municipal park and urban wilderness area in the United States— and a well-used, well-loved backyard for this city of 3.5 million.

★ An awesome 130-acre garden, formerly the grounds of railroad tycoon Henry E. Huntington's hilltop estate, forms the foundation of the **Huntington Library, Art Collections, and Botanical Gardens**—still one of the most extraordinary cultural complexes in the world.

Hotels

★ Individual bungalows at the famed **Beverly Hills Hotel** have wood-burning fireplaces, period furniture, and even (in some cases) grand pianos; outside are 12 acres of landscaped (and carpeted!) walkways. *$$$$*

★ In a secluded wooded canyon, the ultraluxurious **Hotel Bel-Air** feels like a grand country home; you can even request a room with a private whirlpool bath on the patio. *$$$$*

★ Newport Beach is a sybarite's dream, and there's no more luxurious hostelry here than the **Four Seasons Hotel,** a full-service resort with weekend golf packages, fitness weekend packages, and extensive fitness facilities. *$$$$*

★ The grand, French grand, French Renaissance–style **Peninsula Beverly Hills** has gorgeous rooms with fine antiques and marble floors; the fifth-floor pool overlooks the Hollywood Hills. *$$$$*

★ An unrivaled setting on the edge of the Pacific, combined with the hallmark Ritz-Carlton service, have made the **Ritz-Carlton, Laguna Niguel** justifiably famous. *$$$$*

★ A less-expensive alternative to the glitzier hotels in Beverly Hills, the 50-room **Beverly Hills Inn** has a courtyard with a pool, and extras like complimentary breakfast, and cheese and fruit in the evening. *$$$*

Restaurants

★ The wellspring from which Joachim Splichal's Pinot bistrots have sprung, Hollywood's **Patina** remains one of L.A.'s best restaurants, with a spare elegance and outstanding contemporary cuisine. *$$$$*

★ **Aubergine** is *the* place to eat in Newport Beach, with modern takes on classical French cuisine. *$$$–$$$$*

★ At **Campanile,** Mark Peel and Nancy Silverton (also the force behind the adjacent La Brea Bakery)—two of the finest modern American chefs in the country— blend robust Mediterranean flavors with homey Americana. Save room for dessert. *$$$–$$$$*

★ Saffron-marinated scallops, jasmine tea–smoked squab, and lobster risotto are among the novelties you might try at **Nouveau Café Blanc,** in Beverly Hills. *$$$*

★ For a taste of authentic northern Italian cooking, head to **Vincenti,** where meats roasted to perfection are carved and served tableside. $$$

⭐ In West Hollywood head to **Boxer** for young chef Mark Plapp's excellent and affordable seasonal classics like striped bass in cardamom broth; it's BYO, but there's a well-stocked wine shop next door. $$–$$$

⭐ Crisp and clean with white walls and plain wooden chairs, **Cafe Bizou** serves top-notch California–French bistro fare at bargain prices in Sherman Oaks. $$

⭐ Fresh, high-quality seafood is the draw at the vast, marble-clad, aquarium-lined **Ocean Star,** an outpost of great Chinese cooking in Monterey Park. $$$

⭐ **La Serenata Gourmet** is tops for casual Mexican on the Westside. $–$$

⭐ A taste of the dense and complex mole sauce at West Hollywood's **Monte Alban** may forever transform your impressions of Mexican cuisine. $

Only in L.A.

⭐ Take a quiet walk around **Lake Hollywood** for spectacular views of the HOLLYWOOD sign.

⭐ Set out in the car after dark for **Mulholland Drive,** and the lights of the City of Angels will appear to stretch into infinity.

⭐ When the urban action is too much, escape to Malibu's **El Matador, La Piedra,** and **El Pescador** state beaches, where huge, craggy boulders and spectacular views will bring you back down to earth.

⭐ Learn about the inner workings of movie production on the walking tour of **Paramount Studios.**

⭐ Watch television stars at work by attending a **television taping** at one of L.A.'s TV studios.

⭐ Be part of the scene at the **Venice Boardwalk,** where chainsaw jugglers, fortune tellers, street artists, musicians, tattooed weight lifters, and tourists from all over the world converge.

⭐ Take a sunset stroll along the seaside bluff of **Palisades Park** in Santa Monica.

⭐ After dark, cruise the **Sunset Strip** in West Hollywood, where clubs like Whiskey A Go Go and House of Blues jam until the wee hours.

⭐ Pack a picnic dinner for an outdoor concert at the **Hollywood Bowl,** a summertime tradition.

⭐ From December to March, go on a **whale-watching cruise,** or grab binoculars and head to the high ground of the Palos Verdes Peninsula to watch the annual migration of the California gray whales.

FESTIVALS AND SEASONAL EVENTS

WINTER

➤ JAN.: The annual **Tournament of Roses Parade and Football Game** (☎ 626/449–7673) takes place in Pasadena on New Year's Day, with flower-decked floats, marching bands, and equestrian teams, followed by the Rose Bowl game.

➤ FEB.: Los Angeles's large Chinese-American community brings in the **Chinese New Year** with a parade, beauty pageant, street fair, and fun run (☎ 213/617–0396). **African-American History Month** (☎ 323/295–0521) celebrations include films, exhibits, performances, and more. Events take place throughout Los Angeles. Long Beach holds the **Queen Mary Scottish Festival** in mid-February. Expect pipe bands, Highland dancing, and performances by Scottish theater groups. The **Los Angeles Bach Festival** (☎ 213/385–1345) runs from February into March, with all concerts held in the Gothic First Congregational Church building.

SPRING

➤ MAR.: The **Los Angeles Marathon** (☎ 310/444–5544) involves thousands of runners, plus bicyclists and in-line skaters, dozens of bands and musical groups, and 1 million spectators. The **Sierra Madre Wisteria Festival** (☎ 626/355–5111) has crafts and small-town charm, but the main attraction is the world's largest living plant, with more than 1 million blossoms. Malibu greets spring with the **Spring Wildflower show** (☎ 310/457–8142), which includes short guided walks and displays of more than 100 native species. At the **Blessing of the Animals,** (☎ 213/625–5045) pets and livestock are blessed by the Cardinal of Los Angeles amid the historic splendor of Olvera Street.

➤ APR.: The **Toyota Grand Prix** (☎ 562/981–2600) in Long Beach, the largest race car competition in North America, draws top competitors from all over the world.

➤ MAY: Early May brings **Cinco De Mayo** (☎ 213/485–9777) to Los Angeles. Mexico's victory over the French is celebrated with food, music, and dance, traditional and contemporary. The **Los Angeles Asian-Pacific Film and Video Festival** (☎ 213/680–3004) showcases works by Asian and Pacific filmmakers worldwide. Artists have always lived in Venice, drawn by its ocean views and easy-going lifestyle, and the **Venice Art Walk** (☎ 310/392–8630, ext. 333) provides the chance to tour their studios and see their work. The **Beach Fest** (☎ 562/434–5408) in Long Beach has live music and what's purported to be the world's largest chili cook-off.

SUMMER

➤ JUNE: During the first weekend in June, Pasadena City Hall Plaza hosts the **Absolut Chalk street painting festival** (☎ 626/449–3689), where more than 300 artists use the pavement as their canvas. There are also musical performances and exotic dining kiosks. The proceeds benefit arts and homeless organizations of the Light-Bringer Project. Late June brings the two-day explosion of sequins, dancing, and floats that is **Christopher Street West's Gay & Lesbian Pride Celebration** (☎ 323/860–0701). The parade that wraps up the event is the third largest in California.

➤ JULY: **Outfest: Los Angeles Gay and Lesbian Film Festival** (☎ 323/951–1247) presents a wide range of films by, for, and about gays and lesbians. The **Lotus Festival** (☎ 213/485–8745), celebrating Asian and Pacific culture, is held each year in Echo Park, which boasts the largest lotus bed outside of China. Starting in July and running through August, the **Festival of the Arts and Pageant of the Masters** (☎ 949/494–1145), in Laguna, presents the works of 160 artists in a juried show, along with a unique pageant where masterpieces of art and sculpture are depicted as tableaux vivants.

➤ AUG.: The **Industry Hills Charity Pro Rodeo** (☎ 626/961–6892), in City of Industry, includes a professional rodeo, a petting zoo, and pony rides. The **Long Beach Jazz Festival** (☎ 562/436–7794) lures internationally recognized musicians.

L.A.'s Japanese community celebrates the summer season with **Nisei Week** (☎ 213/687–7193), a Japanese festival featuring arts-and-crafts fairs, plays, and other events.

AUTUMN

➤ SEPT.: The **Los Angeles City Birthday Celebration** (☎ 213/485–9777) commemorates the city's founding with historical reenactments, demonstrations, and art exhibits.

The **Los Angeles County Fair** (☎ 909/623–3111), in Pomona, said to be the largest county fair in the world, hosts entertainment, exhibits, livestock, horse racing, food, and more. In Lancaster, the **American Indian Celebration** (☎ 805/946–3055) includes storytelling and traditional dance. Olvera Street comes alive during the weekend-long **Mexican Independence Day** (☎ 213/625–5045) festival, with arts-and-crafts exhibits, historic displays, and occasional carnival rides.

➤ NOV.: Look for faces painted like skeletons in honor of **Dia de los Muertos** (☎ 213/625–5045), an ancient Mexican celebration honoring the dead. Held at the historic El Pueblo de Los Angeles on Olvera Street, the event features beautifully decorated altars, entertainment, and a solemn procession. Pasadena's

Doo Dah Parade (☎ 626/449–3689), a fun-filled spoof of the annual Rose parade, features the Lounge Lizards, who dress as reptiles and lip sync to Frank Sinatra favorites, and West Hollywood cheerleaders in drag.

➤ DEC.: The **Hollywood Christmas Parade** (☎ 323/469–8311) features floats, high school marching bands, equestrian displays, a mammoth sleigh-riding Santa, and celebrities. Song and candlelight are the hallmarks of **Las Posadas** (☎ 213/625–5045), a traditional Mexican event depicting the journey of Joseph and Mary. The procession starts at the Avila Adobe and continues on to Olvera Street. Newport Beach celebrates Christmas on the ocean with more than 200 festooned boats at the **Newport Harbor Christmas Boat Parade** (☎ 949/729–4400).

2 Exploring Los Angeles

Few cities in the world capture the imagination like Los Angeles does— from the bronze stars in the sidewalk along Hollywood's Walk of Fame to the Spandex-clad in-line skaters zipping along the Venice Boardwalk. Visitors flock to Hollywood in search of film and television stars; to Beverly Hills and Malibu, for a glimpse of glamour and privilege; and to the beaches all along the coast, where the sunny, laid-back California good life is alive for all to see.

Revised and
updated by
Stephen
Dolainski

SEEING LOS ANGELES REQUIRES COVERING a lot of territory—the city sprawls across 467 square miles. Add in the surrounding five-county metropolitan area, and you've got an area of more than 34,000 square mi. Contrary to popular myth, however, that doesn't mean you have to spend all your time in a car. In fact, getting out of your car is the only way to really get to know Los Angeles. The following tours, designed to cover the highlights, should give you a glimpse of what makes this city unique.

We've divided the major sightseeing areas of Los Angeles into nine driving and walking tours:

Downtown, the historical and cultural heart of Los Angeles, has a vibrant, multicultural personality.

Hollywood still reigns as the entertainment capital of the world after nearly a century; there's magic to be found here if you know where to look.

Museum Row and Farmers Market make for an entertaining day of novelties, such as a fossil-filled tar pit and a museum of miniatures, as well as high culture (the L.A. County Museum of Art)—all jump-started with coffee and pastries at L.A.'s most colorful marketplace.

Beverly Hills and Century City is the best place to go if you're looking for glamour and glitz; here are some of the most expensive shops and real estate in California, if not in the country.

Westside has become a hot destination with the arrival of the Getty Center; this is also where you'll find the Museum of Tolerance and UCLA

Santa Monica, Venice, and Malibu are the coastal communities that give Los Angeles its sunny, surf-swept image.

The San Fernando Valley, home to Universal Studios, Warner Bros., and NBC, has a mix of legitimate film and TV production studios and Hollywood-themed entertainment, as well as a historic mission.

Pasadena, famed for the town's annual Tournament of Roses parade, also has a rich legacy of historic architecture, mostly from the early 20th century, as well as a top-notch museum, a botanic garden, a historic mission, and an old town with a lively street scene.

Palos Verdes, San Pedro, and Long Beach are South Bay communities with a working harbor, a historic luxury liner, and an aquarium as their main draws.

Within the exploring sections, **Off the Beaten Path** includes sights outside the map areas but worth visiting.

Orientation

Looking at a map of sprawling Los Angeles, first-time visitors are sometimes overwhelmed. Where to begin? What to see first? And what about all those freeways? Here's some advice: relax. There is no cookie-cutter version of Los Angeles; you get to dream up your own perfect visit. Begin by setting your priorities—movie and television fans should first head to Hollywood, Universal Studios, and a taping of a television show. Beach lovers and outdoorsy types might start out in Santa Monica or Venice or Malibu, or spend an afternoon in Griffith Park, the largest city park in the country. Those with a cultural bent will probably make a beeline for the new Getty Center in Brentwood (bear in mind that you have to make parking reservations far in advance) or the reorganized Los Angeles County Museum of Art (LACMA). And urban explorers might begin with downtown Los Angeles.

As for the freeways—well, they're really not so bad. For one thing, they're well marked and for non–rush hour travel still the best route from one end of the city to the other. But here are a couple tips: Most freeways are known by a name and a number; for example, the San Diego Freeway (I–405), the Hollywood (U.S. 101) or Ventura (U.S. 101) freeways, the Santa Monica Freeway (I–10), and the Harbor Freeway (I–110). It helps, too, to know which direction you're traveling; say, west toward Santa Monica, or east toward downtown Los Angeles. Distance in miles doesn't mean much, depending on the time of day you're traveling: The short 10-mi distance between the San Fernando Valley and downtown Los Angeles might take an hour to travel during rush hour, but only 20 minutes at other times.

Finally, don't believe everything you may have heard about Los Angeles, because chances are you've heard some exaggerated claim, good or bad. The truth, of course, lies somewhere in between. Now you can find out for yourself.

DOWNTOWN LOS ANGELES

Most visitors to Los Angeles who aren't staying at one of the big convention hotels downtown never make it to this part of the city. After Beverly Hills, Disneyland, and Universal Studios, downtown L.A. is an afterthought. Understandable, but a shame, because downtown is the heart of this great city, despite long-standing rumors to the contrary. It's the financial core of the city, as well as the historical and cultural soul of Los Angeles. Architectural landmarks like the Bradbury Building and the old movie palaces along Broadway are glimpses into the past, while the Museum of Contemporary Art (MOCA) steers a steady course into the present. And the dynamic ethnic enclaves on Broadway and in Chinatown and Little Tokyo are reminders of L.A.'s extraordinary multicultural makeup.

A Good Tour
Numbers in the text correspond to numbers in the margin and on the Downtown Los Angeles map.

A convenient and inexpensive minibus service—DASH, or Downtown Area Short Hop—has several routes that travel past most of the sights on this tour, stopping every two blocks or so. Each ride costs 25¢, so you can hop on and off without spending a fortune. Special (limited) routes operate on weekends. Call DASH(☎ From all Los Angeles area codes, 808–2273) for routes and hours of operation.

Begin a downtown tour by heading north on **Broadway** ① from 8th or 9th street. Around 3rd Street, look for cheap weekend parking at one of the small lots that charge a flat all-day rate (Joe's Auto Park at 236 S. Broadway charges about $3). At the southeast corner of Broadway and 3rd is the **Bradbury Building** ②. Across the street is the **Grand Central Market** ③—once you've made your way through its tantalizing stalls you'll come out the opposite side onto Hill Street.

Cross Hill Street and climb aboard **Angels Flight Railway** ④, a funicular that sweeps you up a steep incline to a courtyard called Watercourt (it's surrounded by bubbling, cascading fountains). From here, walk toward the glass pyramidal skylight topping the **Museum of Contemporary Art** ⑤, which is visible half a block north on Grand Avenue.

Exploring Los Angeles *(Boxes Refer to Detail Maps)*

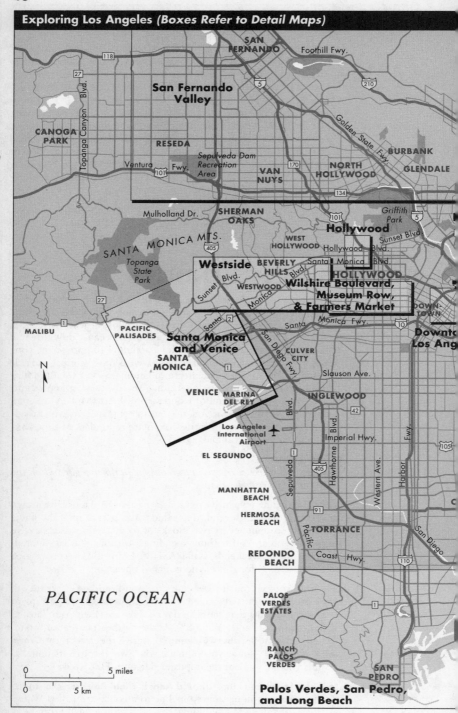

SAN FERNANDO

San Fernando Valley

Foothill Fwy.

118

27

Topanga Canyon Blvd.

CANOGA PARK

RESEDA

Sepulveda Dam Recreation Area

VAN NUYS

NORTH HOLLYWOOD

BURBANK

GLENDALE

Golden State Fwy.

Ventura Fwy.

170

134

SHERMAN OAKS

Mulholland Dr.

Hollywood

Griffith Park

SANTA MONICA MTS.

Topanga State Park

405

WEST HOLLYWOOD

Hollywood Blvd.

Sunset Blvd.

Santa Monica Blvd.

Westside

BEVERLY HILLS

Sunset Blvd.

WESTWOOD

HOLLYWOOD

DOWN-TOWN

Wilshire Boulevard, Museum Row, & Farmers Market

Monica

27

1

MALIBU

PACIFIC PALISADES

Santa Monica and Venice

SANTA MONICA

2

San Diego Fwy.

Santa Monica Fwy.

10

Downtown Los Ang

1

CULVER CITY

VENICE

MARINA DEL REY

Slauson Ave.

INGLEWOOD

42

Los Angeles International Airport

EL SEGUNDO

Blvd.

Imperial Hwy.

Hawthorne Blvd.

Western Ave.

Harbor Fwy.

105

MANHATTAN BEACH

Sepulveda

1

405

HERMOSA BEACH

91

REDONDO BEACH

TORRANCE

Pacific

Coast Hwy.

San Diego

110

PACIFIC OCEAN

PALOS VERDES ESTATES

1

RANCH PALOS VERDES

SAN PEDRO

N

0 — 5 miles
0 — 5 km

Palos Verdes, San Pedro, and Long Beach

SAN GABRIEL MOUNTAINS

Angeles Crest Hwy. 2

Mt. Wilson

LA CAÑADA
FLINTRIDGE

PASADENA

HIGHLAND
PARK

Pasadena Area

Foothill Fwy. 210

SAN
MARINO

Pasadena Fwy.

2

110

ALHAM-
BRA

SAN
GABRIEL

EL
MONTE

San Bernardino Fwy. 10

Dodger
Stadium

MONTEREY
PARK

ntown
ngeles

60   Pomona Fwy.

Santa Ana Fwy.

Rosemead Blvd.

San Gabriel River Fwy.

WHITTIER

72

HUNTINGTON
PARK

710

19

42

DOWNEY

105

39

COMPTON

5

Long Beach Fwy.

Riverside Fwy.

91

Fwy.

710

605

LAKEWOOD

ANAHEIM

19

Pacific Coast Hwy.

GARDEN
GROVE

San Diego Fwy. 39

LONG
BEACH

55

1

You can now either retrace your steps to Watercourt for the Angels Flight descent to Hill Street, Grand Central Market, and your car; or walk two blocks south on Grand to 5th Street. There you'll find two of downtown's historical and architectural treasures: the **Regal Biltmore Hotel** ⑥ and the **Central Library** ⑦. Behind the library are the tranquil MacGuire Gardens. Across 5th Street are the **Bunker Hill Steps** ⑧, L.A.'s version of Rome's Spanish Steps.

Back in your car, continue north on Broadway to 1st Street. A right turn here will take you into **Little Tokyo** ⑨ and the **Japanese American National Museum** ⑩. The **Geffen Contemporary** ⑪ art museum, an arm of MOCA, is just one block north on Central. For a tranquil respite, backtrack on Central to 2nd Street and head two blocks north to Los Angeles Street to get to the rooftop **Japanese Garden** ⑫ at the New Otani Hotel.

From Little Tokyo, turn left (north) from 1st onto Alameda Street. As you pass over the freeway, you'll come to the next stop, **Union Station** ⑬, on the right. Street parking is limited, so your best bet is to park in the pay lot at Union Station (about $5). After a look inside this grand railway station, cross Alameda to **Olvera Street** ⑭.

From Union Station, turn right on Alameda and then immediately left on Cesar Chavez Avenue for three blocks. At Broadway, turn right to **Chinatown** ⑮. If you have kids in tow, reverse your route on Broadway from Chinatown; cross back over the freeway, and at Temple Street make a left for the three-block drive to the **Los Angeles Children's Museum** ⑯ at the Los Angeles Mall. Look to the right as you drive down Temple to see the back of **Los Angeles City Hall** ⑰. Head out of downtown Los Angeles (take Los Angeles Street south to 11th Street, turn west on 11th to Figueroa, then south on Figueroa Street) to **Exposition Park,** site of two museums: the **California Science Center** ⑱ and the **Natural History Museum of Los Angeles County** ⑲. Adjacent to Exposition Park is the **University of Southern California** ⑳.

Return to downtown at night for a performance at the **Music Center** ㉑, and then take in the bright lights of the big city after the show at Bona-Vista, the revolving rooftop lounge atop the **Westin Bonaventure Hotel** ㉒.

TIMING

The weekend is the best time to explore downtown: There's less traffic, parking is easier to find on the streets (bring quarters for meters) and cheaper day rates prevail in the lots. Seeing everything mentioned on this tour would take at least a full day, if not two. Expect to spend at least an hour in Chinatown, Olvera Street, and Little Tokyo—longer if you stop to eat, watch a parade, or visit a museum. The **Los Angeles Conservancy** (☎ 213/623–2489) regularly conducts Saturday morning walking tours of downtown architectural landmarks and districts; call for reservations.

Sights to See

❹ **Angels Flight Railway.** The turn-of-the-century funicular dubbed "the shortest in the world" began operating again in 1996 after having been closed for nearly 30 years. Two original orange-and-black wooden cable railway cars take riders on a 70-second ride up a 298-ft incline from Hill Street (between 3rd and 4th streets) to the fountain-filled Watercourt at California Plaza at a show-stopping 4 mph. ☎ *213/626-1901.* 🚋 *25¢ one-way.* ☻ *Daily 6:30 AM–10 PM.*

★ ❷ **Bradbury Building.** Designed in 1893 by a novice architect who drew his inspiration from a science-fiction story and a conversation with his dead brother via a Ouija board, this classy office building is a mar-

Downtown Los Angeles

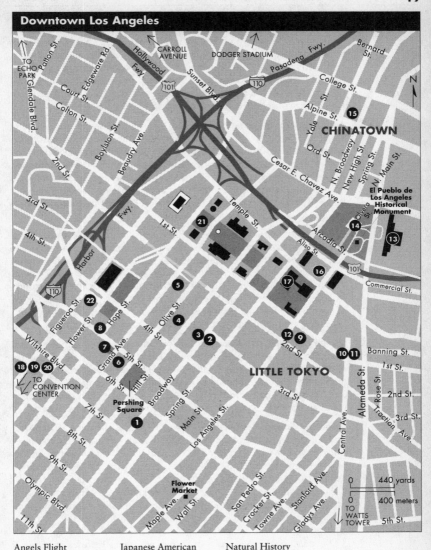

Angels Flight Railway, **4**

Bradbury Building, **2**

Broadway, **1**

Bunker Hill Steps, **8**

California Science Center, **18**

Central Library, **7**

Chinatown, **15**

Geffen Contemporary, **11**

Grand Central Market, **3**

Japanese American National Museum, **10**

Japanese Garden, **12**

Little Tokyo, **9**

Los Angeles Children's Museum, **16**

Los Angeles City Hall, **17**

Museum of Contemporary Art at California Plaza (MOCA), **5**

Music Center, **21**

Natural History Museum of Los Angeles County, **19**

Olvera Street, **14**

Regal Biltmore Hotel, **6**

Union Station, **13**

University of Southern California (USC), **20**

Westin Bonaventure Hotel & Suites, **22**

velous specimen of Victorian-era commercial architecture. Originally the site of turn-of-the-century sweatshops, it now houses somewhat more genteel firms beyond the pink marble staircases. The interior atrium courtyard, with its glass skylight and open balconies and elevator, is frequently used as a movie locale (*Blade Runner* was filmed here). The building is open weekdays from 9 to 6 and on weekends until 5 for a peek, as long as you don't wander past the lobby. ⊠ *304 S. Broadway (southeast corner Broadway and 3rd St.),* ☎ *213/626–1893.*

❶ Broadway. From the late 19th century to the 1950s—before shopping malls and freeways—Broadway was the main shopping and entertainment street downtown. Photos taken during those glory days show sidewalks crowded with shoppers and lights ablaze on movie marquees. About the only evidence of that period are the few movies palaces still in operation between 8th and 5th streets: Look for the **Orpheum** (⊠ 842 S. Broadway) and the **Million Dollar** (⊠ 307 S. Broadway) in particular.

Much of the historical character of Broadway has suffered over the years, but the avenue today is as colorful, vibrant, and noisy as ever. Shops and businesses catering to a mostly Mexican and Central American immigrant clientele have moved into the old movie palaces; between 1st and 9th streets you'll find *mariachi* and *banda* music blaring from electronic-store speakers, street-food vendors hawking sliced papaya sprinkled with chili powder, and fancy dresses for a young girl's *quinceanera* (15th birthday) trumpeting their bright colors above store entrances.

❽ Bunker Hill Steps. A "stream" flows down the center of this monumental staircase into a small pool at its base. The stream originates at the top of the stairs where Robert Graham's nude female sculpture *Source Figure* stands atop a cylindrical base that mimics the shape of the trunks of surrounding palm trees. The figure's hands are open, as if to offer water to the city. ⊠ *5th St., between Grand Ave. and Figueroa St.*

★ ☺ ❶⑧ **California Science Center.** Formerly called the California Museum of Science and Industry, the science center has grown considerably, especially in recent years: In 1997 its original 1912 buildings were incorporated into a new 245,000-square-ft structure. Inside, interactive exhibits illustrate the relevance of science to everyday life. Tess, the 50-ft Animatronic star of "Body Works," demonstrates how the body's organs work together to maintain balance. In other exhibits you can build a structure to see how it stands up to an earthquake, or ride a high-wire bicycle to learn about gravity. The new IMAX theater, with 3-D capabilities and a seven-story movie screen, features science-related films. ⊠ *700 State Dr., Exposition Park,* ☎ *213/744–7400; IMAX 213/744–2014.* ☒ *Free; IMAX $7.25; parking $5.* ☉ *Daily 10–5.*

OFF THE
BEATEN PATH   **CARROLL AVENUE –** The 1300 block of Carroll Avenue in Angelino Heights, now designated a historical monument in one of Los Angeles's oldest neighborhoods, has the city's highest concentration of Victorian houses; look for the Sessions House (No. 1330) and the Haunted House (No. 1345)—the latter seen in Michael Jackson's *Thriller* video. To get to Carroll Avenue from downtown take Temple Street west to Edgeware Road, turn right onto Edgeware and go over the freeway. Carroll Avenue is on the left.

★ ❼ **Central Library.** Major fires in the 1980s closed the library for six years. Today, at twice its former size, it's the third-largest public library in the nation. The original building, designed by Bertram Goodhue, was completely restored to its 1926 condition, with the pyramid tower and its torch symbolizing the Light of Learning still crowning the building. Take the elevator up to the second floor for a look at Dean Cornwell's murals depicting the history of California. The new Tom Bradley Wing, with a soaring eight-story atrium, was named for the former mayor of Los Angeles. A 1½-acre outdoor garden within the library complex has a pricey, but good, restaurant. ⊠ *630 W. 5th St. (corner of 5th and Flower Sts.),* ☎ *213/228–7000.* ⊠ *Free.* ☉ *Mon. and Thurs.–Sat. 10– 5:30, Tues.–Wed. noon–8, Sun. 1–5; docent tours weekdays at 12:30, Sat. at 11 and 2, Sun. at 2.*

⓯ Chinatown. Los Angeles's Chinatown may not compare in size and scope to San Francisco's or Vancouver's, but this downtown sector across from Union Station still represents an authentic slice of Southeast Asian life. The neighborhood is bordered by Yale, Bernard, Ord, and Alameda streets, but North Broadway is the heart—especially during Chinese New Year, when giant dragons snake down the street. More than 15,000 Chinese and Southeast Asians actually live in the Chinatown area, but many thousands more regularly frequent the savory markets, which are filled with dried squid, roots, shark's fin, and other exotic foods. Dim sum parlors are another big draw; **Empress Pavilion** (⊠ 988 N. Hill St., ☎ 213/617–9898) is one of the best. Call the **Chinatown Chamber of Commerce** (☎ 213/617-0396) for information about Chinese New Year and other events.

El Pueblo de Los Angeles Historical Monument. This site that commemorates Los Angeles's heritage encompasses many significant buildings, a park, and festive **Olvera Street** (☞ *below*). ⊠ *Olvera and Temple Sts.*

Exposition Park. Originally developed in 1880 as an open-air farmers' market, this 114-acre public space hosted Olympic festivities in 1932 and 1984 in conjunction with the adjacent Memorial Coliseum and Sports Arena. Today the park is beginning to show signs of exhaustion and neglect, but it remains home to two fascinating museums, the **California Science Center**(☞ *above*) and the **Natural History Museum of Los Angeles County** (☞ *below*). ⊠ *Between Exposition and Martin Luther King Jr. Blvds.*

⓫ Geffen Contemporary at MOCA. Back in 1982, Los Angeles architect Frank Gehry transformed a warehouse in Little Tokyo into a temporary space while the permanent home for the Museum of Contemporary Art (MOCA) (☞ *below*) was being built a mile away. The Temporary Contemporary, with its large, flexible space allowing for wacky installations and big multimedia projects, was such a hit that it remains part of the museum facility. The Geffen houses part of MOCA's permanent collection, which spans the years from the 1940s to the present, and usually one or two temporary exhibits. "Elusive Paradise: Los Angeles Art from the Permanent Collection" will be on view through the end of 1999. ⊠ *152 N. Central Ave.,* ☎ *213/626-6222.* ⊠ *$6, free with MOCA admission on same day; free Thurs. 5–8.* ☉ *Tues.–Wed. and Fri.–Sun. 11–5, Thurs. 11–8.*

★ ❸ Grand Central Market. The city's largest and most active food market is also a testament to Los Angeles's diversity. This block-long marketplace of colorful and exotic produce, herbs, and meat draws a faithful clientele from the Latino community, senior citizens on a budget, and Westside matrons for whom money is no object. Even if you don't plan to buy anything, the market is a delightful place to browse: The butcher shops display everything from lambs' heads to bulls' testicles and pigs' tails; the produce stalls are piled high with locally grown avocados and very ripe, very red tomatoes. Several taco stands make for a tasty on-the-go meal; you can even watch tortillas being flattened on a conveyor belt. ⊠ *317 S. Broadway,* ☎ *213/624-2378.* 🎟 *Free.* ☉ *Mon.–Sat. 9–6; Sun. 10–5:30.*

★ ⑩ **Japanese American National Museum.** What was it like to grow up on a coffee plantation in Hawaii? How difficult was life for Japanese Americans interned in concentration camps during World War II? These questions are addressed by changing exhibits at this museum in Little Tokyo. Volunteer docents are on hand to share their own stories and experiences, making a visit here insightful and personal. Presently housed in a renovated 1925 Buddhist temple, the museum plans to expand into an additional building across the street in January 1999. ⊠ *369 E. 1st St., at Central Ave.,* ☎ *213/625–0414.* 🎟 *$4.* ☉ *Tues.–Thurs. and Sat.–Sun. 10–5; Fri. 11–8; closed Mon..*

⑫ **Japanese Garden.** Landscape architect Sentaru Iwaki modeled this rooftop oasis at the New Otani Hotel and Garden after a 400-year old garden in Tokyo. Like all Japanese gardens, this ½-acre plot of land represents the universe and its elements: a rock could symbolize a mountain or continent, and a plot of combed sand might represent an ocean. ⊠ *New Otani Hotel and Garden, 120 S. Los Angeles St.,* ☎ *213/629–1200.* 🎟 *Free.*

⑨ **Little Tokyo.** The original neighborhood of Los Angeles's Japanese community, this downtown area has been deserted by most of those immigrants, who have moved to suburban areas such as Gardena and West Los Angeles. Still, Little Tokyo remains a cultural focal point. Nisei Week ("nisei" is the name for second-generation Japanese) is celebrated here every August with traditional drums, dancing, a carnival, and a huge parade. Bounded by 1st, San Pedro, 3rd, and Los Angeles streets, Little Tokyo has dozens of sushi bars, tempura restaurants, and trinket shops. **The Japanese American Cultural and Community Center** (⊠ 244 S. San Pedro St., ☎ 213/628–2725) presents such events as Kabuki theater straight from Japan.

🐚 ⑯ **Los Angeles Children's Museum.** Hands-on exhibits allow kids to record a song, make a TV show, learn about recycling, create arts and crafts, build a city out of pillows, and practice being a firefighter. ⊠ *310 N. Main St.,* ☎ *213/687–8800.* 🎟 *$5.* ☉ *Sat.–Sun. 10–5 (during summer vacation, daily 10–5).*

⑰ **Los Angeles City Hall.** This often-photographed, very recognizable building has made numerous appearances on *Superman, Dragnet,* and other popular television shows. Erected in the late 1920s with a pointy spire at the top, the 28-story art deco treasure remained the only structure to break the 13-story height limit until 1957. The building is presently closed for seismic renovations, and probably won't be open again until after the turn of the century. ⊠ *200 N. Spring St.*

★ ⑤ **Museum of Contemporary Art at California Plaza.** The 5,000-piece permanent collection of MOCA is split between Geffen Contemporary (☞ *above*) and the galleries of this site, a red sandstone building designed by Japanese architect Arata Isozaki. The collection represents art from 1940 to the present, including works by Mark Rothko, Franz Kline, Susan Rothenberg, Diane Arbus, and Robert Frank. MOCA also sponsors at least 20 exhibitions a year by both established and new artists in all visual media. ⊠ *250 S. Grand Ave.,* ☎ *213/626–6222.* 🎟 *$6; free Thurs. 5–8.* ☉ *Tues.–Wed. and Fri.–Sun. 11–5, Thurs. 11–8.*

NEED A BREAK?	**Patinette at MOCA** (⊠ Courtyard at MOCA at California Plaza, ☎ 213/626–1178) is a quick-stop cafeterialike set up, but with an imaginative menu of salads and sandwiches designed by one of L.A.'s most renowned chefs, Joachim Splichal.

OFF THE BEATEN PATH	**MUSEUM OF NEON ART (MONA)–** In the Renaissance Tower, you'll discover one of the world's few tributes to the art of neon—a form of lighting that evolved from advertising status to fine art in less than half a century. Changing exhibits focus on contemporary neon, electric, and kinetic art. The art moves, hisses, and flashes, bringing the entire room to life. In spring and summer, MONA schedules nighttime bus tours to historic and contemporary neon signs throughout the city. ⊠ *501 W. Olympic Blvd.; enter on Hope St.,* ☎ *213/489–9918.* ⊡ *$5; free 2nd Thurs. of month (5–8 only).* ⊙ *Wed.–Sat. 11–5, Sun. noon–5.*

㉑ **Music Center.** L.A.'s major performing arts center since its opening in 1969, the Music Center is home to the Los Angeles Philharmonic, the Los Angeles Opera, and the Center Theater Group. In the past the Music Center has alternated with the Moorish Shrine Auditorium as the site of the Academy Awards; however, the Awards are expected to receive a permanent new home in 2000, when the Hollywood and Highland complex is scheduled for completion. Limousines arrive for the big-screen event at the Hope Street drive-through, and celebrities are whisked through the crowds to the largest and grandest of the three theaters, the **Dorothy Chandler Pavilion,** named after the wife of former *Los Angeles Times* publisher Norman Chandler (she was instrumental in raising the money to build the complex). The philharmonic and opera perform here. The round building inthe middle, the **Mark Taper Forum,** is a smaller theater showing mainlyexperimental works, many on a pre-Broadway run. The **Ahmanson,** at the north end, is the venue for big musicals. The vast complex's cement plaza has a fountain and a Jacques Lipchitz sculpture. ⊠ *135 N. Grand Ave. at 1st St.,* ☎ *213/972–7211; 213/972–7483 tour information.* ⊡ *Free.* ⊙ *75-min tour Tues.–Fri. 10–1:30, Sat. 10–noon; no tours on Fri. Nov.–Apr.*

★ ☙ ⑲ **Natural History Museum of Los Angeles County.** With more than 3.5 million specimens in its halls and galleries, this is the third-largest museum of its type in the United States. The museum has a rich collection of prehistoric fossils and extensive bird, insect, and marine-life exhibits. A brilliant display of stones can be seen in the Gem and Mineral Hall. An elaborate taxidermy exhibit shows North American and African mammals in detailed replicas of their natural habitats. Exhibits typifying various cultural groups include pre-Columbian artifacts and a display of crafts from the South Pacific. The Times-Mirror Hall of Native American Cultures delves into the history of Los Angeles's earliest inhabitants. The Ralph M. Parsons Discovery Center for children has hands-on science-oriented exhibits. ⊠ *900 Exposition Blvd.,* ☎ *213/763–3466.* ⊡ *$6; free 1st Tues. of month.* ⊙ *Tues.–Sun. 10–5; 1-hr tours at 1.*

★ ☙ ⑭ **Olvera Street.** Lively, one-block Olvera Street tantalizes with tile walkways, piñatas, mariachis, and authentic Mexican food. Restored as an open-air Mexican market in 1930, the street is the symbol of the city's beginnings when the original settlers—11 families of Indian, Spanish, Black, and mixed heritage—built earthen and willow huts near the river. Vendors sell puppets, tooled leather goods, sandals, serapes, and other items from little stalls that line the center of the narrow street. On weekends the restaurants are packed, and there is usually music in the plaza and along the street. Two Mexican holidays, Cinco de Mayo (May 5) and Independence Day (September 16), also draw huge crowds. To see Olvera Street at its quietest and perhaps loveliest, visit late on a week-day afternoon, when long shadows heighten the romantic feeling of the passageway. For information, stop by the **Olvera Street Visitors Center,** housed in the Sepulveda House (✉ 622 N. Main St., ☎ 213/628–1274), a Victorian built in 1887 as a hotel and boardinghouse. The center is open from Monday through Saturday between 10 and 3.

Pelanconi House (✉ W-17 Olvera St.), built in 1855, was the first brick building in Los Angeles and has been home to La Golondrina restaurant for 60 years. **Avila Adobe** (✉ E-10 Olvera St.), built in 1818, is considered the oldest building still standing in Los Angeles. This graceful, simple adobe with a traditional interior courtyard is furnished in the style of the 1840s. It is open daily from 9 to 5 (until 4 in winter).

Another Olvera Street landmark is at the **Italian Hall building** (✉ 650 N. Main St.), whose south wall bears a controversial mural. Famed Mexican muralist David Alfaro Siqueiros shocked his patrons in the 1930s by depicting the oppressed workers of Latin America held in check by a menacing American eagle. The anti-imperialist mural was promptly whitewashed into oblivion. The whitewash has since been removed and work is underway to shelter the mural permanently and allow public viewing of it.

At the beginning of Olvera Street is **The Plaza,** a wonderful Mexican-style park shaded by a huge Moreton Bay fig tree. There are plenty of benches here, or perhaps you'd rather stroll on one of the park's many walkways. On weekends, mariachis and folkloric dance groups often perform. Two annual events particularly worth seeing are the Blessing of the Animals and Las Posadas. The blessing takes place on the Saturday before Easter. Residents bring their pets (not just dogs and cats but horses, pigs, cows, birds, hamsters) to be blessed by a priest. For Las Posadas (every night between December 16 and 24), merchants and visitors parade up and down the street, led by children dressed as angels, to commemorate Mary and Joseph's search for shelter on Christmas Eve.

The Old Firehouse, an 1884 building on the south side of the Plaza, contains early fire-fighting equipment and old photographs. Free 50-minute walking tours start from the docent office next door and take in the Merced Theater, Masonic Hall, Pico House, and Garnier Block—all ornate examples of the late 19th-century style. On request, the docent will show you the tunnel passageways under the buildings that were once used by Chinese immigrants. Tours leave on the hour, from 10 to 1 every day but Monday.

NEED A
BREAK?
Dining choices on Olvera Street range from fast-food stands to comfortable, sit-down restaurants. The most authentic Mexican food is at **La Luz del Dia** (✉ 107 Paseo de la Plaza, ☎ 213/628–7495), for traditional favorites such as *chile rellenos* and pickled cactus, as well as handmade tortillas patted out in a practiced rhythm by the women behind the counter. **La Golondrina** (☎ 213/628–4349) and **El Paseo** (☎ 213/626–1361) restaurants, across from each other mid-block, have delightful patios and extensive menus.

❻ Regal Biltmore Hotel. The beaux-arts Biltmore, a creation of Shultze and Weaver, also the architects for New York City's Waldorf-Astoria, opened in 1923. The lobby has the feel of a Spanish palace, and the indoor pool looks like a Roman bath. Afternoon tea is served in the ornate Rendezvous Court. The Academy Awards were held here in the 1930s, and the hotel has also been the site of many films, such as *Chinatown, The Fabulous Baker Boys, The Poseidon Adventure*, and *Independence Day.* ⊠ *506 S. Grand Ave.*, ☎ *213/624–1011.*

★ ⑬ **Union Station.** This building is familiar to moviegoers the world over. It was built in 1939 in a Spanish-mission style that subtly combines Streamline Moderne and Moorish design elements. The waiting room alone is worth a look, its majestic scale so evocative of movies past that you'll half expect to see Carole Lombard or Barbara Stanwyck to step off a train and sashay through. The station's new restaurant, **Traxx** (☞ Chapter 3) is equally atmospheric.

Union Station is also the departure point for the **Metro Rail's Red Line** (☎ 800/COMMUTE, ⊠ $1.35), L.A.'s long-awaited subway system. The subway has been a long time coming and fraught with all sorts of public-relations horrors, including portions of Hollywood Boulevard sinking during tunneling operations. The Red Line, which follows a westward route, has been completed in segments, first from Union Station to MacArthur Park, then to Wilshire Boulevard and Western Avenue. The segment stretching into Hollywood was scheduled to become operational by January 1999. Eventually the Red Line will extend to Hollywood Boulevard and Highland Avenue before jogging northwest to the San Fernando Valley (underneath Hollywood Hills). ⊠ *800 N. Alameda St.*

⓴ **University of Southern California (USC).** Join a free 45-minute campus tour on weekdays, taking in the more notable of its 191 buildings, like the Romanesque **Doheny Memorial Library; Widney Alumni Hall,** a two-story clapboard dating to 1880; and **Mudd Memorial Hall of Philosophy,** which contains a rare book collection of missives from the 13th through 15th centuries. ⊠ *Guest Relations, 615 Childs Way, University Park, adjacent to Exposition Park*, ☎ *213/740–6605.* ☉ *Call for tour schedule.*

OFF THE
BEATEN PATH

WATTS TOWERS – The jewel of rough South Central L.A. is the legacy of Simon Rodia, a tile setter who emigrated from Italy to California and erected one of the world's greatest folk-art structures. From 1921 until 1954, without any help, this eccentric man built the three main cement towers, using pipes, bed frames, and anything else he could find. He embellished them with bits of colored glass, broken pottery, and more than 70,000 seashells. The towers still stand preserved, now the centerpiece of a state historic park and cultural center. It's best to visit during the day, as the area can be dangerous at night. ⊠ *Watts Towers Arts Center, 1727 E. 107th St. (take I–110 to I–105 east; exit north at S. Central Ave., turn right onto 108th St., left onto Graham Ave.).* ⊠ *Free; weekend tours (scheduled to resume summer 1999), $1.* ☉ *Tues.–Sun. 9–5, closed Mon.*

⓶ **Westin Bonaventure Hotel & Suites.** In 1976 John Portman designed these five shimmering cylinders in the sky, with nary a 90° angle. Sheathed in mirrored glass, the building looks like a science-fiction fantasy; it's considered by some to be emblematic of postmodern architecture. The only elevator open to the public rises through the roof of the lobby to soar through the air outside to the revolving restaurant and bar on the 35th floor. ⊠ *404 S. Figueroa St.*, ☎ *213/624–1000.*

HOLLYWOOD AND SUNSET BOULEVARD

For nine decades Hollywood has lured us with its carefully manufactured images promising show-biz glitz and glamour. As visitors, we just want a glimpse of that sexy sophistication, a chance to come close enough to be able to say, "I was there!" Reality check: The magic of Hollywood takes place, for the most part, on sound stages that are not even in Hollywood anymore, and in nondescript film-processing labs and editing bays. Go to Beverly Hills and look at jewelry store windows if you want glitz. As for glamour, well, Hollywood is really a working town. Granted, many of the people who work in Hollywood—actors, directors, writers, composers—are among the highest paid and most celebrated workers in the world. But most of them face the same workaday grind as the rest of us, commuting daily at a factory—that is, a movie, television, or recording studio—and working long hours every day. So much for glamour. No matter. Hollywood is still the entertainment capital of the world. It fires our imaginations with glittering images of romance and adventure, and we must pay homage. Here's a tour that will get you as close to some of that magic as possible.

A Good Tour
Numbers in the text correspond to numbers in the margin and on the Hollywood map.

Start off by driving up into the Hollywood Hills on Beachwood Drive (off Franklin Avenue, just east of Gower Street) for an up-close look at one of the world's most familiar icons: the **HOLLYWOOD sign** ①. Follow the small sign pointing the way to the LAFD Helispot. Turn left onto Rodgerton Drive, which twists and turns higher into the hills. At Deronda Drive, turn right and drive to the end. The Hollywood sign looms off to the left. Turn around and retrace your route down the hill, back to Beachwood for the drive into Hollywood.

Make a right (west) at Franklin Avenue, and prepare to turn left at the next light at Gower Street. Stay on Gower, driving through the section of Sunset Boulevard known as **Gower Gulch.** At Gower and Santa Monica Boulevard, look for the entrance to **Hollywood Memorial Park Cemetery** ②, half a block east on Santa Monica. If you visit the park, retrace your route back to Gower Street and turn left to drive along the western edge of the cemetery flanking Gower. Abutting the cemetery's southern edge is **Paramount Pictures** ③. The famous gate Norma Desmond (Gloria Swanson in *Sunset Boulevard*) was driven through is no longer accessible to the public, but a replica marks the new entrance on Melrose Avenue: turn left from Gower Street to reach the gate.

Next, drive west (right off Gower) on Melrose for three blocks to Vine Street, turn right, and continue to **Hollywood** (Boulevard) **and Vine** ④—an intersection whose fame is worldwide. Across the street, the so-called "record stack" **Capitol Records Tower** ⑤ resembles—to those who remember vinyl—a stack of 45s. Look west to **Ivar Street** ⑥ for a glimpse of the former homes of literary giants William Faulkner and Nathanael West.

Drive west along Hollywood Boulevard for a look at the bronze stars that make up the **Hollywood Walk of Fame** ⑦. If you want to stop along the way to visit the Lingerie Museum at the purple **Frederick's of Hollywood** ⑧ or the **Hollywood Wax Museum** ⑨—both shrines to Holly-

Hollywood

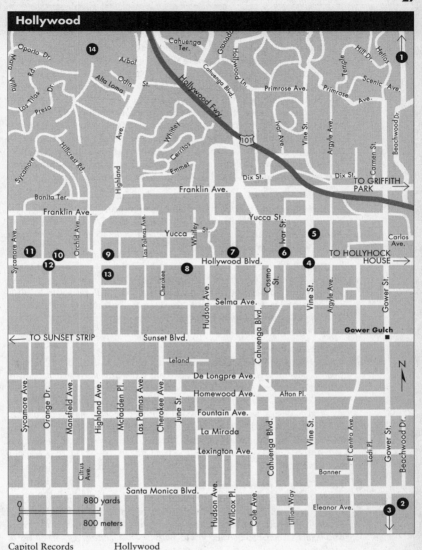

Capitol Records
Tower, **5**

Frederick's of
Hollywood, **8**

Hollywood
Bowl, **14**

Hollywood
Entertainment
Museum, **11**

Hollywood
History Museum, **13**

Hollywood
Memorial Park
Cemetery, **2**

Hollywood
Roosevelt Hotel, **12**

Hollywood Sign, **1**

Hollywood and
Vine, **4**

Hollywood Walk
of Fame, **7**

Hollywood Wax
Museum, **9**

Ivar Street, **6**

Mann's Chinese
Theatre, **10**

Paramount Pictures, **3**

wood camp—metered parking is fairly easy to find. If not, small lots just north and south of the boulevard have reasonable hourly rates.

The biggest draw along Hollywood Boulevard is the elaborate pagoda-style movie palace **Mann's Chinese Theatre** ⑩, a genuine, if kitschy, monument to Hollywood history. Across the street, the Disney folks have impeccably restored the El Capitan theater to its original, exuberant, elaborate facade. Stay on the north side of Hollywood Boulevard and continue west to the **Hollywood Entertainment Museum** ⑪. From the museum, cross Hollywood Boulevard and loop back east along the boulevard past the historic **Hollywood Roosevelt Hotel** ⑫, also the site of the Cinegrill cabaret (☞ Chapter 5). Continue east on Hollywood Boulevard; on Highland Avenue just south of the boulevard is the **Hollywood History Museum** ⑬, housed in the old Max Factor building.

Several blocks north of the Max Factor building on Highland Avenue is the **Hollywood Bowl** ⑭, where summertime concerts take place. The first feature-length film shot in Hollywood, Cecil B. DeMille's *The Squaw Man,* was produced across from the Bowl in 1913 in the building at 2100 North Highland Avenue.

TIMING

Plan to spend the better part of a morning or afternoon taking in Hollywood and Sunset Boulevard. A walking tour of Paramount Studios will add at least two and half hours to your itinerary. Hollywood Boulevard attracts a sometimes-bizarre group of folks; your best bet for a safe walk down the boulevard is during the day.

Sights to See

★ ❺ **Capitol Records Tower.** The romantic story about the origin of this symbol of '50s chic is that singer Nat King Cole and songwriter Johnny Mercer suggested that the record company's headquarters be shaped to look like a stack of 45s. Architect Welton Beckett claimed he just wanted to design a structure that economized space. On its south wall, L.A. artist Richard Wyatt's mural *Hollywood Jazz, 1945–1972,* immortalizes musical greats Duke Ellington, Billie Holiday, Ella Fitzgerald, and Miles Davis. The blinking light at the top of the tower spells out "Hollywood" in Morse code. ✉ *1750 N. Vine St.*

❽ **Frederick's of Hollywood.** Though you can stock up on risqué (and trashy) lingerie here, the real reason to visit Frederick's is to view the undergarments of some of Hollywood's legends: In the **Lingerie Museum,** Madonna's bustier shares space with Cher's kinky underwear and Marilyn Monroe's merry widow from *Let's Make Love.* ✉ *6608 Hollywood Blvd.,* ☎ *323/466–8506.*

Gower Gulch. Small B-picture Poverty Row studios once filled this area. Radio broadcasts with Edgar Bergen and Charlie McCarthy originated at the CBS studio on the northwest corner of Gower and Sunset. At the southeast corner of the same intersection is the old Columbia Pictures studio (*Gilda, All the King's Men, Born Yesterday, From Here to Eternity, The Caine Mutiny*), now known as **Sunset-Gower Studios,** where television shows like *America's Funniest Home Videos* are taped.

Griffith Park. Like Central Park in Manhattan, or Golden Gate Park in San Francisco, Griffith Park is the Angeleno's great escape (☞ Closeup: Griffith Park, *below*). Though most people come here simply to take in the tranquility of open space, several attractions are worthwhile in their own rights. Among them are the **Griffith Observatory and Planetarium,** the **Los Angeles Zoo,** the **Autry Museum of Western Heritage,** and the **Greek Theatre.** Kids love **Travel Town** and the

Griffith Park & Southern Railroad; there are also pony rides and a vintage carousel. ⊠ *Los Feliz Blvd. at Western Canyon Rd., Vermont Ave., Crystal Springs Dr., and Riverside Dr.* ☏ *Observatory and planetarium, 323/664–1191; laserium, 818/901–9405; zoo, 323/644–6400; museum, 323/667–2000; theater, 323/665–1927; Travel Town, 323/662–5874; railroad, 323/664–6903; pony rides, 323/664–3266; carousel, 323/665–3051.* ☐ *Observatory and Hall of Science free; planetarium $4; laserium $7–$8; zoo $8.25 (Safari Shuttle Tour $3); museum $7.50; Travel Town free, railroad $1.75; pony rides $1.50; carousel $1.* ⊙ *Observatory and planetarium, daily 12:30 PM–10 PM in summer (Tues.–Fri. 2 PM–10 PM, weekends 12:30 PM–10 PM rest of yr); zoo, daily, 10–5 (animals removed from view starting at 4:30); museum, Tues.–Sun. 10–5; theater performances Apr.–Oct.; Travel Town weekdays 10–4, weekends and holidays 10–5; railroad daily 10–5; carousel, weekends only (daily in summer); pony rides, Tues.–Sun. 10–5, weather permitting.*

OFF THE BEATEN PATH	**HOLLYHOCK HOUSE** – The first of several houses Frank Lloyd Wright designed in Los Angeles, this 1921 manse was commissioned by heiress Aline Barnsdall. A perfect example of the pre-Columbian style of which Wright was so fond at that time, the house features a stylized hollyhock flower, which appears in a broad band around the house's exterior and even on the dining room chairs. The restored Hollyhock House includes original, Wright-designed furniture. ⊠ *4800 Hollywood Blvd.,* ☏ *323/913-4157.* ☐ *$2.* ⊙ *Tours Wed.–Sun., noon, 1, 2, and 3.*

⓮ **Hollywood Bowl.** Summer evening concerts have been a tradition since 1922 at this amphitheater cradled in the Hollywood Hills. The Bowl is the summer home of the Los Angeles Philharmonic, but musical fare also includes pop and jazz. The 17,000-plus seating capacity ranges from boxes (where fancy alfresco preconcert meals can be catered) to concrete bleachers in the rear. Some prefer the back rows for their romantic appeal. Come early for a picnic in the surrounding grounds. Before the concert, or during the day, visit the **Hollywood Bowl Museum** (☏ 323/850–2058) for a capsulized version of the Bowl's 75-year history. Display drawers open to reveal vintage programs or letters written by Aaron Copland and Eugene Ormandy; headphones let you listen to an 80-year-old recording of soprano Amelita Galli-Curci, a superstar of her day, singing "Caro Nome" from Verdi's *Rigoletto*— or Ella Fitzgerald or Paul McCartney, all of whom performed at the Bowl. ⊠ *2301 N. Highland Ave.,* ☏ *323/850–2000.* ⊙ *Museum, Tues.–Sat. 10–4; grounds daily sunrise–sunset (call for performance schedule).*

⓫ **Hollywood Entertainment Museum.** A multimedia presentation in the main rotunda and interactive exhibits track the evolution of Hollywood, from the low-tech silent era to today's hyper-tech world of special effects. Highlights are the marvelously detailed miniature model of 1936 Hollywood, and sets from television shows such as the bar from TV's *Cheers,* into which the series' stars carved their names. Another exhibit displays the Max Factor makeup first used by movie stars, complete with an old-fashioned vanity table with Hollywood-style mirror lights. ⊠ *7021 Hollywood Blvd.,* ☏ *323/465-7900.* ☐ *$7.50.* ⊙ *Tues.– Sun. 11–6.*

⓭ **Hollywood History Museum.** The legendary Max Factor building, once home to make-up czar Max Factor and his beauty empire, is a fitting place in which to present Hollywood's glamorous history. Opened in fall 1998 after a two-year restoration, the grand Art Deco building houses exhibits and displays from the film capital's most memorable eras: "Hollywood, a New Town and Infant Industry," "The Silent Era," and "Talkies and Color" cover Tinseltown's fledgling years. People from all generations will most likely identify with "The Westerns," "Hollywood's Golden Era," and "Adventure Films." Then come "The War Years" and "The Musical Comedies," testaments to an extraordinary era; and the more modern "Spies and Detectives," "Sci Fi," "The Art of Advanced Technology," and "Hollywood in the New Millennium." Costumes, artifacts, and props from famous and rare Hollywood motion pictures are also on display, as are artifacts such as movie posters, scripts, cameras, and projectors. Adjoining the museum is Chasen's Hollywood Café, named after the legendary restaurant where the stars used to gather for cocktails and conversation. ⊠ *1660 N. Highland Ave.,* ☎ *323/464–7776.* ☒ *$8.* ☉ *Mon.–Sun. 9–9; call to confirm.*

②　Hollywood Memorial Park Cemetery. Rudolph Valentino, Tyrone Power, and Jayne Mansfield are among the celebrities buried here. Sadly, the cemetery has fallen into a state of neglect: Weeds have sprung up around many tombstones, and the place feels abandoned. Still, if you're intent on seeing the graves of the stars, you can pick up a map of the grounds in the office at the entrance. At the lake area you'll find the crypt of Cecil B. DeMille and the graves of Nelson Eddy and Douglas Fairbanks, Sr. Inside the Cathedral Mausoleum is Rudolph Valentino's crypt (the mysterious Lady in Black, who for years visited on the anniversary of his death, comes no more). Other stars interred in the mausoleum are Peter Lorre and Eleanor Powell. Norma Talmadge and Clifton Webb rest in the Abbey of Palms Mausoleum. In Pineland, the headstone on the grave of Mel Blanc, voice of Bugs Bunny and other Warner Bros. cartoon characters, reads, "That's all, folks!" ⊠ *6000 Santa Monica Blvd.,* ☎ *323/469–1181.* ☉ *Daily 8–5.*

⑫　Hollywood Roosevelt Hotel. The first Academy Awards banquet was held here in 1927. A display of vintage Hollywood photographs and other historical memorabilia occupies the hotel's mezzanine level. Also located in the hotel is Cinegrill, a cabaret steeped in Hollywood history. Have a look at the pool out back: David Hockney was commissioned to paint the "mural" at the bottom (actually nothing more than a series of blue blotches). ⊠ *7000 Hollywood Blvd.,* ☎ *323/466-7000.*

★　**①　Hollywood Sign.** With letters 50 ft tall, Hollywood's trademark sign can be spotted from miles away. The sign, which originally spelled out "Hollywoodland," was erected in the Hollywood Hills in 1923 to promote a real-estate development. In 1949 the "land" portion of the sign was taken down. Over the years pranksters have altered it, albeit temporarily, to spell out "Hollyweed" (in the 1970s, to commemorate lenient marijuana laws), "Go Navy" (before a Rose Bowl game), and "Perotwood" (during the 1992 presidential election). In 1994, however, a fence and surveillance equipment were installed surrounding the sign to deter intruders.

④　Hollywood and Vine. The mere mention of this intersection inspires images of a street corner bustling with movie stars, starlets, and moguls passing by, on foot, or in snazzy Duesenbergs and classy Rolls-Royces. In the old days this was the hub of the radio and movie industry, and there was nothing unusual about film stars like Gable and Garbo hurrying in or out of office buildings at the intersection on their way to or from their agents' offices. These days, Hollywood and Vine is far from the action, and foot traffic is rather pedestrian, so to speak. The Brown Derby restaurant once stood a half-block south of the intersection

(⊠ 1628 N. Vine St.). Nearby is the Palace Theater (⊠ 1735 N. Vine St.), where the 1950s TV show *This Is Your Life* was recorded; it's now a rental venue for rock shows. Within a block or two of the intersection, however, you can still see the **Capitol Records** building (☞ *above*) and **Pantages Theater** (⊠ 6233 Hollywood Blvd.), a former opulent movie palace now used to house large-scale Broadway musicals on tour. The arrival of the Metro Rail Red Line subway in 1999 may revive some activity around the intersection.

★ ❼ **Hollywood Walk of Fame.** All along this mile-long stretch of Hollywood Boulevard sidewalk, entertainment legends' names are embossed in brass, each at the center of a pink star embedded in dark-gray terrazzo. The first eight stars were unveiled in 1960 at the northwest corner of Highland Avenue and Hollywood Boulevard: Olive Borden, Ronald Colman, Louise Fazenda, Preston Foster, Burt Lancaster, Edward Sedgwick, Ernest Torrence, and Joanne Woodward (some of these names have stood the test of time better than others). Since then, more than 2,000 others have been immortalized, though that honor doesn't come cheap—upon selection by a special committee, the personality in question (or more likely his or her movie studio or record company) must pay $7,500 for the privilege. Naturally, many so-called celebs are allowed to buy their way in, which means that many names are not all that familiar. To aid in the identification, celebrities are classified by one of five logos: a motion-picture camera, a radio microphone, a television set, a record, and a theatrical mask. Here's a miniguide to a few of the more famous celebs' stars: Marlon Brando at 1765 Vine, Charlie Chaplin at 6751 Hollywood, W. C. Fields at 7004 Hollywood, Clark Gable at 1608 Vine, Marilyn Monroe at 6774 Hollywood (in front of McDonalds), Rudolph Valentino at 6164 Hollywood, Michael Jackson at 6927 Hollywood, and John Wayne at 1541 Vine. You can always call the **Hollywood Chamber of Commerce** (⊠ 7018 Hollywood Blvd., ☎ 323/469–8311) or the **Hollywood Visitor Information Center** (⊠ 6541 Hollywood Blvd., ☎ 323/236–2331) to find out where your favorite celebrity's star can be found. Ask when the next sidewalk star installation ceremony is scheduled to take place; the honoree usually shows up for the event.

❾ **Hollywood Wax Museum.** Here you'll spot celebrities that real life can no longer provide (Mary Pickford, Elvis Presley, and Clark Gable) and a few that even real life never did (such as the *Star Trek* cast). Other living legends on display include actors Kevin Costner and Brad Pitt. A short film on Academy Award winners screens daily. ⊠ *6767 Hollywood Blvd.,* ☎ *323/462–8860.* ☞ *$8.95.* ⊙ *Sun.–Thurs. 10 AM–midnight, Fri.–Sat. 10 AM–2 AM.*

NEED A BREAK? **Musso & Frank Grill** (⊠ 6667 Hollywood Blvd., ☎ 323/467–5123), open since 1919, is the last remaining Old Hollywood watering hole. Wash down a plate of lamb chops, spinach, and sourdough bread with a martini, or just stop in for a Coke and soak up some atmosphere. Expect high prices and some attitude.

❻ **Ivar Street.** William Faulkner wrote *Absalom, Absalom!* while he lived at the old Knickerbocker Hotel (⊠ 1714 N. Ivar St.), and Nathanael West wrote *The Day of the Locust* in his apartment at the Parva Sed-Apta (⊠ 1817 N. Ivar St.).

★ ❿ **Mann's Chinese Theatre.** The former "Grauman's Chinese," a fantasy of Chinese pagodas and temples, is a place only Hollywood could turn out. Although you have to buy a movie ticket to appreciate the inte-

GRIFFITH PARK

WITH SO MUCH OF LOS Angeles paved in cement and asphalt, the 4,100-acre Griffith Park stands out as a special place. In the northwest corner of the city, it's the largest municipal park and urban wilderness area in the United States, and a communal backyard for this city of 3.5 million. On hot summer weekends, the park becomes a bucolic escape for inner-city families who spread out in the shade. Joggers, cyclists, and walkers course its roadways, and golfers play its four municipal courses in rain or shine. Within the park, there are tennis courts, horse stables, a zoo, a collection of vintage locomotives and railroad cars, a fern garden, merry-go-round, observatory and planetarium, Western heritage museum, and the 6,100-seat Greek Theatre, where Rod Stewart, Tina Turner, and the Gipsy Kings have all performed.

The park was named after Griffith J. Griffith, a mining tycoon who donated 3,000 acres of land to the city for the park in 1896. Additional donations and land purchases by the city expanded the park to its present size. If some of this terrain, which ranges from forested valleys to semi-arid foothills, seems familiar, it will come as no surprise to learn that the park has been used as a film and television location since the early days of motion pictures. One Hollywood producer is reported to have advised, "A tree is a tree, a rock is a rock, shoot it in Griffith Park!" Since then, those trees and rocks have appeared in countless films and television shows, including features like the (original) *The Invasion of the Body Snatchers, Batman,* and *Jurassic Park,* as well as TV shows such as *Bonanza.*

One of the park's most obvious filming sites is the **Griffith Observatory and Planetarium.** Sitting on a promontory overlooking Hollywood and downtown, this art deco landmark off Vermont Avenue was immortalized in *Rebel Without a Cause,* and *The Terminator* was also filmed here. A different kind of film shot in Griffith Park—the Western—is celebrated at the **Autry Museum of Western Heritage,** in the northeast corner of the park at the junction of Western Heritage Way and Zoo Drive. Here, memorabilia, art, and artifacts conjure up the American West—both the movie and real-life versions: You'll find Teddy Roosevelt's Colt revolver, Buffalo Bill Cody's saddle, and Annie Oakley's gold-plate Smith and Wesson guns, along with video screens showing clips from old Westerns.

Not far from the museum, at the junction of the Ventura Freeway (Highway 134) and Golden State Freeway (I–5), the 80-acre **Los Angeles Zoo** is noted for its breeding of endangered species like the California condor. Other points of interest are **Amir's Gardens,** a lovely picnic spot accessible only by fire-road trail (climb up the hill from Mineral Springs Picnic, off Griffith Drive); **Dante's View,** another garden spot en route to the top of Mt. Washington (elev. 1,652 ft); and Ferndell, where California sycamores shade more than 50 fern species (look for the dell off the park's Western Canyon entrance off Los Feliz Boulevard and Western Avenue.

rior trappings, the courtyard is open for browsing. Here you'll see those oh-so-famous cement hand- and footprints. This tradition is said to have begun at the theater's opening in 1927, with the premiere of Cecil B. DeMille's *King of Kings,* when actress Norma Talmadge accidentally stepped into the wet cement. Now more than 160 celebrities have contributed imprints of their appendages for posterity, along with a few other oddball imprints, like the one of Jimmy Durante's nose. ⊠ *6925 Hollywood Blvd.,* ☎ *323/464–8111.*

OFF THE BEATEN PATH	**PACIFIC DESIGN CENTER –** These two architecturally intriguing buildings known as the "Blue Whale" and the "Green Whale" are interior-decorating showrooms open only to the trade. Cesar Pelli designed the blue structure in the mid-1970s; the center added the green one, also by Pelli, in 1998. ⊠ *8687 Melrose Ave.,* ☎ *310/657–0800.*

❸ **Paramount Pictures.** The last major studio still located in Hollywood is the best place to see what a real Hollywood movie studio looks like. Two-hour guided walking tours of the 85-year-old studio include historical narrative about Rudolph Valentino, Mae West, Mary Pickford, Lucille Ball, and other stars who worked on the lot. Movies and TV shows are still filmed here; if you're lucky you might see a show being produced. Tours are first come, first served and leave from the pedestrian walk-up gate on Melrose Street; park in the lot at Bronson and Melrose avenues. Children under 10 are not admitted. ⊠ *5555 Melrose Ave.,* ☎ *323/956–5575.* ➾ *$15.* ☉ *2-hr tour weekdays on the hr, 9–2.*

Sunset Strip. For 60 years the Hollywood nighttime crowd has headed for the 1¾-mi stretch of Sunset Boulevard between Crescent Heights Boulevard on the east and Doheny Drive on the west, known as the Sunset Strip. In the 1930s and '40s, stars like Tyrone Power, Errol Flynn, Norma Shearer, and Rita Hayworth got themselves gussied up in tuxedos and fancy gowns for wild evenings of dancing and drinking at nightclubs like Trocadero, Ciro's, and Mocambo. By the '60s and '70s, the Strip had become the center of rock 'n' roll: Johnny Rivers, the Byrds, the Doors, Elton John, and Bruce Springsteen gave legendary performances on stages at clubs like the **Whisky** (⊠ 8901 Sunset Blvd., ☎ 310/652–4202) and **Roxy** (⊠ 9009 Sunset Blvd., ☎ 310/276–2222). Nowadays it's the **Viper Room** (⊠ 8852 Sunset Blvd., ☎ 310/358–1880), the **House of Blues** (⊠ 8430 Sunset Blvd., ☎ 323/848–5100), and **The Key Club** (⊠ 9039 Sunset Blvd., ☎ 310/274–5800) that keep young Hollywood busy after dark. The Strip lies entirely within the incorporated city of West Hollywood, one of L.A.'s trendiest areas.

Universal Studios Hollywood. ☞ The San Fernando Valley tour, *below.*

WILSHIRE BOULEVARD, MUSEUM ROW, AND FARMERS MARKET

Just east of Fairfax Avenue in the Miracle Mile district is the three-block stretch of Wilshire Boulevard known as Museum Row, with four museums of widely varying themes and a prehistoric tar pit to boot. Only a few blocks away is the historic Farmers Market, a great place to jumpstart a day of museum-hopping with coffee and pastries and people-watching. Wilshire Boulevard itself is something of a cultural monument, as well. It begins its grand, 16-mi sweep to the sea in downtown Los Angeles. Along the way it passes through once-grand but now-rundown neighborhoods near MacArthur Park, the elegant old-money enclave of Hancock Park, Miracle Mile and Museum Row, the showy city of Beverly Hills, and the high-priced high-rise condo corridor in Westwood, before ending its march at the cliffs above the Pacific Ocean. The drive from downtown to the ocean can be traffic-clogged; Wilshire is a major thoroughfare and tends to be busy all day long. For avid urban explorers, the most interesting stretch historically is the boulevard's eastern portion, from Fairfax Avenue to downtown.

A Good Tour

Numbers in the text correspond to numbers in the margin and on the Wilshire Boulevard, Museum Row, and Farmers Market map.

Start the day with coffee and fresh-baked pastries at **Farmers Market** ①, a few blocks north of Wilshire Boulevard at 3rd Street and Fairfax Avenue. Drive south on Fairfax Avenue to the **Miracle Mile** ② district of Wilshire Boulevard. The black-and-gold Art Deco building on the northeast corner is a former department store that now houses exhibition galleries shared by the Los Angeles County Museum of Art and the **Southwest Museum** at LACMA West. Turn left onto Wilshire and proceed to Ogden Drive or a block farther to Spaulding Avenue, where you can park the car and set out on foot to explore the museums.

The large complex of contemporary buildings surrounded by a park (on the corner of Wilshire and Ogden Drive) is **The Los Angeles County Museum of Art** ③, also known as LACMA. It's the largest museum west of Chicago and houses works spanning the history of art from ancient times to the present. Also occupying the park are the prehistoric **La Brea Tar Pits** ④, where many of the fossils displayed at the adjacent **George C. Page Museum of La Brea Discoveries** ⑤ were found. Across Wilshire are the **Carole & Barry Kaye Museum of Miniatures** ⑥ and, back at the corner of Wilshire and Fairfax, the **Petersen Automotive Museum** ⑦, which surveys the history of the car in Los Angeles.

From Museum Row and Miracle Mile, a drive east along Wilshire Boulevard to downtown gives you a minitour of a historical and cultural cross-section of Los Angeles. At Highland Avenue you enter the old-money enclave of **Hancock Park** ⑧. At Western Avenue the **Wiltern Theater** ⑨ stands across the street from the intersection's newest landmark, the Metro station. The frequency of Korean-language signs in this area is a clue that you're now driving along the edge of **Koreatown** ⑩. Just past Normandie Avenue is the **Ambassador Hotel** ⑪, now abandoned. Farther on, as Wilshire crosses Vermont Avenue toward downtown Los Angeles, you'll pass the magnificent **Bullock's Wilshire** ⑫ building before coming to **MacArthur Park** ⑬, the heart of a burgeoning Central American community.

TIMING

The museums open between 10 and noon, so plan your tour around the opening time of the museum you wish to visit first. LACMA is open Monday but closed Wednesday, and has extended hours into the evening, closing at 8 (9 on Friday). The other museums are closed on Monday. Weekends bring the largest crowds to Farmers Market and the museums. Budget-minded visitors may want to plan a visit to LACMA on the second Tuesday of the month, when admission to all but ticketed exhibits is free. Set aside a day to do this entire tour: an hour for the Farmers Market, three to four hours for the museums, and an hour for the Wilshire Boulevard sights.

Sights to See

⑪   **The Ambassador Hotel.** Now closed and fenced off, this legendary former hotel opened in 1921, at which time it housed the famed Coconut

35

Wilshire Boulevard, Museum Row, and Farmers Market

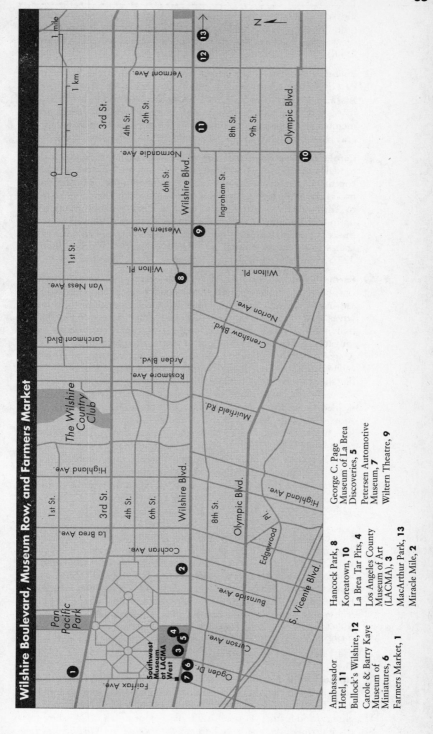

Ambassador Hotel, 11
Bullock's Wilshire, 12
Carole & Barry Kaye Museum of Miniatures, 6
Farmers Market, 1
Hancock Park, 8
Koreatown, 10
La Brea Tar Pits, 4
Los Angeles County Museum of Art (LACMA), 3
MacArthur Park, 13
Miracle Mile, 2
George C. Page Museum of La Brea Discoveries, 5
Petersen Automotive Museum, 7
Wiltern Theatre, 9

Grove nightclub. In the '30s and '40s several Academy Awards presentations took place here. On a more somber note, it was here that presidential nominee Robert F. Kennedy was assassinated on June 5, 1968. ⊠ *3400 Wilshire Blvd.*

⑫ Bullock's Wilshire. The copper-trimmed Art Moderne building just east of Vermont Avenue used to house Bullock's department store, the first Los Angeles store built to showcase the automobile, in 1929. Later it was known for its tea room, a place many longtime Angelenos remember visiting on special occasions. The store has been closed for several years but is still a sight to behold. ⊠ *3050 Wilshire Blvd.*

❻ Carole & Barry Kaye Museum of Miniatures. Besides scaled-down models of the Hollywood Bowl, the Vatican, and several famous European châteaux, the George Stuart Gallery of miniature historical figures is one of the highlights of this pint-sized world. There's also a tribute to America's First Ladies (as far back as Martha Washington), dolled up in their inaugural ball gowns, as well as a rendition of a turn-of-the-century soda fountain, complete with silver spoons the size of eyelashes and a cherry as small as a fly's eye. ⊠ *5900 Wilshire Blvd.,* ☎ *323/937–6464.* ⊡ *$7.50.* ⊙ *Tues.–Sat. 10–5, Sun. 11–5.*

★ ❶ Farmers Market. In July 1934, two entrepreneurs envisioned a European–style open-air market, to be built near the corner of 3rd Street and Fairfax, where farmers would sell their produce to local housewives. The idea was an instant success: Farmers agreed to pay the 50¢ daily parking fee; in exchange, they got to display their wares on the tailgates of their trucks. Soon after the marketplace opened, Blanche Magee, a local restaurateur, drove by and saw a crowd of customers buying produce and flowers from the backs of the trucks. The next day she returned with a hamper full of sandwiches and soft drinks, which she sold to the farmers and customers. Convinced that the marketplace needed a restaurant, she made her case to the market's administration; soon afterwards, **Magee's Kitchen and Deli** became the Farmers Market's first restaurant. (The restaurant is still there, run by Blanche's daughter-in-law, Phyllis.) Today the market has more than 110 stalls and more than 20 restaurants, many with alfresco dining under umbrellas. Close to CBS Television Studios, the market is a major hub for stars and stargazers, tourists and locals—it's one of the few community gathering points in the sprawling city of L.A. Parking is free. ⊠ *6333 W. 3rd St.,* ☎ *323/933–9211.* ⊙ *Mon.–Sat. 9–7, Sun. 10–6 (later in summer).*

NEED A BREAK?   Stop for a BLT on sourdough (rated one of *L.A. Magazine's Los Angeles Magazine* favorite 100 dishes of L.A.), a chicken–chopped salad chock-full of veggies, or a slice of apple–ginger–buttermilk coffeecake and a mocha-french-roast malt at **Kokomo Café,** (☎ 213/933-0773), a favorite fueling station among celebs, black-clad hipsters, and people who like good food. Even the most ardent purists are sure to approve of the melt-in-your mouth donuts at **Bob's Coffee & Donuts** (☎ 213/933-8929), where Bob Tusquellas, a.k.a. "the Donut Man" churns out nearly 2,000 fresh-made jelly-filled, cinnamon-rolled, and glazed creations every day.

❽ Hancock Park. Highland Avenue marks the western perimeter of Hancock Park. In the 1920s, old-money families came here to build English Tudor–style homes with East Coast landscaping that defied local climate and history. For a closer look, detour north off Wilshire for a drive through the residential area. ⊠ *Bordered by Wilshire and Beverly Blvds., Highland Ave., and Wilton Pl.*

⑩ **Koreatown.** Although L.A.'s sizable Korean population is scattered throughout the city, it's especially concentrated in the area known as Koreatown, along Olympic Boulevard between Vermont and Western avenues. Here you'll find Korean specialty food stores among other stores selling everything from furniture to electronics. The area is also home to many Central Americans. ⊠ *Bordered by Vermont and Western Aves., 8th St., and Pico Blvd.*

★ ④ **La Brea Tar Pits.** About 40,000 years ago, deposits of oil rose to the Earth's surface, collected in shallow pools, and coagulated into sticky asphalt. In the early 20th century, geologists discovered that the sticky goo contained the largest collection of Pleistocene, or Ice Age, fossils ever found at one location: more than 600 species of birds, mammals, plants, reptiles, and insects. More than 100 tons of fossil bones have been removed in excavations over the last seven decades. Statues of a family of mammoths in the big pit near the corner of Wilshire and Curson depict how many of them were entombed: Edging down to a pond of water to drink, animals were caught in the tar and unable to extricate themselves. There are several pits scattered around Hancock Park; construction in the area has often had to accommodate these oozing pits and, in nearby streets and along sidewalks, little bits of tar occasionally ooze up, unstoppable.

⑤ **George C. Page Museum of La Brea Discoveries.** At the La Brea Tar Pits, this member of the Natural History Museum family is set, bunker-like, half underground. A bas-relief around four sides depicts life in the Pleistocene era, and the museum has more than three million Ice Age fossils. Exhibits include reconstructed, life-size skeletons of mammoths, wolves, sloths, eagles, and condors. A permanent installation shows a robotic saber-toothed cat attacking a huge ground sloth. The glass-enclosed Paleontological Laboratory permits observation of the ongoing cleaning, identification, and cataloging of fossils excavated from the nearby asphalt deposits. *The La Brea Story,* a short documentary film, is shown every 15–30 minutes. A hologram magically puts flesh on 9,000-year-old "La Brea Woman," and an interactive tar mechanism shows just how hard it would be to free oneself from the sticky mess. ⊠ *5801 Wilshire Blvd.,* ☎ *323/936–2230.* ⌨ *$6, free 1st Tues. of month.* ☉ *Tues.–Sun. 10–5.*

③ **Los Angeles County Museum of Art (LACMA).** Still a young museum—only 32 years old—LACMA has assembled an encyclopedic collection of more than 150,000 works from around the world; its collection is widely considered the most comprehensive in the western United States. Islamic, South and Southeast Asian, Far Eastern, and American works are especially well-represented. The museum's five buildings also house fine collections of modern and contemporary art, costumes and textiles, decorative arts, European paintings and sculpture, photography, drawings, and prints.

A major reorganization project has made the museum easier to navigate. Galleries of Islamic art are now arranged chronologically, emphasizing visual connections and recurrent themes. South and Southeast Asian galleries, which contain one of the finest collections outside Asia, contain several new acquisitions, including the *Hindu Saint Manikkavacakar,* an elegant 12th-century South Indian bronze statue, and *Buddha Calling the Earth to Witness,* a bronze image from 11th-century Tibet. The Far Eastern art galleries have also been expanded and improved.

LACMA's collection of American art—paintings, sculpture, furniture, and decorative arts from the Colonial era to early 20th century—is one of the finest in the nation, and now, for the first time ever, a core of galleries presents these works together. In addition to furniture, silver, glass, ceramics, paintings, and sculpture of the same periods, there are landscape genre paintings from the Federal period, frontier art, works from the Ash Can School, and regional developments such as California impressionism and surrealism. Masterworks such as George Bellows's *Cliff Dwellers,* Mary Cassatt's *Mother About to Wash Her Sleepy Child,* and Winslow Homer's *The Cotton Pickers* have been cleaned and restored.

Throughout the museum, wall panels introduce themes that provide a framework for viewing. A new CD-ROM audio guide narrated by LACMA curators provides overviews and insights into the permanent collection. ⊠ *5905 Wilshire Blvd.,* ☎ *323/857–6000; 323/857–0098 TDD.* 🎟 *$6, free 2nd Tues. of month.* ⊙ *Mon, Tues., Thurs. noon–8, Fri. noon–9, weekends 11–8.*

NEED A BREAK? Unfortunately, the café at LACMA is little more than an airport-style cafeteria, with plastic-wrapped food and Styrofoam cups. Instead, walk one block east to the corner of Wilshire and Curson to **Callender's Wilshire** (⊠ 5773 Wilshire Blvd., ☎ 323/937-7952), where focaccia-bread sandwiches, grilled portabello-mushroom burgers, and pastas are served on an inviting umbrella-shaded brick patio.

⑬ **MacArthur Park.** Grassy knolls and a lake with paddleboats for rent present a welcome break from the crowded, rundown neighborhoods surrounding the park—once an enclave of wealth and prestige, as evidenced by many fine old apartment buildings in the surrounding streets. These days the community is largely Central American. Crime and drug-dealing were rampant in the area a few years ago, but cleanup efforts have helped reduce those incidents. MacArthur Park is a major stop on the Red Line subway. ⊠ *Wilshire Blvd. and Alvarado St.*

❷ **Miracle Mile.** The strip of Wilshire Boulevard between La Brea and Fairfax avenues was vacant land in the 1920s, when a developer bought the parcel to develop into a shopping and business district. The auto age was just emerging and nobody thought the venture could be successful, so the strip became known as Miracle Mile. It was the world's first linear downtown, with building designs incorporating wide store windows to attract attention from passing automobiles. The area went into a decline in the '50s and '60s, but it's now enjoying a comeback, as Los Angeles's Art Deco architecture has come to be appreciated, preserved, and restored. Exemplary architecture includes the **El Rey Theater** (⊠ 5515 Wilshire Blvd., ☎ 323/936–6400), which is now a sometimes-nightclub.

★ ❼ **Petersen Automotive Museum.** More than just a building full of antique or unique cars, the Petersen proves highly entertaining and informative, thanks to the lifelike dioramas and street scenes that help establish a context for the history of the automobile and its influence on our lives. Rotating exhibits on the second floor may include Hollywood-celebrity and movie cars (for example, Fred's rockmobile from *The Flintstones* flick), "muscle" cars (like a 1969 Dodge Daytona 440 Magnum), motorcycles, and commemorative displays of the Ferrari. You'll also learn about the origins of our modern-day car-insurance system, as well as the history of L.A.'s formidable freeway network. A children's interactive Discovery Center illustrates the mechanics of the automobile; a gift shop and research library are also within the museum. ⊠ *6060 Wilshire Blvd.,* ☎ *323/930–2277.* ⊒ *$7.* ⊙ *Tues.–Sun. 10–6.*

Southwest Museum at LACMA West. L.A.'s oldest museum expanded in 1998 from its main facility on Mt. Washington into this 8,000-square-ft satellite location. The additional space gives the museum a chance to present even more of its fine collection of American Indian material culture and art dating from 1800 to the present. At press time, admission fees and schedules had not yet been determined. ⊠ *Northeast corner of Fairfax Ave. and Wilshire Blvd.,* ☎ *323/221–2163.*

❾ Wiltern Theatre. This magnificent example of all-out Art Deco architecture is still used for major performances (☞ Major Concert Halls *in* Chapter 5). The 1930s zigzag design was restored to its splendid turquoise hue in 1985. ⊠ *3790 Wilshire Blvd., at Western Ave..*

BEVERLY HILLS AND CENTURY CITY

If you've got money to spend—lots of it—then come to Beverly Hills. Its main shopping street, Rodeo Drive, is the platinum vein of its commercial district (a.k.a. the Golden Triangle) and has been likened to Rome's Via Condotti and London's Bond Street, though to most of the city's 12 million annual visitors the comparisons are meaningless. What everybody does understand, however, is that Beverly Hills means expensive retailers like Tiffany, Fendi, Gucci, and Cartier; sky-high real estate prices; legendary hotels; high-powered restaurants; and—most of all—movie stars. Like Siamese twins, fable-making Hollywood and fabled Beverly Hills are inseparably linked in the popular imagination. Mary Pickford and Douglas Fairbanks Sr. led the way 80 years ago by setting up house in an old hunting lodge in Benedict Canyon, renovating it into what became known as Pickfair. Hollywood royalty followed suit, and pretty soon Beverly Hills, once a tract of bean patches known as Morocco Junction, was on its way to becoming hometown to Hollywood's royalty. Movie stars still live in Beverly Hills, though nowadays, while their agents package mega-million dollar deals in offices on Wilshire Boulevard, the stars are just as likely to be found hiding out on a ranch in Montana or Argentina. But the allure of Beverly Hills continues to draw armies of visitors on the lookout for a famous face and a glimpse of an opulent lifestyle most mortals are left only to imagine.

A Good Tour
Numbers in the text correspond to numbers in the margin and on the Westside map.

Begin a tour of Beverly Hills with a drive into the hills above Sunset Boulevard for a look at **Greystone Mansion** ① on Loma Vista Drive. Less than a mile west on Sunset is the landmark **Beverly Hills Hotel** ②. Behind the hotel, on Elden Way, is the **Virginia Robinson Gardens** ③, the oldest estate in Beverly Hills and now open to the public for walking tours (by appointment only).

Across the street from the hotel is the pretty little triangular park named for the cowboy-philosopher Will Rogers, who was once honorary mayor of Beverly Hills. Turn south here onto **Rodeo Drive** ④ (pronounced ro-*day*-o). You'll pass through a residential neighborhood before hitting the shopping stretch of Rodeo south of Santa Monica Boulevard. This is where you'll want to get out of the car and walk around. At Rodeo Drive and Dayton Way, the **Beverly Hills Trolley** ⑤ departs for 40-minute tours of the city (between May and December). Across Wilshire, the **Regent Beverly Wilshire Hotel** ⑥ serves as a temporary residence for the rich, famous, and cultured. The **Museum of Television & Radio** ⑦ stands a block east of Rodeo, on Beverly Drive at Little Santa Monica Boulevard. Other tenants on Beverly Drive include more moderately priced retailers like the Gap, Banana Republic, and the 10,000-square ft flagship store for Williams-Sonoma. Adjacent to Beverly Hills on the west is the high-rise office-tower and shopping-center complex known as **Century City** ⑧.

TIMING

After a drive along Sunset Boulevard and a foray or two up into the hills for a look at the opulent homes, plan to arrive in the Golden Triangle of Beverly Hills at midday. Park the car in one of several municipal lots (the first one or two hours are free at most), and spend as long as you like strolling along Rodeo Drive. There are plenty of reasonably priced cafés and restaurants for lunch. The major routes in and out of Beverly Hills—Wilshire and Santa Monica boulevards—get very congested during rush hours.

Sights to See

★ ❷ **Beverly Hills Hotel.** Built in 1912, the Pink Palace is steeped in Hollywood lore. Greta Garbo, Howard Hughes, and other movie-industry guests kept low profiles when staying at this pastel landmark, while other film luminaries, notably Cecil B. DeMille, cut very visible deals in the **Polo Lounge.** ⊠ *9641 Sunset Blvd., 1 mi west of Doheny Dr.,* ☎ *310/276–2251.*

❺ **Beverly Hills Trolley.** The 40-minute "Sights and Scenes" tour gives you a bit more to see of Beverly Hills than just glitzy storefronts. The trolley swings through the Golden Triangle and past the Beverly Hills Hotel before heading into the residential area for a look at former homes of Hollywood celebrities, such as Edgar Bergen, Doris Day, and Mel Blanc. ⊠ *Dayton Way and Rodeo Dr.,* ☎ *310/285–2438.* 🚃 *$5.* ☉ *May–Dec., daily 11–5.*

NEED A
BREAK?

Try the courtyard of the unpretentious and not terribly expensive **Café Rodeo** (⊠ Summit Hotel, 360 N. Rodeo Dr., ☎ 310/273-0300). Ham sandwiches made with panini bread are enormous; salads and pizzas are big enough to split. Pizza lovers, especially transplanted New Yorkers, have created a buzz about the **Mulberry Street** pizzerias (⊠ 240 S. Beverly Dr., ☎ 310/247-8100; and ⊠ 347 N. Cañon Dr., ☎ 310/247-8998), which are owned by actress Cathy Moriarity *(Raging Bull)*.

❽ **Century City.** This 280-acre mixed-use development of office buildings, a shopping center, hotels, an entertainment complex, and housing was built in the '60s on what used to be the backlot of the film studio Twentieth Century Fox. The studio is not open to the public (though a portion of it may be glimpsed from Pico Boulevard and Avenue of the Stars as well as from the garden of the Park Hyatt hotel). The focal point is the pair of silvery triangular **Century City Towers** (⊠ Ave. of the Stars and Constellation Blvd.), designed by Minoru Yamasaki, who also designed New York's World Trade Center. The **Century City Shopping Center** (☞ Chapter 7) is one of the last open-air retail centers, with a festive, marketplacelike arrangement of eateries and cinemas. At the cavernous **Shubert Theater** in the ABC Entertainment Center (☞ Theaters *in* Chapter 5), big Broadway musicals perform.

❶ **Greystone Mansion.** Doheny Drive is named for oilman Edward Doheny, the original owner of this 1927 neo-Gothic mansion of 46,000-

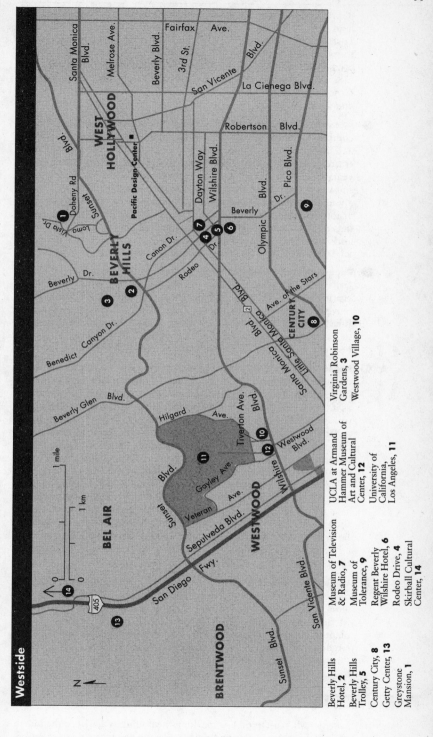

Westside

Santa Monica Blvd.

Fairfax Ave.

Melrose Ave.

Beverly Blvd.

3rd St.

San Vicente

Blvd.

La Cienega Blvd.

WEST HOLLYWOOD

Robertson Blvd.

Doheny Rd

Sunset

Loma Vista Dr.

Pacific Design Center ■

Dayton Way

Wilshire Blvd.

Beverly

Blvd.

Dr. Pico Blvd.

Canon Dr.

Beverly

Dr.

BEVERLY HILLS

Rodeo

Dr.

Olympic

Ave. of the Stars

CENTURY CITY

Benedict Canyon Dr.

Santa Monica Blvd.

Little Santa Monica Blvd.

Beverly Glen Blvd.

Hilgard Ave.

Tiverton Ave.

Blvd.

Westwood Blvd.

mile

Sunset

Blvd.

Gayley Ave.

Ave.

Veteran

Wilshire

WESTWOOD

1 km

BEL AIR

Sepulveda Blvd.

San Diego Fwy.

San Diego Blvd.

San Vicente Blvd.

BRENTWOOD

Sunset Blvd.

N

405

① ② ③ ④ ⑤ ⑥ ⑦ ⑧ ⑨ ⑩ ⑪ ⑫ ⑬ ⑭

Beverly Hills Hotel, **2**
Beverly Hills Trolley, **5**
Century City, **8**
Getty Center, **13**
Greystone Mansion, **1**

Museum of Television & Radio, **7**
Museum of Tolerance, **9**
Regent Beverly Wilshire Hotel, **6**
Rodeo Drive, **4**
Skirball Cultural Center, **14**

UCLA at Armand Hammer Museum of Art and Cultural Center, **12**
University of California, Los Angeles, **11**

Virginia Robinson Gardens, **3**
Westwood Village, **10**

plus square ft. Now owned by the city of Beverly Hills, it sits on 18½ landscaped acres and has been used in such films as *The Witches of Eastwick* and *Indecent Proposal*. The gardens are open for self-guided tours, and peeking (only) through the windows is permitted. Picnics are permitted in specified areas during hours of operation and, sporadically, concerts are held in the mansion's courtyard on summer afternoons. ⊠ *905 Loma Vista Dr.,* ☎ *310/550–4796.* ☜ *Free .* ☉ *Fall and winter, daily 10–5; spring and summer, daily 10–6.*

❼ Museum of Television & Radio. Revisit the great "Where's the beef?" commercial at this sleek stone-and-glass building, which opened in 1996 as a companion to the Museum of Television & Radio in New York, entirely duplicating its collection of 90,000 programs spanning 77 years. Search for your favorite commercials and television and radio shows on easy-to-use computers, and then watch or listen to them in an adjacent room. The museum also presents special exhibits of television- and radio-related art and costumes, and schedules daily screenings and listening series, as well as frequent seminars with television and radio cast members. ⊠ *465 N. Beverly Dr.,* ☎ *310/786–1000.* ☜ *$6.* ☉ *Wed. and Fri.–Sun. noon–5, Thurs. noon–9.*

❻ Regent Beverly Wilshire Hotel. Anchoring the south end of Rodeo Drive at Wilshire Boulevard since opening in 1928, the hotel often hosts visiting royalty and celebrities; it's where the millionaire businessman played by Richard Gere ensconced himself with the hooker played by Julia Roberts in the movie *Pretty Woman*. Though the lobby is too small to explore, you might stop for a drink or meal in one of the hotel's restaurants. ⊠ *9500 Wilshire Blvd.,* ☎ *310/275–5200.*

★ ❹ Rodeo Drive. No longer an exclusive shopping street where a well-heeled clientele shops for $200 pairs of socks wrapped in gold leaf, Rodeo Drive is one of southern California's bona fide tourist attractions. Just as if they were at Disneyland or in Hollywood, T-shirt-and-shorts-clad tourists wander along this tony stretch of avenue, window shopping at Tiffany & Co., Gucci, Armani, Hermes, Harry Winston, and Lladro. Fortunately the browsing is free, and strolling the section of Rodeo between Santa Monica and Wilshire boulevards is a fun way to spend the afternoon. Some of the shops may sound familiar to you since they supply clothing for major network television shows and their names often appear among the credits. Several nearby restaurants have outside patios where you can sip a drink while watching fashionable shoppers saunter by. At the southern end of Rodeo Drive (at Wilshire Boulevard) is **Via Rodeo,** a curvy cobblestone street designed to resemble a European shopping *via*. The cobblestones and flower vendor make for a pretty picture-taking spot.

❸ Virginia Robinson Gardens. The estate, the oldest in Beverly Hills, was owned by department store heir Harry Robinson, and his wife, Virginia, who bequeathed it to the County of Los Angeles. The classic Mediterranean-style villa is surrounded by nearly 6 acres of lush planted grounds. The collection of King palms is reported to be the largest grove outside the tree's native Australia. Fountains and falls flow through a grove of citrus and camellias. Call in advance to schedule a tour. ⊠ *1008 Elden Way,* ☎ *310/276–5367.* ☉ *Tours by appointment.*

THE WESTSIDE

Like the Mason-Dixon line marking the boundary between the North and the South, La Cienega Boulevard is the de facto demarcation between the east and west sides of Los Angeles. To the east of La Cienega, the city displays its more ethnic heterogeneous side; to the west, consumerism is highly conspicuous, and looking good—and prosperous—is the name of the game. An informal and unscientific survey of Westside districts like West Los Angeles, Westwood, Bel-Air, Brentwood, and Pacific Palisades would probably reveal high concentrations of plastic surgeons and Land Rovers. This, after all, is the part of town where one health club, which costs thousands in annual membership dues, puts celebrity patrons in its magazine ads. The Westside, however, is also rich cultural territory, and the rewards of visiting UCLA's Westwood campus, the Museum of Tolerance, and the new Getty Center in Brentwood are great, even if you just work out at the Y and drive a rented Saturn.

A Good Tour
Numbers in the text correspond to numbers in the margin and on the Westside map.

The major sights on the Westside are spread out, so choosing a starting point is arbitrary; the best strategy is to select one of the major attractions as a destination and plan your visit accordingly. A visit to the **Museum of Tolerance** ⑨ in the morning, for example, can be easily followed with lunch and shopping in Beverly Hills or Century City. Afterwards, you might drive through **Westwood Village** ⑩, home of the **UCLA** ⑪ campus, the Fowler Museum of Cultural History, stopping at the **UCLA at the Armand Hammer Museum of Art and Cultural Center** ⑫. The vast **Getty Center** ⑬, fortresslike atop a hill in Brentwood, is currently L.A.'s most high-profile attraction. About 2 mi north on Sepulveda Boulevard is the **Skirball Cultural Center** ⑭ and its gallery exhibition of Jewish life.

For a less destination-oriented tour of the posh Westside, simply follow Wilshire Boulevard west out of low-rise Beverly Hills as it turns into a canyon of million-dollar condos. Once past the San Diego Freeway (I–405), detour to the right onto San Vicente Boulevard and the upscale urban-village center of **Brentwood.** At the Santa Monica city line, turn right on 26th Street and follow it as it turns into Allenford Avenue. The route will loop you around to Sunset Boulevard. A left turn here will take you to Pacific Palisades and the ocean. A right leads back toward Beverly Hills and West Hollywood, past the Getty Center and Bel-Air mansions, all but invisible behind high walls and lush landscaping.

TIMING
Advance reservations are required for visits to the Museum of Tolerance, which is closed Saturday, and the Getty Center, which is closed Monday—so plan accordingly. Each museum merits an entire half-day. In the evening and on weekends, Westwood Village and Brentwood's commercial district on San Vicente Boulevard come alive with a busy restaurant, café, and street scene. The afternoon rush hour is predictably congested along Wilshire and Sunset boulevards.

Sights to See
Brentwood. Though this is the part of town that gained such notoriety during O.J. Simpson's murder trial, don't come expecting to find the clues to the crime. The restaurant Mezzaluna has long since closed, Nicole Simpson Brown's condo on Bundy Drive has been sold and re-landscaped so it's hardly recognizable, and O.J.'s Rockingham estate has been demolished. Nevertheless (or perhaps as a result), Brentwood remains a ritzy neighborhood, with San Vicente Boulevard as the main stretch of restaurants, cafés, and trendy shops.

★ ⑬ **Getty Center.** Not since the 1984 Los Angeles Olympic Arts Festival did a cultural event so completely capture the city as the opening of the billion-dollar Getty Center in December 1997. The overwhelming success of this new cultural venue has put such a demand on the limited parking facilities that parking reservations, essential for guaranteed admission, are necessary months in advance. And no wonder. The opening was the climax of nearly a decade of anticipation. Architect Richard Meier designed the white city on a hill to house the world's richest museum, and for years, commuters on the San Diego Freeway (I–405) watched construction proceed on the Brentwood hillltop. (In a departure from tradition, the museum has free admission but paid parking, by reservation only.) Unexpected crowds have resulted in traffic jams and limited access to the facility: Many people who arrive by bus without parking reservations have been turned away. The museum expects more than a million visitors each year, and is certain to be a major attraction in Los Angeles for years to come.

J. Paul Getty, the billionaire oil magnate and art collector, began collecting Greek and Roman antiquities and French decorative arts in the 1930s. He opened the J. Paul Getty Museum at his Malibu estate in 1954; in the 1970s, he built a re-creation of an ancient Roman villa to house his initial collection. When Getty died in 1976, the museum received an endowment of $700 million that has grown to a reported $4.2 billion. The Malibu villa closed in 1997. It will reopen in 2001, to house only the antiquities. The new Brentwood Getty Center unites the museum, various research institutes, and grant programs on one site.

Visitors park, or arrive by bus or cab, at the bottom of the hill and take a tram to the top. The principal destination for most visitors is the museum, a series of five pavilions built around a central courtyard and bridged by walkways. Outside, the structures are clad primarily in cleft-cut Italian travertine stone. From the courtyard, plazas, and walkways, you can survey the city from the San Gabriel Mountains to the Pacific Ocean and, on a clear day, beyond to Catalina Island. In a ravine separating the museum and one of the Getty research institutes, artist Robert Irwin created the **Central Garden,** whose focal point is an azalea maze in a pool. Inside the pavilions are the permanent collections of European paintings, drawings, sculpture, illuminated manuscripts, and decorative arts, as well as American and European photographs. For the first time, the Getty's entire renowned collection of French furniture and decorative arts is on view, including a paneled Régence salon from 1710 and a neoclassical salon from 1788. In the paintings galleries, a computerized system of louvered skylights allows natural light to filter in, creating a closer approximation of the conditions in which the artists painted. Notable among the paintings are Rembrandt's *Portrait of Marten Looten* and *The Abduction of Europa,* Van Gogh's *Irises,* Monet's *Wheatstack, Snow Effects, Morning,* and James Ensor's *Christ's Entry Into Brussels.*

Interconnected pavilions around the courtyard allow you to choose various paths through the museum, so you may head straight for the pavilion that interests you most. The curators have also organized a quick tour that takes in 15 highlights of the collection; it's outlined in a brochure available in the entrance hall. There's also an instructive audio tour ($2) with commentaries by art historians. Art information rooms with multimedia computer stations contain more information about the collections. ✉ *1200 Getty Center Dr.,* ☎ *310/440–7300.* 🎫 *Free, $5 parking.* ☉ *Tues.–Wed. 11–7, Thurs.–Fri. 11–9, weekends 10–6; call several months ahead for parking reservations.*

★ **9** **Museum of Tolerance.** Using state-of-the-art interactive technology, this important museum adjacent to the Simon Wiesenthal Center challenges visitors to confront bigotry and racism. One of the most affecting sections covers the Holocaust, with actual film footage of deportation scenes and simulated sets of concentration camps. Each visitor is issued a "passport" bearing the name of a child whose life was dramatically changed by the German Nazi rule and by World War II; later, you learn the fate of that child. Anne Frank artifacts are part of the museum's permanent collection. Plan to spend at least three hours to see the whole museum. Testimony from Holocaust survivors is offered at specified times. ⊠ *9786 W. Pico Blvd.,* ☎ *310/553–8403.* ⊡ *$8.* ☼ *Sun. 10:30–5, Mon.–Thurs. 10–4, Fri. 10–1.*

14 **Skirball Cultural Center.** This concrete-and-steel building rising out of the Santa Monica Mountains opened in 1996. The complex, designed by Moshe Safdie, contains conference and educational centers, but the big draw is the museum, where the core exhibition is "Visions and Values: Jewish Life from Antiquity to America." Twelve galleries use artifacts, building reconstructions, and multimedia installations to tell the story of the Jewish immigration experience. Highlights include a large collection of Judaica, a two-thirds-size replica of the torch of the Statue of Liberty, and a Hannukah lamp with each of the eight branches fashioned after the Statue of Liberty. Children can participate in an outdoor simulated archaeological dig at the interactive Discovery Center. ⊠ *2701 N. Sepulveda Blvd.,* ☎ *310/440–4500.* ⊡ *$8.* ☼ *Tues.–Sat. noon–5, Sun. 11–5.*

12 **UCLA at the Armand Hammer Museum of Art and Cultural Center.** The eclectic permanent collection at this comparatively small museum includes thousands of works by Honoré Daumier, as well as a handful by Van Gogh, Gauguin, Degas, and Mary Cassatt. In addition to French Impressionist and post-Impressionist works, there's an important collection of art by the Old Masters, including drawings by Michelangelo, Raphael, and Rembrandt. Free poetry readings take place Thursday evenings, art lectures and workshops are held many weekdays, and most Saturdays there are music and art events for children. ⊠ *10899 Wilshire Blvd.,* ☎ *310/443–7000.* ⊡ *$4.50, free Thurs. 6– 9; parking $2.75.* ☼ *Tues.–Wed. and Fri.–Sat. 11–7, Thurs. 11–9, Sun. 11–5. Tours Sun. at 1.*

11 **University of California, Los Angeles (UCLA).** With spectacular buildings such as a Romanesque library, the parklike UCLA campus makes for a fine stroll. In the heart of the north campus, the **Franklin Murphy Sculpture Garden** contains more than 70 works of artists such as Henry Moore and Gaston Lachaise. The **Mildred Mathias Botanic Garden** is in the southeast section of the campus and is accessible from Tiverton Avenue. West of the main campus bookstore, the **Morgan Center Hall of Fame** displays the sports memorabilia and trophies of the university's athletic departments. Many visitors head straight to the **UCLA Fowler Museum of Cultural History** (☎ 310/825-4361), which presents changing exhibits on the art and culture of past and present peoples of Latin America, Oceania, Africa, and Asia.

Campus maps and information are available at drive-by kiosks at major entrances seven days a week, and free 90-minute walking tours of the campus are given on weekdays at 10:30 and 2:30. The tour begins at the West Alumni Center, next to Pauley Pavilion; call 310/206– 0616 for reservations, which are required at least one day in advance. The campus has several indoor and outdoor cafés, plus bookstores selling UCLA Bruins paraphernalia. The main entrance gate is on Westwood Boulevard. Campus parking costs $5. ⊠ *Main entrance on*

STARGAZING

YEARS AGO, IT IS SAID, Lucille Ball would come out of her house on Roxbury Drive in Beverly Hills and wave as tour buses full of camera-clicking tourists came by. Can you just see Demi Moore or Barbra Streisand mugging for your camcorder nowadays? Ironically, in a town that lives and dies on publicity, there are precious few ways of guaranteeing a celebrity sighting. In the end, tenacity wins out when it comes to star-gazing, because it's mostly a question of being in the right place at the right time—in the bleachers at the entrance to the annual Academy Awards, for example. (The awards are held at the Dorothy Chandler Pavilion in downtown Los Angeles in March, 1999.) Another public event that guarantees a star's presence is the dedication of a celebrity's bronze star in the Hollywood Walk of Fame (☞ Hollywood Walk of Fame, *above*). Appearances by celebrities at movie premieres and charity events (watch the papers for these events) also provide good opportunities for a sighting or two.

Stars have to eat, so dining at high-profile celebrity restaurants like **Morton's** or the perennial **Spago** (see Chapter 3 for both) ups your chances of spotting a star. Celebs often blend in with the crowds strolling through **Farmers Market** (☞ Wilshire Boulevard, Museum Row, and Farmers Market, *above*). Less fancy eateries near studios where celebrities work can be good hunting grounds too. **Jerry's** and **Art's** (see Chapter 3 for both) are near CBS's satellite facility where *Seinfeld* and other sitcoms are taped.

Of the studio tours, **Paramount Pictures** (☞ *above*), **NBC Studios** (☞ the San Fernando Valley tour, *below*), and

Warner Bros. (☞ San Fernando Valley tour, *below*) are your best bets. Each of these tours gives you a behind-the-scenes look at film and television production and, depending on the studio's schedule, you may even visit the set of a show being filmed.

Watching television stars at work by attending a taping of a television show requires some advance planning. From August through March, dozens of television shows—*Suddenly Susan, Caroline in the City,* and *Third Rock from the Sun,* for example—are taped in front of live audiences. **Audiences Unlimited** (✉ 100 Universal City Plaza, Bldg. 153, ☎ 818/753–3483) is the best source for tickets to many television shows. For tickets and information about *The Tonight Show Starring Jay Leno,* contact **NBC** (☎ 818/840–3537); *Politically Incorrect,* CBS (☎ 323/852–2458); and *Leeza,* **Paramount Studios** (☎ 323/956–5575). Game show hosts Alex Trebek, Pat Sajak, Vanna White, and Bob Barker command their own loyal followings, so get in touch with **Sony Studios** (☎ 310/280–8856) for *Jeopardy* and *Wheel of Fortune* tickets; **CBS** (☎ 323/852–2458) for *The Price Is Right* tickets.

One way practically to guarantee that you won't see a celebrity is to buy one of the souvenir maps to stars' homes that are hawked along Hollywood and Sunset boulevards for about $7 or $8. The addresses of homes of stars, many of whom no longer live at the addresses listed (or no longer live at all), are keyed into a map of a portion of Beverly Hills and Bel-Air. A drive along these posh, tree-lined, winding streets is scenic indeed, but high walls and protective landscaping obscure all but the briefest of glimpses of celebrity digs.

Westwood Plaza; Le Conte, Hilgard, and Gayley Aves. and Sunset Blvd. border the campus. ✉ *Campus free; Fowler Museum $5 (free Sun. and Thurs.)*

⑩ Westwood Village. Laid out nearly 70 years ago as a master-planned shopping district next to the Los Angeles campus of the University of California, Westwood Village is now one of the busiest places in the city on weekend evenings. The lures are a concentration of first-run movie theaters, eateries, and a lively youth-oriented street scene that gets so busy during the summer that many streets are closed to car traffic and visitors must park at the Federal Building (✉ Wilshire Blvd. and Veteran Ave.) and shuttle over. Besides having surpassed Hollywood as the city's moviegoing center, Westwood is the unlikely site of a cemetery, with one of the world's most famous graves. Tucked behind one of the behemoth office buildings on Wilshire Boulevard is **Westwood Village Memorial Park** (✉ 1218 Glendon Ave.). Marilyn Monroe is buried in a simply marked crypt on the north wall. For 25 years after her death, her former husband Joe DiMaggio had six red roses placed on her crypt three times a week. Also buried here are Truman Capote and Natalie Wood.

SANTA MONICA, VENICE, AND MALIBU

In Los Angeles all roads lead, eventually, to the beach and the coastal communities of Santa Monica, Venice, and Malibu. These communities hug the Santa Monica Bay, in an arc of diversity, from the rich-as-can-be Malibu to the bohemian-seedy mix of Venice. What they have in common, however, is cleaner coastal air and an emphasis on being out in the sunshine, always within sight of the Pacific.

Santa Monica—which, because of its liberal-leaning populace, has been dubbed "the People's Republic of Santa Monica"—is a tidy little city, about 8⅓ square mi, with a diverse population of artists and writers, expatriate Brits (there's an English music hall and several pubs here), celebrities, educators, and retired people, all attracted by the cooler, sometimes-foggy climate. The sense of order is reflected in the economic-geographic stratification: The most northern section has broad streets lined with superb, older homes. As you drive south, real estate prices drop $50,000 or so every block or two.

Venice was a turn-of-the-century fantasy that never quite came true. Abbot Kinney, a wealthy Los Angeles businessman, envisioned this little piece of real estate, which then seemed so far from downtown, as a romantic replica of Venice, Italy. He developed an incredible 16 mi of canals, floated gondolas on them, and built scaled-down versions of the Doge's Palace and other Venetian landmarks. Some canals were rebuilt in 1996, but don't reflect the Old World connection quite as well as they could. Figures. Ever since Kinney first planned his project, it was plagued by ongoing engineering problems and disasters and drifted into disrepair. Three small canals and bridges do remain and can be viewed from the southeast corner of Pacific Avenue and Venice Boulevard. Another great glimpse of the canals can be caught when walking along Dell Avenue from Washington Street north to Venice.

By the late 1960s, however, actors, artists, musicians, hippies, and anyone who wanted to live near the beach but couldn't afford to, were attracted by the low rents in Venice, and the place quickly became SoHo-by-the-Sea. The trade-off was that the area was pretty rundown, and the remaining canals were stagnant and fairly smelly, but as the area's appeal grew and a more upscale crowd started moving

Santa Monica, Venice, and Pacific Palisades

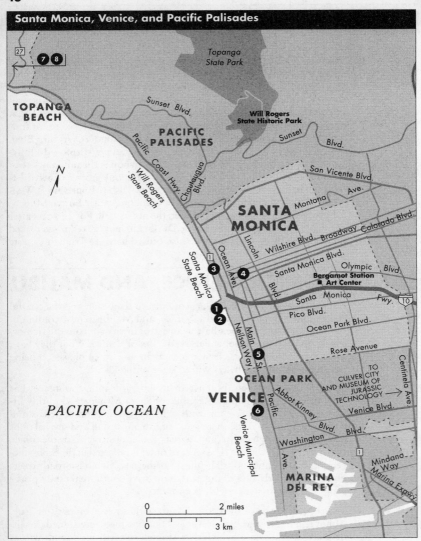

Adamson House and
Malibu Lagoon
Museum, **8**

California Heritage
Museum, **5**

Malibu Lagoon State
Beach, **7**

Pacific Park, **2**

Palisades Park, **3**

Santa Monica Pier, **1**

Third Street
Promenade, **4**

Venice Boardwalk, **6**

in, these drawbacks were rectified. Venice's locals today are a grudgingly thrown-together mix of aging hippies, yuppies with disposable income to spend on inflated rents, senior citizens who have lived here for decades, and homeless people.

North of Santa Monica is Malibu, which nature has blessed with a gorgeous 23-mi stretch of mountains-meet-the-sea coastline that has lured zillions of television- and film-star residents to build swank homes on the beach. Nature keeps it all in perspective, however, with a calamitous brush fire or mud slide every so often.

A Good Drive

Numbers in the text correspond to numbers in the margin and on the Santa Monica, Venice, and Pacific Palisades map.

Look for the arched neon sign at the foot of Colorado Avenue marking the entrance to the **Santa Monica Pier** ①, the city's number-one landmark, built in 1906. Park on the pier and take a turn through **Pacific Park** ②, a 2-acre amusement park. The wide swath of sand on the north side of the pier is Santa Monica Beach, on hot summer weekends one of the most crowded beaches in southern California. From the pier, walk to Ocean Avenue, where **Palisades Park** ③, a strip of lawn and palms above the cliffs, provides panoramic ocean views. Three blocks inland is **Third Street Promenade** ④, an active outdoor mall with shopping, dining, and entertainment.

Retrieve the car and drive two blocks inland on Colorado to Main Street. Turn right and continue to Ocean Park Boulevard. Look for a colorful mural on the side of the building on the southeast corner. On the southwest corner you'll find the **California Heritage Museum** ⑤. The next several blocks south along Main Street are great for browsing.

Next stop: **Venice Boardwalk** ⑥. Walk up Main Street through the trendy shopping district until you hit Rose Avenue. Ahead on the left you'll spot an enormous pair of binoculars, the front of the Frank Gehry–designed Chiat-Day Mojo building. Turn right toward the sea. The main attraction of this dead end is the boardwalk, where the classic California beach scene is in progress.

For the drive to Malibu, retrace your route along Main Street. At Pico Boulevard, turn west, toward the ocean, and then right on Ocean Avenue. When you pass the pier, prepare to turn left down the California Incline (the incline is at the end of Palisades Park at Wilshire Boulevard) to Pacific Coast Highway (Highway 1), also known as PCH. About 5 mi north, you may be able to spot the red-tile roof of an enormous rendition of an Italian villa high on the cliffs to your right. That's the J. Paul Getty Museum (not to be confused with the Getty Center in Brentwood). Closed now for renovations, it will reopen in 2001 as America's only museum devoted to Greek and Roman antiquities. Another 6 mi or so will bring you into Malibu proper. Unfortunately, Malibu Pier is closed indefinitely due to storm damage and a lack of funds to repair it. But you can park in the adjacent lot and take a walk on **Malibu Lagoon State Beach** ⑦, also known as Surfrider Beach. On the highway side of the beach is the Moorish-Spanish **Adamson House and Malibu Lagoon Museum** ⑧, a tiled beauty with a great Pacific view. From here, you can walk along the strand of beach that fronts the famed Malibu Colony, the exclusive residential enclave of film, television, and recording stars.

TIMING

If you've got the time, break your coastal visit into two excursions: Santa Monica and Venice in one, and Malibu in another. The best way to "do" L.A.'s coastal communities is to park the car, rent a bike or a pair of Rollerblades in Santa Monica or Venice, and walk, cycle, or skate along the 3-mi beachside bike path. For this, of course, a sunny day is best; on all but the hottest days, when literally millions of Angelenos flock to the beaches, late morning is a good time to get started. Places like Santa Monica Pier, Main Street, and the Venice Boardwalk are more interesting to observe as the day progresses. Only the boardwalk should be avoided at night, when the crowd becomes unsavory. You can park on the Santa Monica Pier and in small lots close to the beach in Venice (the smart thing to do, since break-ins are common in the area) and Malibu. Main Street is a good place to head for lunch and spend an hour or so shopping for gifts and souvenirs; Third Street Promenade is more interesting in the evening, when cafés and restaurants are packed and strollers throng the promenade. Avoid driving to Malibu during rush hour, when traffic along the Pacific Coast Highway moves at a snail's pace—but do try to be there at sunset to watch the sun dip into the mighty Pacific.

Sights to See

8 **Adamson House and Malibu Lagoon Museum.** The Rindge family, which owned much of the Malibu area in the early part of the 20th century, also originally owned this home. Malibu was quite isolated then, with all visitors and supplies arriving by boat at the nearby Malibu Pier (and it can still be isolated these days when rock slides close the highway). The Moorish Spanish–style structure was built in 1929. The Rindges led an enviable Malibu lifestyle, decades before the area was trendy. The house, covered with magnificent tile work from the now-defunct Malibu Potteries in rich blues, greens, yellows, and oranges, is right on the beach—high chain-link fences keep out curious beachgoers. Even an outside dog shower, near the servants' door, is a tiled delight. Docent-led tours provide insights on family life here as well as the history of Malibu and its real estate (you can't have one without the other). Signs posted around the grounds outside direct you on a self-guided tour as well. Park in the adjacent county lot, or in the lot at Pacific Coast Highway and Cross Creek Road. ⊠ *23200 Pacific Coast Hwy.,* ☎ *310/456–8432.* ⊠ *House tours, $2.* ☉ *Wed.–Sat. 11–3.*

OFF THE
BEATEN PATH

BERGAMOT STATION –This collection of old railroad cars behind the city recycling center houses more than 30 galleries and design studios featuring the work of some of the area's best artists. It's also the home of the Santa Monica Museum of Art, which opened here in 1998, showcasing exhibits of lesser-known painters and sculptors, as well as performance and video art. The museum features free films, discussions, and readings on Friday evenings. ⊠ *2525 Michigan Ave.,* ☎ *310/829–5854 Bergamot, 310/586–6488 museum.* ⊠ *Galleries free, Santa Monica Museum suggested donation $4.* ☉ *Wed.–Sun. 11–6, Fri. 11–10.*

---

5 **California Heritage Museum.** Occupying an 1894-vintage, late-Victorian house built by the founder of Santa Monica, this museum was moved to its present site on Main Street in the late 1970s. Three rooms have been fully restored: the dining room in the style of 1890–1910; the living room, 1910–1920; and the kitchen, 1920–1930. The second-floor galleries contain photography and historical exhibits as well as shows by contemporary California artists. ⊠ *2612 Main St.,* ☎ *310/392–8537.* ⊠ *$3.* ☉ *Wed.–Sat. 11–4, Sun. 10–4.*

NEED A BREAK?	Try **Windsail Malibu** (✉ 22706 Pacific Coast Hwy., ☎ 310/456–0900), just south of the Malibu Pier at the edge of the ocean, for sandwiches, vegetarian curry, salmon salad, or warm roast-lamb salad. A glass wall and open patio provide year-round ocean views.

OFF THE BEATEN PATH	**MARINA DEL REY** – A brilliant sight on a sunny day, this enormous man-made marina with moorings for 10,000 boats is just south of Venice. Stop by Burton Chace Park (at the foot of Mindanao Way) to watch the wind carry colorful sailboats out to sea. Small "Mother's Beach" (Marina Beach) has calm, protected waters ideal for young children. Call **Hornblower Dining Yachts** in Fisherman's Village (✉ 13755 Fiji Way, ☎ 310/301–9900) to arrange marina and dining cruises.

❼ **Malibu Lagoon State Beach.** Visitors are asked to stay on the boardwalks at this 5-acre haven for native and migratory birds so that the egrets, blue herons, avocets, and gulls can enjoy the marshy area. The signs listing opening and closing hours refer only to the parking lot; the lagoon itself is open 24 hours and is particularly enjoyable in the early morning and at sunset. Street-side parking is available at those times, but not at midday. ✉ *23200 Pacific Coast Hwy.*

OFF THE BEATEN PATH	**MUSEUM OF JURASSIC TECHNOLOGY** – Don't bring the kids here expecting to see dinosaur bones or memorabilia from *Jurassic Park*. This unusual place, in a realm somewhere between a museum and an art installation, has a permanent collection of natural (and perhaps fictional) wonders such as the African stink ant and the "piercing devil" (a tiny bat that uses radar to fly through solid objects), as well as an exhibit on the obscure figure of memory theorist Geoffrey Sonnabend. Temporary exhibits cover a grab-bag of topics: old wives' tales, miniaturism, or perhaps the culture of the mobile home. ✉ *9341 Venice Blvd., Culver City,* ☎ *310/836–6131.* ⊞ *$4.* ☉ *Thurs. 2–8, Fri.–Sun. noon–6.*

❷ **Pacific Park.** The 12 rides at Santa Monica Pier's 2-acre amusement facility include a giant Ferris wheel, a flying submarine, and a motion-simulated action ride. ✉ *380 Santa Monica Pier, Santa Monica,* ☎ *310/260–8747.* ⊞ *Rides $1–$4, all-day pass $15.* ☉ *Summer, entire park open 7 days May–Sept.; winter, Ferris wheel and selected rides Mon.–Thurs., entire park Fri. evening–Sun. evening; call for hrs.*

❸ **Palisades Park.** The ribbon of green that runs along the top of the cliffs from Colorado Avenue to just north of San Vicente Boulevard has flat walkways where casual strollers and joggers come to enjoy spectacular views of the Pacific. Sunsets here are hard to beat.

★ ❶ **Santa Monica Pier.** Eateries, souvenir shops, a psychic adviser, arcades, and the Pacific Park amusement facility are all part of this truncated pier at the foot of Colorado Boulevard below Palisades Park. The pier's trademark 46-horse carousel, built in 1922, has appeared in many films, including *The Sting.* ✉ *Colorado Ave. and the ocean,* ☎ *310/458–8900.* ⊞ *Rides 25¢ and 50¢.* ☉ *Carousel summer, daily 11–6; winter, weekends 10–5.*

❹ **Third Street Promenade.** Only foot traffic is allowed along a three-block stretch of 3rd Street, just a whiff away from the Pacific, which is lined with jacaranda trees and accented with ivy-topiary dinosaur fountains. Outdoor cafés, street vendors, several movie theaters, and a rich nightlife (the mix of folks down here is great, from elderly couples out for a bite to skateboarders and street musicians) make this one of Santa Monica's main gathering spots. ✉ *3rd St. between Wilshire Blvd. and Broadway.*

★ **❻** **Venice Boardwalk.** "Boardwalk" may be something of a misnomer—
it's really a paved walkway—but this L.A. must-see delivers year-
round action: Bicyclists zip along and bikini-clad roller and in-line skaters
attract crowds as they put on impromptu demonstrations, vying for
attention with magicians, fortune tellers, a chain-saw juggler, and
street artists. A local bodybuilding club works out on the adjacent "Muscle Beach—it's nearly impossible not to stop and ogle the strongmen's
pecs. You can rent in-line skates, roller skates, and bicycles (some with
baby seats) at the south end of the boardwalk (which is also known
as Ocean Front Walk), along Washington Street, near the Venice Pier.

NEED A BREAK?	For a beach picnic you can buy food at one of the many fast-food stands that line the boardwalk. For a more relaxing meal, stand in line for a table at **Sidewalk Café** (✉ 1401 Ocean Front Walk, ☎ 310/399–5547). It's worth the wait for a patio table, where you can watch the free spirits on parade.
OFF THE BEATEN PATH	**WILL ROGERS STATE HISTORIC PARK** – The late cowboy-humorist Will Rogers lived on this site in the 1920s and 1930s. His 187-acre estate is a folksy blend of Navajo rugs and Mission-style furniture. A nearby museum features Rogers memorabilia and a short film that presents his roping technique and homey words of wisdom. Rogers was a polo en-thusiast, and in the 1930s, his front-yard polo field attracted such friends as Douglas Fairbanks, Sr., for weekend games. The tradition continues, with free games scheduled when weather allows. The park's broad lawns are excellent for picnicking, and there's hiking on miles of eucalyptus-lined trails. From Pacific Coast Highway, turn inland at Sunset Boule-vard. Follow Sunset for about 5 mi to the park entrance. ✉ 1501 Will Rogers State Park Rd., Pacific Palisades, ☎ 310/454–8212. ☜ Free, parking $6. ☼ Park, daily 8–sunset daily; house tours, daily 10:30–4:30.

THE SAN FERNANDO VALLEY

There are other valleys in the Los Angeles area, but this is the one that
people refer to simply as the Valley. Sometimes, there is a note of de-
rision in their tone; to city people, the Valley just isn't cool. That's not
altogether untrue, since large portions of the Valley are bedroom communities of neat bungalows and shopping centers. But the last decade
has seen several fine restaurants opening here, and this is also home
to most of the major film and television studios, such as Warner Bros.
and NBC. The Valley is also home to one of the most historical sites
in Los Angeles, Mission San Fernando Rey de España.

Within the Valley, Universal City is a one-industry town, and that industry is Universal Studios. The studio has been at this site since 1915,
and even then it allowed visitors to watch movies being made for 25¢.
Its history goes back decades as a major film and television studio, but
in the past few years Universal has also become a major tourist attraction.
Today this hilly area contains the Universal Studios Hollywood theme
park, the Universal Amphitheater, CityWalk (fun shopping and dining
along a narrow thoroughfare that resembles a movie back lot), a major
movie complex, and two major hotels.

A Good Drive

*Numbers in the text correspond points of interest on the San Fernando
Valley map.*

On a clear day or evening, a drive along **Mulholland Drive** gives you a spectacular view of the sprawling San Fernando Valley below. Just over the hill from Hollywood via the Hollywood Freeway (U.S. 101 North) is Universal City, which has its own freeway off-ramp (Universal Center Drive). **Universal Studios Hollywood** ① is on a large hill overlooking the San Fernando Valley, a city-within-a-city. As you exit Universal, follow signs to Barham Boulevard. At Barham, turn left toward Burbank. After driving about a mile, the street curves around **Warner Bros. Studios** ②, whose outside wall is covered with billboards of current films and television shows. After the curve, you will be on West Olive Avenue. Keep to the right and look for the entrance to Gate No. 4 at Hollywood Way.

Just a minute away at the second big intersection, West Olive and Alameda avenues, is the main entrance to **NBC Television Studios** ③. Continue east on Alameda; on the next block to your right is **Disney Studios** ④, a very colorful bit of architecture. Drive south on Buena Vista and then turn left on Riverside to get a good look at the whimsical architecture.

To reach **Mission San Fernando Rey de España** ⑤, drive north on either the San Diego (I–405) or Golden State (I–5) freeways; Alameda Avenue will lead you to I-5, as will the Hollywood Freeway (Highway 170 North). Drive about 12 mi and exit at Fernando Mission Boulevard. From I–405, drive east; from I–5, drive west. The mission is about ½ mi from either freeway on the north side of the street. (A scenic, and often less traffic-clogged, route back to L.A. is via Mulholland Drive, whose exit is about 15 mi, or 20 minutes, from the mission off I–405.)

TIMING

The Valley is surrounded by mountains and the major routes to and from it go through mountain passes. During rush hour, traffic jams on the Hollywood Freeway (U.S. 101/Highway 170), San Diego Freeway (I–405), and Ventura Freeway (U.S. 101/Highway 134) can be brutal, so avoid trips to or from the Valley at those times. Expect to spend a full day at Universal Studios Hollywood and CityWalk; studio tours at NBC and Warner Bros. last about two hours. A visit to the mission will eat up more time driving to and from than touring the grounds.

Sights to See

OFF THE
BEATEN PATH

DESCANSO GARDENS – Once part of the vast Spanish Rancho San Rafael that covered more than 30,000 acres, this lovely oasis encompasses 165 acres of native chaparral–covered slopes and lushly planted gardens. A forest of California live oak trees furnishes a dramatic backdrop for thousands of camellias, azaleas, and a breathtaking 5-acre International Rosarium holding 1,700 varieties of antique and modern roses. The Tea House operates on weekends between February and November and, with its Zen garden, is a nice place spot to stop for refreshments and reflection. There's also a gift shop. Tram tours traverse the grounds (on a limited schedule), but be sure to spend some time strolling on your own to appreciate the gardens up close. ⊠ *1418 Descanso Dr., La Cañada/Flintridge,* ☎ *818/952-4400.* ⊞ *$5, $2.50 3rd Tues. of month.* ☉ *Daily 9–4:30.*

❹ **Disney Studios.** Although tours of this state-of-the-art animation studio are not available, a peek from Riverside Drive shows you Disney's innovations go beyond the big and small screens to fanciful touches of architecture as well (note the little Mickey Mouse heads mounted on the surrounding fence). You can't miss this Michael Graves–designed

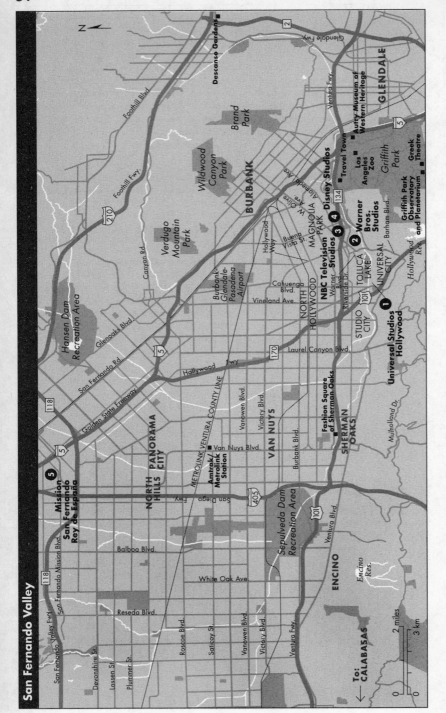

San Fernando Valley

Descanso Gardens

Glendale Fwy.

2

Brand Park

Wildwood Canyon Park

Foothill Blvd.

BURBANK

GLENDALE

Ventura Fwy.

Autry Museum of Western Heritage

Travel Town

Los Angeles Zoo

Griffith Park

Greek Theatre

Disney Studios

Warner Bros. Studios

Griffith Park Observatory and Planetarium

5

134

Verdugo Mountain Park

Foothill Fwy.

210

Canyon Rd.

W. Olive Ave.

Alameda Ave.

NBC Television Studios

3 4

2

Hollywood Way

Buena Vista St.

MAGNOLIA PARK

NORTH HOLLYWOOD

Warner Blvd.

Riverside Dr.

Barham Blvd.

TOLUCA LAKE

UNIVERSAL CITY

Hollywood Res.

Burbank-Glendale-Pasadena Airport

Glenoaks Blvd.

Hansen Dam Recreation Area

Cahuenga Blvd.

Vineland Ave.

101

1

STUDIO CITY

Universal Studios Hollywood

San Fernando Rd.

5

Hollywood Fwy.

170

Laurel Canyon Blvd.

Mulholland Dr.

118

Golden State Freeway

NORTH HILLS

PANORAMA CITY

Vanowen Blvd.

Victory Blvd.

VAN NUYS

Burbank Blvd.

Fashion Square of Sherman Oaks

SHERMAN OAKS

METROLINK / VENTURA COUNTY LINE

Amtrak/ Metrolink Station

Van Nuys Blvd.

5

Mission San Fernando Rey de España

5

San Fernando Mission Blvd.

San Diego Fwy.

405

101

Sepulveda Dam Recreation Area

Ventura Blvd.

Balboa Blvd.

ENCINO

Encino Res.

White Oak Ave.

118

San Fernando Valley Fwy.

Devonshire St.

Lassen St.

Plummer St.

Reseda Blvd.

Roscoe Blvd.

Saticoy St.

Vanowen Blvd.

Victory Blvd.

Ventura Fwy.

TO: CALABASAS

0   2 miles

0   3 km

N

building, erected in 1995—almost entirely made of glass, it looks like the hull of an enormous ocean liner. ☒ *500 S. Buena Vista, Burbank.*

❺ Mission San Fernando Rey de España. An important member of a chain of 21 California missions established by Franciscan friars, Mission San Fernando was founded in 1797 and named in honor of King Ferdinand III of Spain. Fifty-six Native Americans joined the mission and made it a self-supporting community, growing and harvesting its own wheat, corn, beans, and olives; raising cattle, sheep, and hogs; and establishing workshops to produce metalwork, leather goods, cloth, soap, and candles. In 1834, after Mexico extended its rule over California, a civil administrator was appointed for the mission and the priests were restricted to religious duties. The Native Americans began leaving, and what had been flourishing one year before became unproductive. Twelve years later the mission, along with its properties (those being the entire San Fernando Valley), was sold for $14,000. During the next 40 years, the mission buildings were neglected; settlers stripped roof tiles, and the adobe walls were ravaged by the weather. Finally in 1923 a restoration program was initiated. Today, as you walk through the mission's arched corridors, you may experience déjà vu—and you probably have seen it before, in an episode of *Gunsmoke, Dragnet,* or in any number of movies. (Notably, in 1991, scenes from the Steve Martin comedy *L.A. Story* were filmed here.) Inside the mission, Native American designs and artifacts of Spanish craftsmanship depict the mission's 18th-century culture. Look for the small museum and gift shop.☒ *15151 San Fernando Mission Blvd., Los Angeles,* ☎ *818/361–0186.* ☒ *$4.* ☉ *Daily 9–4:30.*

Mulholland Drive. The dividing line between the San Fernando Valley and Los Angeles proper is one of the most famous thoroughfares in this vast metropolis. Driving the length of the hilltop road is slow and can be treacherous, but the rewards are sensational views of valley and city on each side and expensive homes along the way. From Hollywood reach Mulholland via Outpost Drive off Franklin Avenue or Cahuenga Boulevard West via Highland Avenue north.

❸ NBC Television Studios. This major network's headquarters is in Burbank, as any regular viewer of *The Tonight Show* can't help knowing. For those who wish to be part of a live studio audience, free tickets are made available for tapings of the various NBC shows, and 70-minute walking tours of the studio are given on weekdays. ☒ *3000 W. Alameda Ave., Burbank,* ☎ *818/840–3537.* ☒ *$7.* ☉ *Tour weekdays 9–3.*

★ ❶ Universal Studios Hollywood. Though you probably won't see anything that actually has to do with making a real film, visiting the theme park is an enlightening (if somewhat sensational) introduction to the principles of special effects. Seated aboard a comfortable tram (narrated, hour-long tours traverse the 420-acre complex all day long), you can experience the parting of the Red Sea, an avalanche, and a flood; meet a 30-ft-tall version of King Kong; live through an encounter with a runaway train; be attacked by the ravenous killer shark of *Jaws* fame; and endure a confrontation by aliens armed with death rays. An all-too-real simulation of an earthquake that measured 8.3 on the Richter scale—complete with collapsing earth. If you missed Kevin Costner's epic film *Waterworld,* Universal delivers a facsimile in the form of a sea-war extravaganza. *Jurassic Park—The Ride* is a tour through a jungle full of dinosaurs with an 84-ft water drop. Long lines form at *Back to the Future,* a flight simulator disguised as a DeLorean car that shows off state-of-the-art special effects. At *Lucy: A Tribute to Lucille Ball,* a 2,200-square-ft heart-shape museum contains a re-creation of the set from the *I Love Lucy* television show. Throughout the park, costumed characters mingle with guests and pose for photos. Within the slew of shops and restaurants known as **CityWalk**, the Wolfgang Puck Café is a poor man's version of Spago, Puck's star-studded Sunset Strip restaurant. ⊠ *100 Universal City Pl., Universal City,* ☎ *818/508–9600.* ◪ *$36.* ⊙ *Daily 9–7.*

❷ Warner Bros. Studios. Two-hour tours at this major studio center in Burbank involve a lot of walking, so dress comfortably and casually. Somewhat technically oriented and centered more on the actual workings of filmmaking than the ones at Universal, tours here vary from day to day to take advantage of goings-on at the lot. Most tours take in the back-lot sets, prop construction department, and sound complex. A museum chronicles the studio's film and animation history. Reservations are strongly recommended one week in advance; children under 10 are not admitted. Call for special needs. ⊠ *4000 Warner Blvd., Burbank,* ☎ *818/954–1744.* ◪ *$30.* ⊙ *Tours weekdays 9–3 on the hour.*

PASADENA AREA

Although now fully absorbed into the general Los Angeles sprawl, Pasadena is a separate and distinctly defined—and very refined—city. Its varied residential architecture, augmented by lush landscaping, is among the most spectacular in southern California. Nearby Highland Park has a two excellent museums, and San Marino is home to the famous Huntington Library, Art Collections, and Botanical Gardens.

To reach Pasadena from downtown Los Angeles, drive north on the Pasadena Freeway (Highway 110), which follows the curves of the arroyo (creek bed). This was the main road north during the early days of Los Angeles, when horses and buggies made their way through the chaparral-covered countryside to the small town of Pasadena. In 1939 the road became the Arroyo Seco Parkway, the first freeway in Los Angeles, later renamed the Pasadena Freeway. The freeway remains a pleasant drive in non–rush hour traffic, with old sycamores winding up the arroyo in a pleasant contrast to the more common 10-lane freeways of Los Angeles.

From Hollywood use the Glendale Freeway (Highway 2 North), and from the San Fernando Valley use the Ventura Freeway (Highway 134 East), which cuts through Glendale, skirting the foothills, before arriving in Pasadena.

A Good Tour
Numbers in the text correspond to numbers in the margin and on the Pasadena Area map.

A good place to start a short driving tour of Pasadena is on Orange Grove Boulevard, a.k.a. Millionaire's Row, where wealthy Easterners built grand mansions in this area at the turn of the century. One mansion that remains is the **Wrigley Mansion** ①, a Mission-style structure with grounds and gardens reminiscent of the old neighborhood. To get to the mansion, take the Orange Grove exit off the Ventura Freeway (Highway 134); turn right at Orange Grove and travel five blocks. From the Pasadena Freeway (Highway 110), stay on the freeway until it ends at Arroyo Parkway. From Arroyo Parkway turn left at California Boulevard and then right at Orange Grove.

From the Wrigley Mansion, travel north on Orange Grove to Walnut Street and the **Fenyes House** ②, now headquarters of the Pasadena Historical Society. Continue on Orange Grove to Arroyo Terrace, where a left turn will take you into an architectural wonderland. Greene and Greene, the renowned Pasadena architects, designed all of the houses on Arroyo Terrace, as well as others in the area. To view their Crafts-man masterpiece, the three-story, shingled **Gamble House** ③, turn right on Westmoreland Place. Also in this section is the Frank Lloyd Wright–designed Millard House ("La Miniatura") on Prospect Crescent (from Westmoreland, turn left onto Rosemont Avenue, right on Prospect Ter-race, and right onto Prospect Crescent to No. 645). The famous **Rose Bowl** ④ is nestled in a gulley just to the west off Arroyo Boulevard. Leave this area via Rosemont Avenue, driving away from the hills to the south. From Rosemont, turn right onto Orange Grove Boulevard. Then, at Colorado Boulevard, turn left. Immediately on the left is the contemporary, austere **Norton Simon Museum** ⑤, a familiar backdrop to so many viewers of the annual New Year's Day Tournament of Roses Parade. Continue east on Colorado Boulevard and, after a few blocks, you'll cross the historic concrete-arched Colorado Street Bridge, built in 1913, rising 160 ft above the Arroyo Seco gorge. Some called this Suicide Bridge during the Depression, as this was a place where many people ended their lives.

After leaving the block-long overpass, you'll enter **Old Town Pasade-na** ⑥. You'll want to walk around this section of Pasadena, heading east. For a look at domed Pasadena City Hall, turn left on Fair Oaks Avenue, then right on Holly Street. Garfield Avenue will bring you back to Colorado. The next intersection is Los Robles Avenue. One-half block north on Los Robles is an Oriental-style building housing the **Pacific Asia Museum** ⑦. Back on Colorado, head three blocks east to El Molino Avenue. Turn right past the Pasadena Playhouse (✉ 39 S. El Molino, ☎ 626/356–PLAY) and, if you have youngsters, continue along four blocks to **Kidspace** ⑧.

From this point it's a short drive south on El Molino to California Boule-vard, where a left turn will take you into San Marino and the **Hun-tington Library, Art Collections, and Botanical Gardens** ⑨ (follow the signs). Also in this area is the historic **El Molino Viejo** ⑩.

TIMING
Get a late-morning or early afternoon start to see the important ar-chitectural sights on this tour, saving Old Pasadena for last. The lat-ter has one of the best evening street scenes in southern California: Shops remain open late, bringing plenty of pedestrian traffic to Colorado Boule-vard; and restaurants and cafés do a thriving business.

You'll want to allow half a day for the entire driving tour. A stop at the Gamble House may take an hour, leaving plenty of time for an af-ternoon visit to the Norton Simon Museum. There's no need to stop at the Rose Bowl unless you happen by on the second Sunday of the month, when one of the country's largest flea markets (often called swap meets in California) is underway in the parking lot. With kids in tow, you may want to adjust your schedule to spend at least an hour at Kidspace. Set aside an entire day for the Huntington Library, Art Col-lections, and Botanical Gardens—preferably on a sunny day, when the gardens are most pleasant.

Sights to See
⑩ **El Molino Viejo.** Built in 1816 as a grist mill for the San Gabriel Mis-sion, this is one of the last remaining examples in southern California of Spanish Mission architecture. It's a quiet, restful place, with a flower-decked arbor and peaceful garden shaded by sycamores and old

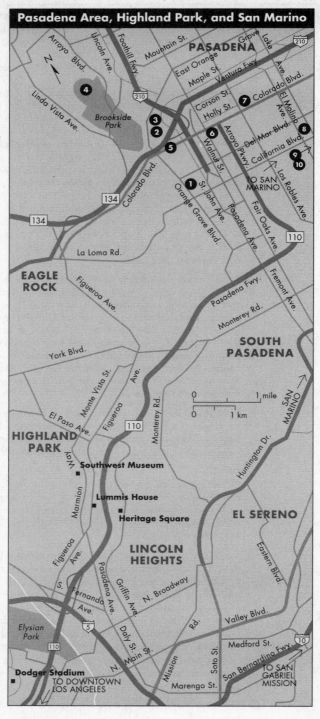

Pasadena Area, Highland Park, and San Marino

oaks. ✉ *1120 Old Mill Road, San Marino,* ☎ *626/449–5458.* 🎫 *Free.* ⊘ *Tues.–Sun. 1–4.*

② **Fenyes House.** The 1905 mansion, now the **Pasadena Historical Society** still has its original furniture and paintings on the main and second floors. Basement exhibits trace Pasadena's history. There are also well-landscaped gardens surrounding the mansion. You may recognize the mansion as the residence of Peter Sellers's simpleminded caretaker character in the film *Being There.* ✉ *470 W. Walnut St., Pasadena,* ☎ *626/577–1660.* 🎫 *$4.* ⊘ *Thurs.–Sun. 1–4, 1-hr docent-led tour.*

★ **③** **Gamble House.** Built by Charles and Henry Greene in 1908, this is a spectacular example of Craftsman-style bungalow architecture. The term "bungalow" can be misleading, since the Gamble House is a huge three-story home. To wealthy Easterners such as the Gambles (as in Procter & Gamble), this type of vacation home seemed informal compared to their accustomed mansions. What makes visitors swoon is the incredible amount of hand craftsmanship, including a teak staircase and cabinetry, Greene-designed furniture, and an Emil Lange glass door. The dark exterior has broad eaves, with sleeping porches on the second floor. If you want to see more Greene and Greene homes in the neighborhood, buy a self-guided tour map in the bookstore. ✉ *4 West-moreland Pl., Pasadena,* ☎ *626/793–3334.* 🎫 *$5.* ⊘ *Thurs.–Sun. noon–3, 1-hr tour every 15–20 min.*

OFF THE
BEATEN PATH

HERITAGE SQUARE – Five residences, a depot, a church, and a carriage barn have been moved to this small park from all over the city—a result of the ambitious attempt by the Cultural Heritage Foundation of southern California to save from the wrecking ball some of the city's architectural gems of the era from 1865 to 1914. The most breathtaking building in Heritage Square is **Hale House,** built in 1887. The garish colors of both the interior and exterior are not the whim of some aging hippie painter, but rather a faithful re-creation of the palette that was in fashion in the late 1800s. The **Palms Depot,** built around 1886, was moved to the site from L.A.'s Westside. The night the building was moved, down city streets and up freeways, is documented in photomurals on the depot's walls. Docents dress in period costume. ✉ *3800 Homer St., off Ave. 43 exit, Highland Park,* ☎ *626/449–0193.* 🎫 *$5, free Fri. 10–3.* ⊘ *Weekends 11:30–4:30, hourly tours 12–3.*

★ **⑨** **Huntington Library, Art Collection and Botanical Gardens.** If you have time for only one stop in the Pasadena area, it should be San Marino, where railroad tycoon Henry E. Huntington built his hilltop home in the early 1900s. Since then, it has established a reputation as one of the most extraordinary cultural complexes in the world and annually receives more than a half-million visitors. The library contains more than 600,000 books and some 300 manuscripts, including such treasures as a Gutenberg Bible, the Ellesmere manuscript of Chaucer's *Canterbury Tales,* George Washington's genealogy in his own handwriting, and first editions by Ben Franklin and Shakespeare. In the library's hallway are five tall hexagonal towers displaying important books and manuscripts. The Huntington Gallery, housed in the original Georgian mansion built by Henry Huntington in 1911, holds a world-famous collection of British paintings, including the original *Blue Boy* by Gainsborough, *Pinkie,* a companion piece by Thomas Lawrence, and the monumental *Sarah Siddons as the Tragic Muse* by Joshua Reynolds. American paintings (Mary Cassat, Frederic Remington, and more), and decorative arts are housed in the Virginia Steele Scott Gallery of American Art.

An awesome 150-acre garden, formerly the grounds of the estate, the Huntington Gardens now include a 12-acre Desert Garden featuring the world's largest group of mature cacti and other succulents, all arranged by continent. The Japanese Garden holds traditional Japanese plants, stone ornaments, a drum bridge, a Japanese house, a bonsai court, and a Zen rock garden. Besides these gardens, there are collections of azaleas and 1,500 varieties of camellias, the world's largest public collection. The 3-acre rose garden is displayed chronologically, so the development leading to today's strains of roses can be observed; on the grounds is the charming **Rose Tea Garden Room**, where traditional high tea is served. There are also herb, palm, and jungle gardens plus a Shakespeare garden, which blooms with plants mentioned in Shakespeare's works. The Huntington Pavilion, a later addition to the property, has commanding views of the surrounding mountains and valleys, plus a bookstore, displays, and information kiosks. A 1¼-hour guided tour of the gardens is led by docents at posted times, and inexpensive, self-guided tour leaflets are available in the entrance pavilion. ⊠ *1151 Oxford Rd., San Marino,* ☎ *626/405–2100.* ☞ *$8.50, free 1st Thurs. of month.* ☉ *Memorial Day–Labor Day, Tues.–Sun. 10:30–4:30; Labor Day–Memorial Day, Tues.–Fri. noon–4:30, weekends 10:30–4:30.*

⑧ Kidspace. At this children's museum housed in the gymnasium of an elementary school, kids can direct a television or radio station; dress up in the real (and very heavy) uniforms of a firefighter, astronaut, or football player; or play in the sand of an indoor beach. "Critter Caverns" beckons with its large tree house and secret tunnels for exploring insect life firsthand (don't worry, the bugs are fake). Kids can even test their skills at the cash register of a child-size supermarket. ⊠ *390 S. El Molino Ave., Pasadena,* ☎ *626/449–9143.* ☞ *$5.* ☉ *Sept.–July 1, Tues. 1:30–5, Wed.–Thur. 1–5, Sat. 10–5, Sun. 1–5, hrs vary during school vacations.*

OFF THE BEATEN PATH

LUMMIS HOUSE – This was once the home of eccentric Easterner-turned-Westerner Charles Lummis, who edited the magazine *The Land of Sunshine,* later *Out West.* The Harvard dropout and lifelong scholar was captivated by Native American culture (he founded the Southwest Museum), much to the shock of his more staid Angeleno contemporaries. The L-shaped house was built around a large sycamore between 1898 and 1910; stones from the arroyo were used in the facade. California artist Charles Walter Stetson designed the art nouveau fireplace. The grounds include a 2-acre "water-wise" garden. ⊠ *200 E. Ave. 43, entrance on Carlota Blvd., Highland Park,* ☎ *323/222-0546.* ☞ *Free.* ☉ *Fri.–Sun. noon–4.*

OFF THE BEATEN PATH

MISSION SAN GABRIEL ARCHANGEL – In 1771 Father Junípero Serra dedicated this mission to the great archangel and messenger from God, St. Gabriel. As the founders approached the mission site, they were confronted by "savage" Native Americans. In the heat of battle, one of the padres revealed the canvas painting *Our Lady of Sorrows,* which so impressed the Indians that they laid down their bows and arrows. Within the next 50 years, the San Gabriel Archangel became the wealthiest of all California missions. In 1833 the Mexican government confiscated the mission and it began to decline; in 1855 the U.S. government returned the mission to the church, but by this time the Franciscans had departed. In 1908 the Claretian Missionaries took charge, and much care and respect has since been poured into the mission. Today, Mission San Gabriel Archangel's adobe walls preserve an era of history, and the magnificent cemetery stands witness to the many people who lived here. The 1987 Whittier and 1994 Northridge earthquakes damaged the structure, but it has been repaired and strengthened. ⊠ *537 W. Mission Dr., San Gabriel,* ☎ *626/457–3048.* 🖾 *$4.* ☉ *Daily 9:30–5.*

★ **❺ Norton Simon Museum.** Familiar to television viewers of the Rose Parade, this sleek, modern building makes a stunning background for the passing floats. Like the more famous Getty Center, the Norton Simon is a tribute to the art acumen of an extremely wealthy businessman. In 1974 Simon reorganized the failing Pasadena Art Institute and assembled one of the world's finest collections, richest in its Rembrandts, Goyas, Picassos, and most of all, Degas: This is one of the only to U.S. institutions to hold the complete set of the artist's model bronzes (the other is the Metropolitan Museum of Art, in New York). There are also several Rodin sculptures dotted throughout the museum Rembrandt's development can be traced in three oils—*The Bearded Man in the Wide Brimmed Hat, Self Portrait,* and *Titus.* The most dramatic Goyas are two oils—*St. Jerome in Penitence* and the *Portrait of Dona Francisca Vicenta Chollet y Caballero.* Picasso's renowned *Woman with a Book* highlights a comprehensive collection of his paintings, drawings, and sculptures. The museum's collections of Impressionist (van Gogh, Matisse, Cézanne, Monet, Renoir) and Cubist (Braque, Gris) work is extensive. Down the walnut-and-steel staircase is the Asia collection, one of the country's best. The emphasis here is Southeast Asia bronze sculpture; arts from the Indian subcontinent are also on display. Early Renaissance, Baroque, and Rococo artwork are additional specialties: Church works by Raphael, Guariento, Giovanni de Paolo, Filippino Lippi, and Lucas Cranach give way to robust Rubens maidens and Dutch landscapes, still lifes, and portraits by Frans Hals, Jacob van Ruisdael, and Jan Steen. A magical Tiepolo ceiling highlights the Rococo period. A Frank Gehry–designed sculpture garden with a teahouse is the latest addition. ⊠ *411 W. Colorado Blvd., Pasadena,* ☎ *626/449–6840.* 🖾 *$4.* ☉ *Thurs.–Sun. noon–6.*

❻ Old Town Pasadena. Once the victim of seedy decay, the area was revitalized the 1990s as a blend of restored brick buildings with a yuppie overlay. Rejuvenated buildings include bistros, elegant restaurants, and boutiques. On Raymond Street, the former Hotel Green, now the Castle Apartments, is a faded Moorish fantasy of domes, turrets, and balconies. In many respects it's reminiscent of the Alhambra, except that, true to its name, it has a greenish tint. Old Town is bisected by Colorado Boulevard, which, west of Old Town, rises onto the **Colorado Street Bridge,** a raised section of roadway on graceful arches completed in 1913 and restored in 1993. On New Year's Day throngs of people line Colorado Boulevard to watch the Rose Parade.

NEED A BREAK?
Walk down to Fair Oaks Avenue to seek out the **Market City Cafe** (⊠ 33 S. Fair Oaks Ave., ☎ 626/568–0203), which you'll recognize by the life-size black-and-white cow in the window. Imaginative Italian fare, including food from the self-serve antipasto bar, brick-oven pizzas, and charbroiled fish, is served both indoors and alfresco.

❼ Pacific Asia Museum. Designed in the style of a Chinese imperial palace with a central garden, this elaborate building is devoted entirely to the arts and culture of Asia and the Pacific Islands. Changing exhibits of the museum's permanent collection of 17,000 items focus on various aspects of particular regions. ⊠ *46 N. Los Robles Ave.,* ☎ *626/449–2742.* 🖾 *$4, free 3rd Sat. of month.* ☉ *Wed.–Sun. 10–5.*

❹ **Rose Bowl.** With an enormous rose, the city of Pasadena's logo, tattooed onto its exterior, it's hard to miss this 100,000-seat stadium, host of many Super Bowls and home to the UCLA Bruins. Set at the bottom of a wide area of the arroyo in an older wealthy neighborhood, the facility is closed except during games and special events such as the monthly Rose Bowl Swap Meet. Held the second Sunday of the month, it is considered the granddaddy of West Coast flea markets. ✉ *Rosemont Ave., Pasadena,* ☎ *626/577–3100.* ☉ *Daily 9–5*

OFF THE
BEATEN PATH

SOUTHWEST MUSEUM – Readily spotted from the Pasadena Freeway (Highway 110), this huge Mission Revival building stands halfway up Mt. Washington. Inside is an extensive collection of Native American art and artifacts, with special emphasis on the people of the Plains, Northwest coast, Southwest coast, and California. The basket collection is outstanding. Additional galleries of the museum are now housed in the old May Company building, on the corner of Fairfax Avenue and Wilshire Boulevard (☞ Wilshire Boulevard, Museum Row, and Farmers Market, *above*). ✉ *234 Museum Dr., off Ave. 43 exit, Highland Park,* ☎ *323/ 221–2163.* ⛿ *$5.* ☉ *Tues.–Sun. 10–5*

❶ **Wrigley Mansion.** The chewing gum magnate, William Wrigley, purchased this white Italian Renaissance–style house in 1914. The mansion is now the headquarters for the Tournament of Roses Association; though not especially remarkable architecturally, it does give an idea of the grand style of the area in the early 20th century. The house is open for tours on Thursdays only. The gardens, however, with some 1,500 varieties of roses, are open daily. ✉ *391 S. Orange Grove Blvd., Pasadena,* ☎ *626/449–4100.* ☉ *House tours Feb.–Aug., Thurs. 2– 4; gardens, daily sunrise–sunset.*

PALOS VERDES, SAN PEDRO, AND LONG BEACH

If you've planned a visit to the *Queen Mary* or an off-shore excursion to Catalina Island, you'll be headed to metropolitan Los Angeles's South Bay area, home to the hilly Palos Verdes Peninsula and the port cities of San Pedro and Long Beach.

In gentrified Palos Verdes, real estate ranges from expensive to very expensive and is zoned for stables. You'll often see riders along the streets (they have the right of way). Down the hill, San Pedro (pronounced *Pee*–dro) is an old seaport community full of tidy, 1920s-era white clapboards and dozens of boats of all sizes. Greek and Yugoslavian markets and restaurants abound in San Pedro, epitomizing the town's strong Mediterranean and Eastern European flavor. San Pedro and neighboring Wilmington are connected to downtown Los Angeles by a narrow, 16-mi-long strip of land, less than ½ mi wide in most places, annexed in the late 19th century to preserve Los Angeles's transportation and shipping interests.

Across the Vincent Thomas Bridge from San Pedro is Long Beach, wholly separate from the city of Los Angeles. Long Beach began as a seaside resort in the 19th century, and during the early part of the 20th century it was a destination for Midwesterners and Dust Bowlers in search of a better life. In trying to promote Long Beach as a destination in its own right, the city has tried to develop its waterfront with a convention center and most recently, the Long Beach Aquarium of the Pacific, which opened in 1998.

A Good Drive

Numbers in the text correspond to numbers in the margin and on the Palos Verdes, San Pedro, and Long Beach map.

Because a single drive around these three southern towns would encompass more than 100 mi, it's best to approach the area on two separate tours. For an overview of **Palos Verdes and San Pedro,** begin at the **South Coast Botanic Garden** ①, on Crenshaw Boulevard 1 mi south of the Pacific Coast Highway. (Exit I–405 at Crenshaw Boulevard and head west.) Continue west on Crenshaw to Crest Road, and turn right to Hawthorne Boulevard. At Palos Verdes Drive, turn left. Less than a mile farther on your right you'll see Point Vicente Lighthouse, a good spot to watch for whales, and, another 2 mi away, on your left, you'll see the all-glass **Wayfarers Chapel** ②. Continue south and you'll hit San Pedro and the western end of the Los Angeles Harbor. Follow the signs to Cabrillo Beach, where you'll find the stark white building that houses the **Cabrillo Marine Aquarium** ③. To reach the **Banning Residence Museum and Park** ④, take Pacific Avenue north to the Harbor Freeway, and exit at Pacific Coast Highway. This is the former home of the gentleman responsible for developing the harbor you just visited.

A Good Drive

Take Pacific Coast Highway toward **Long Beach,** turn south on Magnolia Avenue, and follow signs leading to the art deco ship, the **Queen Mary** ⑤. Then take the Queensway Bridge back across the bay to the new **Long Beach Aquarium of the Pacific** ⑥. Adjacent **Shoreline Aquatic Park** ⑦ affords the best view of the harbor and the Long Beach skyline. Continue on Shoreline Drive to **Shoreline Village** ⑧, a waterfront outdoor shopping center. Take Ocean Boulevard west (left) to Long Beach Boulevard and head north (right) to San Antonio Drive. Turn left here to Virginia Road and then right, past a golf course, to the historic adobe two-story **Rancho Los Cerritos** ⑨. Then drive south to the San Diego Freeway (I–405), and go south and exit at Palo Verde. Turn right onto Palo Verde, which will dead-end at Bixby Hills Estate, a gated community. Tell the guard at the entrance that you'd like to visit **Rancho Los Alamitos** ⑩ and you'll be sent up the hill to the historic dwelling. After that, take the Pacific Coast Highway south to a southern Californian version of Venice, inaptly called **Naples** ⑪, on Los Alamitos Bay, where—no surprise—the ancient art of gondola riding is all the rage.

TIMING

In Palos Verdes, the South Coast Botanic Garden could occupy you for a couple of hours; the Wayfarers Chapel, less than 20 minutes from the garden, is a half-hour stopover. If you have kids in tow, expect to stay a couple of hours at the San Pedro's Cabrillo Marine Aquarium, longer if you join one of the tidepool walks. An hour should be enough time to walk around the Banning Residence Museum and Park. In Long Beach, guided tours of the *Queen Mary* last an hour, and the new Long Beach Aquarium of the Pacific could occupy most of a morning or an afternoon. Visits to Ranchos Los Cerritos and Los Alamitos will require about an hour each. If you've planned well enough in advance, you could end the day with a sunset gondola cruise on the canals in Naples. Don't forget to factor in at least 20 minutes' driving time between attractions.

Sights to See

④ **Banning Residence Museum and Park.** General Phineas Banning, an early entrepreneur in Los Angeles, is credited with developing the Los

Palos Verdes, San Pedro, and Long Beach

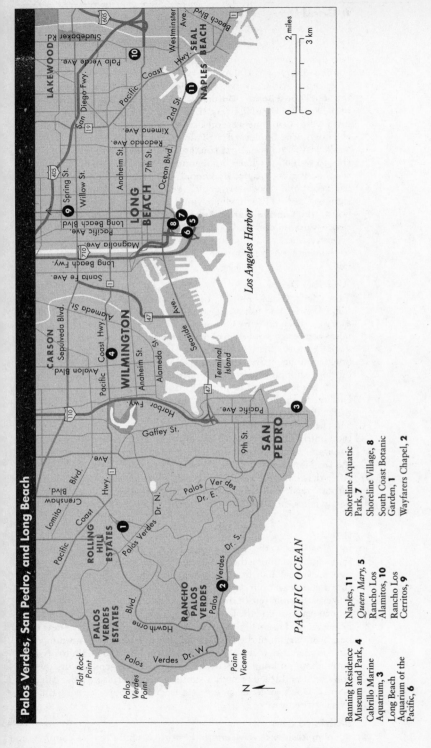

Banning Residence Museum and Park, **4**

Cabrillo Marine Aquarium, **3**

Long Beach Aquarium of the Pacific, **6**

Naples, **11**

Queen Mary, **5**

Rancho Los Alamitos, **10**

Rancho Los Cerritos, **9**

Shoreline Aquatic Park, **7**

Shoreline Village, **8**

South Coast Botanic Garden, **1**

Wayfarers Chapel, **2**

Angeles Harbor into a viable economic entity and naming the area Wilmington (he was from Delaware). Part of his estate has been preserved in a 20-acre park. (The picnicking possibilities here are excellent.) A 100-year-old wisteria, near the arbor, blooms in the spring. You can see the interior of the house on docent-led tours. ⊠ *401 E. M St., Wilmington,* ☎ *310/548–7777.* ⊡ *Suggested donation for house tours, $3.* ⊙ *Guided house tours Tues.–Thurs. 12:30, 1:30, 2:30, weekends 12:30–3:30 on the hr.*

❸ **Cabrillo Marine Aquarium.** This gem of a small museum is dedicated to the marine life that flourishes off the southern California coast. A modern Frank Gehry–designed building right on the beach houses 35 saltwater aquariums. Don't miss the shark tank, the whale and dolphin room, and the see-through tidal tank that enables you to see the long view of a wave. Exhibits are instructive and fun—on the back patio, you can reach into a shallow tidepool tank to touch starfish and sea anemones. ⊠ *3720 Stephen White Dr., San Pedro,* ☎ *310/548–7562.* ⊡ *Suggested donation $2, parking $6.50.* ⊙ *Weekdays noon–5, weekends 10–5.*

❻ **Long Beach Aquarium of the Pacific.** A full-scale model of a blue whale, the largest living creature in the Pacific and on the planet, is suspended above the Great Hall, the entrance to this new aquarium. Seventeen major exhibit tanks and 30 smaller focus tanks contain some 10,000 live marine animals—including seals and sea lions—that inhabit the Pacific Ocean and its environment. The exhibits focus on three regions of the Pacific Ocean: southern California and Baja, the northern Pacific, and the tropical Pacific. You'll also learn about conservation problems that pertain to each area, such as pollution, endangered coral reefs, and overharvesting. ⊠ *100 Aquarium Dr., Long Beach,* ☎ *562/590–3100.* ⊡ *$13.* ⊙ *Daily 10–6.*

⓫ **Naples.** Canals in *Naples,* you ask? Yes, this is a misnomer. But better misnamed and successful than aptly named and a bust. Arthur Parsons, the developer who came up with the Naples canal idea, learned from the mistakes and bad luck that did in those in Venice, just up the coast, and built the canals to take full advantage of the tidal flow that would keep them clean. Actually three small islands in man-made Alamitos Bay, Naples is best experienced on foot. Park near Bay Shore Avenue and 2nd Street and walk across the bridge, where you can meander around the quaint streets with Italian names. This well-restored neighborhood has eclectic architecture: vintage Victorians, Craftsman bungalows, and Mission Revivals. You may spy a real gondola or two on the canals. You can hire them for a ride, but not on the spur of the moment. **Gondola Getaway** offers one-hour rides, usually touted for romantic couples, although their gondolas can accommodate up to six people and serve bread, salami, and cheese—you bring the wine. Reservations are essential at least one week in advance. ⊠ *5437 E. Ocean Blvd., Long Beach,* ☎ *562/433–9595.* ⊡ *Rides $55 per couple, $10 each additional person.* ⊙ *Cruises 11 AM–midnight.*

★ ❺ **Queen Mary.** Be sure to get at least a glimpse of this huge passenger ship, now sitting snugly in Long Beach Harbor. What seemed like sure folly when Long Beach officials bought her in 1967 put the city on the proverbial map. The 80,000-ton *Queen Mary* was launched in 1934, a floating treasure of art deco splendor. It took a crew of 1,100 to minister to the needs of its 1,900 demanding passengers. The former first-class passenger quarters are now a hotel. Allow a generous half day to explore this most luxurious of luxury liners, admiring the extensive wood paneling, the gleaming nickel- and silver-plated handrails, and the hand-cut glass. Tours of the ship are available, and guests are invited to browse the 12 decks and walk around the bridge, staterooms, officers' quarters, and engine rooms. There are several restaurants and shops on board, a gallery of the ship's original art, and even a wedding chapel. From the deck, you can watch bungee jumpers as they fall 21 stories next to the ship. Stay late for fireworks Saturday nights in the summer. ⊠ *Pier H, Long Beach,* ☎ *562/435–3511.* 🎟 *$12, guided 1-hr tour $4 extra.* ☉ *Tours daily 10–4:30, later in summer.*

🔟 **Rancho Los Alamitos.** Said to be one of the country's oldest adobe one-story domestic buildings still standing, this landmark was built circa 1800, when the Spanish flag still flew over California. Docents lead guided tours of the house, and there's a working blacksmith shop in the barn. ⊠ *6400 E. Bixby Hill Rd., Long Beach,* ☎ *562/431–3541.* 🎟 *Donations accepted.* ☉ *Wed.–Sun. 1–5, free 90-min tour every ½ hr 1–4.*

9 **Rancho Los Cerritos.** Two features make this charming Monterey-style adobe house built by the Don Juan Temple family in 1844 easily recognizable: It has two stories and a narrow balcony across the front. It's easy to imagine Zorro, that swashbuckling fictional hero of the rancho era, jumping from the balcony onto a waiting horse and making his escape. The 10 rooms have been furnished in the style of the period and are open for viewing. The gardens were designed in the 1930s by well-known landscape architect Ralph Cornell. ⊠ *4600 Virginia Rd., Long Beach,* ☎ *562/570–1755.* 🎟 *Donations accepted.* ☉ *Wed.–Sun. 1–5, free self-guided tour weekdays, free 50-min guided tour weekends hourly 1–4.*

7 **Shoreline Aquatic Park.** Set literally in the middle of Long Beach Harbor is this much-sought-after resting place for RVers. Kite flyers love the winds here, and casual passersby can enjoy a short walk, where the modern skyline, quaint Shoreline Village, the *Queen Mary,* and the ocean all vie for attention. The park's lagoon is off-limits for swimming, but aquacycles and kayaks can be rented in summer. ⊠ *E. Shoreline Dr.*

8 **Shoreline Village.** This stretch of 24 gift shops and four restaurants between downtown Long Beach and the *Queen Mary* is a good place for a stroll, day or evening (when visitors can enjoy the lights of the ship twinkling in the distance). ⊠ *Shoreline Dr. and Shoreline Village Rd., Long Beach.,* ☎ *562/435–2668.* ☉ *May–Sept., daily 10–10; Oct.– Apr., daily 10–9.*

NEED A
BREAK?   **Parker's Lighthouse** (⊠ Shoreline Village, ☎ 562/432–6500) is the best place to enjoy a view of the *Queen Mary* and surrounding harbor. Sit outside to savor some of the best seafood in town.

★ **1** **South Coast Botanic Garden.** This Rancho Palos Verdes botanical garden began life ignominiously—as a garbage dump-cum-landfill. It's hard to believe that as recently as 1960, truckloads of waste (3.5 million tons) were being deposited here. With the intensive ministerings of the experts from the L.A. County Arboreta Department, the dump soon sprouted lush gardens, with all the plants eventually organized into color groups. Self-guided walking tours take visitors past flower and herb gardens, rare cacti, and a lake with ducks. The Garden for the Senses is devoted to touching and smelling plants; the Water-Wise garden showcases alternatives to grass lawns in the parched southern California climate. Picnicking is limited to a lawn area outside the gates. ⊠ *26300 S. Crenshaw Blvd., Rancho Palos Verdes,* ☎ *310/544–6815.* 🎟 *$5.* ☉ *Daily 9–5.*

② **Wayfarers Chapel.** Architect Lloyd Wright, son of Frank Lloyd Wright, designed this modern glass church in 1949 to blend in with an encircling redwood forest. The redwoods are gone (they couldn't stand the rigors of urban encroachment), but another forest has taken their place, lush with ferns and azaleas, adding up to a breathtaking combination of ocean, vegetation, and an architectural wonder. This "natural church" is a popular wedding site, so avoid visiting on weekends. ✉ *5755 Palos Verdes Dr. S, Rancho Palos Verdes,* ☎ *310/377–1650.* ⊙ *Daily 7–5.*

3 Dining

L.A.'s restaurants reflect both the city's well-deserved reputation for culinary innovation and its rich ethnic cornucopia. Many of the country's star chefs are here—Wolfgang Puck, Joachim Splichal, Michel Richard— but so are many unheralded chefs who delight Angelenos daily with the cuisines of their native Shanghai, Oaxaca, Tuscany, and perhaps more of the world's other gastronomic regions than in any other city. So whether you are looking for a traditionally elegant dinner, a culinary adventure, or just a really good burger, expect to find them all here—in spades.

By Bill Stern

THAT LOS ANGELES IS HOME to some of the best restaurants and chefs in the United States is old news. Wolfgang Puck, for one, has parlayed his West Hollywood Spago success into nationwide name recognition with his chain of restaurants and packaged food business. And with the entrenchment of the contemporary cooking style that Puck helped popularize, innovation has become an institution here, ensuring that you'll almost always find something new to eat in Los Angeles.

That this is one of the least expensive big cities in which to eat well, here or abroad, is less well known. Strong competition for the luxury-class dollar has kept prices at many high-end restaurants under control, and the city's many excellent ethnic restaurants are, with few exceptions, easy on the pocketbook.

Unparalleled dining options for Angelenos have opened up as a result of immigration from regions as diverse as Central America, the Near East, and Southeast Asia. One consequence is that even going out for standard Mexican cooking has become an outdated concept. Now savvy diners seek out the distinctive regional cuisines of Mexico—Jaliscan, Sonoran, and Oaxacan among them. And the availability of culinary diversity has spread far beyond areas with concentrations of immigrant populations. One of the city's best Indian restaurants is in Pasadena; West Los Angeles has a first-rate Oaxacan establishment; and branches of Hong Kong-style seafood houses have found their way from San Gabriel Valley to the West Side as inevitably as fish migrating to richer waters.

In this culinary melting pot, chefs don't have to look far to find the the exotic ingredients that have come to be a staple of contemporary cuisine. Wasabi, phyllo pastry, bok choi, ginger, and fuyu persimmons are just a few of the so-called ethnic products now appearing regularly on the menus of the city's top restaurants—and not just those that see themselves as serving so-called fusion cuisine. Eating out in Los Angeles has never been so exciting.

Naturally, reservations are always essential at most high-end Los Angeles-area restaurants, and on weekend evenings at many others as well. You'll find that Angelenos do not dress up to eat out—even in pricey restaurants, jeans are not uncommon. (Note that state law forbids smoking in any enclosed public place, including all bars and restaurants. Some establishments may, however, allow smoking on outdoor patios—call first to be sure.)

For approximate costs, *see* the dining price chart in On the Road with Fodor's.

Beverly Hills, Century City, Hollywood and West Hollywood

Beverly Hills

AMERICAN

$$–$$$ ✗ **Grill on the Alley.** This fashionable place for power lunching is reminiscent of a traditional San Francisco bar and grill, with its dark-wood paneling and brass trim. The tasty, simple American fare includes high-quality steaks and seafood, as well as chicken potpies, crab cakes, creamy Cobb salad, and homemade rice pudding. ⊠ *9560 Dayton Way,* ☎ *310/276–0615. Reservations essential. AE, DC, MC, V. No lunch Sun. Valet parking evenings.*

Los Angeles Dining *(Boxes Refer to Detail Maps)*

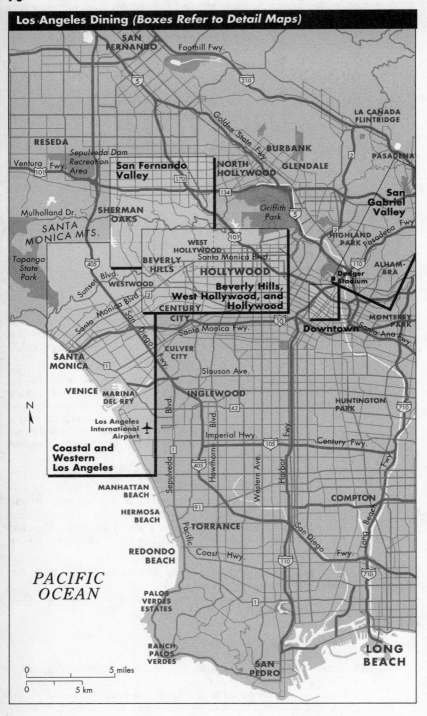

CONTEMPORARY

$$–$$$$ ✕ **The Dining Room at the Regent Beverly Wilshire.** This formal but
★ comfortable room is one of L.A.'s best for an elegant breakfast, lunch,
or dinner. Santa Barbara prawns with sweet-potato *agnolotti* (a type
of ravioli) sometimes appears on the prix-fixe lunch menu, which gen-
erally runs about $25; other fine choices are Chilean sea bass with bok
choy and kefir-lime broth, or Angus steak with curly fries. The prix-
fixe dinner menu ($40–$50) may include mushroom risotto with as-
paragus, foie gras with Thai curry sauce, or Maine lobster with
mascarpone-and-potato gnocchi. A la carte choices are also available.
⊠ *9500 Wilshire Blvd.,* ☎ *310/275–5200. Jacket required. AE, D,
DC, MC, V. No lunch or dinner Sun. Valet parking.*

$$–$$$$ ✕ **Spago Beverly Hills.** Wolfgang Puck has done it again. The chef who
helped define California Cuisine at his original Hollywood Hills venue
now wows celebrity and business circles in a smart Beverly Hills location designed by his wife, Barbara Lazaroff. The restaurant centers
around an outdoor courtyard, from which diners can glimpse the large
open kitchen and, on occassion, Mr. Puck himself. For starters, there's
white-bean and duck-confit soup, warm crayfish salad with mustard
potatoes, and foie gras presented three ways: as a mousse with pan-
roasted apples; as a terrine with quince chutney; and sautéed with Bart-
lett pears and huckleberries. Entrées range from wild striped bass with
celery-root puree to roasted Cantonese duck with persimmons,
pomegranate, and ginger. Also worth trying are Puck's Austrian "child-
hood favorites," such as *Kärntner Käsenudeln* (cheese ravioli) with hazelnut butter, and his renowned pizzas, with or without smoked salmon.
This Spago attracts as many of the who's-who of Hollywood as the
original once did. ⊠ *176 N. Canon Dr.,* ☎ *310/385–0880. Reservations essential. AE, D, DC, MC, V. No lunch Sun.*

$$–$$$ ✕ **Nouveau Café Blanc.** Chef-owner Tommy Harase has made this small,
unpretentious restaurant one of Beverly Hills' unexpected treats.
Lunchtime entrées such as sautéed salmon with basil vinaigrette, or lobster ravioli with vin-blanc cream sauce cost as little as $10. Four- and
five-course prix fixe dinners, $33 and $43, have featured saffron-
marinated scallops, jasmine-tea–smoked squab, lobster risotto, and
roasted lamb steak with ratatouille sauce. Service is gracious and un-
intrusive. ⊠ *9777 Little Santa Monica Blvd.,* ☎ *310/888–0108. Reservations essential. AE, D, MC, V. Closed Sun., Mon.*

CHINESE

$$–$$$ ✕ **Joss.** Industrial design—soaring ceilings, hanging halogen lighting,
and a chic spareness—is softened by upholstered chairs and a tree-lined
patio at this high-end Chinese restaurant popular with Beverly Hills
and Hollywood Hills locals. Try the varied dim sum and the Peking
duck. The sidewalk tables are great for a lunchtime rendezvous, but
service can be haughty and prices high. ⊠ *9255 Sunset Blvd.,* ☎ *310/
276–1886. Reservations essential. AE, DC, MC, V. No lunch weekends. Valet parking.*

$–$$ ✕ **The Mandarin.** The Mandarin serves Szechuan and Chinese coun-
try dishes in a serene, traditional Chinese setting, with roomy bamboo
armchairs, soft Chinese music, and linens and crystal. Specialties include minced chicken wrapped in lettuce leaves, Peking duck (order
ahead of time), beggar's chicken, scallion pancakes, and several noo-
dle dishes. ⊠ *430 N. Camden Dr.,* ☎ *310/859–0926. Reservations
essential. AE, DC, MC, V. No lunch weekends. Valet parking evenings.*

DELI

$$–$$$ ✕ **Barney Greengrass.** This *haute* deli on the fifth floor of Barneys has
★ an appropriately high-class aesthetic: limestone floors, mahogany furniture, and a wall of windows. On the outdoor terrace, tables shaded

72

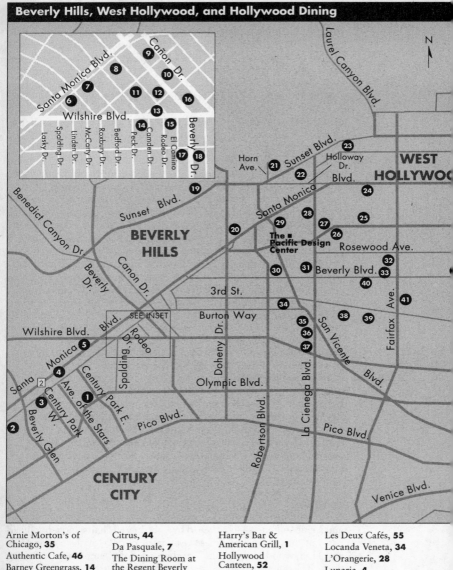

Arnie Morton's of Chicago, **35**
Authentic Cafe, **46**
Barney Greengrass, **14**
Bistro K, **18**
Boxer, **45**
Ca'Brea, **48**
Cadillac Cafe, **31**
California Pizza Kitchen, **17**
Campanile, **49**
Canter's, **32**
Cava, **38**
Cha Cha Cha, **63**
Chan Dara, **54**

Citrus, **44**
Da Pasquale, **7**
The Dining Room at the Regent Beverly Wilshire, **15**
Dive!, **3**
Drai's, **25**
East India Grill, **47**
Ed's Coffee Shop, **29**
El Cholo, **64**
Fenix, **23**
Fred 62, **59**
Grill on the Alley, **13**
Gumbo Pot, **41**

Harry's Bar & American Grill, **1**
Hollywood Canteen, **52**
Hollywood Hills Coffee Shop, **58**
Il Fornaio Cucina Italiana, **12**
Ita-Cho, **51**
Joss, **19**
Jozn, **26**
La Cachette, **2**
Le Chardonnay, **25**
Le Colonial, **30**
Le Dôme, **22**

Les Deux Cafés, **55**
Locanda Veneta, **34**
L'Orangerie, **28**
Lunaria, **4**
The Mandarin, **8**
Matsuhisa, **36**
Mimosa, **33**
Miss Gregory's American Kitchen, **24**
Nate 'n' Al's, **9**
Nouveau Café Blanc, **6**
ObaChine, **16**
The Palm, **20**
Patina, **56**

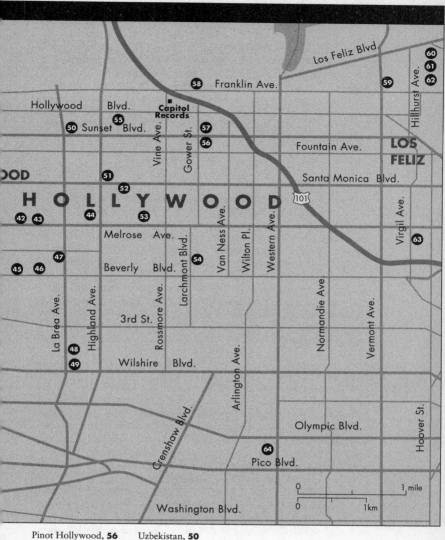

Pinot Hollywood, **56**
Prego, **11**
Restaurant Katsu, **61**
Roscoe's House of
Chicken 'n'
Waffles, **57**
Sofi, **39**
Spago, **21**
Spago Beverly
Hills, **10**
Swingers, **40**
Tavola Calda, **42**
Tommy Tang's, **43**
Trader Vic's, **5**
Trattoria Farfalla, **60**

Uzbekistan, **50**
Vida, **62**
Woo Lae Oak, **37**

by large umbrellas overlook Beverly Hills and Hollywood. Specialties are flawless smoked salmon, sturgeon, and whitefish flown in fresh from New York. The brisket of beef and Mediterranean salads are also worth a try. The deli keeps store hours, closing Thursday at 8, Sunday at 6, and every other day at 7. ✉ *Barneys, 9570 Wilshire Blvd., Beverly Hills,* ☎ *310/777–5877. AE, MC, V. Valet parking.*

$ ✕ **Nate 'n' Al's.** A famous gathering place for Hollywood comedians, gag writers, and their agents, Nate 'n' Al's serves first-rate matzo-ball soup, lox and scrambled eggs, cheese blintzes, potato pancakes, and deli sandwiches. ✉ *414 N. Beverly Dr.,* ☎ *310/274–0101. Reservations not accepted. AE, MC, V. Free parking.*

FRENCH

$$–$$$ **Bistro K.** Seated outside in an ivy-trellised brick courtyard, with a fountain softly gurgling in the background and a glamorous, French waitress taking your order, you'll feel far from urban L.A. Beverly Hills' newest little charmer opened in January 1998 on the site of the former Chez Gilles. At the helm is Brittany-born chef Lionel Deniaud, former executive chef of New York's Ici and The Bistro in Beverly Hills. Flavors are clear and uncomplicated: There's a simple but delectable "triangle of tuna, pink grapefruit, green peppercorns, and broccoli rabe," a delicious seared swordfish with lemon, garlic, and spinach, and of course, bistro classics such as roast beef in burgundy sauce with pommes frites, and classic crème brulée. This is a perfect place for a low-key lunch break when you want to escape the frenetic Beverly Hills scene—or a chic but affordable supper *sans* stars. ✉ *267 S. Beverly Dr.* ☎ *310/276–1558. AE, DC, MC, V. No lunch Sun. Meter parking.*

ITALIAN

$$–$$$ ✕ **Il Fornaio Cucina Italiana.** What started as a bakery-café has been transformed into one of the best-looking contemporary trattorias in California, with cream-color walls and columns, slick little halogen lights, white linens, and a gleaming open kitchen. From the huge brass-and-stainless-steel rotisserie come crispy roasted duck, herb-basted chicken, and juicy rabbit. Nearby, cooks paddle pizzas and calzones in and out of the oak-wood-burning oven. ✉ *301 N. Beverly Dr.,* ☎ *310/550–8330. AE, D, DC, MC, V. Valet parking.*

$$–$$$ ✕ **Prego.** Part of a small, stylish chain of Italian restaurants, Prego is as consistent as it is comfortable, with a bar counter and large wooden booths. Regulars (shoppers, businesspeople, low-key showbiz folks) rely on the baby lamb chops, large broiled veal chop (the specialty), bruschetta Toscana, and agnolotti filled with lobster and ricotta in a lemon-lobster sauce. The bread sticks and pasta are made in-house. ✉ *362 N. Camden Dr.,* ☎ *310/277–7346. AE, DC, MC, V. No lunch Sun. Valet parking evenings.*

$$ ✕ **Da Pasquale.** An affordable meal is hard to find here in the land of Gucci and Bijan, which is one reason to visit Da Pasquale. An even better reason is the pizza topped with ingredients like fresh tomato, garlic, and basil or three cheeses and prosciutto. The skillful kitchen staff also does a good job with standards such as antipasti, pastas, and roast chicken. Walls of glass face the street, giving the black-clad regulars a chance to check out the scene. ✉ *9749 Little Santa Monica Blvd.,* ☎ *310/859–3884. AE, MC, V. Closed Sun. No lunch Sat. Free parking.*

HAWAIIAN

$$$–$$$$ ✕ **Trader Vic's.** Sure, it's corny, but this kitschy restaurant-bar inside the Beverly Hilton is the most restrained of the late Victor Bergeron's South Sea extravaganzas. Besides, who says corny can't be fun? The

Polynesian menu is as quirky as the decor: crab Rangoon, grilled-cheese wafers, skewered shrimp, grilled pork ribs, and peanut butter–coated lamb cooked in huge clay ovens. As for the exotic rum drinks, watch your sips. ⊠ *9876 Wilshire Blvd.,* ☎ *310/276–6345. Reservations essential. AE, D, DC, MC, V. No lunch. Valet parking.*

KOREAN

$$ ✕ **Woo Lae Oak.** This marble-clad, high-ceilinged Beverly Hills restaurant has made Korean food more accessible to a wider audience. It's relatively pricey, but, as at many traditional Korean restaurants, you cook your own meats and seafood on your tabletop grill, which is great fun for a lively group. ⊠ *170 N. La Cienega Blvd.,* ☎ *310/652–4187. AE, DC, MC, V. Valet parking.*

PAN-ASIAN

$$–$$$ ✕ **ObaChine.** Wolfgang Puck and Barbara Lazaroff strike again: this time with pan-Asian food for the Beverly Hills crowd. Prices are more reasonable than at their Santa Monica restaurant, Chinois On Main. Interesting dishes include savory crab *shui mai* (dumplings), Cambodian-style shrimp crepes, and salmon-skin salad with daikon-ponzu sauce (made from Japanese radishes and citrus fruit). ⊠ *242 N. Beverly Dr.,* ☎ *310/274–4440. AE, MC, V. No lunch Sun. Valet parking.*

PIZZA

$ ✕ **California Pizza Kitchen.** This is the original branch of a nationwide chain specializing in wood-fired pizza with a wide, esoteric choice of pizza toppings—from hoisin duck with Portobello mushrooms to a tandoori pie, with or without cheese. (Pizza purists may want to avoid the bacon, lettuce, and tomato variation.) There's friendly counter service by the open kitchen—or take a seat in the immaculate, pleasingly modern dining room. ⊠ *207 S. Beverly Dr.,* ☎ *310/275–1101. Reservations not accepted. AE, D, DC, MC, V. Free parking in lot.*

Century City

AMERICAN/CASUAL

$–$$ ✕ **Dive!** A Steven Spielberg creation, this place is as much a theme park as it is a restaurant. Water gurgles through porthole windows, fish swim by on giant screens, hatches connect the dining areas, and every now and then red lights flash and the whole place makes a simulated submarine dive. Submarine sandwiches, the specialty, go a step beyond ham and cheese: Try the Parisian chicken sub or the brick oven–baked Tuscan steak sub. S'mores and a lemon-bar concoction with white chocolate and raspberry sauce are among the rich desserts. Dive! is a big hit with kids, but prepare them for a long wait. ⊠ *10250 Santa Monica Blvd.,* ☎ *310/788–3483. AE, D, DC, MC, V. Valet parking or free self-parking.*

FRENCH

$$–$$$ ✕ **La Cachette.** Owner-chef Jean-Francois Meteigner cooked in some
★   of France's finest restaurants before coming to L.A., where he developed a following at L'Orangerie and Cicada. Now at his own place, he replaces butter-rich French fare with lighter, more modern French cuisine. L.A.'s fortysomething crowd dresses up (by L.A. standards) to see and be seen at this flower-filled restaurant hidden on an undistinguished stretch of Little Santa Monica Boulevard. ⊠ *10506 Little Santa Monica Blvd.,* ☎ *310/470–4992. Reservations essential. AE, MC, V. No lunch weekends. Valet parking.*

$$–$$$ ✕ **Lunaria.** Bernard Jacoupy, who made Bernard's one of the '80s best restaurants, has done it again at this jazz-friendly bistro. The sunny flavors of tomatoes, fennel, and good fresh fish dominate the Provençal menu; there's also an oyster bar. Roomy wicker armchairs and large tables fill the dining room, which is warmed by watercolors painted by Jacoupy's grandfather. After 8:30 (9:30 on weekends), a wall slides open to reveal the stage and the evening's featured jazz group. ⊠ *10351 Santa Monica Blvd.,* ☎ *310/282–8870. AE, DC, MC, V. Closed Sun. No lunch Sat., no dinner Mon. Valet parking.*

ITALIAN

$$–$$$ ✕ **Harry's Bar & American Grill.** The decor and selection of dishes—paper-thin carpaccio, grilled fish, and several pastas—are intended to evoke Harry's Bar in Venice, but the check will be far lower than it would be in Italy. The restaurant is on the promenade level of the Century City office complex. ⊠ *2020 Ave. of the Stars,* ☎ *310/277–2333. Reservations essential. AE, DC, MC. No lunch weekends. Valet parking.*

Hollywood

AMERICAN

$–$$ ✕ **Miss Gregory's American Kitchen.** Country quilts set the mood at this aptly named restaurant serving inspired American regional cuisine. Look for Rhode Island clam fritters, barbecued lamb steak, and catfish with a lemon-walnut crust. The unusual Sunday brunch features flannel cakes topped with caramelized apples or strawberries and cream. Miss Gregory's is convenient to movie theaters and shops; it's also a hit with children. ⊠ *7986 Sunset Blvd.,* ☎ *323/822–9057. AE, MC, V. Closed Mon. No lunch Sat.*

AMERICAN/CASUAL

$–$$ ✕ **Hollywood Canteen.** In the heart of working Hollywood, near soundstages, recording studios, and lighting companies, this handsome diner functions as a canteen for executives, actors, and technicians, who come here for simple but upscale grub: organic field-green salads, burgers, risotto with wild mushrooms, and various soups. ⊠ *1006 Seward St.,* ☎ *323/465–0961. AE, MC, V. Closed Sun. No lunch Sat. Valet parking.*

$$ ✕ **Hollywood Hills Coffee Shop.** Despite the modest name, this little café often has surprisingly good food. Breakfast promises classics such as corned-beef hash, huevos rancheros, Denver omelets, and even a whole grilled salmon trout, its reddish flesh set off by eggs and red salsa. For dinner, there are vegetarian choices as well as fish and meat (the Blue Plate Special is always chicken-fried steak). Don't be surprised to find yourself sharing the dining room with a troupe of green-haired rockers or the entire Jeanette MacDonald International Fan Club. ⊠ *6145 Franklin Ave.,* ☎ *323/467-7678. Reservations not accepted. MC, V.*

CAJUN/CREOLE

$ ✕ **Gumbo Pot.** While not exactly "down by the levee," this outdoor Cajun/Creole café in the Farmers Market does serve a mean smoky and spicy gumbo rich in shrimp and chicken. It's also the place for *mufalatas* (hero sandwiches), corn-battered shrimp, jambalaya, and *beignets* (deep-fried pastry squares). ⊠ *Farmers Market, 6333 W. 3rd St.,* ☎ *323/933–0358. Reservations not accepted. MC, V.*

CONTEMPORARY

$$$$ ✕ **Patina.** The exterior of Joachim Splichal's flagship restaurant is so
★ understated that it's easy to miss, and the interior is a study in spare elegance. Generally considered one of the best restaurants in Los Angeles, this is the wellspring from which the various Pinot bistros have sprung. Among the mainstays are a corn blini filled with fennel-marinated salmon and crème fraîche, and scallops wrapped in potato slices with brown-butter vinaigrette. Specials might include crispy

whitefish with "not fried" French fries and roasted rabbit leg stuffed with spinach and dried plums. ⊠ *5955 Melrose Ave.,* ☎ *323/467–1108. Reservations essential. AE, D, DC, MC, V. No lunch Wed.–Mon. Valet parking.*

$$–$$$ ✕ **Pinot Hollywood.** A link in the chain of glamorous bistros Joachim "Patina" Splichal has laid out across the city, Pinot Hollywood occupies a walled compound almost next door to Paramount Studios. With an outdoor terrace, martini bar, and lounge in addition to the main dining room, this is a comfortable venue for lunch, dinner, or late-night drinks. Lunch entrées, which range from $13 to $16, include salad Niçoise with grilled ahi tuna, a grilled lamb sandwich with ratatouille and goat cheese, and crispy whitefish with garlic mashed potatoes. For dinner you might find caramelized onion tart with marinated salmon, fresh grilled sardines à la Provençal, or breaded pork tenderloin with mustard greens and plum sauce. There are also daily "bistro" specials such as lobster with sweet garlic-lavender butter. ⊠ *1448 N. Gower St.,* ☎ *323/461–8800. Reservations essential. AE, D, DC, MC, V. No lunch Sat. Closed Sun. Valet parking.*

$$$–$$$$ ✕ **Citrus.** Seated under one of the large umbrellas in Citrus's spacious,
★ landscaped interior patio, you can see Melrose Avenue on one side and a glass-walled kitchen on the other. Chef Michel Richard has opened restaurants elsewhere, but Citrus has remained his hottest ticket, especially within the entertainment industry. Lunch begins on the light side, with starters such as artichoke terrine or a shiitake-mushroom-and-garlic Napoleon, followed by sautéed Chilean sea bass or medium-rare *onglet* (hangar steak). The dinner menu has featured crab cakes with tomato-mustard sauce, salmon with asparagus crust, and roast duck with apple fries and fig sauce. ⊠ *6703 Melrose Ave.,* ☎ *323/857–0034. Reservations essential. AE, MC, V. Closed Sun. Valet parking.*

FRENCH

$–$$$ ✕ **Les Deux Cafés.** Entertainment industryites and young fashion-forward folk known as the New Hollywood have been slowly transforming the formerly tattered tinsel of downtown Hollywood. One of the telltale signs of this renaissance is Les Deux Cafés, a handsomely refitted 1904 house with a hidden dining terrace and an even more intimate herb garden set in a parking lot behind a barbed-wire-topped wall. Chef David Winn appeals to easily bored tastes with inventions such as lobster-and-tabbouleh salad, crayfish gratin, and a salad of beets, spinach, and horseradish; he also turns out a splendid skate sautéed in brown butter; braised chicken in a bouillabaisse of fennel, onions, tomato, and saffron; and prosciutto-wrapped salmon cooked *en papillote* (in parchment paper). Desserts range from a cherry *clafouti* (custard tart) to *fondant au chocolat* (warm molten chocolate in a chocolate crust). ⊠ *1683 Las Palmas Ave., Hollywood,* ☎ *213/465–0509. Reservations essential. Closed Sun. No lunch Sat. AE, MC, V. Valet parking.*

INDIAN

$ ✕ **East India Grill.** With a high-tech aesthetic, zesty food, and speedy courteous service, this indoor-outdoor café is a winner. Traditional dishes such as green-coconut curries, *makhani tikka masalas* (tomato-based curries), and *sagwalas* (spinach dishes) are just as well prepared as the more imaginative, California-influenced novelties—tandoori chicken salad, mango ribs, and garlic-basil nan, to name a few. ⊠ *345 N. La Brea Ave.,* ☎ *323/936–8844. AE, MC, V. Garage parking.*

JAPANESE

$$ ✕ **Ita-Cho.** It may be in a tattered minimall, but Ita-Cho is a chic destination for those in the know. Specializing in *koryori-ya,* the Japa-

nese pub cuisine that features delicately cooked dishes, the small dining room also serves flawless sashimi (but no sushi). Try the tender pork simmered in sake and soy for two days, lightly fried tofu cubes in soy-ginger-scallion sauce, and yellowtail braised with teriyaki. The sake list is excellent. ⊠ *6775 Santa Monica Blvd.,* ☎ *323/871–0236. Reservations essential. AE, MC, V. Closed Sun. Valet parking.*

MEXICAN

$–$$ ✕ **El Cholo.** The progenitor of a chain, this landmark south of Holly-
★   wood has been packing them in since the '20s. A hand-painted adobe ceiling and outdoor patio with a fountain create a partylike atmosphere—it's the kind of place where you order margaritas and all kinds of tacos, some of which you make yourself. L.A.-Mex standards are also served—chicken enchiladas, *carnitas* (pork with rice and beans), and, from July through October, green-corn tamales. Portions are large and prices reasonable. ⊠ *1121 S. Western Ave.,* ☎ *323/734–2773. AE, DC, MC, V. Valet and meter parking.*

RUSSIAN

$–$$ ✕ **Uzbekistan.** Brightly colored murals lend a fittingly folksy air to this restaurant, which serves a mix of Russian and Central Asian cuisine. Start with any of the meat dumplings—*samsa, manti,* or *pelmeni*—and go on to eggplant Samarkand (sautéed with tomatoes and garlic), *lulya-kebab* (skewered ground lamb), or *akurma lagman* (a stir fry of beef, noodles, and vegetables perfumed with cumin). ⊠ *7077 Sunset Blvd.,* ☎ *323/464–3663. MC, V.*

SOUL

$ ✕ **Roscoe's House of Chicken 'n' Waffles.** The name of this casual eatery doesn't sound all that appetizing, considering the strange combination of foods mentioned, but don't be fooled: This is *the* place for real down-home southern cooking. Just ask the patrons, who drive from all over the L.A. basin for Roscoe's bargain-price fried chicken, waffles, and grits. ⊠ *1514 N. Gower St.,* ☎ *323/466–9329. Reservations not accepted. AE, D, DC, MC, V.*

THAI

$–$$ ✕ **Chan Dara.** A rock 'n' roll and showbiz crowd frequents this casual eatery, which occupies an old Spanish house in a block of doctors' offices near Paramount Pictures. Try any of the noodle dishes, especially those with crab and shrimp. Also on the extensive menu are *satay* (appetizers on skewers), barbecued chicken, and catfish. You can dine alfresco on the patio, or just have dessert there (the mango tart is especially good). ⊠ *310 N. Larchmont Blvd.,* ☎ *323/467–1052. AE, D, DC, MC, V. No lunch weekends.*

Los Feliz

CARIBBEAN

$–$$$ ✕ **Cha Cha Cha.** Because it's off the beaten path, Cha Cha Cha attracts a discerning, eclectic crowd. It's hip yet not pretentious or overly trendy; a nice touch is the giant map that pinpoints the restaurant's Caribbean influences. You can sit indoors in a cozy room or on the enclosed tropical-à-la-Carmen-Miranda patio. There's Jamaican jerk chicken, swordfish brochette, fried plantain chips, and assorted flans. Sangria is the drink of choice. ⊠ *656 N. Virgil Ave.,* ☎ *323/664–7723. AE, D, DC, MC, V. Valet parking.*

ECLECTIC

$–$$ ✕ **Fred 62.** Fred Eric, of nearby Vida—a darling of the it-doesn't-matter-what-you-wear-so-long-as-it's-black crowd—opened this 24-hour luncheonette that caters to neighborhood locals and club-goers. "Cream of what you want soup" and "punk tarts" may be too cutesy for some, but if you can get past the scene factor, you're bound to find something you like on the eclectic menu, which includes everything from tofu scrambles to oxtail. ✉ *1850 N. Vermont Ave.,* ☎ *323/667–0062. Reservations not accepted. MC, V.*

$–$$ ✕ **Vida.** Chef-owner Fred Eric's quirky cuisine is anything but predictable—and loaded with cute-as-a-cactus-button puns ("Okra Winfrey" gumbo; spicy Ty Cobb salad complete with duck confit cut into perfect squares). The modern, hip-to-the-hilt dining room, heavy on bamboo, skylights, and shoji screens, is a converted 1920s bungalow. Be sure to book a booth in the front room if you seek privacy. ✉ *1930 N. Hillhurst Ave.,* ☎ *323/660–4446. AE, DC, MC, V. No lunch. Valet parking.*

ITALIAN

$$ ✕ **Trattoria Farfalla.** This hip, brick-walled trattoria brought Los Feliz out of the spaghetti-and-meatballs mode in the '80s and has remained a favorite ever since, thanks in part to its fair prices. The daily specials are always good, but regulars tend to order the Caesar salad on a pizza-crust bed; roasted free-range chicken; and pasta alla Norma, studded with rich, smoky eggplant. ✉ *1978 N. Hillhurst Ave.,* ☎ *323/661–7365. AE, DC, MC, V. No lunch weekends. Street parking.*

JAPANESE

$–$$$ ✕ **Restaurant Katsu.** Exquisitely presented, high-quality sushi is served
★ in this stark, peaceful sushi bar, in addition to other Japanese specialties. Tempura and teriyaki lunches are a good value ($6.50–$9). For dinner try the "dynamite" *yadokari* (a casserole made with scallops and white sauce), or grilled fish or beef. ✉ *1972 N. Hillhurst Ave.,* ☎ *323/665–1891. Reservations essential. AE, DC, MC, V. Closed Sun. No lunch Sat. Valet parking.*

West Hollywood

AMERICAN/CASUAL

$–$$ ✕ **Cadillac Cafe.** This futuristic, Jetsons-inspired eatery is a modestly priced, fun alternative to the food chains in nearby Beverly Center. Goofy-sounding but good-tasting dishes such as Original Turkey Sundae and Burnt Meatloaf Marinara please children as well as adults. There are also more mainstream selections like smoked trout sandwich, grilled ahi tuna salad Niçoise, and angel hair pasta with shrimp. Weekend breakfasts include a vegetarian frittata. ✉ *359 N. La Cienega Blvd.,* ☎ *310/657–6591. AE, MC.*

$ ✕ **Ed's Coffee Shop.** The coffee shop of choice for decorators and clients from the nearby Pacific Design Center, Ed's serves delicious omelets, huevos rancheros, egg salad, stuffed peppers, meat loaf, and homemade pies. It's as homey as a restaurant can be, which partially explains why almost all the customers are regulars. ✉ *460 N. Robertson Blvd.,* ☎ *310/659–8625. Reservations not accepted. No credit cards. No lunch weekends. No dinner.*

$ ✕ **Swingers.** Everyone from power lunchers to Doc Marten–clad posers takes to this all-day, late-night coffee shop, so be prepared for a wait. Eat at sidewalk tables or inside the pseudo-diner on the ground floor of a '60s no-frills hotel. Loud alternative music plays to the Gen-X crowd, and a casual menu—breakfast burritos, hamburgers, ostrich burgers, and chicken breast sandwiches on fresh French bread—appeals to the pocketbook. ⊠ *8020 Beverly Blvd.,* ☎ *323/653–5858. AE, D, MC, V. Meter parking.*

CONTEMPORARY

$$$–$$$$ ✕ **Fenix.** Anticipate abundant art deco splendor from The Argyle Hotel's culinary outpost on the Sunset Strip. The bi-level dining room–bar, accented in dark purple and brushed gold, has plush banquettes, a grand piano, and a romantic city view. Chef Ken Frank is renowned for his rösti potatoes with golden caviar; other signature dishes include porcini-crusted scallops with lobster-crushed potatoes and grilled Texas antelope with foie gras sauce. You may also spot some Asian influences on this Franco-Californian menu, as in the daikon–sesame salad with lobster and toasted salmon skin. Tasting menus may be ordered for the entire table. ⊠ *8358 Sunset Blvd.,* ☎ *323/848–6677. Reservations essential. AE, D, DC, MC, V. Valet parking.*

$$–$$$ **Jozu.** The Japanese name, which means "excellent," and Japanese-theme decor hint at the bias of executive chef Suzanne Tracht's Cal-Asian menu. Start with crisp Sonoma quail with tangerine glaze, mussels with saffron-coconut broth, or deep-fried Ipswich clams. As an entree, you might try grilled Maine scallops with Thai-rolled pasta, roasted tomatoes, and lemongrass butter; or grilled chicken marinated with a kefir-lime leaf on sticky rice, with red curry sauce. The Pacific Rim wine list is augmented by cognacs and vintage ports. ⊠ *8360 Melrose Ave.,* ☎ *323/655–5600. AE, DC, MC, V. No lunch. Valet parking.*

$$–$$$ ✕ **Spago.** This is the restaurant that propelled chef-owner Wolfgang Puck into the international culinary spotlight in the early 1980s. Make reservations far in advance to sample roasted cumin lamb on lentil salad with fresh coriander and yogurt chutney, fresh oysters with green chili and black-pepper mignonette, grilled free-range chickens, and grilled Alaskan baby salmon—all made with the finest West Coast produce. The biggest seller is not on the menu, so ask: It's known as the Jewish pizza, topped with cream cheese and smoked salmon. This is the place to see *People* magazine live, but you'll have to put up with the noise in exchange. ⊠ *1114 Horn Ave.,* ☎ *310/652–4025. Reservations essential. D, DC, MC, V. No lunch. Closed Mon. Valet parking.*

$$–$$$ ✕ **Boxer.** This smart, small restaurant on the newly developing Beverly Boulevard strip is well-served by its young new chef, Michael Plapp, who presents a seasonal menu with French influences. Start with a crab-and-prosciutto salad or a rich roasted vegetable soup made without cream or butter; follow with couscous and rock shrimp, striped bass in cardamom broth, or lamb shanks slow-cooked in red wine. Although the owners have no wine license, you can buy your own bottle from the well-stocked wine shop next door. ⊠ *7615 Beverly Blvd.,* ☎ *323/ 932–6178. AE, MC, V. Closed Sun. Valet parking.*

$$$–$$$$ ✕ **Campanile.** In this stylish, high-ceilinged restaurant that was once
★   Charlie Chaplin's office complex, Mark Peel and Nancy Silverton (also the force behind the adjacent La Brea Bakery)—two of the finest modern American chefs in the country—blend robust Mediterranean flavors with those of homey Americana. Distinguished appetizers include celery-root soup with pesto, grilled sardines with marinated fennel, and grilled squid salad. Entrées include bourride of snapper and manila clams, and pork loin with sweet potatoes and turnip greens. Here is also where you'll find some of the best desserts in town—try the light-as-a-feather bitter-almond *panna cotta* (a custardlike crème brûlée), or tuck into Mom's apple pie. Weekend brunch on the enclosed patio with a vintage fountain should not be missed. ⊠ *624 S. La Brea Ave.,* ☎ *323/938–1447. Reservations essential. AE, D, DC, MC, V. No dinner Sun. Valet parking.*

DELI

$ ✗ **Canter's.** This granddaddy of Los Angeles delicatessens (it opened in 1928) pickles its own corned-beef pastrami and has its own in-house bakery. Next door is the Kibitz Room, where there's live music most nights. ⊠ *419 N. Fairfax Ave.,* ☏ *323/651–2030. Reservations not accepted. MC, V. Parking in lot.*

FRENCH

$$$$ ✗ **L'Orangerie.** Elegant French Mediterranean cuisine is served in this
★ rococo dining room, complete with white flower arrangements and oils depicting European castles. Specialties include coddled eggs served in the shell and topped with caviar, duck with foie gras, John Dory with roasted figs, rack of lamb for two, and a rich apple tart accompanied by a jug of double cream. ⊠ *903 N. La Cienega Blvd.,* ☏ *310/652– 9770. Reservations essential. AE, D, DC, MC, V. Closed Mon. No lunch. Valet parking.*

$$$–$$$$ ✗ **Drai's.** Rolls-Royce and Range Rover owners parade through Victor Drai's see-and-be-seen restaurant, where chef Claude Segal serves up Mediterranean-influenced French-bistro fare. Consider the leg of lamb, cooked for seven hours in its own juices, or such standards as osso buco and beef bourguignonne. Expect attitude from the fashionable crowd as well as the waiters, who have been known to hurry diners. ⊠ *730 N. La Cienega Blvd.,* ☏ *310/358–8585. Closed Sun. No lunch. Valet parking. AE, DC, MC, V.*

$$$–$$$$ ✗ **Le Dôme.** This fancy show- and music-biz bistro mixes French-country dishes and hearty American fare: escargots Burgundy-style (served with garlic, shallots, and parsley), coq au vin, and steamed pig's knuckle appeal to francophiles, while center-cut pork chops and and grilled Sonoma lamb chops satisfy patriots. ⊠ *8720 Sunset Blvd.,* ☏ *310/659–6919. Reservations essential. AE, MC, V. Closed Sun. No lunch Sat. Valet parking.*

$$$ ✗ **Le Chardonnay.** The art nouveau dining room, resplendent with mirrors and polished woodwork, is modeled after the famous 1920s Parisian bistro Vagenende; its comfortable, cozy booths make it ideal for a swank romantic rendezvous. Chef Jean-Pierre Le Manissier has added salmon Parmentier (roasted with potatoes) and venison chops with black-currant sauce to the traditional menu. Older classics are mussels marinière, escargots with garlic butter, and numerous lush desserts. ⊠ *8284 Melrose Ave.,* ☏ *323/655–8880. Reservations essential. AE, D, DC, MC, V. Closed Mon. No lunch Sat.–Thurs. Valet parking.*

$$–$$$ ✗ **Mimosa.** Like this small restaurant's sunny, pale-yellow interior, its menu is country French with a Provençal accent. Chef Jean-Pierre Bosc proudly claims on the menu: "No truffles, no caviar, no bizarre concoctions, simply our interpretation of French regional cuisine with a touch of Italy." Indeed, this is simple, authentic bistro food at its best. Witness the Lyonnaise salad, served with de rigueur poached egg; the *tarte flambée alsacienne,* a pizza-like wood-fired onion tart; and the hearty chicken terrine with onion marmalade. Standout entrées are bouillabaisse, whole snapper à la provençale, and roasted pork with prunes and red cabbage. Home-cured *cornichons* (pickles) are set out on every table, along with crocks of country mustard. A handful of celebrities joins a bevy of neighborhood regulars at Mimosa, but the atmosphere remains intimate, with framed mirrors, red upholstered banquettes, and chalkboard specials. ⊠ *8009 Beverly Blvd., West Hollywood,* ☏ *213/ 655–8895. Closed Sun. No lunch Sat. AE, MC, V. Valet parking.*

GREEK

$$ ✗ **Sofi.** Hidden down a narrow passageway is this friendly little taverna where you can sample such Greek favorites as *dolmades* (stuffed grape leaves), lamb gyros, traditional salads, phyllo pies, spanakopita,

and souvlaki. Sit in the stone-wall dining room or outside on a vine-shaded patio. ⊠ *8030¾ W. 3rd St.,* ☎ *323/651–0346. AE, D, DC, MC, V. No lunch Sun.*

ITALIAN

$$ ✕ **Ca'Brea.** Chef Antonio Tommasi, formerly at Locanda Veneta, turns
★   out lamb chops with black-truffle and mustard sauce, whole boneless chicken marinated and grilled with herbs, and a very popular osso buco. Starters make the meal—try baked goat cheese wrapped in pancetta and served atop a Popeye-size mound of spinach. Daily specials include soup, salad, pasta, and fish dishes. The cozy upstairs loft is ideal for those seeking privacy. ⊠ *346 S. La Brea Ave.,* ☎ *323/938–2863. AE, D, DC, MC, V. Closed Sun. No lunch weekends.*

$$ ✕ **Locanda Veneta.** This up-market Italian trattoria has an open kitchen, terra-cotta walls, and stone floors. Specialties include flattened grilled chicken, veal chops, linguine with clams, lobster ravioli with saffron sauce, and an unusual apple tart with polenta crust and caramel sauce. ⊠ *8638 W. 3rd St.,* ☎ *310/274–1893. Reservations essential. AE, D, DC, MC, V. Closed Sun. No lunch Sat. Valet parking.*

$ ✕ **Tavola Calda.** This low-tech Italian favorite draws a budget-watching crowd, with many entrées priced under $10. Cabaret tables are scattered around the spacious room, which has high ceilings and intimate lighting. Best bets on the limited menu are unusual gourmet pizzas, like the cheese-less vegetarian pie, and also the seafood and porcini risottos. ⊠ *7371 Melrose Ave.,* ☎ *323/658–6340. AE, DC, MC, V. Valet parking.*

JAPANESE

$$$–$$$$ ✕ **Matsuhisa.** Cutting-edge Pacific Rim cuisine is pushed to new lim-
★   its at this modest-looking yet high-profile Japanese bistro. Chef Nobu Matsuhisa creatively infuses his dishes with flavors encountered during his sojourn in Peru. Consider his caviar-capped tuna stuffed with black truffles, and the sea urchin wrapped in a *shiso* leaf. Tempuras are lighter than usual, and the sushi is fresh and authentic. There isn't another restaurant in the country like it—except Matsuhisa's Manhattan outpost, Nobu. Regulars ask the chef to prepare whatever's best that day—and then steel themselves for a daunting tab. ⊠ *129 N. La Cienega Blvd.,* ☎ *310/659–9639. Reservations essential. AE, DC, MC, V. Valet parking.*

SOUTHWESTERN

$–$$ ✕ **Authentic Cafe.** Think Southwestern food has fallen off the map? Then head to this way hip, way fun café for some spicy flavors that are anything but dated. The Gen-X crowd can't get enough of the Santa Fe salad, wood-grilled chicken with mole, chicken casserole with cornbread crust, and excellent vegetarian dishes. You'll have to wait at peak hours, but the reward is high-quality, sun-drenched cooking at reasonable prices. Breakfast is served on weekends. ⊠ *7605 Beverly Blvd.,* ☎ *323/939–4626. Reservations not accepted. MC, V.*

SPANISH

$$–$$$ ✕ **Cava.** This two-level tapas bar and restaurant is in the Beverly Plaza Hotel, not far from the Farmers Market. The artsy dining room has larger-than-life roses painted on the walls, and the atmosphere is a bit noisy but lots of fun. You can graze on tapas—tiny snacks such as baked artichoke topped with bread crumbs and tomato, or a fluffy potato omelet served with crème fraîche. Those with bigger appetites should try the paella, *zarzuela* (lightly baked shrimp, scallops, clams, mussels, and fresh fish in a hearty tomato wine sauce), or *bistec flamenco* (aged New York steak with caramelized onions and a traditional Argentine

steak sauce). Wash it all down with a glass or three of sangría. ✉ *8384 W. 3rd St.,* ☎ *323/658–8898. AE, D, DC, MC, V. Valet parking.*

STEAK

$$$–$$$$ ✕ **Arnie Morton's of Chicago.** The West Coast addition to this ever-expanding national chain brought joy and cholesterol to the hearts of Los Angeles meat lovers, many of whom claim that Morton's serves the best steaks in town. In addition to a 24-ounce porterhouse, a New York strip, and a double-cut filet mignon, there are giant veal and lamb chops, thick cuts of prime rib, swordfish steaks, and imported lobsters at market prices (translation: The tasty crustaceans don't come cheap!). ✉ *435 S. La Cienega Blvd.,* ☎ *310/246–1501. AE, DC, MC, V. No lunch.*

$$$–$$$$ ✕ **The Palm.** All the New York elements are present at this West Coast replay of the famous Manhattan steak house—mahogany booths, tin ceilings, boisterous atmosphere, and New York–style waiters rushing you through your cheesecake (which is flown in from the Bronx). This is where you'll find the biggest and best lobster, good steaks, prime rib, chops, great French-fried onion rings, and paper-thin potato slices. When writers sell a screenplay, they celebrate with a Palm lobster. ✉ *9001 Santa Monica Blvd.,* ☎ *310/550–8811. AE, DC, MC, V. Reservations essential. No lunch weekends. Valet parking.*

THAI

$–$$ ✕ **Tommy Tang's.** A lot of people-watching goes on at this Melrose Avenue grazing ground. Although portions are on the small side, they're decidedly innovative: Try crisp duck marinated in ginger–plum sauce, blackened sea scallops, or the low-calorie spinach salad tossed with grilled chicken. A happening sushi bar overlooks the restaurant's inviting garden patio. Be sure to save room for raspberry–mango crème brûlée or banana spring rolls with vanilla-bean ice cream and chocolate sauce. ✉ *7313 Melrose Ave.,* ☎ *323/937–5733. AE, DC, MC, V. Valet parking.*

VIETNAMESE

$$–$$$ ✕ **Le Colonial.** A bright blue neon sign makes this high-fashion restaurant hard to miss. The inside looks like prewar Saigon, with whirling fans hanging from a burgundy pressed-tin ceiling, shuttered windows, floors done in green-trimmed antique tiles, and mood music such as the *Indochine* soundtrack. Like the original Le Colonial in Manhattan, this is a bi-level restaurant with an opulent bar upstairs, and below, a seductive dining room serving dishes such as roasted chicken with lemongrass; fried spring rolls packed with pork, mushrooms, and shrimp; and shredded chicken and cabbage doused in lime juice. ✉ *8783 Beverly Blvd.,* ☎ *310/289–0660. AE, DC, MC, V. No lunch weekends. Valet parking.*

Coastal Los Angeles

Bel-Air

CONTEMPORARY

$$$–$$$$ ✕ **Hotel Bel-Air.** You couldn't ask for a lovelier setting: Nestled in the
★ midst of luxuriant Beverly Glen, the restaurant in the Hotel Bel-Air spills out into a romantic country garden with gurgling fountains and a swan lake. Chef Peter Roelant, a graduate of L'Orangerie, wows diners with eclectic starters such as grilled asparagus with prosciutto, figs, and chived sour cream; or perhaps a salad of crispy sweetbreads, dates, and apples. Entrées such as duck glazed with sour cherries; venison with port and poached pear; and halibut with a vodka-lime mousseline are exceptional. The Hotel Bel-Air also hosts one of the best high teas in town.

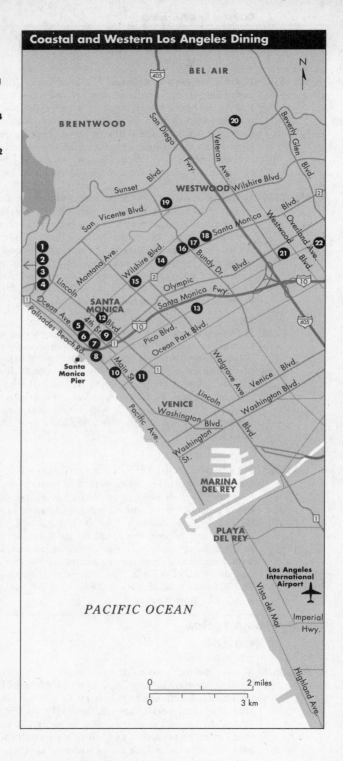

Coastal and Western Los Angeles Dining

✉ *701 Stone Canyon Rd.,* ☎ *310/472–1211. Reservations essential. Jacket and tie. AE, DC, MC, V. Valet parking.*

Malibu

ITALIAN

$$–$$$ ✕ **Tra di Noi.** The name means "between us," and Malibu natives are trying to keep this charming, simple *ristorante* just that—a local secret. It's run by a mama who does the cooking, along with her son and daughter-in-law. Regular customers, film celebrities, and non-showbiz folk turn up here, but it's also a great place to bring kids. Nothing fancy or *nuovo* on the menu, just great lasagna, freshly made pasta, mushroom and veal dishes, and fresh salads. An Italian buffet is laid out for Sunday brunch. ✉ *3835 Cross Creek Rd.,* ☎ *310/456–0169. AE, MC, V.*

CONTEMPORARY

$$$–$$$$ ✕ **Granita.** Wolfgang Puck's famed Granita is an underwater fantasy
★ world of handmade tiles embedded with seashells, blown-glass lighting fixtures, and etched-glass panels with wavy edges (even the blasé Malibu film colony is impressed by its exotic koi pond and waterfall)— and its beachside location adds to the marine mood. Fitting, then, that the menu should favor seafood items such as grilled Atlantic salmon in tomato broth with seared carrots and wild mushrooms. Standard Puck favorites are also available: peppered shrimp pizza with sun-dried tomatoes and herb pesto, roasted Cantonese duck with dried-fruit chutney, sautéed foie gras with ginger–port-wine glaze, and Caesar salad with oven-baked bruschetta. Brunch is served on weekends. ✉ *23725 W. Malibu Rd.,* ☎ *310/456–0488. Reservations essential. D, DC, MC, V. No lunch weekdays.*

FRENCH

$$$–$$$$ ✕ **Beaurivage.** One of the few Malibu restaurants with a view of the beach and ocean, this romantic Mediterranean-villa–style dining room has copper domes and lush landscaping. The menu complements the Provençal mood: roast duck breast served with a wild-cherry sauce, portabello mushrooms served atop polenta with a lemon–ginger sauce, pasta with shellfish, mussel soup, and filet mignon with a mushroom– marsala sauce. ✉ *26025 Pacific Coast Hwy.,* ☎ *310/456–5733. Reservations essential. AE, DC, MC, V. No lunch Mon.–Sat. Parking lot.*

Pacific Palisades

AMERICAN/CASUAL

$$$–$$$$ ✕ **Gladstone's 4 Fish.** Gladstone's is one of the most popular restaurants along the southern California coast; its demand has even spawned a sister restaurant in Universal Studios' CityWalk, whose lack of a beachfront setting makes it far less attractive. The food is notable mostly for its Brobdingnagian portions: giant bowls of crab chowder, mounds of steamed clams, three-egg omelets, heaps of barbecued ribs, and the famous mile-high chocolate cake, which can easily feed a small regiment. The real reason to visit Gladstone's is the glorious vista of sea, sky, and beach. The good cheer of the diners and staff is infectious, too. ✉ *17300 Pacific Coast Hwy., at Sunset Blvd., Pacific Palisades,* ☎ *310/454– 3474. AE, D, DC, MC, V. Valet parking.*

Santa Monica

AMERICAN/CASUAL

$–$$ ✕ **Broadway Deli.** The name is misleading, so don't come here expecting
★ hot corned-beef and pastrami sandwiches. This joint venture of Michel Richard and Bruce Marder is a cross between a European brasserie and an upscale diner. Whatever you feel like eating, you'll probably find it on the menu—a platter of assorted smoked fish or Caesar salad, shep-

herd's pie, carpaccio, or broiled salmon with creamed spinach. Plus, there are great side dishes such as corn muffins, mashed potatoes with mushroom gravy, and potato pancakes. Breads are baked fresh, and there's also a kids' menu. ⊠ *1457 3rd St. Promenade, Santa Monica,* ☎ *310/451–0616. Reservations not accepted. AE, MC, V. Valet parking weekends and evenings.*

CONTEMPORARY

$$$–$$$$
★
× **Chinois on Main.** A once-revolutionary outpost in Wolfgang Puck's repertoire, this is still one of L.A.'s most crowded restaurants—and one of the noisiest. Puck's wife and partner, Barbara Lazaroff, designed the jazzy interior, which is just as loud as the clientele. The happy marriage of Asian and French cuisines yields seasonal dishes such as grilled Mongolian lamb chops with cilantro vinaigrette and wok-fried vegetables, Shanghai lobster with spicy ginger–curry sauce, and rare duck with plum sauce. ⊠ *2709 Main St., Santa Monica,* ☎ *310/392–9025. Reservations essential. AE, D, DC, MC, V. No lunch Sat.–Tues. Valet parking.*

$$$–$$$$
Lavande. How about a lavender sachet to take home with you? The complimentary miniature potpourris are just one of the unexpected pleasures of dining at Lavande, the new Provençal restaurant in the Loews Santa Monica Hotel. Seated on a wicker chair in this huge, peach-walled dining room, gazing through stylized Palladian windows at expansive ocean views, it's not a stretch to imagine yourself in a grand seaside hotel in Cannes. Chef Alain Giraud and manager Michel Keller, who previously worked together at Citrus, have already developed a following for their robust Provençal cuisine: scallop pissaladière tart, striped bass with fennel and Pernod sauce, classic fish soup Provençale with garlic croutons and rouille, and veal stew with red wine and green and black olives are all boldly flavored and beautifully presented. For dessert, the vacherin with lavender ice cream and strawberries is a must. For Sunday brunch, the menu reverts back to standard American hotel fare. ⊠ *Loews Santa Monica Beach Hotel, 1700 Ocean Ave.,* ☎ *310/576–3181. AE, D, DC, MC, V. No dinner Sun. Valet parking.*

$$–$$$
× **JiRaffe.** Nothing about this up-market bistro is as cutesy as its name—which is actually just a contraction of the two chef-owners' names. The gleaming, wood-paneled, two-story dining room with ceiling-high windows is a handsome setting, and the menu is just as tasteful. Inventive pastas, such as butternut squash agnolotti with brown-butter sage sauce and squash chips, are an excellent way to kick off a meal of roasted Chilean sea bass with a ragout of salsify, chanterelles, and pearl onions; or roasted rack of lamb with truffled potato gnocchi. ⊠ *502 Santa Monica Blvd., Santa Monica,* ☎ *310/917–6671. Reservations essential. AE, DC, MC, V. Closed Mon. No lunch weekends. Valet parking.*

IRISH

$$–$$$
× **Gilliland's.** Gerri Gilliland was teaching cooking in her native Ireland, took a vacation in southern California, and never went back. Instead, she stayed and opened this casual bistro with an old mahogany bar and a wonderful rear garden. Chef Gilliland has gradually abandoned the modern Cal-Asian dishes she used to favor, shifting toward light, skillful renditions of her homeland's classics: soda bread; Irish stew; roasted, stuffed pork loin; and bread pudding. She also makes good salads and several low-fat dishes. ⊠ *2424 Main St., Santa Monica,* ☎ *310/392–3901. AE, D, DC, MC, V. No lunch Sat.*

$$–$$$$ ✕ **Valentino.** Rated among the nation's best Italian restaurants, Valentino
★ is also generally considered to have the best wine list outside Western
Europe. In the 1980s, owner Piero Selvaggio introduced Los Angeles
to this style of light, modern Italian cuisine, including superb prosci-
utto, fried calamari, lobster cannelloni, fresh broiled porcini mushrooms,
and osso buco. For a true Valentino experience, order from the lengthy
list of daily specials instead of the more ordinary standard menu. ⊠
3115 Pico Blvd., Santa Monica, ☎ *310/829–4313. Reservations es-
sential. AE, DC, MC, V. Closed Sun. No lunch Sat.–Thurs. Valet
parking.*

$$$ ✕ **Drago.** Authentic Sicilian fare is hard to come by in the City of An-
★ gels, but affable Celestino Drago's culinary outpost is an exception.
The home-style fare, though pricey, is perfectly prepared and attentively
served in stark designer surroundings. White walls and white linen–
covered tables line both sides of a floating service station dressed up
with a massive fresh-flower arrangement. Sample Drago's *pappardelle*
(wide noodles) with rabbit ragout; morel mushroom risotto; or ostrich
breast with red-cherry sauce—or the savory pumpkin soup accompanied by chestnut gnocchi, the perfect starter for any Drago meal. ⊠
2628 Wilshire Blvd., Santa Monica, ☎ *310/828–1585. AE, DC, MC,
V. No lunch weekends. Valet parking.*

$$–$$$ ✕ **Remi.** If you think of Santa Monica's Third Street Promenade as a
canal, this may feel like a swank Venetian trattoria. The menu is diverse: linguine with scallops, mussels, shrimp, and fresh chopped tomatoes; whole-wheat crepes with ricotta and spinach, topped with a
vegetable sauce; and roasted pork chop stuffed with smoked mozzarella
and prosciutto, served with roast potatoes and fennel—all good choices.
⊠ *1451 3rd St. Promenade, Santa Monica,* ☎ *310/393–6545. Reservations essential. AE, DC, MC, V. Parking in nearby mall parking lots.*

$$ ✕ **Border Grill.** Hipsters love this loud, trendy eating hall designed by
★ minimalist architect Josh Schweitzer and owned by the talented team
of Mary Sue Milliken and Susan Feniger. It's the most progressive, eclec-
tic Mexican restaurant in L.A., with a menu ranging from Yucatán
seafood tacos to vinegar-and-pepper-grilled turkey to daily seviche
specials. The margaritas are also top-notch. ⊠ *1445 4th St., Santa Mon-
ica,* ☎ *310/451–1655. AE, D, DC, MC, V.*

$$–$$$$ ✕ **Ocean Avenue Seafood.** Operating since 1946, this cavernous restaurant isn't right on the water, but the Pacific is just across the street—
ask for a table by the window for an ocean view. Low ceilings, dim
lighting, well-spaced tables, and attentive service create an intimate mood.
Standout dishes are the cioppino, a fish stew made with Dungeness crab,
clams, mussels, and prawns; and the Chilean sea bass marinated in a
sake *kasu* sauce (an intoxicating mixture of sake, soy sauce, white wine,
and rice wine vinegar). Daily specials and oyster-bar selections are also
good. For dessert, the apple tart with caramel sauce is tops. ⊠ *1401
Ocean Ave., Santa Monica,* ☎ *310/394–5669. AE, DC, MC, V. Valet
parking.*

West Los Angeles

$–$$ ✕ **JR Seafood.** Westsiders who once had to drive to Monterey Beach
to get a good plate of shrimp in spicy salt have made this place a huge
hit. The Hong Kong–style restaurant serves all the Chinese seafood-
house standards—seafood soup, rock cod in garlic sauce, kung-pao scallops—that are so plentiful in the San Gabriel Valley but so scarce in

these parts. The service can be slow, but as long as the shrimp keeps coming, no one seems to mind. ⊠ *11901 Santa Monica Blvd., West Los Angeles,* ☎ *310/268–2463. MC, V. Free parking.*

CONTEMPORARY

$–$$ ✕ **Jack Sprat's Grill.** In the spirit of its namesake nursery rhyme, Jack Sprat's is as spare in style (lots of wood and a concrete floor) as it is in its caloric approach. Nevertheless, virtue tastes like vice, thanks to inventive light sauces and sassy salsas: Boneless, skinless chicken breasts are perked up with mango-kiwi-mint salsa, and grilled vegetables go well with Dijon mustard sauce. Other guiltless treats: dynamite salads, pita wraps, hummus, and air fries (french fries *sans* grease). One caveat: The service could be better. ⊠ *10668 W. Pico Blvd., West Los Angeles,* ☎ *310/837–6662. AE, MC, V. No lunch Sun. Self parking.*

INDIAN

$–$$ ✕ **Bombay Cafe.** If another meal of tandoori chicken sounds dull, head to this lively minimall café for high-quality Indian street food. Regulars swear by the chili-laden lamb frankies (sausages), various chutneys, *sev puri* (little wafers topped with onions, potatoes, and chutneys), and other vibrant small dishes. ⊠ *12113 Santa Monica Blvd., West Los Angeles,* ☎ *310/820–2070. MC, V. Closed Mon. No lunch weekends.*

ITALIAN

$$$ ✕ **Vincenti.** City Hall clientele may no longer be frequenting this Westside reincarnation of downtown's Rex, the City's former premier Italian restaurant, but the more relaxed, contemporary Vincenti has quickly become one of the Westside's hottest culinary destinations. A big open kitchen is the heart of this handsome, white-tile restaurant, and revolving on its mammoth rotisserie are the mouthwatering meats for which chef Gino Angelini is known. You can order the *misti di carne del giorno* (a platter of the day's meats carved to order), or a whole spit-roasted fish such as Arctic char, served with imaginative sauces made with beets, artichokes, and other unexpected ingredients. Chef Angelini, a native of Rimini on the Adriatic coast, also delivers adept renderings of traditional favorites like *insalata caprese* and fried calamari, and pastas such as pumpkin-squash lasagnette with asparagus-and-sage sauce. For dessert, tiramisu served in a martini glass leads the menu. This is authentic northern Italian cooking as seen through an adept modern sensibility—a welcome addition to L.A.'s dining scene. ⊠ *11930 San Vicente Blvd., Brentwood,* ☎ *310/207–0127. Reservations essential. Closed Sun. and Mon. No lunch Sat. or Tues.–Thurs. AE, MC, V. Valet parking.*

JAPANESE

$–$$ ✕ **U-Zen.** This highly regarded Japanese café serves fresh sushi and sashimi, a good selection of sakes, and pub food such as fried spicy tofu and salmon-skin salad. Prices are modest, unless you get carried away with the sushi and sashimi, which is entirely possible. ⊠ *11951 Santa Monica Blvd., West Los Angeles,* ☎ *310/477–1390. Reservations not accepted. MC, V. No lunch weekends. Self parking.*

MEXICAN

$–$$ ✕ **La Serenata Gourmet.** The crowding in this handsome Westside branch of the East Los Angeles original can be uncomfortable, but the restaurant scores points for its flavorful Mexican cuisine. Moles and pork dishes are delicious, but seafood is the real star—there are chubby *gorditas* (cornmeal pockets stuffed with shrimp), juicy fish enchiladas, a soupy seviche that sings with flavor, and fresh fish with various salsas. Even the chips are noteworthy. ✉ *10924 W. Pico Blvd., West Los Angeles,* ☎ *310/441–9667. Reservations not accepted. AE, D, MC, V. Valet parking.*

$–$$ ✕ **Monte Alban.** Far from the common "rice and beans" stop, this family-owned café serves the subtle cooking of one of Mexico's most respected culinary regions, Oaxaca. Flavors here are intense without being spicy: Try the bright green chile peppers stuffed with chicken, raisins, and ground nuts; tender stewed goat with toasted avocado leaves; and any of the moles—dense and complex green, red, yellow, or black sauces made from dozens of spices and seeds. For dessert, there's fried, sliced sweet plantain topped with sour *crema fresca.* ✉ *11927 Santa Monica Blvd., West Los Angeles,* ☎ *310/444–7736. MC, V.*

Downtown

AMERICAN/CASUAL

$$–$$$ ✕ **Water Grill.** As the name suggests, seafood is the be-all, end-all at this handsome, somewhat noisy brasserie. It's always packed with well-dressed attorneys, brokers, and other downtown business folk who are joined in the evenings by theater and concert goers. The oyster bar alone—stocked with a great variety of shellfish—is worth a trip. Avoid the pastas and complicated dishes and stick with fresh seafood. ✉ *544 S. Grand Ave.,* ☎ *213/891–0900. Reservations essential. AE, DC, MC, V. No lunch weekends. Valet parking next door.*

$
★   ✕ **Philippe's the Original.** This downtown landmark near Union Station and Chinatown has been serving its famous French dip sandwich (made with beef, pork, ham, lamb, or turkey on a freshly baked roll) since 1908. Still a family-run establishment, Philippe's continues its early traditions, from sawdust on the floor to long, wooden tables where customers can sit and socialize like one big, noisy family. The home cooking includes hearty breakfasts, potato salad, coleslaw, sandwiches, salads, and an enormous pie selection brought in fresh daily from a nearby bakery. The best bargain: a cup of java for only 10¢. ✉ *1001 N. Alameda St.,* ☎ *213/628–3781. Reservations not accepted. No credit cards.*

CONTEMPORARY

$$$–$$$$ ✕ **Checkers.** In the rear of the elegant Wyndham Checkers Hotel, this is one of downtown's best business restaurants. Chef Tony Hodges, a nominee for the prestigious 1998 James Beard Award, prepares contemporary American food with Asian influences: lobster, dandelion, and curly endive salad; seared sea bass with rice-shrimp dumpling; and grilled lamb chops in a pumpkinseed crust have been among the tempting lunch or dinner options. Dine outside on the patio or inside the handsome dining room, with its soothing earth tones, soft lighting, and white linens. ✉ *535 S. Grand Ave.,* ☎ *213/624–0000. Reservations essential. AE, DC, MC, V. Valet parking.*

$$–$$$ **Traxx.** One of Downtown's newest restaurants serves contemporary cooking in a spectacular historic building—the 1939 Spanish mission–style Union Station. The Asian–Italian–Californian menu seems just right inside a structure that was created to unite three railroads under one roof. The menu, which changes regularly, has included such fusion dishes as ahi tuna Napoleon with crispy wontons and wasabi caviar; grilled lamb chops with gorgonzola risotto; and crispy white-fish with fennel, arugula, and Niçoise olives. Among the desserts, rosemary bread pudding is an unexpected, but welcome, delight. Dine in the smartly modern interior space, which vaguely resembles an old-fashioned dining car; on the terrace, which extends out into the station's dramatic concourse, with its 50-ft-high vaulted ceiling; or on the

Downtown Los Angeles Dining

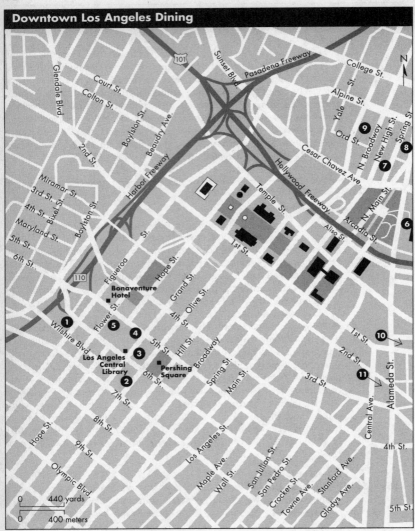

Café Pinot, **5**
Checkers, **4**
Cicada, **2**
La Serenata de Garibaldi, **10**
Mon Kee Seafood Restaurant, **7**
Nicola, **1**
Philippe's the Original, **8**
R-23, **11**
Traxx, **6**
Water Grill, **3**
Yang Chow, **9**

newly restored and handsomely landscaped patio. The well-stocked bar, which specializes in single-malt scotches and 100% blue agave tequilas, occupies what was originally the station's telephone room. ⊠ *Union Station, 800 N. Alameda St.,* ☎ *213/625–1999. AE, D, MC, V. No lunch Sat. Closed Sun. Valet parking or pay parking lot.*

CHINESE

$–$$ ✕ **Mon Kee Seafood Restaurant.** The name tells you what to expect— seafood. However, it doesn't convey the morning-freshness of the fish or the lively flavors of dishes like garlic crab, steamed catfish, or shrimp in spicy salt. This is a crowded place; be prepared for a wait. ⊠ *679 N. Spring St.,* ☎ *213/628–6717. AE, DC, MC, V. Pay parking lot.*

$–$$$ ✕ **Yang Chow.** This long-time Chinatown favorite is known for its slippery shrimp (crisp, juicy, sweet, hot, and sour all at once), fiery Szechuan dumplings, dried-fried string beans, and panfried dumplings. Booths are comfortable, and the service is crackerjack. ⊠ *379 N. Broadway,* ☎ *213/625–0811. Reservations essential. AE, MC, V. Valet parking.*

ECLECTIC

$$–$$$ ✕ **Nicola.** You can dine inside or out on the patio at this smart restaurant on the ground floor of the Sanwa Bank Building. The two rooms— one intimate, the other more open and airy—are the work of architect Michael Rotondi, who gave it a whimsical look by stretching cloth across the ceiling to resemble sails. Owner-chef Larry Nicola's cooking is mainly Mediterranean with Asian accents—vegetable spring rolls with tangerine-sweet-and sour sauce, lasagna Japonaise with rice noodles; but you'll also find fried calamari and seafood risotto on the wide-ranging menu. Nicola also operates the self-service "Kiosko" downtown, at the Wilshire Boulevard end of the Sanwa building, serving breakfast and quick lunch snacks—grilled chicken Caesar salad, penne with roasted tomatoes, Thai chicken salad with papaya—at reasonable prices (cash only). ⊠ *Sanwa Bank Bldg., 601 S. Figueroa St.,* ☎ *213/485–0927 or 213/485–0354 Kiosko. AE, D, DC, MC, V. Closed weekends. No dinner weekdays. Valet parking.*

FRENCH

$$–$$$ ✕ **Café Pinot.** Joachim and Christine Splichal, proprietors of Patina and
★ a growing number of Pinot bistros, have succeeded again with this warm, convivial restaurant housed in a contemporary pavillion in the garden of the Los Angeles Central Library. If the weather's fine, you can eat outside on the terrace under one of the old olive trees. The menu is rooted in traditional French bistro standards—steak frites, roast chicken coated with three mustards, braised lamb shank—but it also delivers some low-fat dishes, fresh fish, and a few worthy pastas. ⊠ *700 W. 5th St.,* ☎ *213/239–6500. Reservations essential. DC, MC, V. No lunch weekends. Self and valet parking.*

ITALIAN

$$–$$$ ✕ **Cicada.** Cicada occupies the ground floor of a 1928 architectural landmark, the Art Deco Oviatt Building: the glass doors are Lalique; carved wood interior columns rise two-stories; and from the balcony, a glamorous bar overlooks the spacious dining room. Modern Italian best describes the menu: lobster salad with black olives, crab meat risotto, goat cheese ravioli, turbot with porcini mushrooms, and lamb chops with fresh basil. ⊠ *617 S. Olive St.,* ☎ *323/655–5559. Reservations essential. AE, DC, MC, V. Closed Sun. No lunch Sat.*

JAPANESE

$$–$$$ ✕ **R-23.** Just a few blocks east of Little Tokyo you'll find this dramatic redbrick, beamed dining room, carved out of a former railroad loading dock—a surprisingly peaceful and visually stunning place for lunch or dinner. R-23 is at its best with sashimi, sushi, and *chirashi sushi* (raw fish on rice)—and almost as adept with such deceptively simple preparations as flash-fried blue crabs and grilled yellowtail tuna. For dinner, uncomplicated entrées are best. ⊠ *923 E. 3rd St.,* ☎ *213/687–7178. AE, DC, MC, V. No lunch Sat., closed Sun. Self-parking.*

MEXICAN

$–$$ ✕ **La Serenata de Garibaldi.** Behind a modest door on a shabby urban
★   block lies a handsome dining room enlivened with Mexican textiles, contemporary paintings, and an intelligent serving staff. A large board here lists the day's fresh-fish offerings. Try the fat little masa pockets called *gorditas,* stuffed with shrimp; the seafood enchiladas; or any fish or seafood in the fabulous *mojo de ajo* (garlic) sauce, chipotle sauce, or fresh spinach sauce. Even the beans and chips are memorable. To get here, head east from downtown on 1st Street into East L.A.—you'll be rewarded with some of the best Mexican cooking in the region. ⊠ *1842 E. 1st St., East L.A.,* ☎ *213/265–2887. AE, MC, V. Closed Mon. Self park in rear.*

Pasadena Area and Glendale

CONTEMPORARY

$$$ ✕ **Dickinson West.** This very California restaurant brings Pasadena into the '90s with its smart Asian-tinged cuisine. Dinner might start with seared foie gras on a bed of Japanese persimmons; or a salad of fuyu persimmon, cucumber, and Bosc pears—followed by seared salmon served with lentils and roasted asparagus, or osso buco with risotto and braised vegetables. Pear-almond upside-down cake and bread pudding with a ginger créme anglaise are among the great desserts. ⊠ *181-185 E. Glenarm St., Pasadena,* ☎ *626/799–5252. AE, D, MC, V. Closed Sun., Mon. No lunch Sat.*

$$ ✕ **Shiro.** Chef Hideo Yamashiro made quite a splash when he first began
★   serving sizzling whole catfish with a tangy soy–citrus–ponzu sauce. Not surprisingly, the dish started showing up on other menus, but Yamashiro's is still the best—and his contemporary, Asian–influenced cooking style remains exciting and fresh: Where else can you start a meal with Chinese ravioli filled with shrimp mousse, or calamari–basil–tomato soup? Beyond the signature catfish you'll find duck with orange sauce; lobster and scallops with saffron sauce; and herb-mustard chicken. For a sweet conclusion, try the warm souffléed lemon pudding. ⊠ *1505 Mission St., Pasadena,* ☎ *626/799–4774. Reservations essential. AE, DC, MC, V. Closed Mon. No lunch Tues.–Sun.*

$$–$$$ ✕ **Cinnabar.** Glendale's revitalized downtown has plenty of major department stores and movie complexes, but few distinguished restaurants. Enter Cinnabar, a hip, contemporary dining room occupying the double-height ground floor of an early 1930s art deco commercial building. At the elaborate, vintage bar, you half expect to find Sidney Greenstreet and Humphrey Bogart sharing secrets over a Singapore Sling. But the menu is by no means vintage: Charbroiled ostrich tenderloin, spicy lemongrass bouillabaisse, and Colorado lamb chops with smoked-pepper relish are a few of the of-the-moment selections. ⊠ *933 S. Brand Blvd., Glendale,* ☎ *818/551–1155. D, DC, MC, V. Closed Mon. No lunch weekends.*

$–$$$ ✕ **Twin Palms.** Lots of hoopla accompanied the opening of Twin Palms
★   a couple years ago, thanks to Kevin Costner, one of the original co-owners. Now that Kevin is out (his ex-wife, Cindy, won ownership in

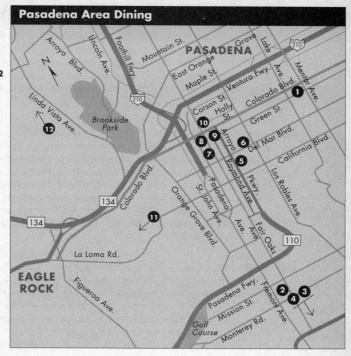

Pasadena Area Dining

the divorce proceedings), the attention has died down, but Twin Palms still attracts a crowd. With a covered patio overlooking a central outdoor piazza, and a deep-hued, more formal dining room, the complex can hold a staggering 400 people: On warm evenings, there's an infectious air of bonhomie, influenced no doubt by two large bars and loud-and-swinging live music. Chef Michael Roberts' French Provençal cooking also keeps spirits high. This garlic-rich, feel-good food—fish soup, portobello sandwich with pistou, succulent chicken cooked over a huge rotisserie—perfectly suits such a profoundly Californian setting. ⊠ *101 W. Green St., Pasadena,* ☎ *626/577–2567. AE, DC, MC, V. Valet parking.*

CHINESE

$$–$$$ ✕ **Yujean Kang's Gourmet Chinese Cuisine.** Forget any and all pre-
★ conceived notions of what Chinese food should look and taste like—Kang's cuisine is nouvelle-Chinese. Start with tender slices of veal on a bed of enoki mushrooms, topped with a tangle of quick-fried shoestring yams; or sea bass with kumquats and passion-fruit sauce. Finish off with poached plums or watermelon ice under a mantle of white chocolate. ⊠ *67 N. Raymond Ave., Pasadena,* ☎ *626/585–0855. AE, D, DC, MC, V.*

$ ✕ **Lake Spring Cuisine.** Of the countless good Chinese restaurants in the south San Gabriel Valley, Lake Spring is one of the best. Unlike its more hectic counterparts, the dining room is subdued and relatively plush, filled with serious food-lovers intent on their meals. Regulars come for the tender, slow-cooked pork rump; grass-green jade shrimp; cured pork with bamboo-shoot casserole; and many more dishes infused with the rich, complex flavors of Shanghai. ⊠ *219 E. Garvey Ave., Monterey Park,* ☎ *626/280–3571. MC, V. Self parking.*

\$\$–\$\$\$ ✕ **Ocean Star.** This vast, marble-clad, aquarium-lined palace is know
★ for the quality and freshness of its fish and shellfish. Try the boiled-
live shrimp with soy-chili dipping sauce, huge scallops served in their
shell, king crabs with garlic sauce, any of the whole steamed fish, and
the delicately sautéed snow-pea sprouts. Bring lots of friends—the
more dishes you try, the more fun you'll have. ⊠ *145 N. Atlantic Blvd.,
Monterey Park,* ☎ *626/308–2128. Reservations not accepted. MC,
V. Free garage parking.*

ECLECTIC

\$\$–\$\$\$ ✕ **Parkway Grill.** This is Pasadena's answer to Wolfgang Puck. The
setting is all-American—brick walls, wood floors, a carved-wood bar,
lots of greenery, and a khaki-clad waitstaff. The always-interesting dishes
incorporate all kinds of influences, from Italian to Mexican to Chinese:
In one sitting you might have a roasted *pasilla* chili stuffed with smoked
chicken, corn, and cilantro; then Chinese-style roasted crispy duck—
and s'mores for dessert. ⊠ *510 S. Arroyo Pkwy., Pasadena,* ☎ *626/
795–1001. Reservations essential. AE, DC, MC, V. No lunch weekends. Valet parking.*

FRENCH

\$\$\$ ✕ **Bistro 45.** As stylish and sophisticated as any Westside hot spot, Bistro
45 blends rustic French cooking—cassoulet, bouillabaisse, caramelized
apple tarts—with more modern and fanciful California hybrids, like
seared ahi tuna with pickled vegetables and pomegranate dressing. Add
a superb wine list and smart service, and you've got a place that makes
almost everyone happy. ⊠ *45 S. Mentor Ave., Pasadena,* ☎ *626/795–
2478. Reservations essential. AE, MC, V. Closed Mon., except for wine-
maker dinner 4th Mon. of month. No lunch weekends. Valet parking.*

INDIAN

\$–\$\$ ✕ **All India Cafe.** Old Town Pasadena may be the last place you'd ex-
pect to find an authentic Indian restaurant, but authentic it is. Ingredients are fresh, and flavors are bold without depending on overpowering
spiciness. Crisp rice wafers jazzed up with chutneys, lime, and cilantro
are a nice way to start a meal; follow this with the *bhel puri,* a savory
puffed rice-and-potatoes dish. In addition to meat curries and tikkas,
there are many vegetarian selections. The prices are as palatable as the
meals: A full lunch costs less than \$6, and dinner isn't much more. ⊠
39 Fair Oaks Ave., Pasadena, ☎ *626/440–0309. Reservations recommended on weekends. AE, MC, V. City parking garage across the
street.*

THAI

\$–\$\$ ✕ **Saladang.** Southern California is rife with Thai restaurants, but few
stand out from the crowd as much as this chic bistro. Although it's
a bit off the beaten track—several blocks south of Old Pasadena—its
reasonably-priced spinach and duck salad, seafood soup, rice noodles
with basil and bean sprouts, and beef panang have ensured Saladung
a lively following. ⊠ *363 S. Fair Oaks Blvd., Pasadena,* ☎ *626/793–
8123. Reservations essential. AE, DC, MC, V. Free parking in lot.*

San Fernando Valley

Calabasas

CONTEMPORARY

\$\$\$–\$\$\$\$ ✕ **Saddle Peak Lodge.** When you've had enough big-city attitude,
★ head for this paradisical retreat in the Santa Monica Mountains. What
was once allegedly a bordello is now a restaurant oozing with Ralph
Lauren–style rugged romance. One dining room is lined with old

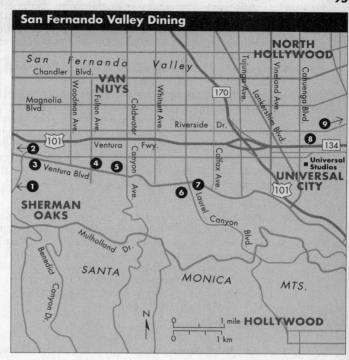

San Fernando Valley Dining

books, another is warmed by a big fireplace, and still another has views
of the rustic mountain ridges. The sprawling terrace is a coveted spot
for Sunday brunch. The food is a perfect match for the upscale lodge
setting: updated American classics with an emphasis on game. Try the
venison with burgundy-poached pear and potato pancakes. ⊠ *419 Cold
Canyon Rd., Calabasas,* ☎ *818/222–3888. Reservations essential on
weekends. AE, MC, V. Closed Mon.–Tues. No lunch, except Sun.
brunch. Valet available.*

North Hollywood
ITALIAN

$–$$ ✕ **Ca'del Sole.** With antique wood hutches, copper moldings, and a
★ fireplace, this studio-area establishment draws showbiz and non-show-
biz types in search of such classics as sautéed fresh rock shrimp in a
spicy garlic–tomato sauce; citrus-marinated chicken wings braised
with Italian bacon, rosemary, and sage; radicchio-and-arugula salad
tossed in a creamy Venetian dressing; and linguine with scallops and
Manila clams. Finish up with a giant hunk of Italian-style cheesecake
covered with marinated strawberries. ⊠ *4100 Cahuenga Blvd., North
Hollywood,* ☎ *818/985–4669. Reservations essential on weekends.
AE, DC, MC, V. No lunch Sat. Valet parking.*

Sherman Oaks
CONTEMPORARY

$$ ✕ **Cafe Bizou.** Crisp and clean, with white walls, black-and-white
★ photos, and plain wooden chairs, Cafe Bizou is *the* place for fine Cal-
ifornia-French bistro fare at bargain prices in Sherman Oaks. Entrée
sauces are classic, soups are rich (try the luscious potato-leek), and com-
binations are creative. If it's on the menu, order the homemade ravi-
oli appetizer, stuffed with lobster and salmon purée; a winning entrée
is the sesame-seed-coated salmon on potato-pancake triangles. For

dessert, the caramelized tart Tatin is tops. Those who bring their own bottle pay a mere $2 corkage fee. ⊠ *14016 Ventura Blvd., Sherman Oaks, Los Angeles,* ☎ *818/788–3536. Reservations essential. AE, MC, V. Valet parking.*

$$–$$$ ✕ **JoeJoe's.** This spin-off of Joe's in Venice follows the current trend—plain decor, high noise levels, and low prices. (The food is cooked with a level of skill that could demand twice the price in West Hollywood.) This is American cooking for the next century: meaty grilled shiitakes with smoked mozzarella, roasted peppers and a red-onion salad; smoky grilled shrimp on creamy saffron risotto with a delicate crown of fried carrots; juicy roast beef with tangy balsamic vinegar sauce, buttery mashed potatoes, and spinach. To end, a zippy lemon tart. ⊠ *13355 Ventura Blvd., Sherman Oaks,* ☎ *818/990–8280. Reservations essential. AE, MC, V. Closed Mon. Valet parking.*

ITALIAN

$$$ ✕ **Posto.** Thanks to owner Piero Selvaggio, Valley residents no longer have to drive to the Westside for good modern Italian cuisine. At Posto there's a tissue-thin pizza topped with flavorful ingredients, plus chicken, duck, and veal sausages made fresh each morning. Other specialties are the risotto with porcini mushrooms and the veal saltimbocca with sage and prosciutto. For dessert, try the pumpkin cheesecake. ⊠ *14928 Ventura Blvd., Sherman Oaks,* ☎ *818/784–4400. AE, D, DC, MC, V. Closed Sun. No lunch Sat.*

Studio City

DELI

$ ✕ **Art's Delicatessen.** One of the best Jewish-style delicatessens in the
★ city, this mecca serves mammoth corned beef and pastrami sandwiches. Matzo-ball soup and sweet-and-sour cabbage soup are specialties, and there is good chopped chicken liver. ⊠ *12224 Ventura Blvd., Studio City,* ☎ *818/762–1221. Reservations not accepted. AE, D, DC, MC, V.*

FRENCH

$$$ **Perroche.** It's worth going out of your way to eat at this neighborhood newcomer. The ambience is quiet and comforting but far from stuffy. And chef Grady Atkins's cuisine, prepared from organic ingredients, is equally appealing. Refreshing two- and three-course lunches, $15 and $18 respectively, can begin with house-made gravlax or tomato-and-sweet-garlic soup, or an airy parfait of chicken livers. Entrées include grilled pork loin, sautéed halibut, and a cassoulet of vegetables. On the dinner menu you might also find sweetbreads with potato mousseline and sautéed bay scallops. Save room for desserts like hot peach-and-blueberry crumble. ⊠ *1929 Ventura Blvd., Studio City,* ☎ *818/766–1179. AE, MC, V. Closed Sun. No lunch Sat. Valet parking.*

$$–$$$ ✕ **Pinot Bistro.** Another Joachim Splichal creation (he's also the owner-chef of top-rated Patina, ☞ *above*), this tony evocation of a Parisian bistro has butter-yellow walls, polished wood, comfortable banquettes, and framed displays of old postcards. Dishes are high-tone Gallic: fresh oysters, country pâtés, bouillabaisse, braised tongue and spinach, pot-au-feu, and steak with French fries. The pastry chef specializes in chocolate desserts. ⊠ *12969 Ventura Blvd., Studio City,* ☎ *818/990–0500. D, DC, MC, V. No lunch weekends. Valet parking.*

Toluca Lake

AMERICAN

$ ✕ **Paty's.** Near NBC, Warner Bros., and the Disney Studio, this homey coffee shop is a good, affordable place for stargazing. Breakfasts include plump omelets and homemade biscuits served with high-quality jam. For lunch or dinner there are hearty, comforting dishes such as

In case you want to see the world.

At American Express, we're here to make your journey a
smooth one. So we have over 1,700 travel service locations
in over 120 countries ready to help. What else would you
expect from the world's largest travel agency?

do more

http://www.americanexpress.com/travel

Travel

In case you want to be welcomed there.

We're here to see that you're always welcomed at establishments everywhere. That's why millions of people carry the American Express® Card – for peace of mind, confidence, and security, around the world or just around the corner.

do more®

AMERICAN EXPRESS

Cards

In case you're running low.

We're here to help with more than 118,000 Express Cash locations around the world. In order to enroll, just call American Express before you start your vacation.

do more

Express Cash

And just in case.

We're here with American Express® Travelers Cheques and Cheques *for Two*.® They're the safest way to carry money on your vacation and the surest way to get a refund, practically anywhere, anytime.
Another way we help you...

do more ®

Travelers Cheques

Swiss steak, roast turkey, or beef stew served in a hollowed-out loaf of home-baked bread. A standout dessert is New Orleans bread pudding with hot brandy sauce. If you're in a hurry, call ahead with your order and the restaurant will deliver directly to your car. ⊠ *10001 Riverside Dr., Toluca Lake,* ☎ *818/761–9126. Reservations not accepted. AE, DC, MC, V.*

4 Lodging

Whether you stay in West Hollywood's groovy digs or Santa Monica's surfside rooms, an art deco tower or a bougainvillea-drenched villa, a night in Los Angeles is a night to remember.

BECAUSE LOS ANGELES IS SO SPREAD OUT, it's good to select a hotel room not only for its ambience, amenities, and price, but also for a location that's convenient to where you plan to spend most of your time. Planning to hit the beach? Give some thought to Santa Monica. Nightlife aficionados might enjoy the funky hostelries of West Hollywood. The Hollywood Boulevard area has its own funky charm, though not everyone will like the neighborhood. For upscale and posh, you can't do better than Beverly Hills. The downtown area, though gaining ground in the tourist department, is still frequented mostly by conventioneers and business travelers.

Revised and
updated by
Lisa
Oppenheimer

Prices for Los Angeles hotels run the gamut from bargain basement to sky high. Tax rates for the area will add 9%-14% to your bill depending on where in Los Angeles you stay. Because you will need a car no matter where you stay in Los Angeles, parking is another expense to consider: Though a few hotels have free parking, most charge for the privilege—and some resorts have valet parking only.

Most hotels have air-conditioning, TVs, and in-room irons and boards. Those in the moderate and expensive price ranges often have voice mail and hair dryers as well. If a particular amenity is important to you, ask; many hotels will provide extras upon request.

If you're traveling with children, look for hotels with "kids stay free" programs. Few hotels have baby-sitters on site, but many contract with outsider services and can help you find someone on demand. There are a few supervised kiddie clubs in Los Angeles, but many are seasonal— mostly in summer—so be sure to ask when making reservations.

When looking for a hotel, don't write off the pricier establishments just because they're in the $$$$ price category. Price categories are determined by rack rates—prices that are often discounted (industry experts say only about 5% of rooms are actually rented at rack rates). Specials abound, particularly downtown on the weekends. A club-floor room at the opulent Regal Biltmore in downtown L.A. drops from $310 on weekdays to about $159 on weekends. Some specials come with meals or tickets to nearby attractions.

Finally, when making reservations, particularly last-minute ones, call the hotel directly. On-site reservations agents often know of specials not available through agents working the 800 lines. The few extra pennies you spend dialing long distance (instead of toll free) could wind up saving you many dollars.

Hotels listed below are organized according to their location, then by price category. For approximate costs, *see* the lodging price chart in On the Road with Fodor's.

Downtown

$$$$ ▣ **Hotel Inter-Continental Los Angeles.** The Los Angeles version of the Inter-Continental might seem a little bland compared with some of its urban siblings around the country, but the service is still A-one. Rooms in the residential-style building are your basic business contemporary, although floor-to-ceiling windows add a dash of excitement; little extras include separate bath and shower stalls (in some rooms) and TV sound in the bathrooms. Located at the top of Olive Street, the hotel is within walking distance of Watercourt and the Museum of Contemporary Art. The 17th-floor concierge level has a comfortable business center–lounge. ⊠ *251 S. Olive St., 90012,* ☎ *213/617–3300 or*

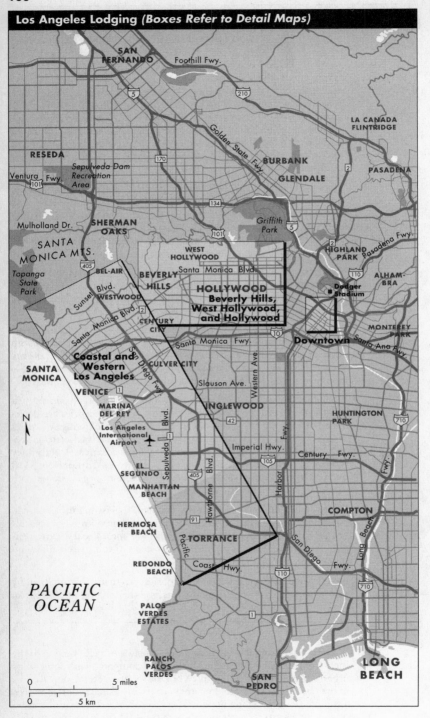

Los Angeles Lodging (Boxes Refer to Detail Maps)

PACIFIC
OCEAN

WEST HOLLYWOOD

HOLLYWOOD
Beverly Hills,
West Hollywood,
and Hollywood

Downtown

Coastal and
Western
Los Angeles

0   5 miles
0   5 km

Downtown Los Angeles Lodging

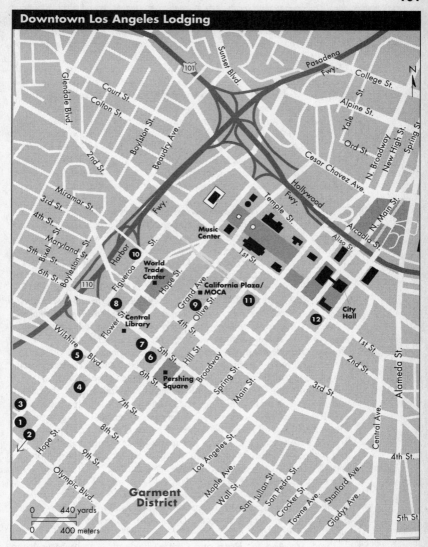

Figueroa Hotel and
Convention Center, **3**

Hotel
Inter-Continental
Los Angeles, **9**

Hyatt Regency
Los Angeles, **4**

Inn at 657, **2**

The InnTowne, **1**

Kawada Hotel, **11**

Los Angeles Marriott
Downtown, **10**

Omni Los Angeles
Hotel and Centre, **5**

New Otani Hotel
and Garden, **12**

Regal Biltmore
Hotel, **6**

Westin
Bonaventure
Hotel & Suites, **8**

Wyndham Checkers
Hotel, **7**

800/442–5251, FAX *213/617–3399. 433 rooms, 18 suites. Restaurant, bar, minibars, no-smoking floors, 24-hour room service, pool, exercise room, piano, laundry service and dry cleaning, concierge, concierge floor, business services, parking (fee). AE, D, DC, MC, V.*

$$$$ 🏨 **Hyatt Regency Los Angeles.** Windows with dramatic city views jazz up the mahogany- and cherry-wood–filled rooms at this hotel near the Music Center. If you're here to work, ask for the Business Plan, available on floors above the 18th—you'll have access to laptop computers and fax machines. The Pavan Pacifico restaurant has a karaoke lounge with 3,000 Japanese and American CDs. ⊠ *711 S. Hope St., 90017,* ☎ *213/683–1234 or 800/233–1234,* FAX *213/629–3230. 485 rooms, 41 suites. 2 restaurants, 2 bars, in-room modem lines, no-smoking floors, room service, exercise room, laundry service and dry cleaning, concierge, concierge floor, business services, meeting rooms, parking (fee). AE, D, DC, MC, V.*

$$$$ 🏨 **Los Angeles Marriott Downtown.** The 14-story building near the First
★ Interstate World Trade Center and the Pacific Stock Exchange has business written all over it. Guest rooms are oversize with marble baths, and wall-to-wall windows with city views. The extensive business center provides secretarial services. Guests have complimentary use of a fitness center one block away. Complimentary limo service is provided within a 5-mi radius. ⊠ *333 S. Figueroa St., 90071,* ☎ *213/617–1133 or 800/260–0227,* FAX *213/613–0291. 469 rooms. 3 restaurants, 2 bars, in-room safes, minibars, no-smoking floors, room service, pool, 4 cinemas, piano, laundry service and dry cleaning, concierge, business services, travel services, parking (fee). AE, D, DC, MC, V.*

$$$$ 🏨 **New Otani Hotel and Garden.** "Japanese Experience" rooms at the
★ New Otani have Tatami Mats instead of beds, and extra-deep bathtubs; you can also have tea and shiatsu massage in the comfort of your own room. Shoji screens on windows lend an Asian touch to the otherwise somewhat plain American-style rooms. Like the hotel, the cuisine in all three of the hotel's restaurants is authentically Japanese, although American fare is also served. The hotel is on the edge of Little Tokyo, within walking distance of many other ethnic neighborhoods and the city's cultural center. There's a ½-acre Japanese garden on the roof. ⊠ *120 S. Los Angeles St., 90012,* ☎ *213/629–1200, 800/421–8795 in CA, 800/421-8795 in the U.S. and Canada;* FAX *213/622–0989. 434 rooms, 20 suites. 3 restaurants, 3 bars, in-room safes, minibars, no-smoking rooms, refrigerators, room service, sauna, health club, piano, baby-sitting, laundry service and dry cleaning, concierge, business services, car rental, parking (fee). AE, D, DC, MC, V.*

$$$$ 🏨 **Omni Los Angeles Hotel and Centre.** Wedged in among the other high-rises at the start of Wilshire Boulevard, the 16-story Omni is convenient to Dodger Stadium, museums, Chinatown, and the Music Center. The sparse-looking guest rooms are done in shades of beige, blue, and green. In-room movies are available. ⊠ *930 Wilshire Blvd., 90017,* ☎ *213/629–4321 or 800/843–6664,* FAX *213/612–3977. 868 rooms, 35 suites. 4 restaurants, bar, in-room modem lines, minibars, no-smoking rooms, room service, pool, beauty salon, exercise room, laundry service and dry cleaning, concierge, travel services, car rental, parking (fee). AE, D, DC, MC, V.*

$$$$ 🏨 **Regal Biltmore Hotel.** This elegant landmark building has a notable past; the lobby (formerly the Music Room) was the headquarters of JFK's democratic campaign, and the Biltmore Bowl ballroom hosted some of the earliest Academy Awards. The Spanish–Italian Renaissance building has rooms you can sink into (flowing draperies, French-style armoires, and overstuffed chairs), making even one night feel like a great escape. Afternoons and evenings, soak up some atmosphere in the beau-

tifully restored Rendezvous Court (the original lobby). Guests on level 10 will find a concierge and a lounge with Continental breakfast and afternoon tea, and a big-screen TV. Eleventh-floor rooms cater to business travelers. A complimentary shuttle travels within a 3-mi radius of the hotel. ⊠ *506 S. Grand Ave., 90071,* ☎ *213/624–1011 or 800/ 245–8673,* FAX *213/612–1545. 627 rooms, 56 suites. 3 restaurants, 3 bars, 2 cafés, minibars, in-room safes, no-smoking floors, refrigerators, room service, indoor pool, hot tub, spa, health club, laundry service and dry cleaning, concierge, concierge floor, business services, travel services, car rental, parking (fee). AE, D, DC, MC, V.*

$$$$ 🏨 **Westin Bonaventure Hotel & Suites.** You can't miss this hotel's image on the downtown L.A. skyline: Its five cylindrical towers are tall (35 stories) and mirrored. Inside is a futuristic lobby with fountains, an indoor lake, and lots of activity. Rooms are fairly basic and on the small side, but floor-to-ceiling glass windows provide terrific views. The all-suites "Green" tower is geared toward business travelers, with fax machines and modem hookups. In addition to the revolving rooftop restaurant (a great viewpoint), there are 16 other eateries within the hotel, including several lobby restaurants and fast-food outlets such as Subway. ⊠ *404 S. Figueroa St., 90071,* ☎ *213/624–1000 or 800/ 937–8461,* FAX *213/612–4800. 1,354 rooms, 135 suites. 17 restaurants, 5 bars, minibars, no-smoking floors, room service, pool, beauty salon, 7 tennis courts, health club, baby-sitting, laundry service and dry cleaning, concierge, business services, meeting rooms, travel services, car rental, parking (fee). AE, D, DC, MC, V.*

$$$$
★ 🏨 **Wyndham Checkers Hotel.** Opened as the Mayflower Hotel in 1927, Checkers has more character than most downtown hotels, with a lobby full of fine antique furniture, and rooms with oversize beds and upholstered easy chairs—there are even bathtub thermometers in the marble bathrooms. Enjoy afternoon tea in the wood-paneled library, and complimentary hors d'oeuvres every day in the lounge. The hotel's highly regarded restaurant, Checkers, (☞ Chapter 3) is one of downtown's best business restaurants. There's complimentary limo service mornings and evenings within a 2-mi radius, but the financial district is within walking distance. ⊠ *535 S. Grand Ave., 90071,* ☎ *213/624– 0000 or 800/996–3426,* FAX *213/626–9906. 188 rooms, 15 suites. Restaurant, bar, minibars, no-smoking floors, room service, pool, hot tub, spa, exercise room, library, baby-sitting, laundry service and dry cleaning, concierge, business services, travel services, car rental, parking (fee). AE, D, DC, MC, V.*

$$$
★ 🏨 **Inn at 657.** Apartment-size suites at this small bed-and-breakfast– style inn near the University of Southern California have down comforters on the beds, Oriental silks on the walls, and huge dining tables that can also be used for spreading out work. Homey touches include full kitchens with microwave, and private room entrances off the garden. Room rates include a hearty breakfast, homemade cookies, and local phone calls. ⊠ *657 W. 23rd St., 90007,* ☎ *213/741–2200 or 800/ 347–7512. 5 suites. In-room modem lines, kitchenettes, no-smoking suites, refrigerators, in-room VCRs, hot tub, laundry service, business services, free parking. Full breakfast. No credit cards.*

$$ 🏨 **Kawada Hotel.** This eclectic three-story redbrick hotel near the Music Center and local government buildings has European flair. Immaculate guest rooms are on the small side, but come with two phones and a wet bar. Two bonuses here are the Epicentre restaurant (named tongue-in-cheek upon its opening on the heels of the 1994 earthquake), the domain of award-winning chef Michael Olmeda; and the Epi Deli, serving breakfast standards. A complimentary shuttle traverses the downtown area. ⊠ *200 S. Hill St., 90012,* ☎ *213/621–4455 or*

800/752–9232, FAX 213/687–4455. *116 rooms, 1 suite. Restaurant, bar, deli, kitchenettes, no-smoking rooms, refrigerators, room service, in-room VCRs, coin laundry, laundry service and dry cleaning, concierge, business services, meeting rooms, car rental, parking (fee). AE, DC, MC, V.*

$–$$ 🔛 **Figueroa Hotel and Convention Center.** The Spanish feel of this 12-story hotel built in 1926 is accented by terra-cotta-color rooms, hand-painted furniture, wrought-iron beds, and, in many rooms, ceiling fans. The hotel's Clay Pit restaurant serves aromatic Indian food. ⊠ *939 S. Figueroa St., 90015,* ☎ *213/627–8971 or 800/421–9092,* FAX *213/689–0305. 285 rooms, 2 suites. 2 restaurants, 2 bars, café, in-room modem lines, refrigerator, pool, hot tub, coin laundry, dry cleaning, concierge, travel services, car rental, free parking. AE, DC, MC, V.*

$ 🔛 **The InnTowne.** This modern three-story hotel just 1½ blocks from the convention center has large rooms with beige-and-white or gray-and-white color schemes. Palm trees and a small garden surround the swimming pool. ⊠ *913 S. Figueroa St., 90015,* ☎ *213/628–2222 or 800/457–8520,* FAX *213/687–0566. 168 rooms, 2 suites. Bar, coffee shop, room service, pool, laundry service and dry cleaning, car rental, free parking. AE, D, DC, MC, V.*

Beverly Hills, Century City, West Hollywood, and Hollywood

Beverly Hills and Vicinity

$$$$ 🔛 **Beverly Hills Hotel.** Even before Beverly Hills existed as a neigh-★   borhood, the "Pink Palace" was attracting Hollywood legends such as Gloria Swanson, Clark Gable, and Marilyn Monroe. Celebrities continue to favor the bungalows that have all of life's little necessities: wood-burning fireplaces, period furniture, and even (in some cases) grand pianos—Bungalow 5 even has its own lap pool. Standard rooms are characteristically decadent, with original artwork, butler-service buttons, walk-in closets, and huge marble bathrooms with double-vanity sinks. All rooms are soundproofed and have stereos with CD players, and personal fax machines. Twelve acres of landscaped (and carpeted!) walkways make for prime strolling grounds if you can bear to leave your room. The fabled Polo Lounge, with its banana-leaf wallpaper, remains a Hollywood meeting place. ⊠ *9641 Sunset Blvd., 90210,* ☎ *310/276–2251 or 800/283-8885,* FAX *310/887–2887. 203 rooms, 21 bungalows. 4 restaurants, bar, in-room modem lines, in-room safes, kitchenettes, no-smoking rooms, room service, pool, barbershop, beauty salon, hot tub, massage, 2 tennis courts, exercise room, jogging, piano, baby-sitting, laundry service and dry cleaning, concierge, travel services, parking (fee). AE, DC, MC, V.*

$$$$ 🔛 **Beverly Hilton.** With an imposing white exterior and glass- and marble-filled public areas that are the annual site of the Golden Globe awards, the Beverly Hilton is owner Merv Griffin's mix of glitz and luxury. Despite all the flashiness, guest rooms are spacious and tasteful, and service is extra-helpful. All accommodations have fax machines, and most have balconies overlooking Beverly Hills or downtown. The kitschy Trader Vic's restaurant-bar is a classic; and on Friday and Saturday nights, the Grand Ballroom becomes the Coconut Club, with swing dancing and dining à la 1940s (☞ Chapter 5). There are plenty of restaurants and shops nearby (a Robinsons-May department store shares the parking lot), and the hotel provides complimentary transportation within a 3-mi radius for exploring Beverly Hills and nearby Century City. ⊠ *9876 Wilshire Blvd., 90210,* ☎ *310/274–7777 or 1-800–445–8667,* FAX *310/285–1313. 581 rooms, 42 suites. 2 restaurants,* *coffee shop, lobby lounge, minibars, no-smoking floors, refrigerators, room service, pool, massage, exercise room, shops, baby-sitting, laundry service and dry cleaning, concierge, business services, meeting rooms, travel services, parking (fee). AE, D, DC, MC, V.*

$$$$ ⌦ **Beverly Prescott Hotel.** A semi-enclosed patio and a tall atrium give this 12-story luxury hotel an open, airy feel. The stylish, spacious guest rooms are done in warm salmon and caramel tones; all have private balconies, fax machines, stereo/CD players, irons, hair dryers, and coffeemakers. Six suites are equipped with whirlpool tubs. The management hosts a daily wine hour in the lobby, where a fire often roars in the fireplace. ⊠ *1224 S. Beverwil Dr., 90035,* ☎ *310/277–2800 or 800/421–3212,* FAX *310/203–9537. 137 rooms, 18 suites. Restaurant, bar, minibars, no-smoking rooms, room service, in-room VCRs, pool, massage, exercise room, baby-sitting, laundry service and dry cleaning, concierge, concierge floor, business services, meeting rooms, travel services, car rental, parking (fee). AE, D, DC, MC, V.*

$$$$ ⌦ **Four Seasons Hotel Los Angeles at Beverly Hills.** With an employee-
★ to-guest ratio greater than one to one, the Four Seasons takes exemplary care of its guests. Extra touches include everything from complimentary cellular phones to limo service every 15 minutes to Rodeo Drive shops; obliging staff members will even bring you fresh towels as you work out at the delightful poolside fitness center. Impeccable, ivory-hue guest rooms are eclectic, some done in pastels, others in black and beige; all have bathroom TVs. Suites have French doors and balconies. Lavish flower arrangements fill the public spaces, and tropical foliage gardens surround the hotel. ⊠ *300 S. Doheny Dr., 90048,* ☎ *310/273–2222 or 800/332–3442,* FAX *310/859–3824. 179 rooms, 106 suites. Restaurant, café, bar, in-room modem lines, minibars, no-smoking rooms, room service, pool, hot tub, exercise room, baby-sitting, laundry service and dry cleaning, concierge, business services, meeting rooms, car rental, free parking and parking (fee). AE, DC, MC, V.*

$$$$ ⌦ **Hotel Nikko.** High-tech toys are the signature of this Japanese luxury hotel in a busy section of Beverly Hills: Rooms and suites have fax machines and bed-side gizmos that control in-room lighting, temperature, TV, VCR, and CD player. Management thoughtfully tends to even the smallest needs: Weary travelers get to sit, rather than stand, through the check-in process; and nonvalet parking is free. Computers are available in the business center, and the lobby sitting area is a favorite place for "industry" meetings. Try Pangaea, the hotel restaurant, for contemporary, Asian-influenced cuisine. ⊠ *465 S. La Cienega Blvd., 90048,* ☎ *310/247–0400 or 800/645–5687,* FAX *310/247–0315. 297 rooms, 10 suites. Restaurant, bar, in-room modem lines, minibars, no-smoking floors, room service, pool, massage, sauna, exercise room, baby-sitting, laundry service and dry cleaning, concierge, business services, meeting rooms, travel services, car rental, free parking. AE, D, DC, MC, V.*

$$$$ ⌦ **Hotel Sofitel Los Angeles.** Sofitel brings a touch of French country to the city, with gallic touches such as cabaret-style music in the lobby and Pierre Deux fabrics in the rooms. As L.A. suite prices go, the Sofitel's are among the most reasonable. Be sure to ask for a southern-exposure room—these have spectacular views of the Hollywood Hills. (Rooms at the back of the hotel face a wall of the Beverly Center, a less-than-scenic view.) ⊠ *8555 Beverly Blvd., 90048,* ☎ *310/278–5444 or 800/521–7772,* FAX *310/657–2816. 298 rooms, 13 suites. Restaurant, in-room modem lines, minibars, no-smoking rooms, room service, in-room VCRs, pool, sauna, health club, piano, concierge, business services, travel services, car rental, parking (fee). AE, D, DC, MC, V.*

Beverly Hills, West Hollywood, and Hollywood Lodging

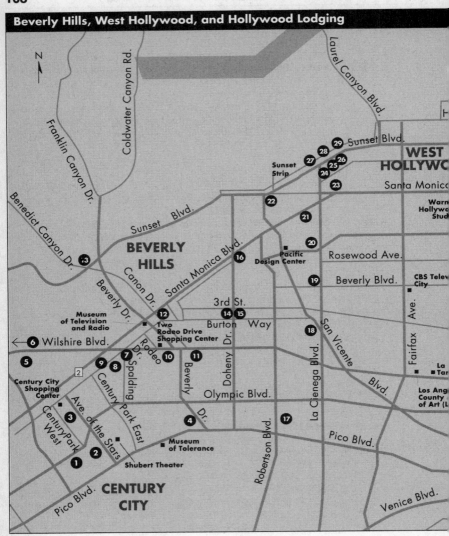

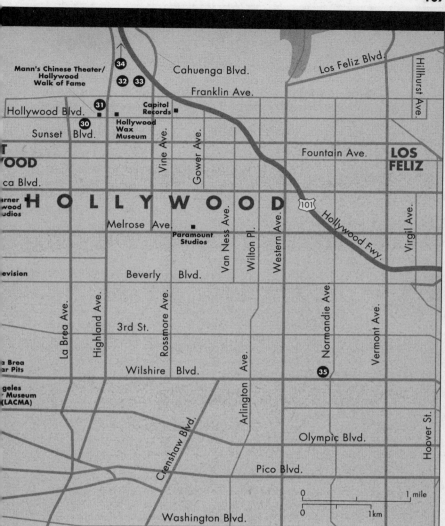

Mann's Chinese Theater/
Hollywood
Walk of Fame

Cahuenga Blvd.

Los Feliz Blvd.

Hillhurst Ave.

34

32 33

Franklin Ave.

Hollywood Blvd.

31

Capitol
Records

Sunset   Blvd.

30

Hollywood
Wax
Museum

Vine Ave.

Gower Ave.

Fountain Ave.

LOS
FELIZ

OOD

ca Blvd.

H O L L Y W O O D

101

Hollywood Fwy.

Virgil Ave.

rner
wood
udios

Melrose Ave.

Paramount
Studios

Van Ness Ave.

Wilton Pl.

Western Ave.

evision

Beverly   Blvd.

La Brea Ave.

Highland Ave.

Rossmore Ave.

3rd St.

Normandie Ave

Vermont Ave.

Ave.

a Brea
ar Pits

Wilshire   Blvd.

35

geles
Museum
(LACMA)

Arlington   Ave.

Crenshaw Blvd.

Olympic Blvd.

Hoover St.

Pico Blvd.

Washington Blvd.

0   1 mile

0   1km

Magic Hotel, **33**
Mondrian, **25**
Park Hyatt, **2**
Park Sunset Hotel, **24**
Peninsula
Beverly Hills, **8**
Radisson Beverly
Pavilion Hotel, **11**
Radisson Wilshire
Plaza Hotel, **35**

Ramada West
Hollywood, **21**
Westin Century Plaza
Hotel and Tower, **3**
Regent Beverly
Wilshire, **10**
Summerfield Suites
Hotel, **23**
Sunset Marquis Hotel
and Villas, **27**

Wyndham Bel Age
Hotel, **22**

$$$$ ⊞ **L'Ermitage Beverly Hills.** After standing vacant for a few years, the once sagging L'Ermitage got a new lease on life with a $60 million face-lift and a rechristening as the L'Ermitage Beverly Hills. The smallish hotel just off Rodeo Drive has spacious, uncluttered rooms with silk bedding, walk-in closets, and French doors that open to views of the city, the Getty Center, Beverly Hills, and the Hollywood Hills. For corporate travelers there are cellular phones with private numbers and contraptions that triple as fax machines, copiers, and printers. Chef Serge Falesitch, who worked with Wolfgang Puck at Spago, is the force behind what the hotel dubs "Cuisine du Soleil": Provençal-Tuscan with an Asian flair. The rooftop pool has drop-dead views and classy poolside cabanas. ⊠ *9291 Burton Way, 90210,* ☎ *310/278–3344 or 800/ 800–2113,* FAX *310/278–8247. 111 rooms, 13 suites. 2 restaurants, 2 bars, in-room modem lines, minibars, no-smoking floors, room service, pool, massage, steam room, exercise room, laundry service and dry cleaning, concierge, business services, meeting rooms, parking (fee). AE, D, DC, MC, V.*

$$$$ ⊞ **Peninsula Beverly Hills.** The interior of this grand, French Renais-
★   sance–style hotel feels a world removed from the bustle on Little Santa Monica Boulevard. Rooms resemble luxury apartments, with fine antiques and marble floors; some suites in the two-story villas have whirlpool tubs, terraces, fireplaces, and CD players. The fifth-floor pool, looking out at the Hollywood Hills, is a gem of a place to relax. Other frivolities include an on-site Bijan store and a courtesy Rolls-Royce for Beverly Hills shopping. Afternoon tea, served in the living room by a crackling fire, has become a popular venue for business meetings. ⊠ *9882 Little Santa Monica Blvd., 90212,* ☎ *310/551–2888 or 800/462– 7899,* FAX *310/788–2319. 196 rooms, 32 suites. 2 restaurants, bar, in-room modem lines, in-room safes, minibars, no-smoking floors, room service, in-room VCRs, lap pool, spa, health club, shops, baby-sitting, concierge, business services, travel services, car rental, parking (fee). AE, D, DC, MC, V.*

$$$$ ⊞ **Radisson Beverly Pavilion Hotel.** This eight-floor boutique hotel is in prime shopping territory, within blocks of Rodeo Drive. Guest rooms and executive suites have private balconies; some also have refrigerators. The well-known restaurant, Colette, serves California cuisine. The Radisson's frequent rate specials make it an economical alternative to some of the neighborhood's pricier establishments. ⊠ *9360 Wilshire Blvd., 90212,* ☎ *310/273–1400 or 800/441–5050,* FAX *310/859–8551. 100 rooms, 10 suites. Restaurant, bar, no-smoking rooms, room service, pool, laundry service and dry cleaning, concierge, business services, parking (fee). AE, D, DC, MC, V.*

$$$$ ⊞ **Regent Beverly Wilshire.** Known of late as the *Pretty Woman* hotel
★   (the presidential suite was the model for the lavish room in the famed Richard Gere/Julia Roberts film), the Regent is a longtime classic. Rooms in the older (1928) Wilshire wing of this landmark Italian Renaissance–style hotel are especially large; those in the Beverly wing (1971) have balconies overlooking the pool. Throughout the hotel, beds are so comfortable that guests have been known to ask where they can buy the mattresses. Personal services include fresh strawberries and cream and bottled water delivered to your room upon arrival. Pets get the welcome treatment, too, with amenities such as Evian water, biscuits served on a silver tray, and a walk by the concierge. Enjoy dinner and dancing in the famed Dining Room on weekends. ⊠ *9500 Wilshire Blvd., 90212,* ☎ *310/275–5200, 800/421–4354 in the U.S., 800/ 427–4354 in CA;* FAX *310/274–2851. 275 rooms, 69 suites. 2 restaurants, bar, lobby lounge, in-room modem lines, in-room safes, mini-*

bars, no-smoking floors, room service, in-room VCRs, pool, beauty salon, spa, health club, piano, baby-sitting, children's programs (ages 4–12), laundry service and dry cleaning, concierge, business services, travel services, car rental, parking (fee). AE, D, DC, MC, V.

$$$–$$$$ ☆ ⭐ **Beverly Hills Plaza Hotel.** A black-and-white lobby has overstuffed sofas and lots of plants. Suites have an airy feel, with white color schemes and plenty of glass; and each has a kitchen. Accommodations come equipped with bathrobes, hair dryers, in-room movies, and Nintendo; some also have VCRs. ⊠ *10300 Wilshire Blvd., 90024,* ☎ *310/275–5575,* FAX *310/278–3325. 116 suites. Restaurant, bar, in-room modem lines, in-room safes, kitchenettes, minibars, pool, massage, exercise room, video games, laundry service and dry cleaning, concierge, business services, parking (fee). AE, D, DC, MC, V.*

$$$ ☆ ⭐ **Beverly Hills Inn.** The 50-room Inn is a nice alternative to the town's more mammoth (and more expensive) luxury hotels. Rooms surround a courtyard with pool; each has a refrigerator, and some have french doors leading to an outdoor sitting area. In addition to complimentary breakfast delivered to your door each morning, cheese and fresh fruit are served every evening, and dried fruits are left instead of mints at nightly turndown. The hotel is just steps away from Wilshire Boulevard and within easy access of all the trendy shopping spots; this convenient location, in addition to reasonable prices and thoughtful service, have ensured the inn a loyal following—be sure to reserve in advance. ⊠ *125 S. Spalding Dr., 90212,* ☎ *310/278–0303, 800/463–4466;* FAX *310/278–1728. 50 rooms, 4 suites. Bar, in-room modem lines, no-smoking floor, refrigerator, pool, sauna, exercise room, baby-sitting, laundry service and dry cleaning, concierge, business services, free parking. Continental breakfast. AE, DC, MC, V.*

$$ ☆ **Beverly Terrace Hotel.** Rooms are basic (except for the leopard-print bedspreads), and bathrooms have shower stalls but not tubs—but the price is right at this hotel on the fringes of Beverly Hills and West Hollywood. On the corner of Santa Monica Boulevard, the hotel is close to the Sunset Strip and the heart of West Hollywood. Complimentary breakfast is served outside by the pool. ⊠ *469 N. Doheney Dr., 90810,* ☎ *310/274–8141,* FAX *310/385–1998 39 rooms. Pool, free parking. Continental breakfast. AE, D, DC, MC, V.*

$$ ☆ **Carlyle Inn.** Complimentary buffet breakfast in the morning and wine in the late afternoon, and in-room extras such as bathrobes, hair dryers, and turndown service make this four-story inn a good choice. It's in a safe neighborhood close to Restaurant Row, Century City, and Beverly Hills; a complimentary shuttle runs within a 5-mi radius. A sun deck and hot tub are added bonuses. ⊠ *1119 S. Robertson Blvd., 90035,* ☎ *310/275–4445 or 800/322–7595,* FAX *310/859–0496. 32 rooms. Restaurant, in-room modem lines, minibars, no-smoking rooms, room service, in-room VCRs, hot tub, exercise room, laundry service and dry cleaning, business services, travel services, parking (fee). Full breakfast. AE, D, DC, MC, V.*

$$ ☆ **Crescent Hotel.** One of the only good values in this swanky neighborhood, the small, European-style Crescent Hotel serves complimentary snacks and fresh fruit all day long. Standard rooms are admittedly on the Spartan side, but unexpected touches such as original paintings on the walls and clothes hangers that double as art spice up the mood. Upper-end suites are a bit expensive considering that the only features that distinguish them from standard rooms are large-screen TVs and tubs. ⊠ *403 N. Crescent Dr., 90210,* ☎ *310/247–0505 or 800/451–1566,* FAX *310/247–9053 39 rooms. No-smoking rooms, refrigerators, free parking. Continental breakfast. AE, D, DC, MC, V.*

Century City

$$$$ ▥ **Westin Century Plaza Hotel and Tower.** Rooms here are lavish, with fine art and antiques, and balconies with ocean or city views. The hotel caters to its small guests as well, with special children's menus and welcome packages that include teddy bears—and strollers are available on request. The Shubert Theatre, ABC Entertainment Center (with 18 cinemas), and Century City Shopping Center are directly across the street, and a complimentary town car takes guests to Beverly Hills. ⊠ *2025 Ave. of the Stars, 90067,* ☎ *310/277–2000 or 800/228–3000,* ☎ *310/ 551–3355. 998 rooms, 74 suites. 2 restaurants, 2 bars, minibars, no-smoking rooms, room service, 2 pools, barbershop, beauty salon, hot tub, 2 exercise rooms, health club, piano, baby-sitting, laundry service and dry cleaning, concierge, business services, car rental, parking (fee). AE, D, DC, MC, V.*

$$$$ ▥ **Park Hyatt.** Rooms at this elegant luxury hotel are big and comfortable, with plants and upholstered furniture. Nice touches include high tea in the Garden Room and complimentary limousine service within Century City and Beverly Hills. A multilingual staff and careful attention to detail make for smooth business meetings. Century City is literally next door, and Rodeo Drive is also nearby. ⊠ *2151 Ave. of the Stars, 90067,* ☎ *310/277–1234 or 800/233–1234,* ☎ *310/785–9240. 367 rooms, 189 suites. Restaurant, 2 bars, in-room modem lines, minibars, no-smoking rooms, 24-hour room service, indoor and outdoor pools, hot tub, massage, sauna, steam room, spa, health club, piano, laundry service and dry cleaning, concierge, business services, convention center, meeting rooms, parking (fee). AE, D, DC, MC, V.*

$$$ ▥ **Century City Courtyard by Marriott.** Near the Century City business complex, this Marriott is well situated and nicely priced. Room amenities include hair dryers, coffeemakers, irons and boards, and Nintendo. A complimentary shuttle zips guests to businesses, shopping, dining, and entertainment within a 3-mi radius. ⊠ *10320 W. Olympic Blvd., 90064,* ☎ *310/556–2777 or 800/321–2211,* ☎ *310/203– 0563. 134 rooms. Restaurant, bar, minibars, no-smoking rooms, room service, hot tub, exercise room, baby-sitting, laundry service and dry cleaning, business services, car rental, free parking. AE, D, DC, MC, V.*

West Hollywood

$$$$ ▥ **The Argyle.** You can't miss the gunmetal-gray, pink, and burgundy
★   art deco facade. Inside, reproduction objets d'art and paintings fill the public spaces. Rooms are also deco; marble bathrooms have black-and-white fixtures. Though small, each accommodation has a separate living room with fax machine, two-line speakerphones, and plenty of plants. The Fenix restaurant (☞ Chapter 3) serves top-notch California-French cuisine. ⊠ *8358 Sunset Blvd., 90069,* ☎ *323/654–7100 or 800/ 225–2637,* ☎ *323/654–9287. 20 rooms, 44 suites. Restaurant, bar, in-room modem lines, in-room safes, minibars, no-smoking floors, room service, in-room VCRs, pool, sauna, exercise room, laundry service and dry cleaning, concierge, business services, meeting rooms, travel services, car rental, parking (fee). AE, DC, MC, V.*

$$$$ ▥ **Hyatt West Hollywood on Sunset Boulevard.** Its proximity to L.A.'s clubs of the moment (it's across the street from the House of Blues) make this Hyatt popular with music-industry types. Rooms that face the boulevard have balconies; those facing the hills do not. Some rooms have aquariums, and all have a deco feel. The view from the Rooftop pool is extraordinary—you can practically see inside some of the Hollywood Hills dwellings. The Silver Screen sports bar and restaurant is a lively nighttime hangout. ⊠ *8401 Sunset Blvd., 90069,* ☎

323/656–1234 or 800/233–1234, FAX *323/650–7024. 262 rooms, 21 suites. Restaurant, sports bar, in-room modem lines, no-smoking floors, room service, pool, laundry service and dry cleaning, business services, parking (fee). AE, D, DC, MC, V.*

$$$$ ▦ **Le Parc Hotel.** Suites in this modern low-rise have sunken living rooms with fireplaces and private balconies; other extras are microwaves, coffeemakers, stereos with CD players, and Nintendo. Cafe Le Parc serves excellent California cuisine to nonguests as well as guests. The hotel is on a residential street close to CBS Television City. ⊠ *733 N. W. Knoll Dr., 90069,* ☎ *310/855–8888 or 800/578–4837,* FAX *310/659–7812. 154 suites. Restaurant, kitchenettes, minibars, no-smoking rooms, in-room VCRs, pool, hot tub, sauna, tennis court, basketball, health club, baby-sitting, coin laundry, concierge, business services, travel services, parking (fee). AE, DC, MC, V.*

$$$$ ▦ **Mondrian.** Ian Schrager, famed for his hipper-than-thou New York
★   City hotels—the Royalton, Paramount, and Morgans—is responsible for this all-white Sunset Strip high rise, which enjoyed a much-publicized reopening in 1997. Mod apartment-size accommodations have floor-to-ceiling windows, slip-covered sofas, and marble coffee tables; many have kitchens. Schrager-esque touches include scented candles, flowers, wool lap blankets, and vintage movie magazines in each room, and a juice bar caters to L.A.'s well-known cult of the body. At 5 PM the lobby lights are dimmed, candles are lit, and a carpet of light creates visual magic. Be sure to meander over to the Sky Bar, Hollywood's club of the moment, where patrons (many celebrities) pay exorbitant prices for the right to drink cocktails out of plastic cups by a pool. ⊠ *8440 Sunset Blvd., 90069,* ☎ *323/650–8999 or 800/525–8029,* FAX *323/650–5215. 53 rooms, 185 suites. Restaurant, 2 bars, outdoor café, in-room modem lines, kitchenettes, no-smoking rooms, refrigerators, room service, pool, massage, sauna, spa, steam room, health club, laundry service and dry cleaning, concierge, business services, meeting rooms, car rental, parking (fee). AE, D, DC, MC, V.*

$$$$ ▦ **Summerfield Suites Hotel.** Suites here are basic, almost dormlike, but frequent specials make them a good value. Each suite has a private balcony, sleeper sofa (in addition to beds), a gas fireplace, separate vanities, and microwave; most have kitchens as well. The staff is as friendly and helpful as any you'd find in L.A.'s most expensive properties; there's even a complimentary grocery-shopping service. On a residential side street, the hotel is steps from Santa Monica Boulevard, close to the Sunset Strip and La Cienega Boulevard's Restaurant Row. ⊠ *1000 Westmount Dr., 90069,* ☎ *310/657–7400 or 800/833–4353,* FAX *310/854–6744. 109 suites. Breakfast room, in-room modem lines, no-smoking suites, refrigerators, in-room VCRs, pool, exercise room, coin laundry, laundry service and dry cleaning, meeting room, parking (fee). Continental breakfast. AE, D, DC, MC, V.*

$$$$ ▦ **Sunset Marquis Hotel and Villas.** Music-industry types love the fact that there's a recording studio on site. Some of the Mediterranean-style accommodations (there are suites and villas), in fact, have their own grand pianos; some also have kitchenettes. A masseuse is on call to iron out the kinks, but a walk in the lush gardens—look for frequent fashion shoots—may also do the trick. Complimentary stereos, VCRs, and fax machines are available on request. Guests are admitted into the hotel's famed (and ultra-exclusive) night spot, the Whiskey Bar. ⊠ *1200 N. Alta Loma Rd., 90069,* ☎ *310/657–1333 or 800/858–9758,* FAX *310/652–5300. 102 suites, 12 villas. Dining room, bar, in-room modem lines, in-room safes, no-smoking floor, refrigerators, minibars, room service, 2 pools, hot tub, sauna, exercise room, baby-sitting, laundry service, concierge, parking (fee). AE, DC, MC, V.*

$$$$ ⊞ **Wyndham Bel Age Hotel.** There's a residential feel to this all-suites
   ★   hotel near the Sunset Strip. South-facing rooms have private terraces
        that look out over the Los Angeles skyline as far as the Pacific. For
        some on-premise pampering, make an appointment at the famed Alex
        Roldan beauty salon, or enjoy a meal at the Diaghilev restaurant,
        where chef Tony Hodges creates Russian dishes with a French flair. The
        hotel caters to the entertainment industry, so keep an eye out for
        celebs. ✉ *1020 N. San Vicente Blvd., 90069,* ☏ *310/854–1111 or 800/
        996–3426,* FAX *310/854–0926. 200 suites. 2 restaurants, bar, in-room
        modem lines, kitchenettes, no-smoking rooms, room service, pool,
        beauty salon, exercise room, laundry service and dry cleaning, concierge,
        travel services, parking (fee). AE, D, DC, MC, V.*

$$$ ⊞ **Ramada West Hollywood.** Though part of a chain, this hotel in the
        largely gay West Hollywood neighborhood has plenty of character. Flashy
        deco rooms have white leather furniture and ultra-comfortable beds,
        and the bilevel loft suites with kitchenettes are an excellent value.
        Pizzeria Uno provides room service, and several restaurants are within
        walking distance—a rare luxury in L.A. ✉ *8585 Santa Monica Blvd.,
        90069,* ☏ *310/652–6400 or 800/845–8585,* FAX *310/652–4207. 135
        rooms, 40 suites. Restaurant, bar, in-room modem lines, no-smoking
        floors, room service, refrigerators, pool, coin laundry, dry cleaning and
        laundry service, concierge, parking (fee). AE, D, DC, MC, V.*

$$ ⊞ **Park Sunset Hotel.** The rooms are basic, but for West Hollywood
        fans, the location can't be beat: It's within walking distance of night
        spots such as the House of Blues (next door) as well as some tony shops.
        Suites have kitchenettes. ✉ *8462 Sunset Boulevard., 90069,* ☏ *323/
        654-6470 or 800/821–3660,* FAX *323/654–2286/. 66 rooms, 18 suites.
        Restaurant, no-smoking rooms, room service, pool, beauty salon, coin
        laundry, laundry services and dry cleaning, parking (fee). AE, D, DC,
        MC, V.*

Hollywood and Vicinity

$$$$ ⊞ **Chateau Marmont Hotel.** You'll know this hotel the minute you see
   ★   it; it's every bit the French castle the name suggests. Entertainment-
        industry moguls have been known to love the hotel's opulent suites,
        cottages, bungalows, and penthouses (notwithstanding John Belushi's
        ill-fated stay here in the 1980s). Though the 1920s feel is authentic,
        some may find the decor looks dated rather than antique. Rooms in
        the cottages have Frank Lloyd Wright–inspired fabrics; the 1956 bun-
        galows are more contemporary. Not all rooms are air-conditioned, but
        the non-AC variety can be cooled with portable units available by re-
        quest. An on-call beauty therapist, masseuse, private trainers, and air-
        port meet-and-greeters are all at your beck and call. The trendy Bar
        Marmont, adjacent to the hotel, has its own kitchen and serves food
        until 1:30 AM—unusual in L.A. ✉ *8221 Sunset Blvd., 90046,* ☏ *323/
        656–1010 or 800/242–8328,* FAX *323/655–5311. 10 rooms, 53 suites.
        Bar, dining room, in-room modem lines, in-room safes, minibars, no-
        smoking rooms, room service, in-room VCRs, pool, massage, exercise
        room, baby-sitting, laundry service and dry cleaning, concierge, busi-
        ness services, car rental, parking (fee). AE, DC, MC, V.*

$$$–$$$$ ⊞ **Radisson Wilshire Plaza Hotel.** One of the mid-Wilshire business dis-
        trict's largest hotels has contemporary rooms with magnificent views
        of Hollywood or downtown through floor-to-ceiling windows. Rooms
        on the two business floors come with coffeemakers, bathrobes, and irons
        and boards. The hotel has a small exercise room, but guests also have
        use of a nearby health club. Starbucks coffee and Ben and Jerry's ice
        cream are both available in the deli. ✉ *3515 Wilshire Blvd., 90010,*
        ☏ *213/381–7411 or 800/333–3333,* FAX *213/386–7379. 380 rooms,*

20 suites. Restaurant, bar, café, deli, in-room modem lines, minibars, no-smoking floor, room service, pool, barbershop, exercise room, laundry service and dry cleaning, concierge, business services, meeting rooms, travel services, parking (fee). AE, D, DC, MC, V.

$$$ ⊞ **Clarion Hotel Hollywood Roosevelt.** The Roosevelt has a hip art deco lobby whose original worn-and weathered steps have been well traveled by Hollywood's golden-age elite. The hotel was the site of the original Academy Awards; now the Hollywood legacy lives on in the little museum on the second floor, and in the 40 suites, which have themes such as Gable and Lombard or Shirley Temple. The Hollywood Walk of Fame, Mann's Chinese Theatre, and the Hollywood Entertainment Museum are all within walking distance, but the neighborhood isn't the best. If you'd rather stay in at night, you can dance to live jazz music at the Cinegrill. ⊠ *7000 Hollywood Blvd., 90028,* ☎ *323/466–7000 or 800/950–7667,* FAX *323/462–8056. 320 rooms, 39 suites. Restaurants, bar, lobby lounge, no-smoking rooms, room service, pool, hot tub, exercise room, laundry service and dry cleaning, baby-sitting, concierge, parking (fee). AE, D, DC, MC, V.*

$$$ ⊞ **Hollywood Holiday Inn.** You can't miss the cylindrical tower of this 23-story hotel, one of Hollywood's tallest buildings. Though rooms are standard-issue Holiday Inn, there's a revolving rooftop restaurant-bar known for its Sunday brunch. You can walk to the Hollywood Walk of Fame and Mann's Chinese Theatre; the Hollywood Bowl and Universal Studios are just a short drive away. ⊠ *1755 N. Highland Ave., 90028,* ☎ *323/462–7181 or 800/465–4329,* FAX *323/466–9072. 470 rooms. Restaurant, bar, coffee shop, in-room modem lines, in-room safes, kitchenettes, no-smoking floors, pool, exercise room, baby-sitting, laundry service, business services, travel services, car rental, parking (fee). AE, D, DC, MC, V.*

$–$$ ⊞ **Magic Hotel.** There's a nice pool here, and parking is free. Some rooms overlook the pool; others face out at the street. Larger rooms have kitchens with eating areas. The hotel is close to the Hollywood Walk of Fame and other Hollywood Boulevard attractions. ⊠ *7025 Franklin Avenue., 90028,* ☎ *323/851–0800 or 800/741–4915,* FAX *323/851–4926. 10 rooms, 30 suites. No-smoking rooms, refrigerator, pool, coin laundry, free parking. AE, D, DC, MC, V.*

$ ⊞ **Banana Bungalow Hotel and International Hostel.** You'll get good value at this friendly hostel on 6.8 acres in the Hollywood Hills. Dorm rooms (only for travelers with international passports) have four bunk beds each and are equipped with lockers; there are also 18 private double-occupancy rooms. You can whip up snacks in the 24-hour common kitchen, and there's internet access in the library. The hostel runs tours of L.A. and provides a free shuttle to Disneyland, Universal Studios, Magic Mountain, Venice, and TV studios. ⊠ *2775 Cahuenga Blvd. W, 90068,* ☎ *323/851–1129 or 800/446–7835,* FAX *323/851–1569. 24 dorm rooms, 18 private rooms. Restaurant, fans, no-smoking rooms, pool, exercise room, billiards, recreation room, theater, coin laundry, travel services, airport shuttle, car rental, free parking. MC, V.*

$ ⊞ **Highland Gardens Hotel.** Studios and standard rooms have kitchens with vinyl chairs and Formica tables that'll have children of the 1950s and 1960s waxing nostalgic. Basic but spacious sleeping areas each have two queen-size beds and a desk and sitting area. The hotel is just blocks from the Walk of Fame and a few minutes' drive to the Sunset Strip. Coffee and donuts are served daily. ⊠ *7047 Franklin Ave., 90028,* ☎ *323/850–0536 or 800/404–5472,* FAX *323/850–1712. 70* *rooms, 48 suites. Kitchenettes, no-smoking rooms, refrigerators, free parking. AE, MC, V.*

Coastal and Western Los Angeles

Bel-Air

$$$$ ⊞ **Hotel Bel-Air.** Locals swear by this luxury treasure tucked in a
★   wooded canyon. Bungalow-style Country French rooms feel like fine
homes with extras such as a stereo with CD player, thick terry bathrobes,
and slippers. Six of the suites have private whirlpool baths on the patio;
some rooms have wood-burning fireplaces (the bell captain will build
a fire for you). The highly regarded Dining Room features a pianist
nightly. For the quietest accommodations, ask for a room near the former stable area. ⊠ *701 Stone Canyon Rd., 90077, ☎ 310/472–1211
or 800/648–4097,* ℻ *310/476–5890. 59 rooms, 33 suites. Restaurant,
bar, in-room modem lines, in-room safes, minibars, no-smoking rooms,
room service, in-room VCRs, pool, beauty salon, hot tubs, massage,
health club, baby-sitting, laundry service and dry cleaning, concierge,
meeting rooms, travel services, parking (fee). AE, DC, MC, V.*

⊞ **Summit Hotel Bel-Air.** There's a southern Californian feel to this Bel-
Air low-rise close to the Getty Museum in Brentwood, with patios and
terraces overlooking 8 acres of gardens. The sleek, modern guest rooms
are deco-inspired. Amenities include bathrobes, coffeemakers, and
hair dryers. ⊠ *11461 Sunset Blvd., 90049, ☎ 310/476–6571 or 800/
468–3541,* ℻ *310/476–1371. 161 rooms, 8 suites. Restaurant, bar,
in-room modem lines, minibars, no-smoking rooms, room service,
pool, massage, spa, 1 tennis court, exercise room, baby-sitting, laundry service and dry cleaning, concierge, business services, meeting
rooms, travel services, car rental, parking (fee). AE, D, DC, MC, V.*

Los Angeles International Airport

$$$$ ⊞ **Summerfield Suites.** This all-suite hotel is ideal for guests who want
★   to spread out. One- and two-bedroom suites are extra large, with
kitchens and bedrooms as well as sleeper sofas in the living room. You
can stock your kitchen at the little shop in the lobby; in-room meals
are available through an outside service. ⊠ *810 S. Douglas Ave., El
Segundo 90266, ☎ 310/725–0100 or 800/833–4353,* ℻ *310/725–
0900. 122 suites. Breakfast room, in-room modem lines, no-smoking
rooms, pool, hot tub, exercise room, coin laundry, laundry service and
dry cleaning, business services, meeting rooms, free parking. Continental
breakfast. AE, D, DC, MC, V.*

$$$ ⊞ **Holiday Inn LAX.** This 12-story international-style hotel appeals to
families as well as businesspeople. Accommodations have dataports and
coffeemakers, and refrigerators can be rented. ⊠ *9901 La Cienega Blvd.,
Los Angeles 90045, ☎ 310/649–5151 or 800/624–0025,* ℻ *310/670–
3619. 401 rooms, 1 suite. Restaurant, bar, in-room modem lines, pool,
exercise room, video games, coin laundry, airport shuttle, parking
(fee). AE, D, DC, MC, V.*

$$$ ⊞ **Los Angeles Airport Marriott.** Convention travelers frequent this 18-
story Marriott. A business center caters to executive needs, and J.W.'s
steakhouse provides a nice setting for business deals. Rooms and suites
have pay-per movies and coffeemakers; VCRs are available on request. The hotel is convenient to Marina del Rey, the Forum, and the
Coliseum; it's about four minutes from the airport. ⊠ *5855 W. Century Blvd., Los Angeles 90045, ☎ 310/641–5700 or 800/228–9290,*
℻ *310/337–5358. 988 rooms, 22 suites. 2 restaurants, sports bar, in-
room modem lines, no-smoking rooms, pool, health club, piano, baby-
sitting, coin laundry, laundry service and dry cleaning, concierge,*

Barnabey's Hotel, **28**
Best Western Ocean
View Hotel, **2**
Best Western Royal
Palace Inn
& Suites, **9**
Century Wilshire
Hotel, **7**
Continental Plaza Los
Angeles Airport, **22**
Crowne Plaza Redondo
Beach & Marina
Hotel, **29**
Furama Hotel Los
Angeles, **20**
Holiday Inn LAX, **24**
Hotel Bel-Air, **5**
Hotel Carmel, **10**
Hotel del Capri, **8**
Hotel Oceana, **1**
Loews Santa Monica
Beach Hotel, **11**
Los Angeles Airport
Marriott, **26**
Marina Beach
Marriott, **15**
Marina del Rey
Hotel, **8**
MarinaInternational
Hotel &
Bungalows, **16**
Marina Pacific
Hotel & Suites, **14**
Miramar Sheraton, **3**
Pacific Shore, **13**
Radisson Los
Angeles, **19**
Ritz-Carlton, Marina
del Rey, **17**
Sheraton Gateway
Hotel at LAX, **23**
Shutters on the
Beach, **12**
Summerfield Suites, **27**
Summit Hotel
Bel-Air, **4**
Westin LAX, **25**
Westwood Marquis
Hotel and Gardens, **6**
Wyndham Hotel at
Los Angeles Airport, **21**

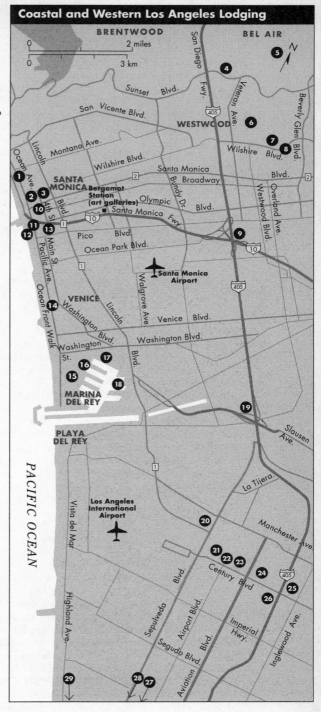

Coastal and Western Los Angeles Lodging

business services, convention center, meeting rooms, airport shuttle, car rental, parking (fee). AE, D, DC, MC, V.

$$$ 🔳 **Sheraton Gateway Hotel at LAX.** There's plenty to do right in your room here, with video games, movies, and 24-hour room service. The hotel also has a currency exchange, business center, and 24-hour shuttle to the airport. Forty-eight rooms were designed especially for people with disabilities. ✉ *6101 W. Century Blvd., Los Angeles 90045,* ☎ *310/642–1111 or 800/325–3535,* FAX *310/410–1267. 518 rooms, 92 suites. 2 restaurants, bar, sushi bar, in-room modem lines, minibars, no-smoking rooms, room service, pool, hot tub, exercise room, laundry service and dry cleaning, concierge, business services, meeting rooms, travel services, airport shuttle, car rental, parking (fee). AE, D, DC, MC, V.*

$$$ 🔳 **Westin LAX.** This is a great place to stay if you want to be pampered
★ but also need to be close to the airport. Rooms and suites are spacious; many suites have private outdoor hot tubs. The Trattoria Grande serves northern Italian cuisine with many seafood specialties. With 42 meeting rooms, a business center, currency exchange, and attentive service, the Westin has been recognized as a "Best of the West" meeting facility. ✉ *5400 W. Century Blvd., Los Angeles 90045,* ☎ *310/216– 5858 or 800/937–8461,* FAX *310/670–1948. 720 rooms, 42 suites. Restaurant, bar, in-room modem lines, minibars, no-smoking rooms, refrigerators, pool, hot tub, sauna, exercise room, laundry service and dry cleaning, business services, meeting rooms, airport shuttle, car rental, parking (fee). AE, D, DC, MC, V.*

$$$ 🔳 **Wyndham Hotel at Los Angeles Airport.** You'll get to your plane in a hurry from this hotel that bills itself as the closest to LAX. Contemporary guest rooms are on the small side (250 square ft) but have plenty of perks, such as fax machines, voice mail, direct-dial phones, and movies. ✉ *6225 W. Century Blvd., Los Angeles 90045,* ☎ *310/ 670–9000 or 800/996–3426,* FAX *310/670–8110. 591 rooms, 12 suites. 2 restaurants, bar, in-room modem lines, in-room safes, minibars, no-smoking floors, refrigerators, pool, hot tub, sauna, exercise room, baby-sitting, laundry service and dry cleaning, concierge, business services, meeting rooms, car rental, parking (fee). AE, D, DC, MC, V.*

$$ 🔳 **Continental Plaza Los Angeles Airport.** Low prices and friendly service make the Continental Plaza a good value among airport hotels. Rooms are well equipped, some with refrigerators, and guests have use of the health club next door. ✉ *9750 Airport Blvd., Los Angeles 90045,* ☎ *310/645–4600 or 800/529–4683,* FAX *310/216–7029. 570 rooms, 12 suites. Restaurant, coffee shop, bar, no-smoking floors, room service, pool, baby-sitting, coin laundry, laundry service and dry cleaning, concierge, business services, meeting rooms, travel services, airport shuttle, car rental, parking (fee). AE, D, DC, MC, V.*

$$ 🔳 **Furama Hotel Los Angeles.** Everything about this hotel has changed in a year, including the name (it was the Airport Marina Resort Hotel) and the color (it's now green). In a quiet, residential area, the hotel is convenient to jogging paths, tennis, and golf. The large marble lobby has writing tables, plants, and cushy sofas for doing business or relaxing. Rooms all have views of either the pool, ocean, or airport. A shuttle service goes to LAX, Marina del Rey, Venice Beach, and the Santa Monica Mall. ✉ *8601 Lincoln Blvd., Los Angeles 90045,* ☎ *310/670–8111 or 800/225–8126,* FAX *310/337–1883. 760 rooms, 6 suites. Restaurant, bar, no-smoking rooms, room service, pool, hot tub, 2 exercise rooms, laundry service and dry cleaning, business services, meeting rooms, airport shuttle, parking (fee). AE, D, DC, MC, V.*

$$ 🔳 **Radisson Los Angeles.** Oversize, art deco guest rooms have in-room movies, coffeemakers, and irons and boards. A live rhythm-and-blues band holds sway at the Culver Club from Thursday through Saturday night; on Sundays it's dancing to a DJ. Just 3 mi north of LAX and a few minutes from Marina del Rey, the hotel is convenient for business travelers. ⊠ *6161 Centinela Ave., Culver City 90231,* ☎ *310/649–1776 or 800/733–5466 ,* FAX *310/649–4411. 368 rooms, 3 suites. Restaurant, bar, coffee shop, no-smoking floors, room service, pool, hot tub, exercise room, nightclub, laundry service and dry cleaning, concierge, business services, meeting rooms, airport shuttle, car rental, free parking. AE, D, DC, MC, V.*

Manhattan Beach

$$$ ★ 🏨 **Barnabey's Hotel.** Modeled after a 19th-century English inn, Barnabey's has tidy rooms with lace curtains, antique furniture, flowered wallpaper, and vintage books. Added luxuries include a heated towel rack in the bathrooms, down comforters on the beds, and video games. The London Pub, styled like a cozy English hangout, has nightly entertainment, and the highly acclaimed Auberge restaurant is a nice place to enjoy Continental and American cuisine in the privacy of curtained booths. (A huge English buffet is served here in the morning.) Doggie and kitty snacks are available for the hotel's four-legged guests. ⊠ *3501 Sepulveda Blvd. (at Rosecrans), Manhattan Beach 90266,* ☎ *310/545–8466 or 800/552–5285,* FAX *310/545–8621. 122 rooms, 1 suite. Restaurant, pub, in-room modem lines, no-smoking rooms, pool, hot tub, bicycles, nightclub, laundry service and dry cleaning, business services, meeting rooms, travel services, airport shuttle, car rental, parking (fee). Full breakfast. AE, D, DC, MC, V.*

Marina del Rey

$$$$ ★ 🏨 **Marina Beach Marriott.** This Mediterranean-style, nine-story highrise has a high-tech design softened by pastel tones and accents of brass and marble. There's a gazebo on the patio, and some rooms have water views—ask for upper-floor rooms that face the marina. The restaurant, Stone's, is known for its fresh seafood. ⊠ *4100 Admiralty Way, 90292,* ☎ *310/301–3000 or 800/228–9290,* FAX *310/448–4870. 375 rooms. Restaurant, bar, minibars, no-smoking rooms, room service, pool, laundry service and dry cleaning, business services, car rental, parking (fee). AE, D, DC, MC, V.*

$$$$ 🏨 **Marina del Rey Hotel.** Rooms at this waterfront property have balconies or patios; many have harbor views. Cruises and charters are easily accessible from the hotel's private slips, and the concierge can arrange boat rentals. You can also take advantage of complimentary access to a fitness club five blocks away, and discounted rates at a nearby tennis club—or simply relax by the pool or gazebo. VCRs are available upon request. ⊠ *13534 Bali Way, 90292,* ☎ *310/301–1000 or 800/882–4000,* FAX *310/301–8167. 156 rooms, 4 suites. Restaurant, bar, in-room modem lines, no-smoking rooms, room service, pool, boating, bicycles, rollerblading, laundry service and dry cleaning, concierge, meeting rooms, travel services, airport shuttle, free parking. AE, DC, MC, V.*

$$$$ ★ 🏨 **Ritz-Carlton, Marina del Rey.** This ritzy, European-style hotel occupies a patch of prime real estate right on the docks of the marina, affording panoramic views of the Pacific. Traditionally styled rooms have French doors, marble baths, and honor bars; there's also twice-daily maid service and 24-hour room service. Bistro cuisine is served in the Terrace Restaurant; there's Mediterranean fare in the more formal Dining Room. ⊠ *4375 Admiralty Way, 90292,* ☎ *310/823–1700 or 800/241–3333,* FAX *310/305–0019. 306 rooms, 12 suites. 2 restaurants, lobby lounge, in-room safes, minibars, no-smoking floors, room service,*

pool, hot tub, massage, spa, tennis court, exercise room, bicycles, baby-sitting, laundry service and dry cleaning, concierge, business services, meeting rooms, travel services, car rental, parking (fee). AE, D, DC, MC, V.

$$$ ⚄ **Marina International Hotel & Bungalows.** A European village-like feel is evoked by white shutters on each window and private balconies overlooking the garden or courtyard (many have unobstructed views of the water). The split-level bungalows, in a flower-filled courtyard, are huge. Across from a sandy beach within the marina, the hotel is a good choice for families with children; it's also close to golf and tennis facilities. ⊠ *4200 Admiralty Way, 90292,* ☎ *310/301–2000 or 800/529–2525,* FAX *310/301–6687. 110 rooms, 25 bungalows. Restaurant, bar, in-room modem lines, minibars, room service, pool, hot tub, health club, laundry service and dry cleaning, concierge, business services, meeting rooms, travel services, airport shuttle, free parking. AE, DC, MC, V.*

Redondo Beach

$$$–$$$$ ⚄ **Crowne Plaza Redondo Beach & Marina Hotel.** This swank five-story hotel overlooking the Pacific has a 2,200-gallon saltwater aquarium as the focal point of its magnificent lobby. Accommodations have wicker furniture and soft colors; those on the fifth-floor concierge level are also equipped with two-line telephones and dataports. There is a Gold's Gym on the premises. Across the street from the King Harbor Marina, the hotel is within walking distance of 15 restaurants. ⊠ *300 N. Harbor Dr., Redondo Beach 90277,* ☎ *310/318–8888 or 800/368–9760,* FAX *310/376–1930. 334 rooms, 5 suites. 2 restaurants, no-smoking rooms, pool, spa, tennis court, exercise room, bicycles, baby-sitting, coin laundry, laundry service and dry cleaning, concierge level, business services, parking (fee). AE, D, DC, MC, V.*

Santa Monica

$$$$ ⚄ **Hotel Oceana.** There's a deco feel to this all-suite boutique hotel across the street from the ocean. Thoughtful touches include desks large enough for a computer (which the concierge will bring upon request) and refrigerators stocked with goodies such as Wolfgang Puck frozen dinners. For those who prefer the real thing, the hotel provides room service via the nearby Wolfgang Puck Café. Some suites have ocean-view patios—a great place to enjoy the complimentary Continental breakfast that's delivered to each room. ⊠ *849 Ocean Ave., 90403,* ☎ *310/393–0486 or 800/777–0758,* FAX *310/458–1182. 63 suites. Bar, in-room modem lines, kitchenettes, no-smoking rooms, refrigerators, room service, pool, spa, exercise room, coin laundry, laundry service and dry cleaning, concierge, business services, parking (fee). AE, D, DC, MC, V.*

$$$$ ⚄ **Loews Santa Monica Beach Hotel.** Proximity to the beach is the selling point of the Loews: The sand's just outside the door. Most of the airy, attractive rooms have spectacular views of the Pacific Ocean; some have balconies. The dramatic atrium lobby is a nice place to sit and soak up the elegant beach atmosphere. In summer there's a supervised "Splash Club" program for children. Children under 18 stay free in their parents' room, or at half price in an adjoining room (summer only). While the kids play, you can get an herbal wrap at the full-service day spa. ⊠ *1700 Ocean Ave., 90401,* ☎ *310/458–6700 or 800/235–6397,* FAX *310/458–6761. 350 rooms, 24 suites. 2 restaurants, café, bar, in-room modem lines, minibars, no-smoking floors, room service, indoor-outdoor pool, beauty salon, hot tub, massage, sauna, spa, steam room, health club, beach, windsurfing, baby-sitting, children's programs (ages 5–12), laundry service and dry cleaning, concierge, business services, meeting rooms, travel services, car rental, parking (fee). AE, D, DC, MC, V.*

$$$$ 🏨 **Miramar Sheraton.** Centrally located for shopping and sunning, the Miramar nevertheless feels like a secluded island resort. There's a bit of Old Hollywood to this 1889 mansion (it was built as a private residence), particularly in the lavish bungalows stocked with huge whirlpool tubs, stereos with CD, and bathroom speakers. (There are even automatic seat warmers on the toilets). Stay in a room in the 10-story tower and you'll be rewarded with spectacular ocean views; there are also residential-style rooms in the historic wing. ⊠ *101 Wilshire Blvd., 90401,* ☎ *310/576–7777 or 800/325–3535,* ℻ *310/458–7912. 213 rooms, 55 suites, 32 bungalows. 2 restaurants, bar, in-room modem lines, in-room safes, minibars, no-smoking floors, pool, beauty salon, health club, spa, piano, laundry service and dry cleaning, concierge, business services, meeting rooms, travel services, car rental, parking (fee). AE, D, DC, MC, V.*

$$$$ 🏨 **Shutters On The Beach.** Weathered-gray shingles and striped awnings
★ call to mind Martha's Vineyard, or a turn-of-the-century beach resort. It's Los Angeles's only hotel sitting directly on the sand, a fact that can easily make you forget you're only minutes from the city. Spacious, luxurious rooms have sliding shutter doors (hence the hotel's name) that open onto tiny balconies, and deep whirlpool tubs from which, in some rooms, you can gaze at the ocean. Suites have fireplaces, and all accommodations have luxurious beds with Frette linens. You'll pay a premium to face the ocean, but the alternative may be a room that faces the street. ⊠ *1 Pico Blvd., 90405,* ☎ *310/458–0030 or 800/334–9000,* ℻ *310/458–4589. 186 rooms, 12 suites. 2 restaurants, bar, lobby lounge, in-room modem lines, in-room safes, minibars, no-smoking floors, room service, in-room VCRs, pool, hot tub, sauna, spa, health club, beach, mountain bikes, baby-sitting, laundry service and dry cleaning, concierge, business services, meeting rooms, travel services, car rental, parking (fee). AE, D, DC, MC, V.*

$$$–$$$$ 🏨 **Pacific Shore.** This modern, eight-story hotel is just 200 steps from the beach and near many highly recommended restaurants. Some rooms have ocean views and small balconies. In-room extras include hair dryers, Nintendo, in-room movies; some also have wet bars and refrigerators. A complimentary shuttle runs to attractions within a 5-mi radius—perfect for seeing Santa Monica. ⊠ *1819 Ocean Ave., 90401,* ☎ *310/451–8711 or 800/622–8711,* ℻ *310/394–6657. 168 rooms. Restaurant, bar, in-room modem lines, in-room safes, pool, hot tub, exercise room, baby-sitting, coin laundry, business services, meeting rooms, travel services, car rental, free parking. AE, D, DC, MC, V.*

$$–$$$$ 🏨 **Best Western Ocean View Hotel.** This relative newcomer (built in 1994) has attractive low-season rates considering its prime real estate just across the street from the ocean. During the summer high season, however, the ocean-view room rate seems high, particularly for a hotel without amenities such as a pool. Guest rooms are small but comfortable; ocean-view rooms have coffeemakers. In addition to its proximity to the surf, the hotel is also just steps from some of Santa Monica's finest restaurants. ⊠ *1447 Ocean Ave., 90401,* ☎ *310/458–4888 or 800/ 528–1234,* ℻ *310/458–0848. 72 rooms. In-room modem lines, no-smoking rooms, refrigerators, laundry service and dry cleaning, business services, parking (fee). AE, D, DC, MC, V.*

$$ 🏨 **Hotel Carmel.** Price and location are the calling cards of this hotel. Basic rooms are spacious; some have ocean views. The hotel doesn't have its own restaurant, but there are plenty of fashionable eateries within walking distance. You can also stroll to the Third Street Promenade or to the beach, just a couple blocks away. In summer rooms often sell out; make reservations months ahead. ⊠ *201 Broadway, 90401,* ☎ *310/451–2469 or 800/445–8695,* ℻ *310/393–4180 . 96* *rooms, 8 suites. Laundry service and dry cleaning, parking (fee). Continental breakfast. AE, D, DC, MC, V.*

Venice

$ ▦ **Marina Pacific Hotel & Suites.** The price is right at this hotel that faces the Pacific and one of the world's most vibrant boardwalks; it's nestled among Venice's art galleries, shops, and elegant, offbeat restaurants. The marina is just a stroll away, giving guests easy access to ocean swimming and roller skating along the strand. Racquetball and tennis courts are also nearby. ⊠ *1697 Pacific Ave. 90291, ☎ 310/399–7770 or 800/421–8151, FAX 310/452–5479. 57 rooms, 35 suites. Restaurant, laundry service, meeting rooms, free parking. AE, D, DC, MC, V.*

Westwood

$$$–$$$$ ▦ **Westwood Marquis Hotel and Gardens.** This 15-story all-suite hotel near UCLA is a favorite of corporate and entertainment types. One-, two-, or three-bedroom suites (some penthouses) have living rooms, dining areas, and views of either Bel-Air, the Pacific Ocean, or Century City. South-facing suites overlooking the pool have expansive views of city *and* sea. Complimentary transportation runs to nearby areas. ⊠ *930 Hilgard Ave., 90024, ☎ 310/208–8765 or 800/421–2317, FAX 310/824–0355. 258 suites. 2 restaurants, bar, café, in-room modem lines, in-room safes, minibars, no-smoking floors, refrigerators, room service, 2 pools, hot tub, exercise room, laundry service and dry cleaning, concierge, business services, meeting rooms, parking (fee). AE, D, DC, MC, V.*

$$–$$$ **Hotel Del Capri.** Despite the modest motel sign, you're just as likely to see Jaguars in the parking lot as Jettas. Midway between Beverly Hills and Westwood, the small hotel has reasonably priced rooms, many with kitchenettes. Most rooms have whirlpool tubs (although some have showers only, so ask in advance if you care), and VCRs can be rented for a small fee. Ask about discounts for those in the arts. ⊠ *10587 Wilshire Blvd., 90024, ☎ 310/474–3511 or 800/444–6835, FAX 310/470–9999. 34 rooms, 45 suites. No-smoking rooms, refrigerators, pool, coin laundry, laundry service and dry cleaning, meeting rooms, free parking. Continental breakfast. AE, D, DC, MC, V.*

West Los Angeles

$$–$$$ ▦ **Century Wilshire Hotel.** This homey, English-style hotel is a favorite among the European crowd. Within walking distance of UCLA and Westwood Village, the hotel has small, well-kept rooms. ⊠ *10776 Wilshire Blvd., 90024, ☎ 310/474–4506 or 800/421–7223, FAX 310/474–2535. 87 rooms, 12 suites. Breakfast room, no-smoking rooms, pool, baby-sitting, laundry service and dry cleaning, concierge, travel services, car rental, free parking. Continental breakfast. AE, DC, MC, V.*

$ ▦ **Best Western Royal Palace Inn & Suites.** Low prices and nice facilities make this Best Western a good deal. Contemporary rooms have microwaves and coffeemakers. ⊠ *2528 S. Sepulveda Blvd. 90064, ☎ 310/477–9066 or 800/251–3888, FAX 310/478–4133. 23 rooms, 32 suites. Refrigerators, pool, hot tub, sauna, exercise room, billiards, coin laundry, laundry service, meeting room, free parking. AE, D, DC, MC, V.*

San Fernando Valley

Burbank

$$$ ▦ **Burbank Airport Hilton.** Across the street from the Burbank Airport, this contemporary Hilton is geared toward business travelers. Guest rooms have coffeemakers, irons and boards, hair dryers, and in-room

Beverly
Garland's
Holiday Inn, **3**

Burbank
Airport
Hilton, **6**

Radisson
Valley Center
Hotel Los
Angeles, **2**

Ritz-Carlton
Huntington
Hotel, **8**

Safari Inn, **7**

Sheraton
Universal, **5**

Sportsmen's
Lodge, **1**

Universal City
Hilton and
Towers, **4**

movies. Ask for a room with a mountain view, unless you prefer looking out at the airport activity across the street. The hotel is close to
Universal Studios and the Media City Centre shopping mall. ✉ *2500
Hollywood Way, 91505,* ☎ *818/843–6000 or 800/468–3576,* FAX
*818/842–9720. 486 rooms, 77 suites. Restaurant, bar, in-room modem
lines, no-smoking floors, room service, 2 pools, outdoor hot tub,
sauna, 2 exercise rooms, coin laundry, laundry service and dry cleaning, concierge, convention center, travel services, airport shuttle, parking (fee). AE, D, DC, MC, V.*

$ 🏨 **Safari Inn.** Often used for location filming, this motel-like hotel 2
mi from Warner Bros. and Universal Studios comprises two buildings.
Common spaces are colorful and fun, with a jungle theme; but rooms
have a conservative, elegant feel, with mahogany furnishings. All accommodations have coffeemakers, irons and boards, and in-room
movies; some have refrigerators. Outside, a sundeck overlooks the pool
with a view to the hills. ✉ *1911 W. Olive Ave., Burbank 91506,* ☎
818/845–8586 or 800/782–4373, FAX *818/845–0054. 103 rooms, 15
suites. Restaurant, lobby lounge, no-smoking rooms, room service, in-
room VCRs, pool, hot tub, laundry service and dry cleaning, business
services, travel services, free parking. AE, DC, MC, V.*

North Hollywood

$$$ 🏨 **Beverly Garland's Holiday Inn.** There's a country-club atmosphere
to this lodgelike hotel in two separate buildings near Universal Studios.
Rooms have an early California look, with distressed furniture and muted
color schemes; private balconies and patios overlook the Sierra Madre
and Santa Monica mountains. The hotel is next to the Hollywood Free-
way, which can be noisy; ask for a room facing Vineland Avenue. ✉
4222 Vineland Ave., 91602, ☎ *818/980–8000 or 800/238–3759,* FAX

818/766–5230. 258 rooms. Restaurant, bar, no-smoking rooms, room service, pool, wading pool, sauna, tennis, laundry service and dry cleaning, meeting rooms, airport shuttle, free parking. AE, D, DC, MC, V.

Sherman Oaks

$$$ ☎ **Radisson Valley Center Hotel Los Angeles.** Standard accommodations here are bolstered by the hotel's excellent service. The hotel is conveniently located at the intersection of I–405 and Highway 101, in the Sherman Oaks business district, close to the Sherman Oaks Galleria shopping mall and excellent restaurants. ✉ *15433 Ventura Blvd., 91403,* ☎ *818/981–5400 or 800/333–3333,* ℻ *818/981–3175. 188 rooms, 12 suites. Restaurant, bar, in-room modem lines, no-smoking floors, room service, pool, beauty salon, hot tub, massage, exercise room, laundry service and dry cleaning, concierge, business services, meeting rooms, car rental, parking (fee). Continental breakfast. AE, D, DC, MC, V.*

Studio City

$$$ ☎ **Sportsmen's Lodge.** A low-slung, English country–style structure, this hotel is surrounded by waterfalls, a swan-filled lagoon, and a gazebo; the pool area and lush garden make you forget you're near a city. The renowned Caribou restaurant adjacent to the main building is housed in a historic lodge. Although service may not be everything you've dreamed of, the accommodations are comfortable and convenient—close to par-3 golf, tennis, and Universal City (the hotel offers discounted tickets to the Universal Studios tour). ✉ *12825 Ventura Blvd., 91604,* ☎ *818/769–4700 or 800/821–8511,* ℻ *323/877–3898. 191 rooms. 3 restaurants, bar, no-smoking floors, room service, pool, barbershop, beauty salon, hot tub, exercise room, baby-sitting, coin laundry, laundry service and dry cleaning, travel services, airport shuttle, car rental, free parking. AE, D, DC, MC, V.*

Universal City

$$$$ ☎ **Sheraton Universal.** You're apt to see movie and TV stars at this large hotel literally on the back lot of Universal Studios, overlooking Hollywood. Rooms have floor-to-ceiling windows that open. Among the amenities are in-room movies, coffeemakers, refrigerators (in some rooms only), and complimentary transportation to Universal Studios— though the studios and CityWalk are within walking distance. ✉ *333 Universal Terrace Pkwy., 91608,* ☎ *818/980–1212 or 800/325–3535,* ℻ *818/509–4980. 442 rooms, 25 suites. Restaurant, bar, in-room modem lines, in-room safes, minibars, no-smoking floors, room service, pool, hot tub, exercise room, baby-sitting, laundry service and dry cleaning, concierge, business services, meeting rooms, car rental, parking (fee). AE, D, DC, MC, V.*

$$$$ ☎ **Universal City Hilton and Towers.** This ultramodern-looking tower has cozy rooms that feel surprisingly homey, with marble baths and nice views from floor-to-ceiling windows. The Sierra Café serves good California cuisine, as well as a daily buffet with some great Chinese dishes. A complimentary limo is on call, and the property is within walking distance of Universal Studios and CityWalk. ✉ *555 Universal Terrace Pkwy., 91608,* ☎ *818/506–2500,* ℻ *818/509–2058. 482 rooms, 8 suites. Restaurant, lobby lounge, in-room modem lines, in-room safes, minibars, no-smoking floors, room service, pool, hot tub, massage, exercise room, piano, baby-sitting, laundry service and dry cleaning, business services, convention center, meeting rooms, travel services, concierge floors, car rental, parking (fee). AE, D, DC, MC, V.*

San Gabriel Valley

Pasadena

$$$$ 🏨 **Ritz-Carlton Huntington Hotel.** The main building of this 1906 land-
★   mark hotel is a Mediterranean-style structure that blends in seamlessly
with the lavish houses of the surrounding San Marino neighborhood.
Past the intimate lobby and the central courtyard, dotted with tiny ponds
and lush plantings, a wood-paneled grand lounge has a sweeping view
of Los Angeles in the distance. Traditionally styled guest rooms are handsome, if a bit small for the price. The landscaped grounds have Japanese gardens and the historic Picture Bridge, with murals depicting scenes
of California along its 20 gables. The Grill, the more formal of the two
dining rooms, is rated among the top 100 five-star restaurants in the
world. ⊠ *1401 S. Oak Knoll Ave., 91106,* ☎ *626/568–3900 or 800/
241–3333,* FAX *626/585–1842. 387 rooms, 31 suites. 2 restaurants, bar,
in-room modem lines, in-room safes, minibars, no-smoking buildings,
room service, in-room VCRs, pool, beauty salon, hot tub, mineral baths,
spa, tennis court, health club, baby-sitting, laundry service and dry cleaning, concierge, business services, meeting rooms, travel services, car rental,
parking (fee). AE, D, DC, MC, V.*

5 Nightlife and the Arts

Most bars, clubs, and bistros in this go-go-go city have a shelf life shorter than the vinyl skirts at Melrose boutiques. Hollywood, the locus of L.A. nightlife, is without question the place to start your search; you can't help but stumble into a happening joint if you cruise the streets long enough. If music is more your tune, L.A. is one of the best cities in the country to catch promising rock bands or check out jazz, blues, and classical acts. Culture vultures will find plenty going on in L.A., from ballet to film to theater.

FOR THE MOST COMPLETE LISTING OF WEEKLY EVENTS, consult the current issue of *Los Angeles* magazine. The Calendar section of the *Los Angeles Times* also lists a wide survey of Los Angeles arts events, as do the more alternative publications, the *L.A. Weekly* and the *New Times Los Angeles* (both free). For a telephone report on current music, theater, dance, film, and special events, plus a discount ticket source, call 213/688–2787.

Revised by
Mark Ehrman

Most tickets can be purchased by phone (with a credit card) from **Ticketmaster** (☎ 213/365–3500), **TeleCharge** (☎ 800/762–7666), **Good Time Tickets** (☎ 323/464–7383), **Tickets L.A.** (☎ 323/660–8587), or **Murray's Tickets** (☎ 323/234–0123). Half-price tickets to many shows are available at **Times Tix** (✉ Beverly Center, 8522 Beverly Blvd., ☎ 310/659–3678), on the 7th floor of Beverly Center, between Club Monaco and Banana Republic. Tickets must be purchased in person, cash only, and availability is never guaranteed.

THE ARTS

Concerts

Major Concert Halls

Part of the Los Angeles Music Center and—with the Hollywood Bowl—the center of L.A.'s classical music scene, the 3,200-seat **Dorothy Chandler Pavilion** (✉ 135 N. Grand Ave., ☎ 213/972–7211) is the home of the Los Angeles Philharmonic. The L.A. Opera presents classics from September through June.

In Griffith Park, the open-air auditorium known as the **Greek Theater** (✉ 2700 N. Vermont Ave., ☎ 323/665–1927) presents classical performances in its mainly pop-rock-jazz schedule from June through October. Its Doric columns evoke the amphitheaters of ancient Greece.

Ever since it opened in 1920, in a park surrounded by mountains, trees, and gardens, the **Hollywood Bowl** (✉ 2301 Highland Ave., ☎ 323/850–2000), has been one of the world's largest outdoor amphitheaters. Its season runs from early July through mid-September; the L.A. Philharmonic spends its summer season here. There are performances daily except Monday (and some Sundays); the program ranges from jazz to pop to classical. Concert goers usually arrive early, bringing or buying picnic suppers. There are plenty of picnic tables, and box-seat subscribers can reserve a table right in their own box. Restaurant dining is available on the grounds (☎ 323/851–3588); reserve ahead. Be sure to bring a sweater—it gets chilly here in the evening. You might also bring or rent a cushion, as the seats are made of wood. A convenient way to enjoy the Hollywood Bowl experience without the hassle of parking is to take one of the Park-and-Ride buses, which leave from various locations around town; call the Bowl for information.

Baghdad and Beyond is an apt description of the **Shrine Auditorium** (✉ 665 W. Jefferson Blvd., ☎ 213/749–5123), which was built in 1926 by the Al Malaikah Temple. Touring companies from all over the world, along with assorted gospel and choral groups, appear in this one-of-a-kind, 6,200-seat theater, as do higher-profile televised awards shows such as the American Music Awards and the Grammys.

The Los Angeles Opera Theatre and a broad spectrum of other musical performers comes to the Spanish-style **Wilshire Ebell Theater** (✉ 4401 W. 8th St., ☎ 323/939–1128), erected in 1924.

The **Wiltern Theater** (✉ 3790 Wilshire Blvd., ☎ 213/380–5005 or 213/388–1400), a green terra-cotta, art deco masterpiece, was constructed in 1930 and is listed in the National Register of Historic Places. A venue for the Los Angeles Opera Theater since 1985, the Wiltern now also schedules pop, rock, and dance performances.

Dance

High-caliber companies dance at various performance spaces around town. Check the *L.A. Weekly* free newspaper under "Dance" to see who is dancing where, or call the Arts Line (☎ 213/688–2787).

Bella Lewitsky Dance Co. (☎ 213/580–6338), one of L.A.'s major resident companies, schedules modern dance performances at various locations.

Cal State L.A.'s Dance Department (✉ 5151 State University Dr., ☎ 323/343–5124) presents several prominent dance events each year—including the Dance Fair in March and Dance Kaleidoscope in July—at their state-of-the-art Luckman Theater.

Shrine Auditorium (✉ 665 W. Jefferson Blvd., ☎ 213/749–5123) hosts touring dance companies, such as the Kirov, the Bolshoi, and the American Ballet Theater (ABT), at various times during the year.

UCLA Center for the Arts (✉ 405 N. Hilgard Ave., ☎ 310/825–2101) welcomes visiting companies, such as Martha Graham, Paul Taylor, and the Hubbard Street Dance Company.

Film

Spending two hours at a movie while visiting Los Angeles needn't mean taking time out from sightseeing. Some of the country's most historic and beautiful theaters are found here, hosting both first-run and revival films. Movie listings are advertised daily in the *Los Angeles Times* Calendar section. The price of admission to first-run movies is, as of this writing, $7.50. Bargain prices as low as $4 are common for the first showing of the day.

Art Houses

The 14-screen **Cineplex** (✉ Beverly Center, 8522 Beverly Blvd., 8th floor, ☎ 310/652–7760) shows foreign films as well as first-run features.

Laemmle Theater chain hosts the best of the latest foreign releases. See its *Los Angeles Times* Calendar ad for listings.

The multiscreen **Los Feliz Theater** (✉ 1822 N. Vermont Ave., Los Feliz, ☎ 323/664–2169) feels more like a neighborhood venue than a chain multiplex.

Melnitz Hall (✉ 405 Hilgard Ave., ☎ 310/825–2345) is UCLA's main film theater; here you'll find the old, the avant-garde, and the neglected.

Film festivals, Hollywood classics, documentaries, and notable foreign films are the fare at the **New Beverly Cinema** (✉ 7165 Beverly Blvd., ☎ 323/938–4038), where there's always a double bill.

Nuart (✉ 11272 Santa Monica Blvd., West L.A., ☎ 310/478–6379) is the best-kept of L.A.'s revival houses, with an excellent screen, good double bills, and special midnight shows.

The **American Cinematèque Independent Film Series** (✉ 6712 Hollywood Blvd., Hollywood, ☎ 323/466–3456) screens rare vintage and current independent films in the atmospheric Egyptian Theater.

New films by independent filmmakers and foreign films are the usual fare at the **Royal Theatre** (✉ 11523 Santa Monica Blvd., Santa Monica, ☎ 310/478–1041).

Rare 16mm film noir clips are screened from Thursday through Sunday at **Tales** (✉ 667 S. La Brea Ave., Mid-Wilshire, ☎ 323/933–2640), an unusual espresso bar and bookstore that's a must for old-movie buffs.

Movie Palaces

Mann's Chinese Theater (✉ 6925 Hollywood Blvd., Hollywood, ☎ 323/464–8111) is perhaps the world's best-known theater, with three movie screens and many gala premieres.

The futuristic, geodesic **Pacific Cinerama Dome** (✉ 6360 Sunset Blvd., Hollywood, ☎ 323/466–3401) was the first theater designed specifically for Cinerama in the United States. The gigantic screen and multitrack sound system create an unparalleled cinematic experience.

Across the street from Mann's Chinese Theater is **Pacific's El Capitan** (✉ 6838 Hollywood Blvd., Hollywood, ☎ 323/467–7674), another classic, art deco masterpiece. First-run movies are on the bill, as are Disney animation debuts.

At the intersection of Hollywood and Sunset boulevards, the 70-year-old **Vista Theater** (✉ 4473 Sunset Dr., Los Feliz, ☎ 323/660–6639) was once Bard's Hollywood Theater, where both moving pictures and vaudeville played. A Spanish-style facade leads to an ornate Egyptian interior.

Television

Audiences Unlimited (✉ 100 Universal City Plaza, Bldg. 153, Universal City, 91608, ☎ 818/506–0043) helps fill seats for television programs (and sometimes theater events, as well). There's no charge, but tickets are distributed on a first-come, first-served basis. Shows that may be taping or filming include *Suddenly Susan, Caroline in the City, Cybil, Third Rock from the Sun,* and *The Drew Carey Show.* Tickets can be picked up at Fox Television Center (✉ 5746 Sunset Blvd., Van Ness Ave. entrance), which is open weekdays from 8:30 to 6. Note: You must be 16 or older to attend a television taping. For a schedule, send a self-addressed, stamped envelope to Audiences Unlimited a few weeks prior to your visit.

Theater

Los Angeles isn't quite the "Broadway of the West" as some have claimed—the scope of theater here doesn't compare to that in New York. Still, the theater scene's growth has been astounding. In 1978 only about 370 professional productions were brought to stages in Los Angeles; now well over 1,000 are scheduled each year. Small theaters are blossoming all over town, and the larger houses, despite price hikes to as much as $60 for a single ticket, are usually full.

Even small productions might boast big names from "the Business" (the Los Angeles entertainment empire). Many film and television actors like to work on the stage between "big" projects or while on hiatus from a TV series as a way to refresh their talents or regenerate their creativity. Doing theater is also an excellent way to be seen by those who matter in the glitzier end of showbiz. Hence there is a need for both large houses—which usually mount road-company productions of Broadway hits or, on occasion, Broadway-bound material—and a host of small, intimate theaters to showcase the talent that abounds in this city.

L. A. Parent, the free monthly tabloid-size magazine, is a great guide for up-to-date theater productions for children (as well as kid-oriented concerts and movies); all listings of performances include a mention of the appropriate ages.

Major Theaters

Jason Robards and Nick Nolte got their starts at **Geffen Playhouse** (⊠ 10886 Le Conte Ave., Westwood, ☎ 310/208–6500 or 310/208–5454), an acoustically superior, 498-seat theater that showcases new plays in the summer—primarily musicals and comedies. Many of the productions here are on their way to or from Broadway.

James A. Doolittle Theatre (⊠ 1615 N. Vine St., Hollywood, ☎ 323/462–6666; 213/365–3500 Ticketmaster), in the heart of Hollywood, has an intimate feeling despite its 1,038-seat capacity. New plays, dramas, comedies, and musicals are presented year-round.

In addition to theater performances, lectures, and children's programs, free summer jazz, dance, and cabaret concerts take place at the **John Anson Ford Amphitheater** (⊠ 2580 Cahuenga Blvd. E, Hollywood, ☎ 323/461–3673), a 1,300-seat outdoor venue in the Hollywood Hills.

There are three theaters in the big downtown complex known as **Music Center** (⊠ 135 N. Grand Ave., ☎ 213/972–7211): The **Ahmanson Theatre** presents both classics and new plays; the 3,200-seat **Dorothy Chandler Pavilion** (☞ *above*) shows a smattering of plays in between performances of the L.A. Philharmonic, L.A. Master Chorale, and L.A. Opera; and the 760-seat **Mark Taper Forum** (☎ 213/972–7353), under the direction of Gordon Davidson, presents new works that often go on to Broadway, such as *Angels in America* and *Master Class.*

Once the home of the Academy Awards telecast and Hollywood premieres, **Pantages** (⊠ 6233 Hollywood Blvd., Hollywood, ☎ 323/468–1700; 213/365–3500 Ticketmaster) is a massive (2,600-seat) but splendid example of high-style Hollywood art deco, although the acoustics could use some updating. Large-scale Broadway musicals are usually presented here.

The 1,900-seat, art deco **Wilshire Theater** (⊠ 8440 Wilshire Blvd., Beverly Hills, ☎ 323/468–1716 or 323/468–1799; 213/365–3500 Ticketmaster) presents Broadway musicals.

Smaller Theaters

The founders of **Actor's Gang Theater** (⊠ 6209 Santa Monica Blvd., Hollywood, ☎ 213/465–0566) include film star Tim Robbins; the fare runs the gamut from Molière to Eric Bogosian to international works by traveling companies.

Bob Baker Marionette Theater has been a staple on the youth scene in Los Angeles since 1963. Kids sit on a carpeted floor and get a close-up view of the intricate marionettes; ice cream and juice are served after the shows. Shows take place Tuesday through Friday at 10:30 AM, and weekends at 2:30. Reservations are required. ⊠ *1345 W. 1st St., at Glendale Blvd., downtown,* ☎ *213/250–9995.* ⊠ *$10.* ☉ *Tues.–Fri. at 10:30, weekends at 2:30.*

Musicals, revivals, and avant-garde improv pieces are performed at the **Cast Theater** (⊠ 804 N. El Centro, Hollywood, ☎ 323/462–0265).

Excellent original musicals and new dramas are the specialties at the 99-seat **Coast Playhouse** (⊠ 8325 Santa Monica Blvd., West Hollywood, ☎ 323/650–8507).

Marian Mercer and Rob Reiner both got their starts at the **Fountain Theater** (⊠ 5060 Fountain Ave., Hollywood, ☎ 323/663–1525), an

BONUS MILES MAKE GREAT SOUVENIRS.

Calling Card

MCI ★

123 456 7891 2345
J.D. SMITH

WorldPhone®

Earn Miles With Your MCI Card.

Take the MCI Card along on this trip and start earning miles for the next one. You'll earn frequent flyer miles on all your calls and save with the low rates you've come to expect from MCI. Before you know it, you'll be on your way to some other international destination.

Sign up for MCI by calling 1-800-FLY-FREE

Is this a great time, or what? :-)

MCI ★

Earn Frequent Flyer Miles.

AmericanAirlines®
AAdvantage®

Continental Airlines
OnePass.

▲**Delta Air Lines**
SkyMiles®

HAWAIIAN
A I R L I N E S

MIDWEST EXPRESS AIRLINES

NORTHWEST
A I R L I N E S
WORLDPERKS®

Rapid Rewards™
SOUTHWEST AIRLINES®

☞ **MILEAGE PLUS.**
United Airlines

US AIRWAYS
DIVIDEND MILES

You've read the book. Now book the trip.

For all the best deals on flights, hotels, rental cars, and vacation packages, book them online at www.previewtravel.com. Then click on our Destination Guides featuring content from Fodor's and more. You'll find hotels, restaurants, attractions, and things to do around the globe. There are even interactive maps, videos, and weather forecasts. You'll have everything you need to make your vacation exactly what you want it to be. All it takes is a trip online.

Travel on Your Terms™
www.previewtravel.com
aol keyword: previewtravel

preview travel℠

80-seat venue for original American dramas and flamenco dance concerts.

At the Japan Cultural Arts Center, the community-oriented **Japan America Theater** (✉ 244 S. San Pedro St., downtown, ☎ 213/680–3700) hosts local theater groups, dance troupes, and the L.A. Chamber Orchestra, plus numerous children's theater groups; it has 880 seats.

Laguna Playhouse's Youth Theater has children's productions such as *The Velveteen Rabbit* and *The Adventures of Stuart Little*. ✉ 606 Laguna Canyon Rd., Laguna Beach, ☎ 714/494–0743.

The **Morgan-Wixon Theatre** presents varied children's fare such as Imagination Station's fractured fairy tale, *Rumpelstiltskin*. Tickets generally cost between $5 and $7. Hours vary, so call ahead. ✉ 2627 Pico Blvd., Santa Monica, ☎ 310/828–7519.

The **Orange County Performing Arts Center** (✉ 600 Town Center Dr., east of Bristol St., Costa Mesa, ☎ 714/556–2787) stages a series of children's plays.

The 99-seat **Santa Monica Playhouse** (✉ 1211 4th St., Santa Monica, ☎ 310/394–9779) is worth visiting for its cozy, librarylike atmosphere, as well as its high-quality comedies, dramas, and children's programs such as *Alice and the Wonderful Tea Party, Cinderella*.

At **Serendipity,** performers from the Actors' Company read children's stories and fairy tales such as *Treasure Island* and *Peter Pan*, encouraging the audience to supply sound effects and giggles. Shows take place Saturday at 1 and Sunday at 1 and 4. ✉ Burbank Little Theatre, 1100 W. Clark Ave., Burbank, ☎ 818/557–0505.

For original children's plays and musical theater (for kids ages 3–8), try the **Storybook Theater.** Past performances have included *The Emperor's New Clothes* and *Sleeping Beauty*. There are plays every Saturday at 1. ✉ 3333 Cahuenga Blvd. W, Hollywood, ☎ 818/761–2203.

Many highly inventive productions have been hosted in the 99-seat **Skylight Theater** (✉ 1816½ N. Vermont Ave., Los Feliz, ☎ 323/666–2202).

Angelenos crowd into the 70-seat **Theatre/Theater** (✉ 1715 Cahuenga Blvd., Hollywood, ☎ 323 /871–0210) to view original works by local authors and international playwrights.

NIGHTLIFE

Despite the high energy level of the L.A. nightlife crowd, don't expect to be partying until dawn—this is still an early-to-bed city. Liquor laws require that bars stop serving alcohol at 2 AM, and it's safe to say that by this time, with the exception of a few after-hours venues and coffeehouses, most jazz, rock, and disco clubs have closed for the night.

Nighttime diversions on the Sunset Strip run the gamut from comedy clubs and hard-rock clubs to cocktail lounges and restaurants with piano bars. There's a good mix of nightlife in the Mid-Wilshire area, which encompasses the area west of the Harbor Freeway (I–110), east of La Cienega Boulevard, south of Beverly Boulevard, and north of the Santa Monica (I–10) Freeway. Local beer bars abound in Westwood, home of UCLA. Downtown Los Angeles has a small contingent of artsy performance spaces and galleries, and a handful of clubs and movie palaces. Some of Los Angeles's best jazz clubs, discos, and comedy clubs are scattered throughout the San Fernando and San Gabriel valleys. In West Hollywood, Santa Monica Boulevard is the heart of the gay-and-lesbian club and coffeehouse scene.

Bars

Despite its well-publicized penchant for hedonism, Los Angeles, unlike New York, Chicago, and San Francisco, is not a saloon town. The practiced art of pub-crawling has never flourished here, mainly because the city has few real neighborhoods and plenty of freeways. Traditionally, unlike New Yorkers, Angelenos rarely pledge loyalty to any libational hangout; they're too nomadic. However, you'll still find hundreds of cozy bars, lively pubs, and festive watering holes to quench your thirst.

Bars in South Bay's beach-adjacent neighborhoods are typically surf-themed or sports-themed affairs that tend to attract a young crowd. Rugby shirts, surfware, and cutoffs are commonplace, as are Dockers and other clothing of professionals at play. This ultracasual atmosphere is less true of Venice, which has an artsy reputation to maintain, and of upscale Santa Monica.

In West Hollywood and Hollywood environs, the attire is even more relaxed: young directors in jogging suits, out-of-work actors in jeans. Here bars buzz with the intoxicating talk of "deals," as in "three-picture deals," "development deals," "album deals." Pasadena, once a nightlife backwater, has livened up, revamping its historic Old Town into an attractive destination day or night. The attire here is still preppy and traditional: button-down shirts, rep ties, blue blazers. Although a few artsy hangouts have sprung up in downtown L.A., the bars in this area are generally a bastion for bankers, brokers, and other business folk; two- and three-piece suits are de rigueur.

Coastal and Western Los Angeles

HERMOSA BEACH

The Irish-themed **Hennessey's Tavern** (⊠ 8 Pier Ave., ☎ 310/372–5759) has two bars, occasional live entertainment, and an outdoor rooftop deck where you and throngs of regulars can take in the ocean breezes.

MANHATTAN BEACH

An eclectic mix of surfers, business folks, and rugby-shirted beach rats frequents **Orville and Wilbur's** (⊠ 401 W. Rosecrans Ave., ☎ 310/545–6639). With its spectacular view of the Pacific, it's a great place to catch the sunset.

Tequila Willy's (⊠ 3290 Sepulveda Blvd., ☎ 310/545–4569) has backgammon boards and is attached to a southwestern-style restaurant.

MARINA DEL REY

Even locals often overlook the **Crystal Fountain Lounge** (⊠ Marina International Hotel, 4200 Admiralty Way, ☎ 310/301–2000), where jukebox music blasts late into the night.

Ex-cinematographer Burt Hixon collected tropical-drink recipes on his South Seas forays. Here, at **The Warehouse** (⊠ 4499 Admiralty Way, ☎ 310/823–5451), he whips up one of the most sinfully rich piña coladas this side of Samoa. The bar gets crowded, so arrive early.

SANTA MONICA

The big open bar at **Brennan's** (⊠ 4089 Lincoln Blvd., ☎ 310/821–6622) is a pleasant backdrop for easy conversation. Thursday-night turtle racing is a tradition here.

Chez Jay (⊠ 1657 Ocean Ave., ☎ 310/395–1741), a shack of a saloon near Santa Monica Pier, has endured for more than 30 years. Warren Beatty, Julie Christie, and former California governor Jerry Brown have all fueled up here.

Named for its 360-degree bar, **The Circle** (✉ 2926 Main St., ☎ 310/392–4898) is the Santa Monica dive to survive Main Street's trendy makeover.

Thick with nautical mementos, the tiny **Galley Steak House** (✉ 2442 Main St., ☎ 310/452–1934) is recommended for nostalgics who want to recapture Santa Monica circa 1940.

As the name implies, **Gotham Hall** (✉ 1431 3rd St. Promenade, ☎ 310/394–8865) is designed like something off the set of Batman. It has the only purple pool tables in town, which, by the way, nicely match the purple walls.

Carved wooden tribal masks and other Indian and Southeast Asian deities make **Monsoon** (✉ 1212 3rd St. Promenade, ☎ 310/576–9996) one of the most elegant spots on the always-jumping Third Street Promenade. The restaurant serves south Asian cuisine and there's usually live entertainment in the rear bar. There's a $10 minimum per person.

From motorcycles to carriages, something old has been glued or nailed to every square inch of **Oar House** (✉ 2941 Main St., ☎ 310/396–4725). Drinks are downright cheap, and it's also a popular place to dance.

At **Typhoon** (✉ 3221 Donald Douglas Loop S, ☎ 310/390–6565), a fun-filled bar right off the Santa Monica Airport runway, beware of the Typhoon Punch (triple sec, rums, and fruit juices)—it's so potent that the umbrella sticking out of the glass is blown inside-out.

Reeking of ale, **Ye Olde King's Head** (✉ 116 Santa Monica Blvd., ☎ 310/451–1402) is a gathering place for Brits eager to hear or dispense news from home.

VENICE

You can watch the cook make tortillas at **Casablanca** (✉ 220 Lincoln Blvd., ☎ 310/392–5751), a Mexican bar and grill.

Abstract art decorates the walls of **Hal's Bar & Grill** (✉ Abbott Kinney Blvd., ☎ 310/396–3105), a regular haunt of local well-to-do professionals.

There's a changing contemporary art show at **James Beach Cafe** (✉ 60 N. Venice Blvd., ☎ 310/823–5396), a gathering place for Westside yuppies.

The very upscale **Rebecca's** (✉ 2025 Pacific Ave., ☎ 310/306–6266) is worth checking out for the outrageous and playful Frank Gehry interior alone, not to mention the opportunity to rub elbows with the Venice Beach elite.

Beverly Hills and Century City

BEL-AIR AND BEVERLY HILLS

There's serene musical entertainment every night (either a pianist or a vocalist) at the romantically secluded **Hotel Bel-Air** (✉ 701 Stone Canyon Rd., Bel-Air, ☎ 310/472–1211).

A quaint bar with an immense wine selection, **La Scala** (✉ 410 N. Canon Dr., Beverly Hills, ☎ 310/275–0579) is honeycombed with celebrities nightly.

Behind the oak bar and brass rail at **R.J.'s** (✉ 252 N. Beverly Dr., Beverly Hills, ☎ 310/274–3474 or 310/274–7427) are 800 bottles stacked to the ceiling. Bend your elbow at the bar with a brace of new buddies during happy hour.

Plush sofas and high tables set the atmosphere at the elegant piano bar of the **Regent Beverly Wilshire** (⊠ 9500 Wilshire Blvd., Beverly Hills, ☎ 310/275–5200).

CENTURY CITY

Windows overlook a reflecting pool and garden in the Lobby Court of the **Century Plaza Hotel and Tower** (⊠ 2025 Ave. of the Stars, ☎ 310/277–2000). Nightly piano music completes the elegant ambience.

Harper's Bar and Grill (⊠ 2040 Ave. of the Stars, ☎ 310/553–1855) is a central place to meet friends for cocktails before a show at the Shubert Theater. The drinks here are generous.

A reasonably authentic version of the famed Florentine bar and grill that Hemingway and other Lost Generation scribblers frequented, **Harry's Bar and American Grill** (⊠ ABC Entertainment Center, 2020 Ave. of the Stars, ☎ 310/277–2333) is unrivaled in L.A. for its potent cappuccino.

Downtown

Downtown's loft-dwelling elite frequent **Boyd Street** (⊠ 410 Boyd St., ☎ 213/617–2491), a downtown bar-restaurant with a streamlined '80s motif.

Stockbrokers favor **Engine Co. #28** (⊠ 644 S. Figueroa St., ☎ 213/624–6996), a bar and restaurant with dark mahogany accents and high-back booths.

In the Biltmore Hotel, the sleek **Grand Avenue Sports Bar** (⊠ 506 S. Grand Ave., ☎ 213/612–1595) serves pricey drinks late into the night.

Little Joe's (⊠ 900 N. Broadway, ☎ 213/489–4900) is a must for sports buffs: Prices are low and the big-screen TV is always tuned to the hottest game. W. C. Fields frequented the bar in the '30s.

Reporters from the *Los Angeles Times* and United Press International pack the gaudy, gabby **Redwood Second Street Saloon** (⊠ 316 W. 2nd St., ☎ 213/617–2867) after 5 PM to trade postmortems of the day's stories or to drink their dinner if they're working nightside.

In warmer months, TGIF celebrants gather at the portable outdoor bars of **Stepps** (⊠ Wells Fargo Ct., 330 S. Hope St., ☎ 213/626–0900), a major business-crowd hangout.

Atop the 32-story Transamerica Building, **The Tower** (⊠ 1150 S. Olive St., ☎ 213/746–1554) is an elegant cocktail bar and restaurant with an unbeatable view.

In the Lobby Court of the **Westin Bonaventure Hotel** (⊠ 5th and Figueroa Sts., ☎ 213/624–1000), nightly music ranges from popular favorites at the piano bar to jazz-oriented musical entertainers.

Hollywood, Los Feliz, and Silver Lake

HOLLYWOOD

For a pick-me-up margarita, stop by the kitschy **El Coyote** (⊠ 7312 Beverly Blvd., ☎ 323/939–7766) restaurant-bar and get a glass of the best—and cheapest—in town.

The old Hollywood restaurant and watering hole known as **Formosa** (⊠ 7156 Santa Monica Blvd., West Hollywood, ☎ 323/850–9050) was featured in the Oscar-nominated film *L.A. Confidential,* though it's long been a favorite of both hipsters and old-timers. It's shaped like an old railroad car with plenty of booths, and lined with pictures of just about every celebrity who ever crossed the silver screen.

A rowdy pool crowd plays billiards at the **Hollywood Athletic Club** (✉ 6525 Sunset Blvd., ☎ 323/962–6600), which doubles as a dance club on Friday and Saturday nights.

Adjacent to the venerable Canter's Restaurant in the predominantly Jewish Fairfax District, the **Kibitz Room** (✉ 419 N. Fairfax Ave., ☎ 323/651–2030) is an of-the-moment gathering place with live music most nights.

Don't be fooled by the seedy, minimall location of **Lava Lounge** (✉ 1533 N. La Brea Ave., ☎ 323/876–6612): Inside you'll find groovy, neo-tiki decor (bamboo and faux-lava walls) and wall-to-wall scenesters dressed as if they stepped out of a fashion magazine. Weeknights there's live music. Occasionally there's a nominal cover.

Film-studio moguls and movie extras flock to **Musso and Franks** (✉ 6667 Hollywood Blvd., ☎ 323/467–5123), where the Rob Roys are just as smooth and the clientele just as eclectic as ever. If the restaurant is too packed, or if you're there alone, you'll be encouraged to dine at the New York–style bar.

The unmarked, nondescript exterior of **3 Of Clubs** (✉ 1123 N. Vine St., ☎ 323/462–1123) hardly prepares you for the plush environment within. This dressy bar is a prime location to scout out L.A.'s young and restless.

On the top floor of the giant Holiday Inn, **Windows on Hollywood** (✉ 1755 N. Highland Ave., ☎ 323/462–7181) spins even if you don't drink too much. The view is, as expected, spectacular, so try to get here as the sun sinks in the West.

A lovely L.A. tradition is to meet at **Yamashiro's** (✉ 1999 N. Sycamore Ave., ☎ 323/466–5125) for cocktails at sunset on the terrace, where a spectacular hilltop view spreads out before you.

LOS FELIZ AND SILVER LAKE

The **Cobalt Cantina** (✉ 4326 Sunset Blvd., Silver Lake, ☎ 323/953–9991), a bar and trendy Tex-Mex restaurant, attracts a mix of daytime business and "biz" folk who take advantage of its proximity to PBS and to ABC's Prospect Studios. At night it draws a mostly gay crowd. The signature drink is a cobalt blue margarita made with blue Curaçao.

An unassuming '40s-style bar that's been rediscovered by a happening '90s crowd, **Dresden Room** (✉ 1760 N. Vermont Ave., Los Feliz, ☎ 323/665–4294) started the whole lounge revival. These days, gold lamé–clad lounge goers flock here to croon along with Marty and Elayne, who perform here nightly (except Sunday) from 9 PM to 1:30 AM. Teenage idol Leonardo DiCaprio has been known to hang out here (he grew up nearby).

The Chinese motif (complete with paper lanterns) at the trendy **Good Luck Bar** (✉ 1514 Hillhurst Ave., Los Feliz, ☎ 323/666–3524) makes you feel as if you just stepped onto the set of a Hong Kong action movie. Be sure to check out the vintage jukebox.

Locals gobble bratwurst and knock back steins at **Lowenbrau Keller** (✉ 3211 Beverly Blvd., Silver Lake, ☎ 213/382–5723)—a bit of Bavaria gone Hollywood. A grand piano accompanies the requisite German drinking songs.

Tiki Ti (✉ 4427 W. Sunset Blvd., Silver Lake, ☎ 323/669–9381), a small cocktail lounge, serves some of the city's best tropical rum drinks in a simulated Tahitian hut. Look out for singles on the make.

Mid-Wilshire Area

Both après-work business types and Gen-Xers frequent **HMS Bounty** (⊠ 3357 Wilshire Blvd., ☎ 213/385–7275), an elegant old watering hole in the historic Gaylord apartment building. Be sure to check out the brass plates above each booth that bear the names of Hollywood heavies who once held court here.

Molly Malone's (⊠ 575 S. Fairfax Ave., ☎ 323/935–1577) is a small, cozy pub with Irish rock and traditional Gaelic music. Harp is the beer of choice.

One of L.A.'s most frequented Irish pubs, **Tom Bergin's** (⊠ 840 S. Fairfax Ave., ☎ 323/936–7151) is plastered with Day-Glo shamrocks bearing the names of the masses of regular patrons who have passed through its door.

Pasadena

Beckham Place (⊠ 77 W. Walnut St., ☎ 626/796–3399), a rather fancy "Olde English" pub, is known for its huge drinks, free roast-beef sandwiches at Happy Hour, and wing chairs placed near a roaring fire.

In Pasadena's Lake District, **Chronicle** (⊠ 897 Granite Dr., ☎ 626/792–1179) is a restaurant-bar with the feel of a turn-of-the-century mansion. Friendly bartenders pour generous drinks.

With two pool tables, a nautical motif, and very reasonable prices, **The Colorado Bar** (⊠ 2640 E. Colorado Blvd., ☎ 626/449–3485) is a divey refuge for art students, Gen-Xers, and aging barflies who are put off by the glitz of Old Town. Shooters are $1.50 and $2 nightly.

Beer is the main attraction at the **Crown City Brewery** (⊠ 300 S. Raymond Ave., ☎ 626/577–5548), but many technophiles are drawn to the on-premises video machines.

At the kitschy, Polynesian-style **Islands** (⊠ 3533 Foothill Blvd., ☎ 626/351–6543), you can order soft tacos, burgers, or chicken sandwiches, and turn drink time into feast time.

John Bull (⊠ 958 S. Fair Oaks Ave., ☎ 626/441–4353) looks as if it came straight from London, even though its Pasadena location draws a more American crowd. English types do come to play pool, though.

In Pasadena's Old Town, **Market City Cafe** (⊠ 33 S. Fair Oaks Ave., ☎ 626/568–0203) draws a crowd at lunchtime and in the early evening.

A young collegiate crowd frequents **Q's** (⊠ 99 E. Colorado Blvd., ☎ 626/405–9777), an upscale bar and pool hall in the middle of Old Town.

With brass fixtures, an oversize fireplace, and a marble-topped bar, the **Ritz-Carlton Huntington Hotel** (⊠ 1401 S. Oak Knoll Ave., ☎ 626/568–3900) is a genteel setting for nighttime drinks.

On the lower level of the Pasadena Hilton, **Sports Edition** (⊠ 150 S. Los Robles Ave., ☎ 626/577–1000) is action-central, with nine TVs, marble tables, and wooden floors.

San Fernando Valley

Commuters traversing the Ventura Freeway often stop to dine and drink in the San Fernando Valley, with its potpourri of French, Italian, Asian, and trendy American bistros.

Residuals (⊠ 11042 Ventura Blvd., Studio City, ☎ 818/761–8301) is so named because actors who present a residual check for less than a dollar can trade it for a free drink here. Naturally, the place is full of struggling thespians and wanna-bes—how very L.A.

The **Smoke House** (✉ 4420 Lakeside Dr., Burbank, ☎ 818/845–3731) has a restaurant and a lounge room with assorted entertainment.

The lounge at **Sportsmen's Lodge** (✉ 12833 Ventura Blvd., Sherman Oaks, ☎ 818/984–0202) has a tranquil setting with brooks and swan-filled ponds.

Sagebrush Cantina (✉ 23527 Calabasas Rd., Calabasas, ☎ 818/222–6062), an indoor-outdoor saloon next to a Mexican restaurant, is the Valley's version of the Via Veneto café scene. Motorcycle hippies mix comfortably with computer moguls and showbiz folk, including a platoon of stunt people. There's classic rock entertainment on weekends.

West Hollywood

A mahogany bar and art nouveau mirrors make **Barefoot** (✉ 8722 W. 3rd St., ☎ 310/276–6223) a swanky place to drink expertly mixed martinis served here.

Dan Tana's (✉ 9071 Santa Monica Blvd., ☎ 310/275–9444) is mainly a restaurant, but the busy bar is a favorite late-night haunt.

A hetero bastion in an ultragay neighborhood, **J. Sloane's** (✉ 8623 Melrose Ave., ☎ 310/659–0250) is a sawdust-on-the-floor, football-on-the-tube (although there's a pretty ample dance floor), frat house kind-of-place.

The circular bar at **Le Dôme** (✉ 8720 W. Sunset Blvd., ☎ 310/659–6919) draws the likes of Rod Stewart and Richard Gere. The best time to visit is after 11 PM, when this upmarket hangout really starts to jump.

Patrons (many celebrities) must either have a Mondrian room key, screen credit, or a model's body to enter **Sky Bar** (✉ 8440 Sunset Blvd., ☎ 323/650–8999), the poolside bar at the Hotel Mondrian. The view is as phenomenal as the clientele.

The bar at the **Sunset Marquis** (✉ 1200 N. Alta Loma Rd., ☎ 310/657–1333) is a convenient watering hole for many visiting celebs (and their entourages). This is the perfect place to catch a glimpse of your favorite Alternative idols.

Westside

Westwood is the front door to UCLA and a popular hangout for kids of all ages. Both it and the neighborhoods around it—Brentwood and West L.A.—have some outstanding bars.

There's a good assortment of Mexican beers at **Acapulco** (✉ 1109 Glendon Ave., Westwood, ☎ 310/208–3884), a convivial Mexican restaurant and bar that's big with the college crowd.

"Cocktail Nation" has finally arrived on the Westside. **Liquid Kitty,** (✉ 11780 W. Pico Blvd., West L.A., ☎ 310/473–3707), with its hip clientele and cool (occasionally live) music, fills the bill. You can't miss this place: Just look for the neon martini glass on the outside.

Neighborhood brat-packers and yuppies gather at **Q's** (✉ 11835 Wilshire Blvd., Brentwood, ☎ 310/477–7550), an upscale pool hall with a dozen tables and a bar.

Old prints adorn the walls and friendly bartenders listen to your troubles at the friendly **San Francisco Saloon** (✉ 11501 W. Pico Blvd., West L.A., ☎ 310/478–0152).

Cabaret, Performance, and Variety

The Cinegrill (✉ Clarion Hotel Hollywood Roosevelt, 7000 Hollywood Blvd., Hollywood, ☎ 323/466–7000) is well worth a visit, if not to hear top-tier jazz performers, just to admire all the Hollywood artifacts lining the lobby of the Hollywood landmark hotel that houses the club.

Gardenia Club (✉ 7066 Santa Monica Blvd., Hollywood, ☎ 323/467–7444) is an elegant, East Coast–style cabaret with singers, comedy, and variety performances. The club is closed Sunday.

Glaxa Studios (✉ 3707 Sunset Blvd., Silver Lake, ☎ 323/663–5295) is a bohemian café-arts venue presenting music, poetry, and performance with an emphasis on the literate, the avant-garde, and the offbeat. Hours and cover (for shows only) vary; call for details.

Westside Bohemians come to **Highways** (✉ 1651 18th St., Santa Monica, ☎ 310/453–1755) to hear and see avant-garde spoken-word and performance artists. Reservations are recommended.

Locally famous drag queens strut their stuff at **Luna Park** (✉ 665 Robertson Blvd., West Hollywood, ☎ 310/652–0611), a self-described "club in progress" featuring an eclectic mix of music, with three stages and two bars.

At **Queen Mary** (✉ 12449 Ventura Blvd., Studio City, ☎ 818/506–5619), female impersonators vamp it up as Diana Ross, Barbra Streisand, and Bette Midler.

Casinos

Just 15 mi south of the Los Angeles Civic Center are six combination card rooms, restaurants, and cocktail lounges. These are not full gaming casinos, and there are no attached hotels. Limits on maximum bets differ: A card room, for example, can have no more than 35 tables. Typically a poker table has eight seats and a designated limit on bets. The minimum bet is $1 before the draw and $2 after the draw, with no limits on the number of raises. Some tables have a "house" dealer; the card room collects a fee from the players, ranging from $1 up to $24 an hour in the $100–$200 games.

Gardena card rooms are open 24 hours a day, and you can play as long as your cash and stamina hold out. Card rooms also have surprisingly good food in their reasonably priced restaurants—but don't expect to have drinks at your table: Law requires that the bars be in separate buildings.

L.A.'s premier racetrack **Hollywood Park Casino** (✉ 3883 W. Century Blvd., Inglewood, ☎ 310/330–2800) has a restaurant and a 24-hour casino. On the "American" side, you can play seven-card stud, hold 'em, Omaha, Texas hold 'em, and lowball. On the "Asian" side, there's Pai Gow poker, Super Pan 9, and California blackjack.

At **Normandie Casino** (✉ 1045 W. Rosecrans Ave., Gardena, ☎ 310/515–1466) you can play seven-card stud, blackjack, Texas hold 'em, and Pai Gow poker. (For the uninitiated, staffers offer free lessons.) There's also Las Vegas–style entertainment with headliners like Freddie Fender. There's a coffee shop on premises.

Coffeehouses

Amidst the murals and neon of downtown's artsy loft district, **Bloom's General Store** (✉ 714 3rd St., downtown, ☎ 213/687–6571) sells cigars, candy, and videos, and is also connected to a soul-food restaurant and art gallery. The couches in the rear make this a community hangout–type place.

Half tiki, half sci-fi, with hand-painted tabletops, the tiny **Cacao** (✉ 11609 Santa Monica Blvd., West L.A., ☎ 310/473–7283) is an aesthetic gem.

At **Cyber Java** (✉ 1029 Abbott Kinney Blvd., Venice, ☎ 310/581–1300) you can log onto the Internet while enjoying coffee and snacks. There's also a cozy patio with a tiny sculpture garden.

Valley poets, artists, and hipsters hang out at **Eagle's** (✉ 5231 Lankershim Blvd., North Hollywood, ☎ 818/760–4212), a laid-back café with occasional live music and spoken-word readings.

Galaxy Gallery (✉ 7224 Melrose Ave., Hollywood, ☎ 323/938–6500) is an "exotic pipe" (read: head) shop, café, art gallery, cigar bar, and smoke shop with occasional live music. Only in L.A.!

With a trippy, sci-fi Tolkienesque motif, **Nova Express Cafe** (✉ 426 N. Fairfax Ave., Hollywood, ☎ 323/658–7533) serves coffee, tea, and other snacks into the wee hours.

Local bohemians idle away countless hours drinking lattes and cappuccinos at Formica tables at **Onyx/Sequel Coffeehouse/Gallery** (✉ 1802 N. Vermont Ave., Los Feliz, ☎ no phone), L.A.'s oldest extant coffeehouse. It's open until 3 AM.

Comedy and Magic

The beachfront **Comedy and Magic Club** (✉ 1018 Hermosa Ave., Hermosa Beach, ☎ 310/372–1193) features many magicians and comedians seen on TV and in Las Vegas: The Unknown Comic, Elayne Boosler, Pat Paulsen, Jay Leno, and Harry Anderson have all played here. Reservations are recommended.

Los Angeles's premier comedy showcase, **Comedy Store** (✉ 8433 Sunset Blvd., West Hollywood, ☎ 323/656–6225) has been going strong for more than a decade. Famous comedians occasionally make unannounced appearances.

Groundlings Theatre (✉ 7307 Melrose Ave., Hollywood, ☎ 323/934–9700) is considered a breeding ground for Saturday Night Live performers, with original skits, music, and improv. Shows take place from Thursday through Sunday.

Three-act shows at **Ice House Comedy Club and Restaurant** (✉ 24 N. Mentor Ave., Pasadena, ☎ 626/577–1894) feature comedians, celebrity impressionists, ventriloquists, and magicians from Las Vegas, as well as from television shows. Shows take place from Wednesday through Sunday.

Liza Minnelli and Richard Pryor got their starts at **The Improvisation** (✉ 8162 Melrose Ave., West Hollywood, ☎ 323/651–2583), a transplanted New York establishment showcasing comedians and some vocalists. You can dine in Hell's Kitchen, inside the Improv. Reservations are recommended for shows.

The two-room **La Cabaret** (✉ 17271 Ventura Blvd., Encino, ☎ 818/501–3737) features karaoke as well as comedy acts, with famous entertainers often making surprise appearances. Light fare is served.

Look for comedy acts and improvisation seven days a week at **Laugh Factory** (✉ 8001 Sunset Blvd., West Hollywood, ☎ 323/656–8860).

Country Music

Learn the two-step or the West Coast swing at **In Cahoots** (⊠ 223 N. Glendale Ave., Glendale, ☎ 818/500–1665), a raucous dance hall à la Nashville. Dance lessons are given twice each night, and there's live music all week long.

Dance Clubs

Though the clubs listed below are predominantly dance clubs as opposed to live music venues, there is quite a lot of overlap. Many places have live music on some nights and dancing on others. In fact, many of the major clubs in Los Angeles are taken over by a different promoter each night of the week and, depending on which night you go, you might find anything from swing to techno to goth.

Merv Griffin's modern-day version of the famed Coconut Grove at the Ambassador Hotel, the **Coconut Club** (⊠ Beverly Hilton, 9876 Wilshire Blvd., ☎ 310/274–7777) has big-band music, on-the-air DJs, and a classic supper-club menu. The club takes over the Grand Ballroom of the Beverly Hilton Hotel on Friday and Saturday nights.

If you're nostalgic for the 1960s, stop by the happening **Crush Bar** (⊠ 1743 Cahuenga Ave., Hollywood, ☎ 323/463–9017), open Friday and Saturday evenings.

Florentine Gardens (⊠ 5951 Hollywood Blvd., Hollywood, ☎ 323/464–0706) is one of Los Angeles's largest dance areas, with spectacular lighting and lots of Latin-fusion. It's open Friday, Saturday, and Sunday.

Big on the swing era, the high-energy **Moonlight Tango Cafe** (⊠ 13730 Ventura Blvd., Sherman Oaks, ☎ 818/788–2000) gets moving in the wee hours, when a conga line inevitably takes shape on the dance floor.

Probe (⊠ 836 N. Highland Ave., Hollywood, ☎ 323/461–8301) has an evening dedicated to a variety of tastes and clientele including gay, goth, industrial, and retro.

Every night of the week, a different promoter takes over **The World** (⊠ 7070 Hollywood Blvd., Hollywood, ☎ 323/467–7070), a large, extremely popular dance venue on the ground floor of a Hollywood office building. You might find anything from house and hip-hop to trance and techno, plus occasional live music. Cover charges vary.

Gay and Lesbian Clubs

Gays and straights mingle easily at **Akbar** (⊠ 4356 Sunset Blvd., Silver Lake, ☎ 323/665–6810), a dark, cozy watering hole with one of the best jukeboxes in town. Local Silver Lake bands get top billing.

Axis (⊠ 652 N. La Peer Dr., West Hollywood, ☎ 310/659–0471) and **Love Lounge** (⊠ 657 N. Robertson Blvd., West Hollywood, ☎ 310/659–0472) share one site but have different entrances and schedule different events. Some nights are for lesbians and some are for gay men, and there are frequent theme parties. The music runs the gamut: new wave, hi-NRG, tribal, rock, and Latin house. Both clubs are open Wednesday through Saturday; Love Lounge also opens its doors for Tuesday-night drag shows.

An ethnically mixed gay and straight crowd flocks to **Circus Disco and Arena** (⊠ 6655 Santa Monica Blvd., Hollywood, ☎ 323/462–1291), two huge side-by-side discos with techno and rock music, as well as a full bar and patio.

With live music and drag shows, **Club 7969** (⊠ 7969 Santa Monica Blvd., West Hollywood, ☎ 323/654–0280) caters to gay, lesbian, and mixed crowds depending on the night. There's a large dance floor and a super sound system.

L.A.'s more glamorous lesbians show up for parties sponsored by **Girl Bar** (☎ 323/460–2531); call the information line for locations. In recent years, Girl Bar has been held on Friday at Axis and on Saturday at the Love Lounge (☞ *above*). Occasional parties are held at West Hollywood hotels such as the Mondrian.

Jewel's Catch One (⊠ 4067 W. Pico Blvd., Mid-Wilshire, ☎ 323/734–8849) attracts gays and straights, blacks and whites, and everyone in between. Its late hours—3 AM weeknights, 4 AM weekends—and its underground vibe make it a prime destination for the serious dance fanatic. The neighborhood can be dicey.

A friendly, publike lesbian bar with a pool table, **The Palms** (⊠ 8572 Santa Monica Blvd., West Hollywood, ☎ 310/652–6188) has DJ dancing six nights a week and live bands on Sunday. One-dollar drinks draw a crowd Wednesday nights, and Sunday's beer bust is a lively affair.

Rage (⊠ 8911 Santa Monica Blvd., West Hollywood, ☎ 310/652–7055) is a longtime favorite of the "gym boy" set. There's also a video lounge.

Jazz

The eclectic entertainment at the **Atlas Bar & Grill** (⊠ 3760 Wilshire Blvd., Mid-Wilshire, ☎ 213/380–8400) includes torch singers as well as a jazz band. The snazzy supper club is inside the historic Wiltern building.

Crowds squeeze in like sardines to hear powerhouse jazz and blues at the tiny **Baked Potato** (⊠ 3787 Cahuenga Blvd. W, North Hollywood, ☎ 818/980–1615). The featured item on the menu is, of course, the baked potato: They're jumbo and stuffed with everything from steak to vegetables.

Birds of Paradise (⊠ 1800 E. Broadway, Long Beach, ☎ 562/590–8773) is a casual art-deco lounge with contemporary jazz and popular happy hours.

Big-name acts and innovators such as Latin-influenced saxophonist Paquito D. Rivera have played at **Catalina Bar and Grill** (⊠ 1640 N. Cahuenga Blvd., Hollywood, ☎ 323/466–2210), a top Hollywood jazz spot. Continental cuisine is served.

You can hear exceptional jazz performers at **Club Brasserie** (⊠ Wyndham Bel Age Hotel, 1020 N. San Vicente Blvd., West Hollywood, ☎ 213/854–1111) from Thursday through Saturday. Impressionist paintings on the wall compete with the expansive city view. Best of all, there's no cover.

In the Crenshaw District's Leimert Park arts enclave, **Fifth Street Dick's Coffee Company** (⊠ 3347½ W. 43rd Pl., Crenshaw District, ☎ 323/296–3970) is a great spot for coffee and traditional jazz. The upstairs performance space has hosted such jazz legends as Billy Higgins and Ronald Muldrow.

Jax (⊠ 339 N. Brand Blvd., Glendale, ☎ 818/500–1604) is an intimate club with a wide variety of food, from ribs to pasta; live music is an added draw.

Come to **Jazz Bakery** (✉ 3221 Hutchison, Culver City, ☎ 310/271–9039), inside the former Helms Bakery, for coffee, desserts, and a nice selection of world-class jazz. Every night and Sunday afternoon, Jim Britt opens his photography studio; the $17–$20 admission (no credit cards) includes refreshments.

Owned by comedy star Marla Gibbs of *The Jeffersons* and *227,* **Marla's Memory Lane Supper Club** (✉ 2323 W. Martin Luther King Jr. Blvd., Crenshaw District, ☎ 323/294–8430) pops with blues, jazz, and easy listening. James Ingram plays here from time to time.

Live Music

In addition to the major music venues listed below, many smaller bars book live music too, sometimes on a nightly basis.

Alligator Lounge (✉ 3321 Pico Blvd., Santa Monica, ☎ 310/449–1844) books various musical acts and serves Cajun cuisine. It's open from Friday through Monday.

One of L.A.'s oldest rock dives, **Al's Bar** (✉ 305 S. Hewitt St., downtown, ☎ 213/625–9703) is still going strong.

The Key Club (✉ 9039 Sunset Blvd., West Hollywood, ☎ 310/786-1712) is a flashy, multitiered Sunset Strip rock club featuring current bands before 11PM and dancing with guest DJs afterward. A restaurant and ATM machine inside make it easy to stay for awhile.

Blue Saloon (✉ 4657 Lankershim Blvd., North Hollywood, ☎ 818/766–4644) is the friendliest club around, with rock and roll, blues, country, and rockabilly. If your seat gets tired while listening to the music, rustle up a game of billiards or darts.

At **Coconut Teaszer** (✉ 8117 Sunset Blvd., West Hollywood, ☎ 323/654–4773) you can dance to live music—raw-rock at its best—for lively fun. The barbecue menu and killer drinks are promising. Another room below, The Crooked Bar, is a low-key sanctuary usually reserved for acoustic acts. Pool tables are always crowded.

L.A. scenesters put on the ritz at **The Derby** (✉ 4500 Los Feliz Blvd., Los Feliz, ☎ 323/663–8979), a spacious, elegant club with a 360-degree brass-railed bar and plush-velvet curtained booths. There's live music nightly—swing, jazz, surf, and rock.

Dark, cozy, mysterious—everything a rock-and-roll dive should be—**Dragonfly** (✉ 6510 Santa Monica Blvd., Hollywood, ☎ 323/466–6111) plays an edgy mix of live and dance music. When you need to cool off, there's an outdoor patio with bar.

The gloriously restored art deco **El Rey Theater** (✉ 5515 Wilshire Blvd., Mid-Wilshire, ☎ 323/936-4790) now showcases top name bands that have included Beck, Bob Dylan, and Willie Nelson. There are also occasional goth, hiphop and swing dance nights and evenings dedicated to local bands.

Chandeliers and hubcaps decorate **The Garage** (✉ 4519 Santa Monica Blvd., Silver Lake, ☎ 213/683-3447), a rock dive with some of the best in local and alternative bands.

At the longtime music industry hangout known as **Ghengis Cohen Cantina** (✉ 740 N. Fairfax Ave., Hollywood, ☎ 323/653–0640), you can hear up-and-coming talent in a refreshingly mellow format reminiscent of MTV's "Unplugged" performances. A plus is the restaurant's updated Chinese cuisine.

Dan Aykroyd and Jim Belushi own the **House of Blues** (✉ 8430 Sunset Blvd., West Hollywood, ☎ 323/650–1451), home to jazz, rock, and blues performers. Past players have included Etta James, Lou Rawls, Joe Cocker, The Young Dubliners, and the Commodores. Some shows are presented cabaret style, including dinner. Every Sunday there's a gospel brunch.

Jack's Sugar Shack (✉ 1707 N. Vine St., Hollywood, ☎ 323/466–7005) features big-name alternative rock, surf, blues, rockabilly, Cajun, and country performers in cartoony, Polynesian-style surroundings. You'll also find an ample selection of umbrella drinks and on-tap microbrews.

Rap music and reggae are served up along with fine Jamaican food at **Kingston 12** (✉ 814 Broadway, Santa Monica, ☎ 310/451–4423), open from Thursday through Sunday.

Vintage LPs hang from the ceiling at **The Mint** (✉ 6010 Pico Blvd., Mid-Wilshire, ☎ 323/954-9630), which features some of the best in blues, jazz, rockabilly and bluegrass. There's also a fine menu and a full bar.

McCabe's Guitar Shop (✉ 3101 Pico Blvd., Santa Monica, ☎ 310/828–4497; 310/828–4403 concert information) is retro-central: Arlo Guthrie sings here on occasion. Folk, acoustic rock, bluegrass, and soul concerts are featured on weekend nights, with coffee, herbal tea, apple juice, and homemade sweets served during intermission. Make reservations well in advance.

The "in" spot for the upwardly mobile, **The Palace** (✉ 1735 N. Vine St., Hollywood, ☎ 323/462–3000) is a multilevel art deco venue that speaks of postwar excess: lively entertainment, a fabulous sound system, laser lights, two dance floors, four bars, a comfortable balcony, and a full bar and dining room on the top-level patio. Patrons here dress to kill. Friday nights are packed.

The Roxy (✉ 9009 Sunset Blvd., West Hollywood, ☎ 310/276–2222) is a Sunset Strip fixture, featuring local and touring alternative, country, blues, and rockabilly bands.

The hottest bands of tomorrow perform at **Spaceland** (✉ 1717 Silver Lake Blvd., Silver Lake, ☎ 213/413–4442), a tacky former disco that's ground zero of the burgeoning, ultratrendy "Silver Lake scene." Mondays are usually free.

The Troubadour (✉ 9081 Santa Monica Blvd., West Hollywood, ☎ 310/276–6168) has weathered the test of time since the '60s, when it first opened as a folk-music club. Once a focal point for the now-moribund L.A. Heavy Metal scene, the old-timer has caught its second wind by booking hot alternative rock acts.

Actor Johnny Depp is part-owner of the **Viper Room** (✉ 8852 Sunset Blvd., West Hollywood, ☎ 310/358–1880), a hangout for musicians and movie stars. There's a different theme going every night, from ballroom and swing to ultrahard rock. Downstairs is a cozy basement room for gabbing and smoking.

Whiskey A Go Go (✉ 8901 Sunset Blvd., West Hollywood, ☎ 310/652–4202) is the most famous rock-and-roll club on the Sunset Strip, with up-and-coming alternative, very hard rock, and punk bands. Mondays launch L.A.'s cutting-edge acts.

6 Outdoor Activities, Beaches, and Sports

Transplants to Los Angeles know they've become acclimated when they go to a movie on a beautiful, sunny day. Although perfect weather is a constant here, visitors should still take advantage of it; Los Angeles supports a range of activities for every level of athlete.

BEACHES

Updated by
Jeanne Fay

The beach scene is an integral part of the southern California lifestyle. There is no public attraction more popular in L.A. than the white, sandy playgrounds that line the deep blue Pacific.

From downtown, the easiest way to hit the coast is by taking the Santa Monica Freeway (I–10) due west. Once you reach the end of the freeway, I–10 runs into the famous Highway 1, better known as the Pacific Coast Highway, or PCH, and continues up to Oregon. Other routes from the downtown area include Pico, Olympic, Santa Monica, Sunset, and Wilshire boulevards. The MTA bus line runs every 20 minutes to and from the beaches along each of these streets.

Los Angeles County beaches (and state beaches operated by the county) have lifeguards. Public parking is usually available, though fees can often be as much as $8; in some areas, it's possible to find free street parking. Generally, the northernmost beaches are best for surfing, hiking, and fishing, and the wider and sandier southern beaches are better for tanning and relaxing. Almost all are great for swimming, but beware: pollution levels in Santa Monica Bay sometimes approach dangerous levels, particularly after storms. Call 310/457–9701 for beach conditions in Malibu, 310/578–0478 for Santa Monica, and 310/379–8471 for Manhattan and Redondo beaches.

The following beaches are listed in north–south order:

Leo Carrillo State Beach. On the very edge of Ventura county, this narrow beach is better for exploring than swimming or sunning. On your own or with a ranger, venture down at low tide to examine the tide pools among the rocks. Sequit Point, a promontory dividing the east and west halves of the beach, creates secret coves, sea tunnels, and boulders on which you can perch and fish. Generally, fishermen stick to the west end of the beach; experienced surfers brave the rocks on the east end. The crowd, like that at many of the beaches in Malibu, is a mix of hippie canyon residents, semiprofessional surfers, and families that make the 25-mi trek from L.A. Picturesque campgrounds are set back from the beach; call to reserve campsites in advance. ✉ *35000 PCH, Malibu, ☎ 818/880–0350 or 800/444–7275 (camping reservations). Parking, lifeguard (summer), rest rooms, showers, fire pits.*

Nicholas Canyon County Beach. Sandier and less private than most of the rocky beaches immediately surrounding it, this little beach is great for picnics: You can sit at picnic tables high up on a bluff, looking out at the ocean. Surfers know it as Zero Beach. ✉ *33904 PCH, Malibu, ☎ 310/457–9891. Parking, lifeguard (winter weekends and summer), rest rooms, showers, barbecues.*

Robert H. Meyer Memorial State Beach. Perhaps Malibu's most beautiful coastal area, this state beach is made up of three separate minibeaches: El Pescador, La Piedra, and El Matador—all with the same spectacular view. Scramble down the steps to the rocky coves where nude sunbathing appears unofficially to be sanctioned. The huge, craggy boulders that make this beach private and lovely also make it somewhat dangerous: Watch the tide and don't get trapped between the boulders when it comes in. ✉ *32350, 32700, and 32900 PCH, Malibu, ☎ 310/457–1324. Parking, rest rooms.*

Zuma Beach Park. Two miles of white sand usually littered with tanning teenagers, Zuma has all the fixin's: concessions, volleyball, and a playground. This is a great beach for swimming and socializing, and it's also a favorite of families with small children; beachgoers looking

Los Angeles Area Beaches

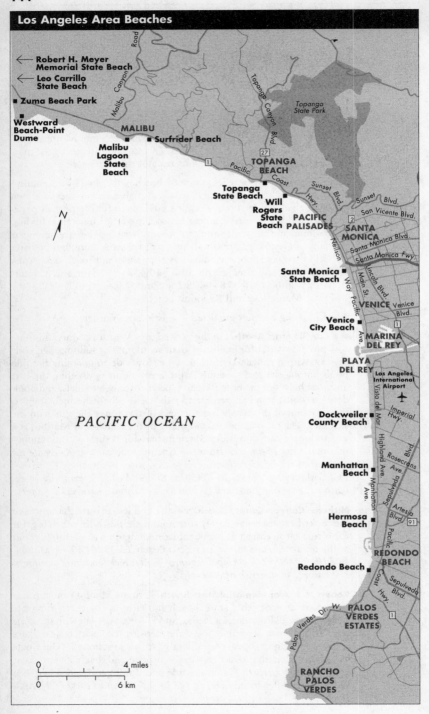

← Robert H. Meyer
Memorial State Beach

← Leo Carrillo
State Beach

■ Zuma Beach Park

■ Westward
Beach-Point
Dume

MALIBU

Malibu
Lagoon
State
Beach

■ Surfrider Beach

Topanga
State Beach ■

**TOPANGA
BEACH**

Will
Rogers
State
Beach

**PACIFIC
PALISADES**

Topanga
State Park

**SANTA
MONICA**

Sunset Blvd.

San Vicente Blvd.

Santa Monica Blvd.

Santa Monica Fwy.

Santa Monica ■
State Beach

VENICE Venice
Blvd.

Venice ■
City Beach

**MARINA
DEL REY**

**PLAYA
DEL REY**

Los Angeles
International
Airport

Dockweiler ■
County Beach

Imperial
Hwy.

Rosecrans
Ave.

Manhattan ■
Beach

Artesia
Blvd.

Hermosa
Beach ■

**REDONDO
BEACH**

Redondo Beach ■

Sepulveda
Blvd.

**PALOS
VERDES
ESTATES**

PACIFIC OCEAN

**RANCHO
PALOS
VERDES**

N

0   4 miles

0   6 km

for maturity or privacy should head elsewhere. The surf is rough but inconsistent. ⊠ *30050 PCH, Malibu,* ☎ *310/457–9891. Parking, lifeguard (year-round), rest rooms, showers, food concessions, playground, volleyball.*

Westward Beach-Point Dume. Though it's a favorite surfing beach, this is no place to take your first lesson—the surf can get steep. Here you can go tidepooling, snorkeling, or hiking to the top of the sandstone cliffs to whale-watch, from November through May. ⊠ *South end of Westward Beach Rd., Malibu,* ☎ *310/457–9891. Parking, lifeguard (year-round), rest rooms, food concessions.*

Malibu Lagoon State Beach/Surfrider Beach. Steady, 3- to 5-ft waves make this beach, just north of the dilapidated and currently closed Malibu Pier, a popular surfing location. The International Surfing Contest is held here in September—the surf is best around that time. Water runoff from Malibu Canyon forms a natural lagoon that's a sanctuary for 250 species of birds. Unfortunately, the lagoon is often polluted and algae-filled, and the debris tends to spill over into the surf. If you're leery of the water, take a walk on one of the nature trails, perfect for romantic sunset strolls. ⊠ *23200 block of PCH, Malibu,* ☎ *818/880–0350. Parking, lifeguard (year-round), rest rooms, picnicking, visitor center.*

Topanga State Beach. The beginning of miles of solid public beach, Topanga has good surfing at the western end (at the mouth of the canyon); the water gets rockier and rougher as you go east. Close to a busy section of the PCH and rather narrow, Topanga is not as serene as other beaches, with hordes of teenagers zipping over Topanga Canyon Boulevard from the Valley. ⊠ *18700 block of PCH, Malibu,* ☎ *310/394–3266. Parking, lifeguard (year-round), rest rooms, food concessions.*

Will Rogers State Beach. A dozen volleyball nets, gymnastics equipment, and playground equipment for kids make this clean, sandy, 3-mi beach a favorite of families and young singles; it all also has a sizeable gay and lesbian following. Surf is even and gentle for swimmers and beginning surfers, but the beach has the dubious distinction of being one of the area's most polluted—beware after a storm. ⊠ *15100 PCH, 2 mi north of Santa Monica pier, Pacific Palisades,* ☎ *310/394–3266. Parking, lifeguard, rest rooms.*

Santa Monica State Beach. The first beach you'll hit when the Santa Monica Freeway (I–10) runs into the PCH, this is one of L.A.'s best-known beaches. Wide, and sandy, it's *the* place for sunning and socializing: Be prepared for a mob scene on summer weekends, when parking becomes an expensive ordeal. The pier has an amusement park with a roller coaster, Ferris wheel, antique carousel, arcade, and food; there are also bicycle paths, volleyball nets, and playgrounds. For a memorable view, climb up the stairway over the PCH to Palisades Park, a grassy strip at the top of the bluffs. Summer-evening concerts are often held here. ⊠ *1642 Promenade, PCH at California Incline, Santa Monica,* ☎ *310/394–3266. Parking, lifeguard (year-round), rest rooms, showers.*

Venice City Beach. The surf and sands of Venice are fine, but the main attraction here is the boardwalk scene: a mile and a half of T-shirt shops, pizza stands, and tattoo parlors. Wander along the path and watch the show, as musicians, magicians, fortune tellers, and dancers of various levels of expertise compete for your spare change. Around 18th Avenue, look for Muscle Beach, a big cage where bodybuilders unabashedly pump iron—grab a seat on the bleachers and gape. If you feel like doing more than watching, there are courts for basketball, paddle tennis, and shuffleboard; or you can rent a bike or some Rollerblades and hit the bike path. For bike rentals try **Venice Pier Bike Shop** (✉ 21 Washington Blvd., ☎ 310/301–4011); **Skatey's** (✉ 102 Washington Blvd., ☎ 310/823–7971) is a good bet for skates. Whatever you do, hold on to your wallet.✉ *West of Pacific Ave., Venice,* ☎ *310/394–3266. Parking, rest rooms, showers, food concessions.*

Dockweiler County Beach. The longest (4-mi) strip of beach in the county, Dockweiler has almost all the makings of a perfect beach: a campground, playground, bike trail, barbecue pits, even surf, nice sand. If only the planes from LAX weren't taking off directly overhead and factories weren't puffing out fumes right behind you. If you don't mind that, you'll find plenty of room to spread out. ✉ *8255 Vista del Mar, at the west end of Imperial Hwy., Playa del Rey,* ☎ *310/322–5008. Parking, lifeguard (year-round), rest rooms, showers.*

Manhattan Beach. Rows of volleyball courts on a wide, sandy strip make this the preferred destination of muscled, tanned young professionals. If you're after bikini watching, this is where you'll find it. ✉ *West of Strand, Manhattan Beach,* ☎ *310/372–2166. Parking, lifeguard (year-round), rest rooms, showers, food concessions, volleyball.*

Hermosa Beach. Just south of Manhattan Beach, Hermosa Beach is just like its neighbor, but it attracts more of a teenage, partying crowd. ✉ *West of Strand, Manhattan Beach,* ☎ *310/372–2166. Parking, lifeguard (year-round), rest rooms, showers, food concessions, volleyball.*

Redondo Beach. The Redondo Beach Pier marks the starting point of this wide, sandy, busy beach, which continues south for about 2 mi along a heavily developed shoreline community. There are plenty of activities here: Restaurants and shops flourish along the pier; excursion boats and privately owned craft depart from launching ramps; and a reef formed by a sunken ship creates prime fishing and snorkeling conditions. A series of rock and jazz concerts takes place at the pier every summer.✉ *Foot of Torrance Blvd., Redondo Beach,* ☎ *310/372–2166. Parking, lifeguard, rest rooms, showers, food concessions, volleyball.*

PARKS AND GARDENS

Parks

In the **Angeles National Forest,** above Pasadena, you can drive to the top of Mount Wilson for spectacular views of Los Angeles. The **Chilao Visitors Center,** 13 mi north of Mount Wilson, has exhibits about the forest, and trails for nature walks.

Above Dodger Stadium (☞ Spectator Sports, *below*), **Elysian Park** is a huge, hilly park that's great for picnics.

The main park in the city of Los Angeles is the 4,000-acre **Griffith Park** (☞ Chapter 2); pick up a map at the visitors center.

Hancock Park, near the L.A. County Museum of Art, is a wide grassy area most notable for the La Brea Tar Pits (☞ Farmers Market and Museum Row *in* Chapter 2).

Near downtown, **MacArthur Park** is a lovely place to rent a pedal boat, though you might feel uncomfortable with some of the shady characters in the neighborhood.

Outdoorspeople cherish the canyons, waterfalls, lake, and more than 30 mi of trails at **Malibu Creek State Park,** at the summit of Malibu Canyon Road.

At **Vasquez Rocks,** in the little town of Agua Dulce in the desert north of Los Angeles, children can scamper around the rock formations used in the shooting of the movie version of *The Flintstones.*

Will Rogers State Historic Park(☞ Santa Monica, Venice, and Malibu *in* Chapter 2) in Pacific Palisades is ideal for children, with broad lawns, walking trails, and even polo games on Saturday and Sunday in summer (☎ 310/454–8212 for polo information).

Playgrounds

Santa Monica's **Douglas Park** (✉ 1155 Chelsea Ave.) has a busy playground at the quiet end of the park, with street parking only a few feet away. An empty cement pond makes a great rink for young rollerbladers and trike riders.

Griffith Park has a small playground near the carousel; there's another one across from the Griffith Park Boulevard entrance, and one more just past the golf course. A free map of the park is available at the rangers station (✉ 4730 Crystal Springs Dr.).

Lacy Park (✉ 3300 Monterey Rd., San Marino, ☎ 818/300–0700) has a playground beside a broad lawn with picnic areas; parents can sit under shade trees while their little ones play.

In Laguna Beach, there's a great seaside playground on **Main Beach,** and a more secluded one on **Cress Street.**

PARTICIPANT SPORTS

If you're looking for a good workout, you've come to the right city. Whether your game is basketball, golf, billiards, or bowling, Los Angeles is a dream town for athletes of all kinds. Not only does the near-perfect climate allow sports enthusiasts to play outdoors almost year-round, but during some seasons it's possible to surf in the morning and snow ski in the afternoon—all in the same county. For information, call the **City of Los Angeles Department of Recreation and Parks** (✉ 200 N. Main St., Suite 1380, City Hall East, 90012, ☎ 213/485–5515) or **Los Angeles County Department of Parks and Recreation** (✉ 433 S. Vermont Ave., 90020, ☎ 213/738–2961).

Bicycling

The most famous bike path in the city, and definitely the most beautiful, can be found on the **Pacific Ocean beach,** a 22-mi route from Temescal Canyon down to Redondo Beach. You can park at one of the many lots along the Pacific Coast Highway (be prepared to pay a high parking fee). Rent bikes at one of many rental shops along the bike path, including **Rental on the Beach** (✉ 2100 Ocean Front Walk, ☎ 310/821–9338), which has several additional locations on the path in Venice: Rates are $5 per hour or $18 a day.

Griffith Park (✉ Entrance at Crystal Springs Dr. and Los Feliz Blvd.) has a tree-lined bike route with several options ranging from easy to hard. Stay on Crystal Springs Drive for an easier ride; turn left up Griffith Park Drive for a tougher ride that rewards with great views. Both routes will take you past Travel Town, with its trains, zoo, and picnic areas where you can take a break. For rentals, try **The Annex** (✉ 3157 Los Feliz Blvd., ☎ 323/661–6665), which charges $15 per day.

In Santa Monica, **San Vicente Boulevard** has a wide, 3-mi cycling lane that parallels the sidewalk. **Balboa Park,** in the San Fernando Valley, is another haven for two-wheelers, as is the flat, 3-mi paved path around **Lake Hollywood**—a great place to take in views of the Hollywood sign. The **L.A. River Bike Path** runs along the river from the intersection of the 5 and 110 freeways, north to Griffith Park. Venture south to the **Palos Verdes Peninsula** for a long, rolling loop around the peninsula on Palos Verdes Drive—the ocean views are superb. Call the **M.T.A.** (☎ 213/626–4455) for a map of more bike trails.

Many of the areas mentioned in Hiking (☞ *below*) have mountain biking paths; Malibu Creek State Park and Topanga State Park are two of your best bets.

Bowling

There are several lanes in town, but the most fun place to bowl is **Hollywood Star Lanes** (⊠ 5227 Santa Monica Blvd., Hollywood, ☎ 323/665–4111), which attracts everyone from quasi-professionals to twentysomething hipsters; it's open 24 hours.

Fishing

The best lakes for freshwater fishing in the Los Angeles area are **Big Bear** and **Arrowhead** in the San Bernardino National Forest, east of the city about two hours(☞ Chapter 8). Rainbow trout, bass, carp, blue gill, and catfish are the typical catch, and the scenery in these mountains will enhance your outing, whether you hook anything or not. Trout are abundant at Juniper Point, on the north shore of Big Bear Lake. Call 909/866–5796 for fishing information in the area.

A sure catch can be found at **Trout Dale** (⊠ Kanan Rd., Agoura, 3 mi south of Ventura Fwy., ☎ 818/889–9993), where they even clean your catch. Two picturesque ponds are set up for picnicking or fishing. A $3 entry fee includes your license and pole, but there's an extra charge for each trout you catch. Trout Dale is open weekdays from 10 to 5, and weekends from 9 to 5.

Shore fishing and surf casting are excellent on many of the beaches, and pier fishing is popular because no license is necessary to fish off public piers. The **Santa Monica** and **Redondo Beach piers** all have nearby bait-and-tackle shops.

If you want to break away from the piers, sign up for a boat excursion with one of the local charters. Requisite fishing licenses ($6.60) are available from the Fish and Game Department (☎ 562/590–5132), and poles can rented for $7–$10. **Marina del Rey Sport Fishing** (⊠ Dock 52, Fiji Way, ☎ 310/822–3625) runs excursions for $20 per half day. **Redondo Sport Fishing Company** (⊠ 233 N. Harbor Dr., ☎ 310/372–2111) has half-day charters starting at $22 per person. Sea bass, halibut, bonita, yellowtail, or barracuda are the usual catch. Both companies run whale-watching excursions in winter.

L.A. Harbor Sportfishing (☎ 310/547–9916) conducts whale-watching excursions off Berth 79 from late December through March at the San Pedro Harbor, in addition to fishing. The cost of boating excursions ranges from $22 to $65; they take you as far as Catalina Island. **Skipper's Twenty Second Street Landing** (⊠ 141 W. 22nd St., San Pedro, ☎ 310/832–8304) leads an overnight charter that lets you look at the stars while waiting for a bite. These boats, complete with bunk beds and full galley, leave at 10 and 10:30 PM and dock between 5 and 9 PM the next night. Per-person price is about $62. Day charters are available as well, at $22 per half day and $32 per day.

The most popular and unquestionably the most unusual form of fishing in the L.A. area involves no hooks, bait, or poles. The great **grunion**

runs, which take place from March through August, are a spectacular natural phenomenon in which hundreds of thousands of small silver fish, called grunion, wash up on southern California beaches to spawn and lay their eggs in the sand. The **Cabrillo Marine Aquarium** (☎ 310/ 548–7562), in San Pedro, has entertaining and educational programs about grunion throughout most of their spawning season (☞ Palos Verdes, San Pedro, and Long Beach *in* Chapter 2). During certain months it is prohibited to touch the grunion; call the Fish and Game Department (☎ 562/590–5132) for details.

Golf

The Parks and Recreation Department lists seven public 18-hole courses in Los Angeles. **Rancho Park Golf Course** (✉ 10460 W. Pico Blvd., ☎ 310/838–7373) is one of the most heavily played links in the country. It's a beautifully designed course, but the towering pines present an obstacle for those who slice or hook. There's a two-level driving range, a nine-hole pitch 'n' putt (☎ 310/838–7561), a snack bar, and a pro shop where you can rent clubs (☎ 310/839–4374).

Several good public courses are in the San Fernando Valley. The **Balboa and Encino Golf courses** (✉ 16821 Burbank Blvd., Encino, ☎ 818/ 995–1170) are next to each other. The **Woodley Lakes Golf Course** (✉ 6331 Woodley Ave., Van Nuys, ☎ 818/780–6886) is flat as a board and has hardly any trees. Summer in the Valley can be quite hot, so be sure to bring lots of sunscreen and water. In Pacoima (the northern part of the Valley), you'll find little escape from the summer heat, but the **Hansen Dam Public Golf Course** (✉ 10400 Glenoaks Blvd., ☎ 818/ 899–2200) has a buffet-style restaurant that serves cold drinks.

Griffith Park has two splendid 18-hole courses along with a challenging nine-hole course. **Harding Municipal Golf Course** and **Wilson Municipal Golf Course** (✉ 4730 Crystal Springs Dr. for both, ☎ 323/ 663–2555) are about 1½ mi inside the park entrance at Riverside Drive and Los Feliz Boulevard. Bridle paths surround the outer fairways, and the San Gabriel Mountains make a scenic background. The nine-hole **Roosevelt Municipal Golf Course** (✉ 2650 N. Vermont Ave., ☎ 323/665–2011) can be reached through the park's Vermont Avenue entrance.

Yet another course in the Griffith Park vicinity, and one at which there's usually no waiting, is the nine-hole pitch 'n' putt **Los Feliz Municipal Golf Course** (✉ 3207 Los Feliz Blvd., ☎ 323/663–7758). Other short courses in Los Angeles include the pitch 'n' putt at **Holmby Park** (✉ 601 Club View Dr., Beverly Hills, ☎ 310/276–1604) and the **Penmar** executive nine-hole course (✉ 1233 Rose Ave., Venice, ☎ 310/ 396–6228).

Health Clubs

There are dozens of health-club chains in the city; some sell daily or weekly memberships. Two that do are **Bodies in Motion** (✉ 1950 Century Park E, Century City, ☎ 310/836–8000), with a full range of aerobics classes including aerobic boxing and kick-boxing classes, and **24 Hour Fitness** (☎ 800/204–2400), with eight locations in the Los Angeles area. Both charge $10 per day.

Probably the most famous body-pumping facility in the city is **Gold's Gym** (✉ 360 Hampton Dr., Venice, ☎ 310/392–6004; ✉ 1016 N. Cole Ave., Hollywood, ☎ 323/462–7012), where local hulks turn themselves into modern art. For $15 a day or $50 a week, several tons of weights and Nautilus machines can be yours. **World Gym** (✉ 812 Main St.,

Venice, ☎ 310/399–9888) is a famous pumping-iron club; it costs $10 a day or $25 a week. **Easton Gym** (✉ 8053 Beverly Blvd., West Hollywood, ☎ 323/651–3636) is a no-frills gym for die-hard lifters; the fee is $13 per day or $40 per week.

Dance and Workout Studios

Partners can learn swing, tango, and ballroom moves at **Arthur Murray Dance Studio** (✉ 262 N. Beverly Dr., ☎ 310/274–8867). Go solo at the neighborhoody **Studio A Dance** (✉ 2306 Hyperion Ave., Silver Lake, ☎ 323/661–8311), convenient to downtown, where aerobics, jazz, and ballet classes taught by friendly instructors cost about $8–$10.

Hiking

With so many different land- and seascapes to explore, hiking is a major pastime for many Angelenos, who head for the hills en masse on weekends, dogs in tow.

One of the best places to begin is **Griffith Park**; pick up a map from the ranger station (✉ 4730 Crystal Springs Dr.). Many of the paths in the park are not shaded and can be quite steep; a nice short hike from Canyon Drive, at the southwest end of the park, takes you to **Bronson Caves,** where the Batman television show was filmed. Begin at the Observatory for a 3-mi round trip hike to the top of **Mount Hollywood.** For more information on parks, *see* Chapter 2.

Other hikes in the Hollywood Hills area include a flat, paved 3⅓-mi path that circles the **Lake Hollywood** reservoir—an easy, scenic walk. Exit the Hollywood freeway at Barham Boulevard and take a right on Lake Hollywood Drive to reach the reservoir. At **Franklin Canyon** you'll find a 2½-mi hike that's often used by film crews. Pick up a map from the visitors center (follow Franklin Canyon Drive to Lake Drive, then turn right to find the Franklin Canyon Ranch House). Docent-led walks are also available.

Head west for ocean, rather than canyon, views. At **Topanga State Park,** miles of trails wind high in the Santa Monica Mountains. **Will Rogers Historic State Park,** off Sunset Boulevard in the Pacific Palisades, abuts Topanga and has a splendid nature trail. A 2-mi hike from Rogers' historic home takes you to a stunning ocean-to-downtown view atop Inspiration Point. From here you can join the **Backbone Trail,** a hiking path that travels the length of the Santa Monicas. Turn north off Sunset Boulevard onto Temescal Canyon Road to reach **Temescal Canyon,** a shorter but equally lovely hike. For an easy hike, walk to the waterfall and then turn back; continue past the fall for a very steep hike that leads to a ridge with spectacular views of the ocean.

In the Malibu area, **Leo Carrillo State Beach,** with its tidepools and coves, and the **Malibu Lagoon State Park** bird sanctuary (☞ Beaches, *above*) are great places to walk. For a more mountainous route, head inland on the trail at the parking area for Leo Carillo to the **Nicholas Flats,** a good place to watch for whales in winter. Another hike in Malibu can be reached by driving 2 mi past Malibu Canyon Road on the PCH to **Corral Canyon,** part of the Santa Monica Mountains National Recreation Area. Drive to the top of Corral Canyon Road to explore trails that stand out for their sweeping mountain and ocean views, as well as interesting geology, flora, and fauna.

Farther away from the city, spectacular mountain hiking trails can be found at **Arrowhead** and **Big Bear,** in the San Bernardino National Forest (☞ Chapter 8), many parts of the **Angeles National Forest,** and the

Angeles Crest area. Much of the terrain here is rugged; contact the National Forest Service (☎ 818/790–1151) before you go. Maps of hiking trails in the Arrowhead and Big Bear areas are available from the Chambers of Commerce in each town.

For further information on hiking locations and scheduled outings in Los Angeles, contact the **Sierra Club** (✉ 3345 Wilshire Blvd., Suite 508, Los Angeles, 90010, ☎ 213/387–4287).

Horseback Riding

More than 50 mi of beautiful bridle trails are open to the public in the Griffith Park area. **Griffith Park Horse Rentals** (✉ 480 Riverside Dr., Burbank, ☎ 818/840–8401) has a going rate of $15 per hour plus a $15 deposit. **Bar S Stables** (✉ 1850 Riverside Dr., Glendale, ☎ 818/242–8443) rents horses for $13 an hour (plus a $10 deposit). **Sunset Ranch** (✉ 3400 Beachwood Dr., Hollywood, ☎ 323/469–5450) also rents horses for $15 an hour, plus a $10 deposit; a Friday-evening package includes a trail ride over the hill into Burbank, where riders tie up their horses and dine at a Mexican restaurant. The package costs $35, not including the cost of dinner.

Ice-Skating

Rinks are all over the city, generally charging about $8 for admission and skate rental. In the Valley, there's the **Pickwick Ice Center** (✉ 1001 Riverside Dr., Burbank, ☎ 818/846–0032). In Pasadena, try the **Ice Skating Center** (✉ 310 E. Green St., ☎ 626/578–0800). Culver City has the **Ice Arena** (✉ 4545 Sepulveda Blvd., ☎ 310/398–5718).

In-Line and Roller Skating

All of the areas mentioned in Bicycling (☞ *above*) are also excellent for in-line and roller skating, though cyclists have the right of way. Venice Beach is the skating capital of the city—and maybe of the world. An 8-mi, almost traffic-free paved trail with underpass dips make the intermittently scenic **Ballona Creek Trail** in Marina del Rey (start at Fisherman's Village) another favorite for skaters.

For Rollerblades, **Boardwalk Skates** (✉ 201½ Ocean Front Walk, Venice, ☎ 310/450–6634) charges $4 an hour or $12 for the day; **Skatey's** (✉ 102 Washington St., Venice, ☎ 310/823–7971) charges $5 per hour or $10 per day.

For indoor skating, head to **Moonlight Rollerway** (✉ 5110 San Fernando Rd., Glendale, ☎ 818/241–3630) or **Skateland** (✉ 18140 Parthenia St., Northridge, ☎ 818/885–1491).

Jogging

A scenic course, popular with students and downtown workers, is found at **Exposition Park.** Circling the Coliseum and Sports Arena is a jogging-workout trail with pull-up bars and other simple equipment placed every several hundred yards. **San Vicente Boulevard** in Santa Monica has a wide grassy median that splits the street for several picturesque miles. The reservoir at **Lake Hollywood,** just east of Cahuenga Boulevard in the Hollywood Hills, is encircled by a 3.3-mi asphalt path with a view of the Hollywood sign. Within hilly **Griffith Park** are thousands of acres' worth of hilly paths and challenging terrain; **Crystal Springs Drive,** from the main entrance at Los Feliz to the zoo, is a relatively flat 5 mi. **Circle Drive,** around the perimeter of UCLA in Westwood, provides a 2½-mi run through academia. The 22-mi **bike path** along

the coast from Venice to Redondo Beach is a great place for a run—
especially in the Venice Beach and Santa Monica sections. Beware of
bikers and skaters zipping by at high speeds.

Racquetball and Handball

Dozens of high schools and colleges all over town have three-walled
courts open to the public. The only catch is you have to wait until after
school's out, or the weekend.

There are several indoor racquetball facilities throughout the city: At
the **Racquet Center** (⊠ 10933 Ventura Blvd., Studio City, ☎ 818/
760–2303), in the San Fernando Valley, court time runs $8–$14 an
hour, depending on when you play. There's another **Racquet Center** (⊠
920 Lohman La., ☎ 323/258–4178) in South Pasadena. The **Hollywood YMCA** (⊠ 1553 Schrader Blvd.; call ☎ 800/872–9622 for other
locations) has racquetball courts among its many facilities; a $12 entry
fee allows you access to all.

Skiing and Snowboarding

Cross-Country

Ski season in Southern California generally runs from Thanksgiving
until Memorial Day. **Idyllwild,** near Palm Springs, has excellent cross-
country trails. For information, call the Idyllwild Chamber of Commerce Information Line (☎ 909/659–3259).

Downhill

A relatively short drive from downtown will bring you to some of the
best snow skiing and snowboarding in the state. Just north of Pasadena,
in the San Gabriel Mountains, are two ski areas: **Mt. Waterman** (☎
626/790–2002) and **Snowcrest Snow Park** (☎ 626/440–9749), both
of which have a couple of lifts and a range of slopes for beginning and
advanced skiers. Farther east is **Mt. Baldy** (☎ 909/981–3344), off
I–10 at the top of Mountain Avenue.

Resorts with accommodations can be found within 90 minutes of Los
Angeles proper. **Big Bear** (☞ Chapter 8) is one of the most popular ski
retreats on the West Coast, with a full range of accommodations, several ski lifts, night skiing, and one of the largest snowmaking operations in California. For information about Big Bear snow conditions,
hotels, and special events, contact the **Chamber of Commerce** (☎ 909/
866–4607).

Other ski and snowboard areas in the vicinity of Big Bear include **Bear
Mountain** (☎ 909/585–2519), **Snow Valley** (☎ 909/867–5151), **Mountain High** (☎ 888/754–7878), and **Snow Summit** (☎ 909/866–5766).
All have snowmaking capabilities, and many have lights for night skiing. Call for directions and information about ski conditions.

Tennis

Many public parks have courts that require an hourly fee. **Lincoln
Park** (⊠ Lincoln and Wilshire Blvds., Santa Monica), **Westwood Park**
(⊠ 1375 Veteran Ave., West L.A.), and **Barrington Recreational Center** (⊠ Barrington Ave., south of Sunset Blvd., West L.A.) all have well-
maintained courts with lights. **Griffith Park** has three sets of lighted courts:
one at Riverside Drive just south of Los Feliz Boulevard; another just
north of the Vermont Avenue entrance; and still another at the intersection of Griffith Park and Crystal Springs drives.

For a shorter wait, and no fee, try the courts at local high schools and
colleges, where gates are often left unlocked on weekends and after

school. Contact the individual schools to obtain the required permit. There are several nice courts on the campus of **USC** (⊠ Off Vermont St. entrance, Downtown), a few on the campus of **Paul Revere Junior High School** (⊠ Sunset Blvd. and Mandeville Canyon Rd., Brentwood), four at **Fairfax High School** (⊠ Fairfax and Melrose Aves., Mid-City), and a few more at **Palisades High School** (⊠ Temescal Canyon Rd., Pacific Palisades), to name just a few.

For a complete list of the public tennis courts in Los Angeles, contact the **L.A. Department of Recreation and Parks** (⊠ 200 N. Main St., Los Angeles, ☎ 213/485–5515).

Water Sports

Boating and Kayaking

Action Water Sports (⊠ 4144 Lincoln Blvd., Marina del Rey, ☎ 310/306–9539) rents single kayaks for $35 and doubles for $45 per day.

Big Bear and Lake Arrowhead(☞ Chapter 8) open up a whole different world of freshwater adventure. Canoes, motorboats, and water-skiing equipment can be rented from outfits in both towns. In summer, Big Bear also has parasailing: Contact **Big Bear Parasailing** (☎ 909/866–4359). For information about both of these lakes and nearby rental facilities, contact the **Big Bear Chamber of Commerce** (☎ 909/866–4607) or **Lake Arrowhead Chamber of Commerce** (☎ 909/337–3715).

Jet Skiing

This is another booming sport on the lakes at Big Bear and Arrowhead, although Jet Skis can be expensive to rent. For information, contact the **Big Bear Chamber of Commerce** (☎ 909/866–4607).

Scuba Diving and Snorkeling

Diving and snorkeling off Leo Carrillo State Beach, Catalina, and the Channel Islands is considered some of the best on the Pacific coast. Dive shops, such as **New England Divers** (⊠ 2936 Clark Ave., Long Beach, ☎ 562/421–8939) and **Dive 'n Surf** (⊠ 504 N. Broadway, Redondo Beach, ☎ 310/372–8423), will provide you with everything you need for your voyage beneath the waves. Snorkeling equipment runs about $10 per day; full scuba gear for certified divers runs $40–$60 per day, with prices cut for subsequent days. Diving charters to Catalina and the Channel Islands as well as certification training can be arranged through these dive shops.

Surfing

The signature water sport in L.A. is surfing: The surfing culture began here, and the area remains a destination for pros from afar. Novices should beware of rocks and undertows; also note that getting in the way of other surfers is considered taboo. There's usually not a lot of leeway granted to new surfers; one beach in Palos Verdes is notorious for having outsiders' tires slashed by local surfer dudes. The best and safest way to learn is by taking a lesson. **Malibu Ocean Sports** (⊠ 22935 PCH, Malibu, ☎ 310/456–6302) gives lessons and rents boards. The main store is near the Malibu pier, but in summer they operate an additional location in Marina del Rey. For a complete listing of the best surfing areas, *see* Beaches, *above*.

Windsurfing

Good windsurfing can be found all along the coast. Certified wind-surfers can rent equipment for about $50 per day through various outfitters, including **Malibu Ocean Sports** (☞ *above*).

SPECTATOR SPORTS

If you enjoy watching professional sports, you'll never hunger for action in this town. Los Angeles is home to some of the greatest franchises in pro basketball and baseball. And although most cities would be content simply to have one team in each of those categories, L.A. fans can root for two teams in many sports like basketball, baseball, and hockey. (Football fans, however, will have to look elsewhere, as L.A.'s two professional teams left the city in 1995.) The best source for tickets to all sporting events is Ticketmaster (☎ 714/740–2000).

Some of the major sports venues in the area are **Edison Field** (✉ 2000 Gene Autry Way, ☎ 714/940–2000), the **Great Western Forum** (✉ 3900 W. Manchester Blvd., Inglewood, ☎ 310/419–3100), **L.A. Sports Arena** (✉ 3939 S. Figueroa St., downtown, next to Coliseum, ☎ 213/748–6136), **L.A. Memorial Coliseum** (✉ 3939 S. Figueroa St., downtown, ☎ 213/748–6131), and **Arrowhead Pond** (✉ 2695 E. Katella Ave., Anaheim, ☎ 714/704–2500).

Baseball

The **Dodgers** take on their National League rivals in another eventful season at the ever-popular Dodger Stadium (✉ 1000 Elysian Park Ave., exit off I–110, Pasadena Fwy., ☎ 323/224–1400 for ticket information). South down the Golden State Freeway, in Anaheim, the **Anaheim Angels** continue their quest for the pennant in the American League West. For Angels ticket information, contact Anaheim Stadium (☎ 714/663–9000).

Basketball

College

The **University of Southern California** (☎ 213/740–8480) plays at the L.A. Sports Arena, and the Bruins of the **University of California at Los Angeles** (☎ 310/825–8699 athletic department, 310/825–2101 tickets) play at Pauley Pavilion on the UCLA campus; these schools go head to head in Pac 10 competition each season. Another local team to watch is the Lions of **Loyola Marymount University** (☎ 310/338–4532).

Professional

The **Los Angeles Lakers** (☎ 310/419–3182) have been virtually untouchable since the arrivals of superstar center Shaquille O'Neal and young star Kobe Bryant in 1996. Their home court is the Forum. L.A.'s "other" team, the much-maligned **Clippers** (☎ 213/748–8000) make their home at the L.A. Sports Arena; tickets are generally cheaper and easier to get than for Lakers' games. New to the pro basketball scene in L.A. is the all-female **Los Angeles Sparks** (☎ 310/419–3193). Though Sparks stars Lisa Leslie and the beloved point guard Jamila Wideman have drawn unexpectedly large crowds to the Forum, tickets are almost always available (the team plays in summer) and quite inexpensive.

Boxing and Wrestling

Championship competitions take place in both of these sports year-round at the **Great Western Forum** (✉ 3900 W. Manchester Blvd., Inglewood, ☎ 310/673–1773).

Football

The L.A. Raiders returned to Oakland in 1995, the same year the Rams moved to St. Louis, leaving Los Angeles without a professional football team; despite constant speculation, it's unlikely a football team will come to town before the end of the decade. The **Anaheim Piranhas** (☎ 714/475–0838) play arena football at the Arrowhead Pond in Anaheim. Football fever in L.A., however, still revolves around the college teams.

College

The **USC Trojans'** (☎ 213/740–8480) home turf is the Coliseum. The **UCLA Bruins** (☎ 310/825–2101) pack 'em in at the Rose Bowl in Pasadena. Each season, the two rivals face off in one of college football's oldest and most exciting rivalries.

Golf

The hot golf ticket in town each February is the PGA **Nissan Open** (☎ 800/752–6736). The tournament attracts the best golfers in the world and is played in Pacific Palisades at the Riviera Country Club.

Hockey

The National Hockey League's **L.A. Kings** (☎ 310/673–6003) put their show on ice at the Forum. Disney's **Mighty Ducks** (☎ 714/704–2701) push the puck at the Pond in Anaheim. Hockey season runs from October through April.

Horse Racing and Shows

Santa Anita Race Track (✉ Huntington Dr. and Colorado Pl., Arcadia, ☎ 626/574–7223) is still the dominant site for exciting Thoroughbred racing. You can always expect the best racing in the world at this beautiful facility, from October to mid-November and late December to late April.

The track next to the Forum in Inglewood in **Hollywood Park** (✉ Century Blvd. and Prairie Ave., ☎ 310/419–1500) is another favorite racing venue. It's open from early November to late December and from late April to mid-July.

Los Alamitos Racecourse (✉ 4961 Katella Ave., Los Alamitos, ☎ 714/995–1234 for track information) has harness racing at night.

Several grand-prix jumping competitions and Western riding championships are held throughout the year at the **Los Angeles Equestrian Center** in Burbank (✉ 480 Riverside Dr., ☎ 818/563–3252). Show jumping and Western riding events are featured at the **Orange County Fair Equestrian Center** (✉ 88 Fair Dr., Costa Mesa, ☎ 714/708–1652); admission is free.

Polo

Will Rogers State Historic Park (✉ 1501 Will Rogers State Park Rd., Pacific Palisades, ☎ 310/454–8212 for polo season information) has picnic grounds where you can enjoy an afternoon chukker of polo between May and September. Games are played Saturday at 2 PM and Sunday at 10 AM, unless the grounds are muddy from rain. Parking costs $5 per car.

Soccer

The **Los Angeles Galaxy** team debuted in April 1996 and plays regular seasons of professional soccer from March through September at the Rose Bowl in Pasadena. Team icons such as Cobi Jones draw enormous crowds. For ticket information, call 888/657–5425.

Tennis

The **Infiniti Open,** held in summer at UCLA, usually attracts some of the top-seeded players on the pro tennis circuit. For information, call 310/824–1010.

7 Shopping

L.A. shoppers are a class unto themselves, with several breeds representing the materialistic melting pot. Rodeo Drive swarms with shoppers in mink coats and sunglasses, cell phones in one hand and designer totes in the other. Santa Monica's shops are filled with svelte men and women in $100 T-shirts, designer jeans, and Gucci shoes. On Melrose Avenue, anarchistic cranberry-haired Gen-Xers in vintage clothes and platform shoes make a statement all their own.

Revised and
updated by
Cynthia
LaFavre Yorks

THE IMAGE OF THE NEWLY OUTFITTED Julia Roberts strolling along Rodeo Drive in *Pretty Woman* remains rife with symbolism. The West Coast's street of dreams is where movie stars, tourists, and even locals come to reinvent themselves. Whether that's your aim or you'd just rather bring a wearable slice of Tinseltown home with you, the funky shops of Melrose, the tony stores of Rodeo Drive, and the offbeat shops along Montana Avenue present infinite possibilities.

Distances between shopping districts can be vast in this notoriously car-dependent city; don't try to hit too many shopping areas in one day, or you'll spend more time driving than spending. When in doubt, ask your hotel concierge to help you approximate driving times.

Most stores in Los Angeles are open from 10 to 6, although many stay open until 9 or later, particularly those on Melrose Avenue and in Santa Monica. Melrose shops, on the whole, don't get moving until 11 AM. In most areas, shops are open for at least a few hours on Sunday. Most stores accept credit cards; traveler's checks are also often allowed with proper identification. Check the *Los Angeles Times* or *L.A. Weekly* for sales, and if you're curious about who's shopping where (after all, this is L.A.), take a peek at *In Style* magazine.

Beverly Hills Vicinity

Shopping in Beverly Hills centers mainly around the three-block stretch of **Rodeo Drive,** between Santa Monica and Wilshire boulevards and the streets surrounding it. Rodeo may be past its heyday of the materialistic '80s, but it's still a shamelessly decadent experience. Though stars are on their guard around this tourist hot spot, many sneak into their favorite shops before or after hours or through back entrances. Be advised: some stores have limited access except by appointment.

Shopping Centers and Malls
The **Beverly Center** (☎ 310/854–0070), bound by Beverly, La Cienega, and San Vicente boulevards and 3rd Street, covers more than 7 acres and contains some 200 stores, including Macy's and Bloomingdale's. The **Rodeo Collection** (✉ 421 N. Rodeo Dr., ☎ 310/276–9600), between Brighton Way and Santa Monica Boulevard, is one of several European-style shopping enclaves in Beverly Hills. Upscale designer boutiques abound in this piazzalike area of marble and brass. **Two Rodeo Drive** (✉ 2 Rodeo Dr., at Wilshire Blvd., ☎ 310/247–7040), a.k.a. Via Rodeo, is a collection of glossy retail shops housed on a private cobblestone street. Amid the outdoor cafés and sculpted fountains of the Italianate piazza are some two dozen boutiques.

Department Stores
Barneys New York (✉ 9570 Wilshire Blvd., ☎ 310/276–4400), the West Coast branch of the Manhattan store, is a favorite among young hipsters who come to at least look at the cutting-edge (and pricey) designer clothing, including threads by Giorgio Armani and Donna Karan. The elaborate home-accessories area showcases unusual pottery, vases, linens, and even baby clothes.
Neiman-Marcus (✉ 9700 Wilshire Blvd., ☎ 310/550–5900), dubbed "Needless Markups" by some shoppers, nevertheless has a spectacular selection of women's fashions and accessories, from the avant garde to the abashedly classic. The store's studio department makes it a magnet for costumers and, consequently, their celebrity clients.

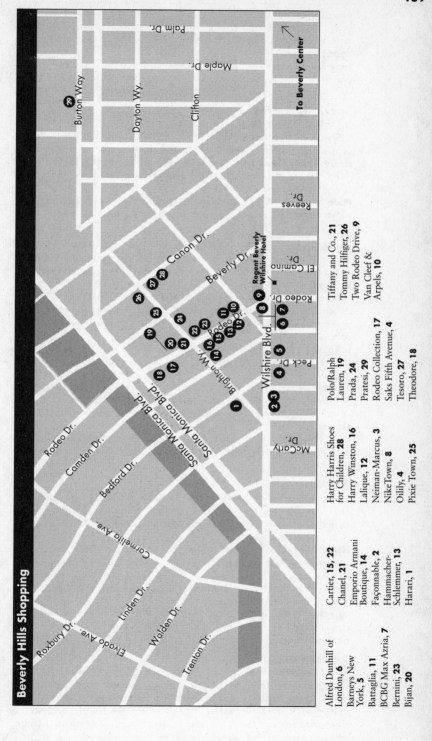

Beverly Hills Shopping

To Beverly Center

Palm Dr.

Maple Dr.

Burton Way

Dayton Wy.

Clifton

Reeves Dr.

Canon Dr.

Beverly Dr.

El Camino Dr.

Regent Beverly Wilshire Hotel

Rodeo Dr.

Wilshire Blvd.

Peck Dr.

Brighton Wy.

Santa Monica Blvd.

Rodeo Dr.

Camden Dr.

Bedford Dr.

Camellia Ave.

Linden Dr.

Roxbury Dr.

Elvado Ave.

Walden Dr.

Trenton Dr.

McCarty Dr.

Alfred Dunhill of London, **6**
Barneys New York, **5**
Battaglia, **11**
BCBG Max Azria, **7**
Bernini, **23**
Bijan, **20**

Cartier, **15, 22**
Chanel, **21**
Emporio Armani Boutique, **14**
Façonnable, **2**
Hammacher-Schlemmer, **13**
Harari, **1**

Harry Harris Shoes for Children, **28**
Harry Winston, **16**
Lalique, **12**
Neiman-Marcus, **3**
NikeTown, **8**
Oilily, **4**
Pixie Town, **25**

Polo/Ralph Lauren, **19**
Prada, **24**
Pratesi, **29**
Rodeo Collection, **17**
Saks Fifth Avenue, **4**
Tesoro, **27**
Theodore, **18**

Tiffany and Co., **21**
Tommy Hilfiger, **26**
Two Rodeo Drive, **9**
Van Cleef & Arpels, **10**

Robinsons-May (✉ 9900 Wilshire Blvd., ☎ 310/275–5464) has seen better days, but is still a reliable source for simple necessities like panty hose or lipstick. It's especially convenient for guests staying at the neighboring Hilton.

Saks Fifth Avenue (✉ 9600 Wilshire Blvd., ☎ 310/275–4211) is still one of the best accessory, shoe, and fragrance resources in town. Expect to find a moneyed celebrity crowd shopping here.

Specialty Stores

CHILDREN'S CLOTHING

Oilily (✉ 9520 Brighton Way, ☎ 310/859–9145) sells whimsical, colorful Dutch clothing and gifts for children, infants, and even their moms.

Harry Harris Shoes for Children (✉ 409 N. Canon Dr., ☎ 310/274–8481) has a wide selection of European leather shoes and sports footwear for kids.

Pixie Town (✉ 400 N. Beverly Dr., ☎ 213/323–6415) has impeccably designed clothing for infants and children up to size 14.

HOME ACCESSORIES AND GIFTS

Del Mano Gallery (✉ 11981 San Vicente Blvd., Brentwood, ☎ 310/476–8508) houses the work of some of the country's best contemporary artists working in a variety of mediums. The store also features wearable art such as handcrafted handbags.

Hammacher Schlemmer (✉ 309 N. Rodeo Dr., ☎ 310/859–7255) is an ideal place to unearth those hard-to-find presents for adults who never grew up, from rocking horses to "programmable hand-assembled robots."

Lalique (✉ 317 N. Rodeo Dr., ☎ 310/271–7892) features the finest in signature crystal objets d'art by the famed French family of talented artisans.

Pratesi (✉ 9024 Burton Way, ☎ 310/274–7661) is a luxurious linen emporium with the very finest in Italian linens for the tabletop, bedroom, and bathroom, as well as home-fragrance accessories.

Tesoro (✉ 401 N. Canon Dr., ☎ 310/273–9890) has everything from trendy Swid-Powell dishware to Southwestern blankets, ceramics, and art furniture. The wide-ranging works by area artists is well worth a browse.

JEWELRY

Cartier (✉ 370 N. Rodeo Dr., ☎ 310/275–4272; ✉ 220 N. Rodeo Dr., ☎ 310/275–5155) carries all manner of luxury gifts and jewelry with the well-known double-C insignia. The branch at No. 220 houses a repair center.

Harry Winston (✉ 371 N. Rodeo Dr., ☎ 310/271–8554) is the preferred destination for many celebrities looking for Oscar-night jewels.

Tiffany & Co. (✉ 210 N. Rodeo Dr., ☎ 310/273–8880), the famous name in fine jewelry, silver, and more, packages each purchase in a signature blue Tiffany box.

Van Cleef & Arpels (✉ 300 N. Rodeo Dr., ☎ 310/276–1161) sells extravagant baubles and fine jewelry to shopping heavyweights with bank accounts to match.

MEN'S FASHIONS

Alfred Dunhill of London (✉ 201 N. Rodeo Dr., ☎ 310/274–5351) caters to dapper gents in search of British-made suits, shirts, sweaters, and slacks. Pipes, tobacco, and cigars are this store's claim to fame.

Battaglia (✉ 306 N. Rodeo Dr., ☎ 310/276–7184) features accessories, shoes, and elegant Italian fashions— luxurious silks, woolens, cottons, and cashmeres—for men who aren't afraid to dress up.

Bernini (✉ 326 N. Rodeo Dr., ☎ 310/246–1121) specializes in contemporary Italian designer fashions. Look for fine leather accessories from Giorgio Armani.

Bijan (✉ 420 N. Rodeo Dr., ☎ 310/273–6544) is a store shrouded in exclusivity; shopping is by appointment only. Bijan claims that many Arabian sheikhs and other royalty shop here, along with some of the wealthiest men in the United States. Many designs are created especially by the owner.

Davidoff of Geneva (✉ 2 Rodeo Dr., ☎ 310/278–8884) carries fine tobacco and related accessories for smoking aficionados.

Façonnable (✉ 9680 Wilshire Blvd., ☎ 310-754-1200) is the place to find elegant French sportswear characterized by classic tailoring and whimsical patterns with bold color combinations.

Sulka (✉ 2 Rodeo Dr., ☎ 310/859–9940) sells high-quality men's suits, shirts, and furnishings off the rack or made to measure.

WOMEN'S FASHIONS

BCBG Max Azria (✉ 201C N. Rodeo Dr., ☎ 310/278–3263) is the designer line of the moment on the West Coast. The tiny boutique carries hip, affordable sportswear.

Chanel (✉ 400 N. Rodeo Dr., ☎ 310/278–5500) houses two floors of ultra-elegant fashions (suits are a signature "must have") and cosmetics. Chanel's collection of fine and costume jewelry includes copies of the original designs popularized by Coco herself in the 1920s and '30s.

Gianfranco Ferre (✉ 2 Rodeo Dr., ☎ 310/273–6311) carries high-quality sportswear and dress apparel for men and women.

Harari (✉ 9646 Brighton Way, ☎ 310/859–1131) is a favorite haunt of shoppers looking for distinctive, forward-looking fashions and accessories that are less about labels than looks.

M.A.C. (✉ Beverly Center, 8500 Beverly Blvd., ☎ 310/659–6201) carries a line of makeup preferred by professional makeup artists.

Mondi (✉ 421 N. Rodeo Dr., ☎ 310/274–8380), another Rodeo Collection boutique, carries high-style German fashions in the Ralph Lauren mode.

Prada (✉ 9521 Brighton Way, ☎ 310/276–8889) is a must for ladies who crave the signature designer bags, as well as the sleek, postmodern sportswear that groovers have come to adore.

WOMEN'S AND MEN'S FASHIONS

Emporio Armani Boutique (✉ 9533 Brighton Way, ☎ 310/271–7790) houses three levels of this famous Italian designer's architecturally inspired sportswear, home and fashion accessories, and perfumes.

Gianni Versace (✉ 421 N. Rodeo Dr., ☎ 310/276–6799), part of the classy Rodeo Collection, has the trendsetting Italian designs that are in such great demand these days.

NikeTown (✉ 9560 Wilshire Blvd., ☎ 310/275–9998) is a fun place to shop for sports garb, with televised sports events and occasional appearances by superstar athletes.

Polo/Ralph Lauren (✉ 444 N. Rodeo Dr., ☎ 310/281–7200) serves up a complete presentation of Lauren's all-encompassing lifestyle philosophy. The men's area, reminiscent of a posh British men's club, delights Ralph disciples with rough wear and active wear. Women can choose from sportswear, career fashions, and special-occasion accessories, as well as a collection of estate-inspired jewelry. One of the world's most extensive selection of Lauren's home-furnishing designs is upstairs.

Shauna Stein (✉ Beverly Center, 8500 Beverly Blvd., ☎ 310/652–5511) is a distinctive destination for female fans of Eurochic. Labels such as Dolce & Gabanna, Moschino, and Jean Paul Gaultier beckon shoppers more concerned with panache than price.

Tommy Hilfiger (⊠ 425 N. Canon Dr., ☎ 310/888−0132) is a relative newcomer to the street, with a 25,000-square-ft antebellum-gone-Hollywood flagship store. Here are athletic-inspired fashions for men, women, and children with an eye for classics in brilliant colors. Natch, there's also the de rigueur espresso bar.

Traffic (⊠ Beverly Center, 8500 Beverly Blvd., ☎ 310/659−4313), for men, and **Traffic Studio** (⊠ Beverly Center, 8500 Beverly Blvd. ☎ 310/659−3438), for women, are adjoining boutiques featuring men's and women's sportswear and dress apparel by such famous names as Dolce & Gabanna, Hugo Boss, Donna Karan, Jean Paul Gaultier, and Alexander McQueen.

Century City Area

Century City is L.A.'s errand central, where entertainment executives and industry types do their serious shopping. More no-nonsense and affordable than Beverly Hills, the malls and speciality shops in this area appeal to a wider audience. There are also many restaurants in the area, as well as the AMC Century 14-screen movie complex.

Shopping Malls

Century City Shopping Center & Marketplace (⊠ 10250 Santa Monica Blvd., ☎ 310/277−3898), set among gleaming, tall office buildings on what used to be Twentieth Century Fox film studios' back lot, is an open-air mall with an excellent roster of shops, including Macy's and Bloomingdale's.

Specialty Stores

BOOKSTORES

Brentano's (⊠ 10250 Santa Monica Blvd., Century City Shopping Center, ☎ 310/785−0204) is the champagne of bookstores, with a particularly good selection of art books and coffee-table books as well as gift merchandise and handcrafted accessories for the home. Well-known authors often do book signings here.

CHILDREN'S CLOTHING AND TOYS

Allied Model Trains (⊠ 4411 S. Sepulveda Blvd., ☎ 310/313−9353) feels like a huge train museum, with dozens of working train sets toot-tooting around the store.

Jacadi (⊠ Century City Shopping Center, 10250 Santa Monica Blvd., Suite 250,, ☎ 310/203−0101) is a children's boutique featuring private-label French layette, playwear, and special-occasion clothing for newborns and children up to age 12, as well as adorable footwear, hats, toiletries, linens, and even luggage.

At **Mille Petites Fleurs** (⊠ Century City Shopping Center, 10250 Santa Monica Blvd., Suite 692, ☎ 310/203−0424) you'll find exclusive boys' and girls' casual and dressy fashions with a *très* French flair. To-die-for accessories such as refined millinery and elaborate headbands for girls are also on hand.

Try **Petit Jardin Children's Shoes** (⊠ Century City Shopping Center, 10250 Santa Monica Blvd., Suite 121, ☎ 310/203−0824) for fine imported footwear for children to wear everywhere from the park to a fancy birthday party. Sizes range from 1 to 5 (European sizes 15 to 37).

HARDWARE

Restoration Hardware (⊠ 10250 Santa Monica Blvd., Century City Shopping Center, ☎ 310/551-4995) is for yuppie do-it-yourself types with an eye for fancy tools, sundry cabinet handles, imported cleaning supplies, and unusual furnishings and accessories for the home and garden.

Downtown

Ever since the closure of I. Magnin in the upper Wilshire district, downtown Los Angeles has lacked any shopping outlets of note, aside from the discount Citadel Factory Store complex. If you're staying downtown, arrange to rent a car and spend time shopping in the other districts.

Shopping Centers

The **Citadel Factory Stores** (✉ 5675 East Telegraph Rd., off I–5, Commerce, ☎ 323/888–1220) are on the historic landmark site of the former Uniroyal Tire factory, whose distinctive 1,750-ft-long concrete wall is adorned with heraldic griffins and Babylonian princes. Behind the wall are the latest in off-price fashions from famous names such as United Colors of Benetton, Joan & David, Ann Taylor, FILA, and Betsey Johnson. There's also an outdoor food court.

Specialty Stores

BOOKSTORES

KOMA Bookstore (✉ 1764 N. Vermont Ave., ☎ 323/665–0956) sells unorthodox magazines and books such as *Laid Bare: A Memoir of Wrecked Lives and the Hollywood Death Trip.*

Designed to appeal to history buffs and students of cultural policy, **Midnight Special Bookstore** (✉ 1318 3rd St., ☎ 310/393–2923) has sections devoted to political science, European world history, and philosophy. Additional sections cover Asian and African-American history.

CANDLES

Soak up the colorful atmosphere of Olvera Street at **Gonzales Candle Shop** (✉ W14 Olvera St., ☎ 213/625–8771), inside the historic Sepulveda House. Since 1929 the artisans here have supplied shoppers with everything from novelty candles to gothic and religious candles, both large and small.

TOYS, GAMES, AND GIFTS

Look for art posters, books, tableware, children's toys, and jewelry by local and international artists at the **Museum of Contemporary Art Store** (✉ MOCA, 250 S. Grand Ave., ☎ 213/621–1710). The museum and store are closed Monday.

Puzzle Zoo (✉ 1413 3rd St., ☎ 310/393–9201) appeals to kids and parents, even though most products are geared toward pint-size players. In addition to jigsaw and beginner puzzles, Disney toys and action figures line the shelves. A cordoned-off play area allows kids to amuse themselves while their parents shop.

Melrose Avenue Vicinity

On Melrose Avenue you're just as inclined to see vampire-slaying Buffy as you are her victim. No longer off the beaten path, thanks to the Fox television show *Melrose Place,* this bohemian shopping street is a great place to pick up everything from inexpensive trinkets and used clothing to pricey Americana antiques in the *Happy Days* tradition. Most shops are concentrated within the 2-mi stretch of Melrose Avenue between La Brea Avenue and the blocks just west of Crescent Heights Boulevard, but there are also some worthwhile stores both east and west of this strip. The stores listed below are scattered throughout West Hollywood, with some along the Sunset Strip.

Melrose Avenue Shopping

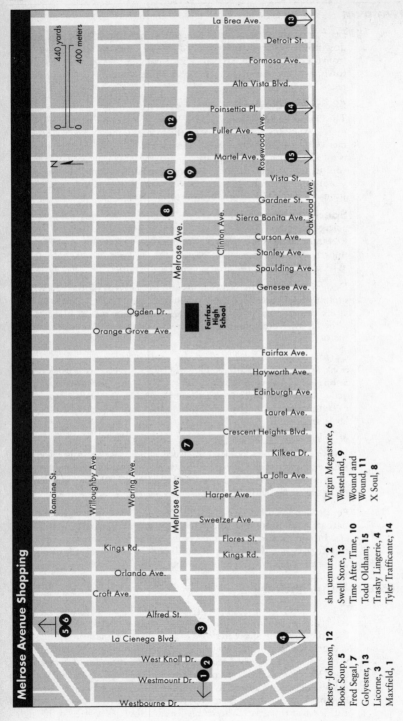

440 yards

400 meters

La Brea Ave.

Detroit St.

Formosa Ave.

Alta Vista Blvd.

Poinsettia Pl.

Fuller Ave.

Martel Ave.

Rosewood Ave.

Vista St.

Gardner St.

Sierra Bonita Ave.

Curson Ave.

Stanley Ave.

Spaulding Ave.

Genesee Ave.

Clinton Ave.

Oakwood Ave.

Melrose Ave.

Ogden Dr.

Orange Grove Ave.

Fairfax High School

Fairfax Ave.

Hayworth Ave.

Edinburgh Ave.

Laurel Ave.

Crescent Heights Blvd.

Kilkea Dr.

La Jolla Ave.

Romaine St.

Willoughby Ave.

Waring Ave.

Melrose Ave.

Harper Ave.

Sweetzer Ave.

Flores St.

Kings Rd.

Kings Rd.

Orlando Ave.

Croft Ave.

Alfred St.

La Cienega Blvd.

West Knoll Dr.

Westmount Dr.

Westbourne Dr.

Betsey Johnson, 12
Book Soup, 5
Fred Segal, 7
Golyester, 13
Licorne, 3
Maxfield, 1

shu uemura, 2
Swell Store, 13
Time After Time, 10
Todd Oldham, 15
Trashy Lingerie, 4
Tyler Trafficante, 14

Virgin Megastore, 6
Wasteland, 9
Wound and
Wound, 11
X Soul, 8

Specialty Stores

ANTIQUES

J. F. Chen Antiques (✉ 8414 Melrose Ave., ☎ 323/655–6310) specializes in ancient Asian pieces, among them Chinese bronzes and lacquered pieces.

Licorne (✉ 8432 Melrose Pl., ☎ 323/852–4765), operated by French emigrants, sells fine 17th-century furnishings.

BOOKSTORES AND MUSIC STORES

Aron's Records (✉ 1150 N. Highland Ave., ☎ 323/469–4700) has an excellent selection of vinyl as well as the latest CD releases.

Book Soup (✉ 8818 Sunset Blvd., ☎ 310/659–3110), one of L.A.'s most prominent literary bookstores, is a frequent book-signing venue for prominent literary and celebrity authors.

Virgin Megastore (✉ 8000 Sunset Blvd., ☎ 323/650–8666) is indeed huge, carrying even tiny indie releases; dozens of listening stations let you sample new and unusual tunes. The classical section is particularly well stocked.

FURNITURE AND HOME ACCESSORIES

Freehand (✉ 8413 W. 3rd St., ☎ 323/655–2607) is an aesthetically pleasing gallery showcasing contemporary American crafts, clothing, and jewelry, mostly by California artists. Owner Carol Sauvion's keen sense of style pays off in the jewelry, ceramics, pottery, and other treasures that she has collected over the years.

Golyester (✉ 136 S. La Brea Ave., ☎ 323/931–1339) sells funky used clothes and home furnishings.

Zipper (✉ 8316 W. 3rd St., ☎ 323/951–0620) focuses on design trends from the 1930s to the 1990s, with everything from furniture and books to candles and shaving kits.

WOMEN'S FASHIONS

Betsey Johnson (✉ 7311 Melrose Ave., ☎ 323/931–4490) epitomizes the neobizarro Melrose look with her whimsical, outlandish women's fashions. The cutting-edge clothing is especially popular with urban nightcrawling hipsters in SoHo, Tokyo, and Hong Kong.

Trashy Lingerie (✉ 402 N. La Cienega Blvd., ☎ 310/652–4543), despite its name, is actually a friendly, family-run establishment; they'll happily make you a custom bra, or anything else you have in mind; there's even a rack of "Officer Naughty" police uniforms. There's a $2 annual membership fee, apparently to keep out the riffraff.

shu uemura (✉ 8606 Melrose Ave., ☎ 800/743-8205) is the makeup emporium choice for celebrity makeup artists and their clients. The store is especially known for their Japanese makeup brushes made of the finest natural sable bristles.

Todd Oldham (✉ 7386 Beverly Blvd., ☎ 323/936–6045) is where you'll find the famous designer's expensive, brightly patterned women's clothes for day and evening, highly favored by celebs including Susan Sarandon.

Tyler Trafficante (✉ 7290 Beverly Blvd., ☎ 323/931–9678) carries designer Richard Tyler's exquisitely tailored, albeit pricey women's sportswear and evening wear, favored by stars such as Julia Roberts. The store occupies a beautiful art deco building.

WOMEN'S AND MEN'S FASHIONS

Maxfield (✉ 8825 Melrose Ave., ☎ 310/274–8800) is among the most elite clothing stores in L.A. Designers carried here include Azzedine Alaia, Comme des Garçons, Issey Miyake, Giorgio Armani, Missoni, and Yamamoto. Maxfield is the supplier of choice for celebs and costumers responsible for dressing the more fashionable shows on television.

Swell Store (⊠ 126 N. La Brea Ave., ☎ 323/937–2096) is a vogue place for shoes (especially the all-American *au courant* Hush Puppies, in any shade including glow-in-the-dark), plus men's and women's clothing and accessories.

X Soul (⊠ 7515 Melrose Ave., ☎ 323/658–5571) is a former Western footwear emporium gone mainstream, with a smattering of boots mixed in with top-of-the-line fashion footwear.

VINTAGE CLOTHING

Time After Time (⊠ 7425 Melrose Ave., ☎ 323/653–8463), decorated to resemble a Victorian garden, has time-honored garments ranging from turn-of-the-century to the 1960s, and a growing assortment of bridal wear, especially antique wedding dresses.

Wasteland (⊠ 7428 Melrose Ave., ☎ 323/653–3028) carries an extensive collection of the kind of retro clothing you might see on Winona Ryder and her stellar celeb contemporaries. The store sells new clothing as well, at reasonable prices. Look for '50s bowling shirts, '40s rayon dresses, funky ties, worn jeans, and leather jackets. Or, if you're low on cash, you might consider selling your worn-out 501s or the fancy gown your mother wore to her prom.

TOYS AND GAMES

Hollywood Magic Shop (⊠ 6614 Hollywood Blvd., ☎ 323/464–5610), a Tinseltown institution, sells costumes year-round and has a wide selection of tricks for beginners and experts.

Wound and Wound (⊠ 7374 Melrose Ave., ☎ 323/653–6703) has a mind-boggling assortment of inexpensive windup toys, robots, music boxes, and rubber animals, as well as a private collection of antique toys not for sale but worthy of a look.

Santa Monica

Less frenetic and status-conscious than Beverly Hills, Santa Monica is an ideal place for a leisurely shopping stroll; the cool ocean breezes felt along the boulevards may tempt you to stay for hours. Most shopping activity takes place at 3rd Street Promenade, the strip of 3rd Street between Broadway and Wilshire Boulevard; Main Street between Pico Boulevard and Rose Avenue; and Montana Avenue, a stretch of a dozen or so blocks from 9th to 17th streets. Beware that on Wednesdays, some of the streets in Santa Monica are blocked off for the weekly farmers market, where parking is usually next to impossible.

Shopping Centers and Streets

3rd Street Promenade is a pedestrian-only street lined with boutiques, movie theaters, clubs, pubs, and restaurants. It's as busy at night as it is in the day, with wacky street performers, missionaries, and protesters hawking their talents, causes, and wares. In addition to chain stores there are several interesting boutiques.

Main Street, which leads from Santa Monica to Venice, is another pedestrian street lined with a mix of mainstream and funky boutiques. Bands occasionally play in local bars for patrons taking in the sea air.

Montana Avenue is a pedestrian street surrounded by quaint residential cottages and bungalows. Now that its boutiques have a following, it's become more than just a neighborhood shopping area. Many of the best shops are between 9th and 17th streets.

Santa Monica Place (⊠ Colorado Ave. and 2nd St.) is a three-story enclosed mall with department stores and chains such as the Wherehouse and Lechter's. Here you'll also find a few uniquely L.A. stores.

Specialty Shops

BOOKSTORES AND MUSIC STORES

Along the 3rd Street Promenade, **Penny Lane** (✉ 1349 3rd St., ☎ 310/319–5333) is an eclectic, funky music store with new and used recordings of artists from the classical, jazz, and rock-and- roll worlds.

CHILDREN'S CLOTHES

And Apple Pie (✉ 1211 Montana Ave., ☎ 310/393–4588) is a tiny store with a big selection of the ever-popular Flapdoodles line, Fitigues, and sweaters from Ball of Cotton, all for newborns and toddlers.

GIFTS, TOYS, AND MEMORABILIA

Imagine (✉ 1001 Montana Ave., ☎ 310/395–9553) carries custom-designed furniture and bedding as well as a large assortment of European wooden toys and gifts.

Star Wares on Main (✉ 2817 Main St., ☎ 310/399–0224) carries authentic and duplicate costumes from films and memorabilia from Loretta Swit, Liz Taylor, and other celebs.

HOME ACCESSORIES AND FURNITURE

Brenda Cain (✉ 1211-A Montana Ave., ☎ 310/395–1559) sells antique jewelry and home accessories, but the hot ticket here is the amazing array of Arts and Crafts pottery by such makers as Roseville and Weller.

Brenda Himmel Stationery (✉ 1126 Montana Ave., ☎ 310/395–2437) is known for its fine stationery, but antiques, frames, photo albums, and books are additional reasons to shop at this quaint boutique.

Sara (✉ 1324 Montana Ave., ☎ 310/394–2900) is a small boutique selling carefully made women's clothing, bags, and home accessories in unusual colors and materials.

WOMEN'S FASHIONS AND ACCESSORIES

Moondance Jewelry Gallery (✉ 1530 Montana Ave., ☎ 310/395–5516) carries an extensive selection of unique jewelry made by 70 some-odd jewelry artists.

Weathervane (✉ 1209 Montana Ave., ☎ 310/393–5344) is one of the street's larger shops, with a friendly staff and fine European women's designer collections, including those of Paul Smith and Victor Victoria.

WOMEN'S AND MEN'S FASHIONS

ABS Clothing (✉ 1533 Montana Ave., ☎ 310/393–8770) sells contemporary California-style sportswear designed in L.A.

A/X Armani Exchange (✉ 2940 Main St., ☎ 310/396–8799) markets the coveted Giorgio Armani label to the masses via T-shirts (the store's best-selling item) as well as other casual and active sportswear for women and men.

San Fernando and San Gabriel Valleys

Over "the Hill" and into the Valleys of Los Angeles lies a long commercial fault line known as Ventura Boulevard, where the lifeblood of Valley shopping is found. Once infamous for the "valley girl" culture born in the 1980s at shopping malls like the Sherman Oaks Galleria (the one and only Galleria in the film *Fast Times at Ridgemont High*), the Valley is still more renowned for shopping malls than any other neighborhood in L.A.

Shopping Malls

Glendale Galleria (✉ 2148 Central Blvd., Glendale, ☎ 818/240–9481) has a Nordstrom, Macy's, and assorted specialty stores.

Media City Center (✉ 201 E. Magnolia Blvd., Burbank, ☎ 818/566-8617) houses a beautiful Macy's as well as Mervyn's and Sears.

The Promenade (✉ 6100 Topanga Canyon Blvd., Woodland Hills, ☎ 818/884–7090), in Woodland Hills at the northern edge of the Valley, has a 24-hour hotline featuring daily bargains and general information about its stores. Within the mall are Macy's and a separate Macy's Men's Store.

Specialty Stores

ANTIQUES, HOME ACCESSORIES, AND GIFTS

Cranberry House (✉ 12318 Ventura Blvd., Studio City, ☎ 818/506–8945) is an expansive shopping co-operative covering half a city block with 140 kiosks run by L.A.'s leading antiques dealers. Visit for vintage furniture, clothing, jewelry, furnishings, and an impressive collection of antique toys and collectibles.

Imagine That! (✉ 13335 Ventura Blvd., Sherman Oaks, ☎ 818/784–8215) is a fun-filled emporium of toys, gifts, decorative accessories, and aromatherapy products for adults and children of all ages. Don't miss the unusual bedding and linen collections.

Pages Books for Children and Young Adults (✉ 18399 Ventura Blvd., Tarzana, ☎ 818/342–6657) sells books for young children and teens.

WOMEN'S, MEN'S, AND CHILDREN'S FASHIONS

Rebel (✉ 6101 Ventura Blvd., Encino ☎ 818/981–5200) is a casually elegant boutique featuring women's and children's fashions with an air of whimsy and flair.

Visit **Scorecard** (✉ 12304 Ventura Blvd., Studio City, ☎ 818/761–0090), where official team gear lines the shelves.

8 Side Trips

Within a couple hours of the metropolitan area, you can plop yourself on a white-sand beach, go skiing in a mountain resort, or swing a golf club in the middle of a cactus-filled desert. The beaches of Orange County are less than an hour's drive, and you can reach Santa Barbara, San Diego, and Palm Springs in about two.

IF YOU'VE GOT THE TIME, A DAY TRIP (or a even a mul-
tiday trip) to the surrounding areas can be very worthwhile. Big Bear and Lake Arrowhead, both about two

Revised and
updated by
Jeanne Fay

to three hours away in the San Bernardino mountains, are rustic resorts with beautiful lakes, crisp air, and snowy winters. Catalina Island, an hour's boat ride off the coast, is the Greek isle of the West
Coast, with crystal blue waters, a gentle climate, and a friendly, small-
town feel. For those curious about California's Spanish heritage, Riverside, an hour southeast of L.A., retains much of its colonial legacy,
including the famed Mission Inn and a number of important museums.
For approximate costs of dining and lodging establishments, *see* the
dining and lodging price charts *in* On the Road with Fodor's.

LAKE ARROWHEAD AND BIG BEAR LAKE

San Bernardino's mountain playground centers around the resorts of
Big Bear and Lake Arrowhead, close together but distinct in appeal.
Big Bear comes alive in winter with downhill ski and snowboard resorts, cross-country trails, lodges, and an active village. Summer draws
crowds to Lake Arrowhead, known for its cool mountain air, trail-
threaded woods, and brilliant lake. Arrowhead is a bit more upscale
than its neighbor, as evidenced by the wealth of its summer residents
and the price tags in its shops.

Even if you're not interested in spending much time at the resorts, the
Rim of the World Scenic Byway, which connects with Lake Arrowhead
and Big Bear Lake, is a magnificent drive. During spring and fall you
can see some amazing views of the San Bernardino Valley from an el-
evation of 8,000 ft.

*Numbers in the margin correspond to points of interest on the Lake
Arrowhead and Big Bear Lake map.*

Lake Arrowhead

*90 mi from Los Angeles, I–10 east to I–215 north to Hwy. 30 east (moun-
tain resorts turnoff) to Hwy. 18 (Waterman Ave.), and then Hwy. 138
north to Hwy. 173 (Lake Arrowhead turnoff); follow signs from there.*

❶ **Lake Arrowhead Village** is an alpine community with offices, shops,
outlet stores, and eateries that descend upon the lake. Although only
residents are permitted to have boats on the lake, you can take a scenic
45-minute cruise on the *Arrowhead Queen,* operated daily by LeRoy
Sports (☎ 909/336–6992) from the waterfront marina. Reservations
are essential. Waterskiing lessons are also available in summer. The **Lake
Arrowhead Children's Museum** (⊠ Lower level of village, ☎ 909/
336–1332) has plenty to entertain pint-size explorers, including hands-
on exhibits, a climbing maze, and a puppet stage.

Just past the town of Rim Forest, follow Bear Springs Road 2 mi north
❷ to the fire lookout tower at **Strawberry Peak.** Brave the steep stairway to the tower, and you'll be treated to a magnificent view and a
lesson on fire spotting by the lookout staff.

❸ If you're up for a barbecue in a wooded setting, visit **Baylis Park Picnic Ground,** farther east on Highway 18.

❹ **Lake Gregory,** at the ridge of Crestline, was formed by a dam constructed
in 1938. Because the water temperature in summer is seldom extremely

Side Trips from Los Angeles

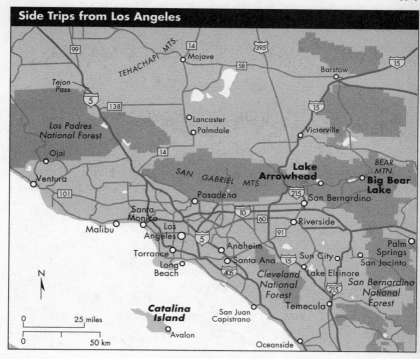

cold—as it can be in the other lakes at this altitude—this is the best swimming lake in the mountains, but it's open in summer only, and there's a nominal charge to swim. The lake allows fishing and has water slides, and you can rent rowboats at Lake Gregory Village.

Dining and Lodging

$$$ ✕ **Casual Elegance.** Just a couple of miles outside Arrowhead Village is this intimate house with a fireplace. The menu changes weekly, and the steaks and seafood remain first-rate. ⊠ *26848 Hwy. 189, Agua Fria*, ☎ *909/337–8932. AE, D, DC, MC, V.*

$$–$$$ ✕ **Royal Oak.** Dimly lit and publike, the Royal Oak has a long history of serving quality food. Among the best dinner choices are pepper steak with baked potato and creamed spinach, and halibut fillet with hollandaise sauce. ⊠ *27189 Hwy. 189, Blue Jay Village*, ☎ *909/337–6018. AE, MC, V. No lunch Sun.–Mon.*

$$$–$$$$ ☷ **Lake Arrowhead Resort.** This lakeside lodge has an Old World feel reminiscent of the Alps. Guests have access to the attached Village Bay Club and Spa for a $5 daily fee. ⊠ *27984 Hwy. 189, Lake Arrowhead Village, 92352*, ☎ *909/336–1511 or 800/800–6792, FAX 909/336–1378. 177 rooms, 4 suites. Restaurant, coffee shop, lobby lounge, pool, health club, beach. AE, D, DC, MC, V.*

$$–$$$ ☷ **Carriage House Bed & Breakfast.** Down comforters and lake views add to the charm of this New England–style bed-and-breakfast. In addition to breakfast, afternoon refreshments are served. ⊠ *472 Emerald Dr., Lake Arrowhead Village 92352*, ☎ *909/336–1400 or 800/526–5070, FAX 909/336–6092. 3 rooms. AE, MC, V. Full breakfast.*

En Route When coming from Los Angeles, you'll reach **Snow Valley** (☎ 909/867–5151) before Big Bear's other ski resorts; it's on Highway 18, 5

Lake Arrowhead and Big Bear Lake

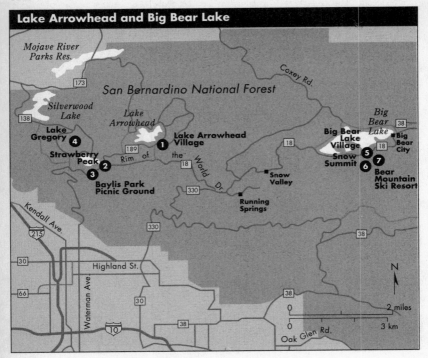

mi east of Running Springs, with snowmaking capabilities and 13 lifts (though the snow isn't always as good here as in Big Bear). Summer visitors can use the trails for hiking, horseback riding, and mountain biking. Call the resort for more information.

Big Bear Lake

110 mi from Los Angeles, I–10 east to I–215 north to Hwy. 30 east; Hwy. 330 north to Hwy. 18 east; chains are sometimes needed in winter.

❺ You'll spot an occasional chaletlike building in **Big Bear Lake,** an alpine- and Western-mountain-style town on the lake's south shore. The paddle wheeler **Big Bear Queen** (☎ 909/866–3218) departs daily from Big Bear Marina, between May and October, for 90-minute scenic tours of the lake; the cost is $9.50. Fishing-boat and equipment rentals are available from several lakeside marinas, including Pine Knot Landing (☎ 909/866–2628), adjacent to Big Bear Village. **Big Bear City,** at the east end of the lake, has more restaurants, motels, and a small airport.

❻ Just southeast of Big Bear Village is **Snow Summit,** one of the area's top ski resorts. It has an 8,200-ft peak and 31 trails, along with two high-speed quads and nine other lifts. Summit has more advanced runs than nearby ski resorts and usually has the best snow. Trails are open to mountain bikers in summer. ✉ *880 Summit Blvd., off Big Bear Blvd.,* ☎ *909/866–5766.*

❼ **Bear Mountain Ski Resort,** also southeast of Big Bear Lake Village, has 11 chairlifts and 35 trails. Bear Mountain is best for intermediate skiers; Summit is more advanced. On busy winter weekends and holidays, it's best to reserve tickets before heading to the mountain. ⊠ *43101 Goldmine Dr., off Moonridge Rd.,* ☎ *909/585–2519.*

Dining and Lodging

$$–$$$ ✕ **Madlon's.** Inside this gingerbread-style cottage, you'll be treated to sophisticated home cooking: lamb chops with Gorgonzola butter, cream of jalapeño soup, or perhaps a fillet with béarnaise sauce. ⊠ *829 W. Big Bear Blvd., Big Bear City,* ☎ *909/585–3762. D, DC, MC, V.*

$$–$$$ ✕ **The Iron Squirrel.** Hearty French fare such as veal Normandie (veal scallopini sautéed with apples, calvados, and cream) and duck à l'orange (roasted duckling with a Grand Marnier sauce) are two specialties at this country French–style restaurant, but you'll also find a big selection of fresh fish and grilled meats on the menu. ⊠ *646 Pine Knot Blvd., Big Bear Lake,* ☎ *909/866–9121. AE, MC, V.*

$–$$ ✕ **Blue Ox Restaurant.** With a simple menu of steaks, ribs, burgers, and chicken, the Blue Ox is best known for its lively bar, where you can munch on peanuts and throw your shells on the floor. ⊠ *441 W. Big Bear Blvd., Big Bear City,* ☎ *909/585–7886. AE, D, DC, MC, V.*

$$$–$$$$ 🏠 **Apples Bed & Breakfast Inn.** Despite its location on a busy road to the
★ ski lifts, the Apples Inn feels remote and peaceful, thanks to the surrounding pine trees. The colorful rooms have names like Golden Delicious, Royal Gala, and Sweet Bough; all have working fireplaces. A common room has a wood-burning stove, a baby grand piano, a game table, and a library loft. ⊠ *42430 Moonridge Rd., Big Bear Lake 92315,* ☎ *909/866–0903. 12 rooms. Hot tub, piano. AE, D, MC, V. Full breakfast.*

$$$–$$$$ 🏠 **Gold Mountain Manor.** This restored log mansion dates back to 1928. Each room has its own theme (ask for the Clark Gable room), and all have fireplaces and old-fashioned beds and quilts. ⊠ *1117 Anita Ave., off North Shore Dr., Big Bear City 92314,* ☎ *909/585–6997 or 800/ 509–2604,* 𝔽𝔸𝕏 *909/585–0327. 4 rooms, 2 suites. AE, D, MC, V. Full breakfast.*

$$–$$$$ 🏠 **The Holiday Inn Big Bear Chateau.** Just two minutes from the lake, Big Bear's grandest hotel resembles a mountain château in the European tradition. Guest rooms have brass beds, antiques, and fireplaces. ⊠ *42200 Moonridge Rd., Big Bear Lake 92315,* ☎ *909/866–6666 or 800/232–7466,* 𝔽𝔸𝕏 *909/866–8988. 76 rooms, 4 suites. Restaurant, lobby lounge, pool, exercise room. AE, MC, V.*

$$–$$$ 🏠 **Northwoods Resort.** Northwoods is a giant log cabin with all the amenities of a resort. The lobby resembles a 1930s hunting lodge, with canoes, antlers, fishing poles, and a grand stone fireplace. Rooms are large but cozy; some have fireplaces and whirlpool tubs. Stillwells Restaurant, next to the lobby, serves hearty American fare. Ski packages are available. ⊠ *40650 Village Dr., Big Bear Lake 92315,* ☎ *909/866–3121 or 800/866–3121,* 𝔽𝔸𝕏 *909/878–2122. 140 rooms, 8 suites. Restaurant, pool, outdoor hot tub, sauna, exercise room. AE, D, DC, MC, V.*

$–$$$ 🏠 **Robinhood Inn.** Centrally located across the street from the Pine Knot Marina, this family-oriented motel has affordable rooms, some with fireplaces or whirlpool tubs. All accommodations face a courtyard with an outdoor whirlpool spa. Also available are several condos just feet from Snow Summit. ⊠ *40797 Lakeview Dr., Big Bear Lake 92315,* ☎ *909/866–4643 or 800/990–9956,* 𝔽𝔸𝕏 *909/866–4645. 17 rooms, 4 suites. Restaurant, outdoor hot tub. AE, MC, V.*

Lake Arrowhead and Big Bear Lake Essentials

Contacts and Resources

LODGING

Rates for Big Bear lodgings fluctuate widely, depending on the season. When winter snow brings droves of Angelenos to the mountains for skiing, expect to pay sky-high prices for any kind of room. Most lodgings require two-night stays on weekends. **Lake Arrowhead Communities Chamber of Commerce** (☞ *below*) has information on camping and lodging. **Big Bear Lake Resort Association** (⌧ Box 1936, Big Bear Lake92315, ☎ 909/866–7000) will help you with lodging arrangements.

VISITOR INFORMATION

Lake Arrowhead Communities Chamber of Commerce (⌧ 28200 Hwy. 189, Bldg. F, Suite 290, Box 219, Lake Arrowhead Village 92352, ☎ 909/337–3715). **Big Bear Chamber of Commerce** (⌧ 630 Bartlett Rd., Box 2860, Big Bear Lake Village 92315, ☎ 909/866–4607).

CATALINA ISLAND

If you dream of an exotic island vacation, and sailing to Hawaii is out of the question, consider taking a cruise to Santa Catalina instead. Just 22 mi across the sea from the L.A. coastline, Catalina has virtually unspoiled mountains, canyons, coves, and beaches; best of all, it gives you a glimpse of what undeveloped southern California once looked like.

Summer, weekends, and holidays, Catalina crawls with thousands of L.A.-area boaters, who tie their vessels at moorings protected in Avalon and other coves. Although Catalina is not known for wide, sandy beaches, sunbathing and water sports are big draws; divers and snorkelers come for the exceptionally clear water surrounding the island. The main town of Avalon is a charming, old-fashioned beach community, where palm trees shade the main street and yachts bob in the crescent-shape bay. White buildings dotting the semi-arid hillsides give it a Greek-island feel.

Cruise ships sail into Avalon twice a week and smaller boats shuttle between Avalon and Two Harbors, a small isthmus cove on the island's western end. You can also take bus excursions beyond Avalon. Roads are limited and nonresident vehicles are prohibited, so hiking (by permit only) is the only other means of exploring.

Perhaps it's no surprise that Catalina has long been a destination for filmmakers and movie stars; in its earlier past, however, the island also sheltered Russian fur trappers (seeking sea-otter skins), pirates, gold miners, and bootleggers (carrier pigeons were used to communicate with the mainland). In 1919, William Wrigley, Jr., the chewing gum magnate, purchased a controlling interest in the company developing the Catalina island, whose most famous landmark, the Casino, was built in 1929 under his orders. Wrigley was also responsible for making Catalina the site of spring training for the Chicago Cubs baseball team (before they moved in 1951).

In 1975 the Santa Catalina Island Conservancy, a nonprofit foundation, acquired about 86% of the island to help preserve the area's natural resources. These days, the conservancy is restoring the rugged interior country with plantings of native grasses and trees. Several bus or van tours bring you into this interior, where you may be lucky enough to see buffalo (brought to the island in the 1920s for the filming of *The Vanishing American*), plus goats, boar, and unusual species of sea life, including such oddities as electric perch, saltwater goldfish, and flying fish.

Although Catalina can be seen in a day, several inviting hotels make it worth extending your stay for one or more nights. A short itinerary might include breakfast along the boardwalk, a tour of the interior, a snorkeling excursion at Casino Point, and dinner in Avalon.

Catalina Island

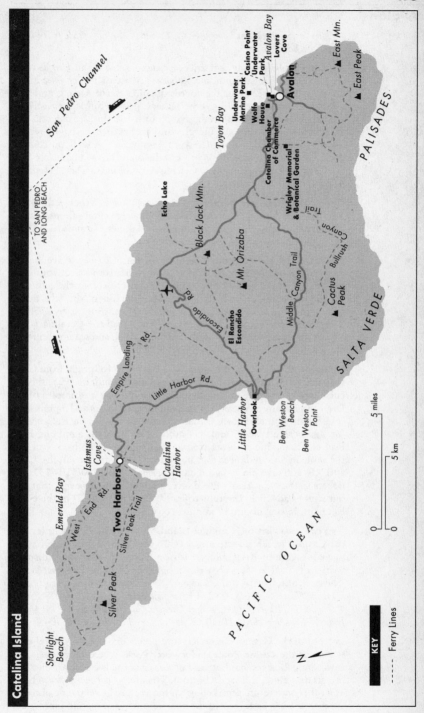

San Pedro Channel

TO SAN PEDRO
AND LONG BEACH

Casino Point
Underwater
Park
Avalon Bay
Lovers
Cove
Underwater
Marine Park
Wolfe
House
Avalon
Catalina Chamber
of Commerce
Wrigley Memorial
& Botanical Garden
East Mtn.
East Peak
PALISADES

Toyon Bay

Echo Lake
Black Jack Mtn.
Mt. Orizaba
Canyon
Trail
Cactus
Peak
Bullrush
Middle Canyon Trail
SALTA VERDE

Escondido Rd.
El Rancho
Escondido
Empire Landing Rd.
Little Harbor Rd.
Little Harbor
Overlook
Ben Weston Beach
Ben Weston Point

Isthmus Cove
Two Harbors
Catalina Harbor

Emerald Bay
West End Rd.
Silver Peak
Silver Peak Trail
Starlight Beach

PACIFIC OCEAN

5 miles
5 km

KEY
----- Ferry Lines

Avalon

1–2-hr ferry ride from Long Beach; 15-min helicopter ride from Long Beach or San Pedro

Avalon, Catalina's only real town, extends from the shore of its natural harbor to the surrounding hillsides. Most of the city's activity, however, is centered along the boardwalk of Crescent Avenue, and most sights are easily reached by foot. Though private autos are restricted and rental cars aren't allowed, taxis, trams, and shuttles can take you anywhere you need to go. Bicycles and golf carts can also be rented; look for rental shops along Crescent Avenue as you walk in from the dock. Permits for hiking the interior of the island are available free from the Catalina Conservancy (☞ Getting Around *in* Catalina Essentials, *below*).

A walk along **Crescent Avenue** is a nice way to begin a tour of the town. You'll notice that vivid art deco tiles adorn the avenue's fountains and planters. Fired on the island by the now defunct Catalina Tile Company, the tiles are a coveted commodity today.

Head to the **Green Pleasure Pier,** at the center of Crescent Avenue, for an overall vantage point of Avalon. From here, stand with your back to the harbor and you'll be in a good position to survey the sights. At the top of the hill on your left, you'll spot the Inn at Mt. Ada, now a top-of-the-line B&B, but once a getaway estate built by William Wrigley, Jr., for his wife. On the pier you'll find the Catalina Island Visitor's Bureau, snack stands, the Harbor Patrol, and scads of squawking seagulls.

On the northwest point of Avalon Bay (looking to your right from Green Pleasure Pier), is the majestic landmark **Casino.** Built in 1929, this circular white structure is considered one of the finest examples of Art Deco architecture anywhere. Its Spanish-inspired floors and murals show off brilliant blue and green Catalina tiles. "Casino" is the Italian word for "gathering place," and has nothing to do with gambling here. Rather, Casino life revolves around the magnificent ballroom; in fact, the same big-band dances that made the Casino famous in the 1930s and '40s still take place on holiday weekends. Call 310/510–1520 for tickets to the New Year's Eve dance, a hugely popular event that sells out well in advance. Daytime tours (☎ 310/510–8687) of the establishment, lasting about 55 minutes, cost $8.50.

You can also visit the **Catalina Island Museum,** in the lower level of the Casino, which investigates 7,000 years of island history; or stop in at the **Casino Art Gallery,** also on the property, which displays works of local artists. First-run movies are screened at the **Avalon Theatre,** noteworthy for its classic 1929 theater pipe organ. ⊠ *1 Casino Way,* ☎ *310/510–2414 for museum, 310/510–0808 for art gallery, 310/510–0179 for Avalon Theatre.* 🎟 *Museum $1.50, art gallery free.* ☉ *Museum daily 10:30–4, art gallery Fri.–Tues. 10:30–4.*

In front of the Casino, snorkelers and divers explore the crystal-clear waters of the **Casino Point Underwater Park,** where moray eels, bat rays, spiny lobsters, halibut, and other sea animals cruise around kelp forests and along the sandy bottom. The area is protected from boats and other watercraft. Snorkeling equipment can be rented on and near the pier. **Lover's Cove,** east of the boat landing, is also good for snorkeling.

Two miles south of the bay via Avalon Canyon Road is the **Wrigley Memorial and Botanical Garden.** Here you'll find plants native to southern California, including several that grow only on Catalina Island:

Catalina ironwood, wild tomato, and rare Catalina mahogany. The Wrigley family commissioned the garden as well as the monument, which has a grand staircase and a Spanish mausoleum inlaid with colorful Catalina tile. Although the mausoleum was never used by the Wrigleys, who are instead buried in Los Angeles, the structure—and the view from it—are worth a look. Tram service between the memorial and Avalon is available daily between 8 AM and 5 PM during summer, less regularly in winter. ⊠ *Avalon Canyon Rd.,* ☎ *310/510–2288.* ☑ *$1.50.* ⊙ *Daily 8–5.*

Walk through the residential hills of Avalon and you'll see such interesting architecture as the contemporary **Wolfe House** on Chimes Tower Road, built in 1928 by noted architect Rudolf Schindler. Its terraced frame is carefully set into a steep site, affording extraordinary views. The house remains a private residence, but you can get a good view of it from the path below and from the street. Across the street, the **Zane Grey Estate** (☎ 310/510–0966 or 800/378–3256) has been transformed into a wonderful rustic hotel. ⊠ *124 Chimes Tower Rd.*

Dining and Lodging

$$–$$$ ✕ **Cafe Prego.** This Italian waterfront restaurant specializes in pasta, seafood, and steak. Reserve ahead, or be prepared for a long wait. ⊠ *603 Crescent Ave.,* ☎ *310/510–1218. AE, D, DC, MC, V.*

$$–$$$ ✕ **Channel House.** A longtime Avalon family owns this restaurant, serv-
★ ing dishes such as Catalina swordfish, coq au vin, and pepper steak with a Continental flair. There's an outdoor patio facing the harbor, as well as a comfortable dining room and beautiful Irish bar. Caesar salad is prepared tableside ⊠ *205 Crescent Ave.,* ☎ *310/510–1617. AE, D, MC, V.*

$$–$$$ ✕ **Pirrone's.** On the second floor of the Hotel Vista del Mar, Pirrone's has a bird's-eye view of the bay. Specialties are local seafood, prime rib, steaks, and pasta; there's a prix fixe brunch on Sundays. ⊠ *417 Crescent Ave.,* ☎ *310/510–0333. AE, D, DC, MC, V. No lunch.*

$$$$ 🏨 **The Inn on Mt. Ada.** Occupying the onetime Wrigley family mansion, the island's most exclusive hotel has all the comforts of a millionaire's mansion—and at millionaire's prices, beginning at $350 a night during the summer season. However, all meals, beverages, snacks, and use of a golf cart are complimentary. The six bedrooms are traditional and elegant; some have canopy beds and overstuffed chairs. The hilltop view of the Pacific is spectacular, and service is discreet. ⊠ *398 Wrigley Rd., 90704,* ☎ *310/510–2030 or 800/608–7669,* ℻ *310/510– 2237. 6 rooms. MC, V. FAP.*

$$$–$$$$ 🏨 **Pavilion Lodge.** Across the street from the beach, this popular motel has simple but spacious rooms. There's a large, grassy courtyard in the center of the complex. ⊠ *513 Crescent Ave., 90704,* ☎ *800/851–0217. 73 rooms. AE, D, DC, MC, V. CP.*

$$–$$$$ 🏨 **Hotel Metropole and Market Place.** This romantic hotel could easily be in the heart of New Orleans's French Quarter. Some guest rooms have balconies overlooking a flower-filled courtyard of restaurants and shops, others have ocean views. Adding to the romance are fireplaces and whirlpool tubs (in some rooms only). For a stunning panoramic view, head for the rooftop sundeck. ⊠ *205 Crescent Ave., 90704,* ☎ *310/510–1884 or 800/541–8528. 42 rooms, 6 suites. AE, MC, V. CP.*

$$–$$$ 🏨 **Hotel Vista del Mar.** Contemporary rooms full of rattan furniture and greenery open onto a skylighted atrium. Some rooms have fireplaces, whirlpool tubs, and wet bars. Two suites have ocean views. ⊠ *417 Crescent Ave., 90704,* ☎ *310/510–1452 or 800/601–3836,* ℻ *310/510–2917. 13 rooms, 2 suites. AE, D, MC, V. CP.*

Nightlife

Warm summer afternoons bring loads of party goers to Catalina's many happy-hour bars, where festivities most assuredly continue into the night. **El Galleon** (✉ 411 Crescent Ave., ☎ 310/510–1188) has microbrews and karaoke. At **Luau Larry's** (✉ 509 Crescent Ave., ☎ 310/510–1919), cocktails are consumed with oyster shooters and calypso hats. The **Catalina Comedy Club** (✉ Glenmore Plaza Hotel, Sumner St., ☎ 310/510–0017) books comic acts all week in summer and on weekends in winter.

Two Harbors

45–60-min ferry ride (summer only) or 90-min bus ride from Avalon; 3-hr ferry ride (summer only) from Los Angeles.

This fairly primitive resort toward the western end of the island has long been a summer boating destination. The area is named for its two harbors, which are separated by a ½-mi-wide isthmus. Once inhabited by pirates and smugglers, Two Harbors recalls the days before tourism was the island's major industry. This side of the island is more untamed, with abundant wildlife, including a herd of buffalo that were initially imported to Catalina as extras in the 1925 film *The Vanishing American*. Activities here include swimming, diving, boating, hiking, mountain biking, beachcombing, kayaking, and sportfishing.

Lodging

Tiny Two Harbors has limited overnight accommodations, including a few campgrounds. All reservations are made through the **visitor services** office (✉ Box 5086, Two Harbors 90704, ☎ 310/510–7265), which you'll no doubt spot upon arriving.

$$–$$$$ 🏨 **Banning House Lodge.** This turn-of-the-century lodge is as close as you'll find to luxury on this end of the island. Rooms have oak furniture and lace curtains. A free shuttle takes guests to and from the village. ✉ *Check-in at visitor services,* ☎ *310/510–7265. 11 rooms. D, MC, V. CP.*

$ ⛺ **Two Harbors Cabins.** These simple, two-person camping cabins have full beds or bunk beds, refrigerators, and a nearby cooking facility. It takes three minutes to reach the cabins by foot from the pier. ✉ *Check-in at visitor services,* ☎ *310/510–7265. 21 cabins. Shower and rest-room facilities. D, MC, V. Closed certain months; call ahead.*

$ ⛺ **Two Harbors Campground.** A quarter-mile outside the village, this campground on the beach has great swimming and snorkeling. Spaces have fire pits and picnic tables. ✉ *Check-in at visitor services,* ☎ *310/510–7265. 54 sites. Shower and rest-room facilities. D, MC, V. Closed during rainstorms; call ahead.*

Catalina Island Essentials

Arriving and Departing

BY BOAT

Catalina Cruises (☎ 800/228–2546) departs Long Beach several times daily, taking an hour and 45 minutes to reach Avalon before continuing to Two Harbors. The fare to either destination is $25 round-trip. **Catalina Express** (☎ 310/519–1212 or 800/995–4386) makes an hour-long run from Long Beach or San Pedro to Avalon and Two Harbors; round-trip fare to either destination from Long Beach and San Pedro is $36. Reservations are advised in summer and on weekends.

Service from Newport Beach is available through **Catalina Passenger Service** (☎ 949/673–5245). Boats leave from Balboa Pavilion at 9 AM, take 75 minutes to reach the island, and cost $36 (reservations are advised). Return boats leave Catalina at 4:30 PM. You can make arrangements to boat in one direction and fly in the other, but reservations must be made separately.

BY BUS
Catalina Safari Shuttle Bus (☎ 310/510–7265) has regular bus service between Avalon and Two Harbors; the trip takes 90 minutes and costs $18 one-way.

BY HELICOPTER
Island Express (☎ 310/510–2525) flies hourly from San Pedro and Long Beach. The trip takes about 15 minutes and costs $66 one-way, $121 round-trip.

Getting Around
BY BICYCLE
Bike rentals are widely available in Avalon; the going rate is about $6 per hour. Look for rental stands on Crescent Avenue and Pebbly Beach Road. Try **Brown's Bikes** (✉ Across from basketball court, ☎ 310/510–0986).

ON FOOT
The requisite permits for hikes into the island's interior are available daily from 9 to 5 at the **Santa Catalina Island Conservancy** (✉ Corner of 3rd and Claressa Sts., ☎ 310/510–2595) and at **visitor services** in Two Harbors (✉ Box 5086, Two Harbors 90704, ☎ 310/510–7265). No permit is required for shorter hikes, such as the one from Avalon to the Botanical Garden. The Conservancy has maps of the island's east-end hikes, such as Hermit's Gulch trail. If you plan to backpack overnight, you'll need a separate camping permit. The interior is dry and desertlike; bring plenty of water.

BY GOLF CART
Golf carts constitute the island's main form of transportation. You can rent them along Avalon's Crescent Avenue and Pebbly Beach Road for about $30 per hour. Try **Island Rentals** (✉ 125 Pebbly Beach Rd., ☎ 310/510–1456).

Contacts and Resources
GUIDED TOURS
Santa Catalina Island Company (☎ 310/510–8687 or 800/322–3434) runs the following tours: a summer-only coastal cruise to Seal Rocks; the *Flying Fish* boat trip (summer evenings only); the inland motor tour; the Skyline Drive; the Casino tour; the Avalon scenic tour; and a submerged glass-bottom-boat tour, where the vessel sinks 5 ft under. Reservations are highly recommended for the inland tours. Tours cost from $8.50 to $26.50; there are ticket booths on the Green Pleasure Pier, at the Casino, in the plaza, and on Metropole Street. **Catalina Adventure Tours** (☎ 310/510–2888), which has booths at the boat landing and on the pier, arranges similar excursions at comparable prices.

LODGING
Between Memorial Day and Labor Day, be sure to make reservations *before* heading here. After Labor Day, rooms are much easier to find on shorter notice, rates drop dramatically, and many hotels offer packages that include transportation from the mainland and/or sightseeing tours.

VISITOR INFORMATION
The **Catalina Island Visitor's Bureau** (✉ Green Pleasure Pier, Box 217, Avalon 90704, ☎ 310/510–1520, FAX 310/510–7606) is a good place to get your bearings, check into special events, and plan your itinerary. The staff will help you find lodgings.

9 Orange County

No place in southern California evokes the stereotype of the California good life quite the way Orange County does: Million-dollar mansions dot the coastline, golf courses meander through inland hills, and convertibles swarm Pacific Coast Highway. But, while the coastal cities are all about relaxing under swaying palm trees, the inland cities are alive with amusement parks, professional sports events, and dozens of hotels and restaurants, all within minutes of each other. You can have it all in one place in Orange County, for better or for worse.

FEW OF THE CITRUS GROVES that gave Orange County its name remain. This region south and east of Los Angeles is now a high-tech business hub where tourism is the number-one industry. Anaheim's theme parks lure hordes of visitors; numerous festivals celebrate the county's culture and relatively brief history; and the area supports fine dining, upscale shopping, and several standout visual and performing arts facilities. With its tropical flowers and palm trees, the stretch of coast between Seal Beach and San Clemente is often called the "American Riviera." Exclusive Newport Beach, artsy Laguna, and the up-and-coming surf town of Huntington Beach are the stars, but lesser-known gems such as Corona del Mar are also worth visiting.

Updated by
Megan Pincus
and Allison
Joyce

Pleasures and Pastimes

Dining
Predictably, Italian restaurants and burger joints abound, but you'll also find French, Chinese, Thai, Scandinavian, Cuban, and other types of cuisine, in every type of setting—from the elegant Dining Room at the Ritz-Carlton, Laguna Niguel, to the ramshackle Ruby's, a diner on the Newport Pier. For approximate costs, *see* the dining price chart *in* On the Road with Fodor's.

Lodging
In a uniquely So-Cal way, accommodations here fulfill their patrons' paradoxical need for serenity and glamour. Limos speed in and out of hotel driveways, ferrying people aching to be noticed; but despite all the palm trees, fountains, and glitz, the pace is far too hurried and the people way too self-conscious for a tropical getaway. Still, a few nights at the Four Seasons Hotel in Newport Beach, or the Ritz-Carlton, Laguna Niguel in Dana Point may well be the next best thing to a Caribbean vacation.

The prices listed in this chapter are based on summer rates. Prices are often lower in winter, especially near Disneyland, unless there's a convention in Anaheim, and weekend rates are often rock-bottom at business hotels; it's worth calling around to find bargains. For approximate costs, *see* the lodging price chart *in* On the Road with Fodor's.

Outdoor Activities and Sports
Predictably, water sports rule the coast of Orange County, but other sports don't lag far behind: The sight of people jogging, walking, biking, and blading is nearly inescapable.

Wave action along Orange County's coastline ranges from beginner to expert. Beginners can get a feel for the waves by riding a Boogie board at Seal Beach, north of Huntington, or at the Newport River Jetties. Surfing is permitted at most beaches year-round (check local newspapers or talk to lifeguards for conditions), and surfboard rental stands line the coast. The best waves are usually at San Clemente, Newport Beach, and Huntington Beach.

From June through September the ocean temperature tops 70° and lifeguards patrol almost every beach. Keep a lookout for signs warning of dangerous conditions: Undertow, strong currents, and big waves can all be hazardous. Never go in the water when flags with a black circle are flying, and avoid swimming near surfers. Many beaches close at night.

Golf and tennis are two more reasons to visit Orange County, thanks to the area's great weather and dozens of facilities. A few public golf courses are listed in this chapter; for more information contact the Southern California Golf Association or the Southern California Public Links Golf Association (☞ Visitor Information *in* Orange County A to Z). Many hotels have tennis courts, and there are public tennis facilities throughout the county. Some courts are listed below; consult your hotel concierge for other options.

For those who wish to enjoy the coastline by bike or by foot, the Santa Ana Riverbed Trail hugs the Santa Ana River for 20½ mi between Pacific Coast Highway (PCH) at Huntington State Beach and Imperial Highway in Yorba Linda. Joggers enjoy an uninterrupted path the entire way and don't have to run alongside cars. There are entrances, rest rooms, and drinking fountains at all crossings. A bike path winds south from Marina del Rey all the way to San Diego with only minor breaks. Most beaches have bike rental stands.

Scenic Drives

A drive up or down Pacific Coast Highway reveals the contradictions of southern California—the pristine ocean vistas and the scars of commercial exploitation, the appealingly laid-back beach life, and the tacky bric-a-brac of the tourist trail. Oil rigs line the road from Long Beach south to Huntington Beach before giving way suddenly to unblemished shoreline and dramatic hillsides.

For a scenic mountain drive, try Santiago Canyon Road, which winds through the Cleveland National Forest in the Santa Ana Mountains. Tucked away in these mountains are Modjeska Canyon, Irvine Lake, and Silverado Canyon. In addition to the natural views, this route showcases some of the most spectacular homes in Orange County.

Exploring Orange County

Like Los Angeles, Orange County stretches over a large area, lacks a focal point, and has limited public transportation. You'll need a car and a sensible game plan to make the most of your visit. If you're headed to Disneyland, you'll probably want to stay in or near Anaheim, organize your activities around the inland-county attractions, and take excursions to the coast. If the mouse's kingdom is not part of your itinerary, try staying at a midpoint location such as Irvine or Costa Mesa, both equidistant from inland tourist attractions and the coast. These towns are less crowded than Anaheim and less expensive than the beach cities. Of course, if you can afford it, staying at the beach is always recommended.

Numbers in the text correspond to numbers in the margin and on the Orange County map.

Great Itineraries

IF YOU HAVE 1 DAY

You're going to **Disneyland** ①.

IF YOU HAVE 3 DAYS

You're still going to **Disneyland** ① (stay overnight in 🏨 **Anaheim**), but on day two, head to the coast and explore **Newport Harbor** ⑰. Have lunch at Ruby's on the pier, and then take a 90-minute harbor cruise. Spend the night in 🏨 **Newport Beach.** On day three, visit **Laguna Beach** and, if there's time, **Dana Point** or **Huntington Beach,** then either hang out on the beach or head inland to **Costa Mesa,** where you can browse through **South Coast Plaza** ⑬, one of the world's largest retail, entertainment, and dining complexes.

When to Tour Orange County

The sun shines year-round in Orange County, but you can beat the crowds and the heat by visiting during spring and fall. Smart parents give kids their Disney fix during these periods (though you should still expect fairly long waits for many rides and shows). If you're traveling with children, you could easily devote several days to the theme parks—a day or two at the Magic Kingdom, a day at Knott's Berry Farm, and perhaps an additional day driving to some of the area's lesser-known diversions.

INLAND ORANGE COUNTY

About a 35-minute drive from downtown Los Angeles on I–5 (also known as the Golden State Freeway) is Anaheim, Orange County's tourist hub, which centers around the big D.

Anaheim

26 mi southeast of Los Angeles, I–5.

The snowcapped Matterhorn, the centerpiece of the Magic Kingdom, dominates Anaheim's skyline, an enduring reminder of the role Disneyland has played in the urbanization and growth of Orange County. Disneyland has attracted millions of visitors and thousands of workers, and Anaheim has been their host, becoming Orange County's most populous city and accounting for more than half the county's 40,000 hotel rooms. To understand the symbiotic relationship between Disneyland and Anaheim, one need only look at the $1 billion-plus being spent to expand the park and renovate run-down areas of the city. Anaheim's vast tourism complex also includes Edison International Field, home of the Anaheim Angels baseball team; the Arrowhead Pond, where the Mighty Ducks hockey team plays; and the enormous Anaheim Convention Center.

★ ♺ ❶ One of the biggest misconceptions tourists have about **Disneyland** is that they've "been there, done that" if they've visited either the more mammoth Disney World or one of the two Disney parks overseas. But Disneyland occupies a unique place in the Disney legend, the only one of the four Kingdoms overseen by Walt himself. Mr. Disney's personal stamp has made an imprint that, while perhaps not specifically quantifiable, can be felt in the park's genuinely historic feel.

There's plenty here that you won't find anywhere else. Storybook Land, with its miniature replicas of classic animated Disney scenes, is a Fantasyland favorite. The kitschy 20,000 Leagues Under the Sea submarine ride can be found only in Anaheim. The Matterhorn, The Indiana Jones Adventure and, at least for the moment, the nighttime show Fantasmic! are unique to Disneyland.

You can start your Disneyland visit with a stroll along **Main Street,** a romanticized image of small-town America, circa 1900. Trollies, double-decker buses, and horse-drawn wagons travel up and down a quaint thoroughfare lined with rows of interconnected shops selling everything from Disney products to magic tricks, crystal ware, sports memorabilia, and photo supplies.

Rides at Disneyland (more than four dozen of them) are divided into themed lands. **Fantasyland,** its entrance marked by Sleeping Beauty Castle, is where you can fly on Peter Pan's Flight, go down the rabbit hole with Alice in Wonderland, take an aerial spin with Dumbo the Flying Elephant, twirl around in giant cups at the Mad Tea Party, bobsled through the Matterhorn, or visit It's a Small World, where Animatron children from 100 countries sing the well-known song.

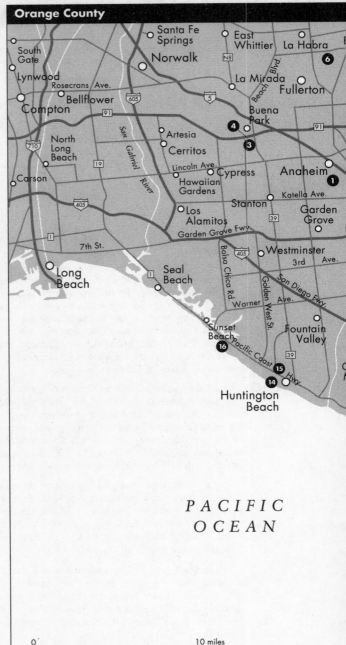

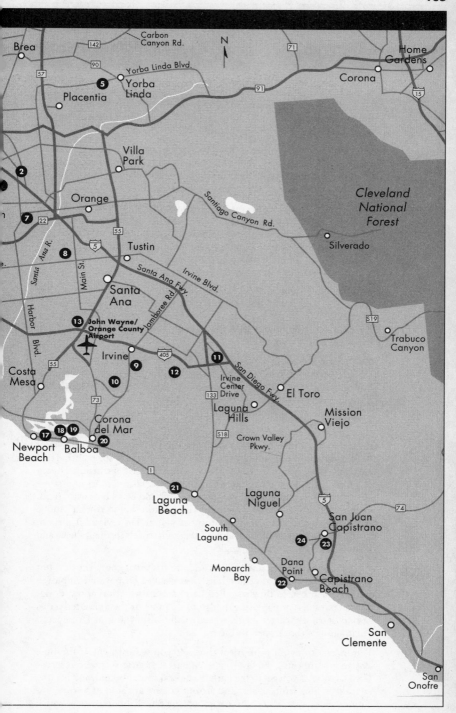

In **Frontierland** you can take a cruise on the steamboat *Mark Twain* or the sailing ship *Columbia*. Kids of every age enjoy rafting to Tom Sawyer Island for an hour or so of climbing and exploring. Some visitors to **Adventureland** have taken the Jungle Cruise so many times that they know the operators' patter by heart. Special effects and decipherable hieroglyphics entertain guests on line for the Indiana Jones Adventure, a don't-miss thrill ride through the Temple of the Forbidden Eye. Also here are the animated bears of **Critter Country; Splash Mountain,** Disney's steepest, wettest adventure; the Enchanted Tiki Room; and shops with African and South Seas wares.

A recent upgrade completed in May 1998 has given **Tomorrowland** a fictional "Buck Rogers" feel. Here you can ride on the futuristic Astro Orbitor rocket, zip along on the Rocket Rods or Space Mountain, or tinker with the toys of tomorrow at Innoventions.

You can browse and shop your way through the twisting streets of **New Orleans Square,** in the company of strolling Dixieland musicians; this is also where you'll find the ever-popular Pirates of the Caribbean ride. The Haunted Mansion, populated by 999 holographic ghosts, is also nearby. Theme shops sell hats, perfume, Mardi Gras merchandise, and gourmet foods, and the gallery carries original Disney art.

At **Mickey's Toontown** kids can climb up a rope ladder on the *Miss Daisy* (Donald Duck's boat), talk to a mailbox, and walk through Mickey's House to meet Mickey. Here is also where you'll find the Roger Rabbit Car Toon Spin, the largest and most unusual black-light ride in Disneyland history.

The Magic Kingdom's crowd-pleasing live-action and special-effects show, Fantasmic! features exhilarating music and just about every animated Disney character ever drawn. Daytime and nighttime Main Street parades are often based on the Disney classic of the moment.

During the busy summer season, Disneyland can be mobbed. If possible, visit on a rainy midweek day instead. In summer, try to avoid the hot midday hours; though most Disney attractions are indoors, you'll be standing in direct sunlight as you wait in lines. Also, try to arrive early; the box office opens a half hour before the park's scheduled opening time. (On most days, guests of the Disneyland Resort and some Anaheim hotels are admitted before other visitors.) Brochures with maps, available at the entrance, list show and parade times. You can move from one area of Disneyland to another via the Disneyland Railroad; in addition to touring all the "lands," the train travels through the Grand Canyon and a prehistoric jungle.

Characters appear for autographs and photos throughout the day, but you'll probably have to wait in line. Check with a Disneyland employee (or cast member, as they're called here) for information about designated character stops. You can also meet some of the animated icons at one of the character meals served at the Disneyland or Disneyland Pacific hotels (both open to the public).

Plan meals to avoid peak meal times. If you want to eat at the Blue Bayou restaurant in New Orleans Square, it's best to make reservations as soon as you get to the park. Fast-food spots abound, and healthy snacks such as fruit, pasta, and frozen yogurt are sold at various locations. For a quick lunch on the go, try the Blue Ribbon Bakery, which sells gourmet sandwiches.

You can store belongings and purchases in lockers just off Main Street; purchases can also be sent to the Package Pickup desk at the front of the park. If you're planning on staying for more than a day or two, ask about the Flex Pass, which gives you five-day admission to Disneyland for roughly the same price as a two-day passport (about $68 at press time). The caveat is that the passes are not sold at the park itself: you can buy them through travel agents and at most area hotels. ⊠ *1313 Harbor Blvd.,* ☎ *714/781–4565.* ⊞ *$38.* ☽ *June–mid-Sept., Sun.–Fri. 9*AM*–midnight, Sat. 9* AM*–1* AM; *mid-Sept.–May, weekdays 10–6, Sat. 9–midnight, Sun. 9–10.*

❷ A 1908 Carnegie Library building houses the **Anaheim Museum,** which documents the history of Anaheim. Changing exhibits include art collections, women's history, and hobbies. A hands-on children's gallery keeps the kids entertained. ⊠ *241 S. Anaheim Blvd. and Broadway,* ☎ *714/778–3301.* ⊞ *$2 donation requested.* ☽ *Wed.–Fri. 10–4, Sat. noon–4, Sun.–Tues. by appointment only.*

Dining and Lodging

Most Anaheim hotels have complimentary shuttle service to Disneyland, though many are within walking distance.

$–$$$$ ✕ **Yamabuki.** Part of the Disneyland Pacific Hotel complex, this stylish Japanese restaurant serves traditional dishes and has a full sushi bar. The plum-wine ice cream is a treat. ⊠ *Disneyland Pacific Hotel, 1717 S. West St.,* ☎ *714/956–6755. AE, DC, MC, V. No lunch weekends.*

$$–$$$ ✕ **The Catch/Hop City Blues and Brew.** Across from Anaheim Stadium, this combination sports bar and House of Blues–style dinner-and-entertainment venue draws a crowd at night. The Catch serves hearty portions of steak, seafood, pasta, and salads. The adjacent Hop City steak house serves up live blues along with 14-ounce blackened rib eyes and 20-ounce T-bones. Try the spicy Wings from Hell or the tamer honey-ginger version. ⊠ *1929 and 1939 S. State College Blvd.,* ☎ *714/634– 1829 (The Catch), 714/978–3700 (Hop City). AE, DC, MC, V.*

$$–$$$ ✕ **JW's.** This subdued steak house inside the Anaheim Marriott specializes in aged beef but also serves seafood. It's a great place for business or romance. ⊠ *Anaheim Marriott, 700 W. Convention Way,* ☎ *714/750–8000. AE, D, DC, MC, V. No lunch. Valet parking.*

$$–$$$ ✕ **Mr. Stox.** Oriental rugs, intimate booths, and linen tablecloths create an elegant setting at this family-owned restaurant. Prime rib, mesquite-grilled rack of lamb, and fresh fish specials are excellent; the pasta, bread, and pastries are homemade; and the wine list wins awards. ⊠ *1105 E. Katella Ave.,* ☎ *714/634–2994. AE, D, DC, MC, V. No lunch weekends. Valet parking.*

$$–$$$ ✕ **The White House.** Several small dining rooms are set with crisp linens, candles, and flowers in this 1909 mansion. The northern Italian menu includes pasta, veal scallopini, and a large selection of fresh seafood. A three-course prix-fixe lunch, served weekdays only, costs $16. ⊠ *887 S. Anaheim Blvd.,* ☎ *714/772–1381. AE, DC, MC, V. No lunch weekends.*

$–$$$ ✕ **Luigi's D'Italia.** Despite the simple surroundings——red vinyl booths and plastic checkered tablecloths—Luigi's serves outstanding Italian cuisine: spaghetti marinara, cioppino, and all the classics. Kids will feel right at home here; there's even a children's menu. ⊠ *801 S. State College Blvd.,* ☎ *714/490–0990. AE, MC, V.*

$$$–$$$$ 🏨 **Anaheim Hilton and Towers.** Next to the Anaheim Convention Center, this busy Hilton is the largest hotel in southern California: It even has its own post office, as well as shops, restaurants, and cocktail lounges. A shuttle runs to Disneyland, or you can walk the few blocks. Special summer children's programs include a "Vacation Station Lending Desk" with games, toys, and books, as well as children's menus. There's a $10 fee to use the health club. ⊠ *777 Convention Way, 92802,* ☎ *714/750–4321 or 800/445–8667,* FAX *714/740–4460.*

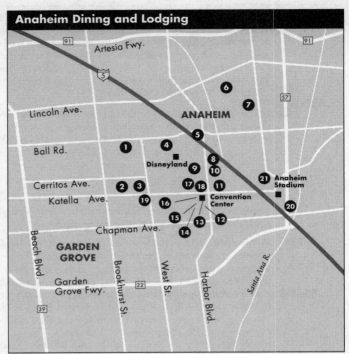

Anaheim Dining and Lodging

1,574 rooms, 95 suites. 4 restaurants, 2 lounges, no-smoking floors, room service, pool, hot tub, health club, beauty salon, massage, sauna, piano, children's programs (under 12), baby-sitting, laundry service and dry cleaning, concierge, meeting rooms, business services, travel services, car rental, airport shuttle, parking (fee). AE, D, DC, MC, V.

$$$–$$$$ ⊡ **Anaheim Marriott.** Rooms at this busy convention hotel are well equipped for business travelers, with desks, two phones, and modem hookups. Some rooms have balconies. Accommodations on the north side have good views of Disneyland's summer fireworks shows. Discounted weekend and Disneyland packages are available. ⊠ *700 W. Convention Way, 92802,* ☎ *714/750–8000 or 800/228–9290,* FAX *714/750–9100. 1,033 rooms, 52 suites. 2 restaurants, 2 lounges, in-room modem lines, in-room safes, no-smoking rooms, room service, 2 pools, 2 hot tubs, health club, piano, coin laundry, laundry service and dry cleaning, concierge, concierge floor, meeting rooms, car rental, parking (fee). AE, D, DC, MC, V.*

$$$–$$$$ ⊡ **Disneyland Hotel.** This Disney-owned resort has a kitschy, 1950s
★ charm that completes the Disney vacation. Disney products are for sale everywhere, and Disney music plays nonstop. You can swim at either the pool or "beach," and paddle boats or steer remote-control tugboats on the lagoon. In Goofy's Kitchen, kids can dine with their favorite Disney characters. Rooms in the Bonita tower overlook the Fantasy Waters, a fountain that's illuminated at night. On most days, guests staying at the hotel are admitted to the park before the gates open to

the general public. Room-and-ticket packages are available. ✉ *1150 W. Cerritos Ave., 92802,* ☎ *714/778–6600,* FAX *714/956–6510. 1,074 rooms, 62 suites. 6 restaurants, 5 bars, in-room safes, minibars, refrigerators, room service, 3 pools, hot tub, health club, beach, paddle boating, skating, baby-sitting, laundry service and dry cleaning, concierge, concierge floor, business services, rental car, travel services, airport shuttle, parking (fee). AE, D, DC, MC, V.*

$$$–$$$$ 🖭 **Disneyland Pacific Hotel.** The newest addition to the Disneyland hotel empire has many of the same Disney touches as the Disneyland Hotel, but the atmosphere is a bit quieter and more ordinary. From here you can walk to Disneyland or pick up a shuttle or monorail. The Pacific has a Japanese restaurant with a sushi bar as well as a contemporary California grill. Start the day with the Minnie and Friends character breakfast at the PCH Grill, or visit with Mary Poppins in her parlor at the Practically Perfect Tea. ✉ *1717 S. West St., 92802,* ☎ *714/956– 6424,* FAX *714/956–6582. 488 rooms, 14 suites. 2 restaurants, 2 lounges, patisserie, no-smoking rooms, room service, pool, hot tub, exercise room, laundry service and dry cleaning, concierge, concierge floor, parking (fee). AE, D, DC, MC, V.*

$$$ 🖭 **Sheraton Anaheim Hotel.** If you're hoping to escape the commer-
★ cial atmosphere of the hotels surrounding Disneyland, consider this sprawling replica of a Tudor-style castle. In the flowers-and-plants-filled lobby you're welcome to sit by the grand fireplace, watching fish swim around in a pond. The sizable rooms open onto interior gardens. A Disneyland shuttle is available. ✉ *1015 W. Ball Rd., 92802,* ☎ *714/ 778–1700 or 800/325–3535,* FAX *714/535–3889. 475 rooms, 16 suites. Restaurant, bar, deli, in-room modem lines, in-room safes, no-smoking rooms, room service, pool, outdoor hot tub, health club, baby-sitting, coin laundry, laundry service and dry cleaning, concierge, concierge floor, meeting rooms. AE, D, DC, MC, V.*

$$$ 🖭 **West Coast Anaheim Hotel.** Service is extra helpful at this hotel near the convention center. Guest rooms all have balconies; those in the tower have good views of Disneyland's summer fireworks shows. Guest are invited to relax in the nicely landscaped pool area. ✉ *1855 S. Harbor Blvd., 92802,* ☎ *714/750–1811 or 800/353–2773,* FAX *714/971–3626. 494 rooms, 6 suites. Restaurant, coffee shop, lounge, no-smoking rooms, refrigerators, room service, pool, outdoor hot tub, piano, laundry service and dry cleaning, concierge, meeting rooms, car rental, parking (fee). AE, D, DC, MC, V.*

$$–$$$ 🖭 **Holiday Inn Anaheim at the Park.** Families frequent this Mediterranean-style hotel. Some rooms have separate sitting areas. Complimentary shuttle service shuttles guests to nearby attractions, including Disneyland, Knott's Berry Farm, the Movieland Wax Museum, Medieval Times, and the Main Place and Anaheim Plaza shopping areas. ✉ *1221 S. Harbor Blvd., 92805,* ☎ *714/758–0900 or 800/545–7275,* FAX *714/533–1804. 252 rooms, 2 suites. Restaurant, bar, no-smoking rooms, room service, pool, outdoor hot tub, concierge, meeting rooms, travel service, free parking. AE, D, DC, MC, V.*

$$–$$$ 🖭 **Radisson Maingate.** This friendly hotel received numerous overhauls when it changed its name (and ownership) from Holiday Inn in 1997. Rooms in the two eight-story buildings have all-new furniture, and some have pull-out sofas as well as beds. Regular shuttles can zip you to Disneyland or Knott's Berry Farm. ✉ *1850 S. Harbor Blvd., 92802,* ☎ *714/750–2801 or 800/333-3333,* FAX *714/971–4754. 487 rooms, 15 suites. Restaurant, bar, no-smoking rooms, room service, pool, coin laundry, laundry service and dry cleaning, concierge, meeting rooms, travel services, free parking. AE, D, DC, MC,V.*

$-$$$ ⚕ **Candy Cane Inn.** One of the Disneyland area's first hotels (deeds
★   were executed Christmas Eve, hence the name) the Candy Cane was
       completely rebuilt in 1991, earning it a reputation as Anaheim's most
       beautiful commercial property. Rooms are spacious (though on the basic
       side); deluxe rooms have refrigerators and coffeemakers. Though the
       hotel is just steps from the Disneyland parking lot, you may have to
       walk a bit to circumnavigate street construction. A free Disneyland shut-
       tle runs every half hour. ⊠ *1747 S. Harbor Blvd., 92802,* ☎ *714/774–
       5284 or 800/345–7057,* FAX *714/772–5462 or 714/772–1305. 172
       rooms. No-smoking rooms, refrigerators, pool, wading pool, outdoor
       hot tub, coin laundry, laundry service and dry cleaning, free parking.
       Continental breakfast. AE,D, DC, MC, V.*

$-$$$ ⚕ **Desert Palm Inn and Suites.** This hotel midway between Disneyland
       and the convention center is a great value, with $99 one-bedroom suites
       that can accommodate the whole family. All rooms, including the stan-
       dard variety, have microwaves. Book well in advance, especially when
       large conventions are in town. ⊠ *631 W. Katella Ave., 92802,* ☎ *714/
       535–1133 or 800/635–5423,* FAX *714/491–7409. 50 rooms, 50 suites.
       In-room modem lines, no-smoking rooms, refrigerators, pool, outdoor
       hot tub, sauna, coin laundry, laundry service and dry cleaning, free park-
       ing. AE, D, DC, MC, V.*

$$ ⚕ **Best Western Stovall's Inn.** Nice touches at this well-kept motel in-
       clude a topiary garden, a free shuttle to Disneyland, and Nintendo and
       movie rentals. Ask about discounts if you're staying several nights. ⊠
       1110 W. Katella Ave., 92802, ☎ *714/778–1880 or 800/854–8175,* FAX
       *714/778–3805. 290 rooms. Bar, no-smoking rooms, room service, 2
       pools, outdoor hot tub, coin laundry, laundry service and dry clean-
       ing, business services, meeting rooms, travel services, free parking. AE,
       D, DC, MC, V.*

$$ ⚕ **Holiday Inn Express–Anaheim.** This limited-service Holiday Inn has
       scaled-back amenities (there's no room service or restaurant), but it's
       only about a block from Disneyland, and the price is right. Rooms are
       spacious; a few have whirlpool tubs. Minisuites, with two queen beds
       and a pull-out sofa, are a particularly good value. ⊠ *435 W. Katella Ave.,
       92802,* ☎ *714/772–7755 or 800/833–7888,* FAX *714/772–2727. 74
       rooms, 30 suites. No-smoking rooms, refrigerators, pool, outdoor hot
       tub, in-room VCRs, laundry service and dry cleaning, business services,
       meeting room, car rental, free parking. AE, D, DC, MC,V. CP.*

$$ ⚕ **Ramada Inn Conestoga at Disneyland.** Pint-size cowboys will love
       this Old West–style hotel with swinging saloon doors and a *Bonanza*-
       style lobby. The restaurants look like saloons, and there's a nice pool
       area for relaxing after a day in the saddle. The residential location makes
       for quiet evenings. A complimentary shuttle heads to Disneyland every
       hour. ⊠ *1240 S. Walnut Ave., 92802,* ☎ *714/535–0300 or 800/824–
       5459,* FAX *714/999–1727. 252 rooms. Restaurant, bar, no-smoking
       rooms, room service, pool, outdoor hot tub, laundry service and dry
       cleaning, airport shuttle, free parking. AE, D, DC, MC,V.*

$-$$ ⚕ **Anaheim Fairfield Inn by Marriott.** The hotel was completely redone
       after Marriott took over in 1997; the finished product has a bit more
       character than the typical Fairfield, with detail-oriented service and spa-
       cious rooms with sleeper sofas as well as beds. Across the street from
       Disneyland, the hotel runs a free shuttle service to the park. A nearby
       restaurant provides room service, but kids usually prefer McDonald's
       Happy Meals, delivered right to your room. ⊠ *1460 S. Harbor Blvd.,
       92802,* ☎ *714/772–6777 or 800/854–3340,* FAX *714/999–1727. 467
       rooms. Restaurant, no-smoking rooms, refrigerators, room service, pool,
       outdoor hot tub, concierge, travel services, meeting rooms, free park-
       ing. AE, D, DC, MC,V.*

$–$$ ☷ **Castle Inn and Suites.** Faux-stone trim and towers, shield decor, and replica gas lamps dress up the Castle Inn. Children under 18 stay free; other perks include microwaves (in suites only) and refrigerators. Some rooms also have whirlpool tubs. Across the street from Disneyland, the hotel runs a complimentary shuttle to the park. ⊠ *1734 S. Harbor Blvd., 92802,* ☎ *714/774–8111 or 800/521–5653,* ℻ *714/956–4736. 150 rooms, 50 suites. Refrigerators, no-smoking rooms, pool, wading pool,outdoor hot tub, coin laundry, laundry service and dry cleaning, free parking. AE, D, DC, MC, V.*

$ ☷ **Alpine Motel.** With a lobby that looks like a snow-covered lodge, this convenient hotel is just steps from Disneyland and the convention center. Two-room suites are a great value, even during the busy summer season. ⊠ *715 W. Katella Ave., 92802,* ☎ *714/535–2186 or 800/772–4422,* ℻ *714/535–3714. 41 rooms, 8 suites. No-smoking rooms, pool, coin laundry, laundry service and dry cleaning, free parking. AE, D, DC, MC,V. CP.*

INEXPENSIVE MOTELS

☷ **Days Inn Suites** (⊠ 1111 S. Harbor Blvd., ☎ 714/533–8830, ℻ 714/758–0573) and **Days Inn Maingate** (⊠ 1604 S. Harbor Blvd., ☎ 714/635–3630, ℻ 714/520–3290) are two options on Disneyland's eastern boundary. **Motel 6** (⊠ 100 W. Freedman Way, ☎ 714/520–9696, ℻ 714/533–7539) is about three blocks from the park.

Nightlife

There's country music with line-dancing lessons on three dance floors from Tuesday through Saturday at **Cowboy Boogie Co.** (⊠ 1721 S. Manchester Ave., ☎ 714/956–1410). Sunday nights usually feature a different style of music; call in advance to see what's on. The club is closed Monday.

Outdoor Activities and Sports

Pro baseball's **Anaheim Angels** play at Edison International Field (⊠ 2000 Gene Autry Way, ☎ 714/634–2000). The National Hockey League's **Mighty Ducks of Anaheim** play at Arrowhead Pond (⊠ 2695 E. Katella Ave., ☎ 714/740–2000).

GOLF

Dad Miller Golf Course (⊠ 430 N. Gilbert St., ☎ 714/774–8055), an 18-hole par-71 course, requires reservations seven days in advance. Greens fees range from $19 to $25; optional cart-rental is $22.

TENNIS

There are six public tennis courts at **Pearson Park** (⊠ 400 N. Harbor Blvd., at Sycamore St.); call the **Parks and Recreation Department** (☎ 949/765–5191) for details.

Buena Park

25 mi south of Los Angeles, I–5.

A humble farmer in Buena Park created the boysenberry by mixing red raspberries, blackberries, and loganberries; now on his land is Knott's Berry Farm, a major amusement park. Buena Park can be seen in a day, but plan to start early and finish fairly late.

★ ☾ ➌   **Knott's Berry Farm** got its start in 1934, when Cordelia Knott began serving chicken dinners on her wedding china to supplement her family's income. Or so the story goes. The dinners and her boysenberry pies proved more profitable than husband Walter's berry farm, so the two moved first into the restaurant business and then into the entertainment business. Their park is now a 150-acre complex with 100-

plus rides and attractions, 60 food concessions and restaurants, and 60 shops.

The first thing you'll encounter is **Ghost Town,** whose authentic old buildings have been relocated from their original mining-town sites. You can stroll down the street, stop and chat with the blacksmith, pan for gold, crack open a geode, ride in an authentic 1880s passenger train, or take the Gold Mine ride and descend into a replica of a working gold mine. A real treasure here is the antique Dentzel carousel.

Kids will likely head straight for **Camp Snoopy,** a miniature High Sierra wonderland where Snoopy and his friends from the "Peanuts" comic strip hang out. Nearby is **Wild Water Wilderness,** where you can ride white water in an inner tube in Big Foot Rapids and commune with the native peoples of the Northwest coast in the spooky Mystery Lodge. For more water thrills, check out the dolphin and sea lion shows in the Pacific Pavilion at **The Boardwalk;** here you'll also find the 3-D Nu Wave Theater.

Thrill rides are placed throughout the park: Try the **Boomerang** roller coaster; **X-K-1,** a living version of a video game; **Kingdom of the Dinosaurs,** a *Jurassic Park*–like thrill ride; and **Montezooma's Revenge,** a roller coaster that goes from 0 to 55 mph in less than five seconds. **Jaguar!** simulates the motions of a cat stalking its prey, twisting, spiraling, and speeding up and slowing down as it takes guests on its stomach-dropping course. The park's newest ride, **Wind Jammer,** is the country's first outdoor dual-action roller coaster, with two cars racing simultaneously through twists and turns at top speed. Shows are scheduled in Ghost Town, the Bird Cage Theater, and the Good Time Theater throughout the day. ⊠ *8039 Beach Blvd., between La Palma Ave. and Crescent St.,* ☎ *714/220–5200.* ⊠ *$36.* ☉ *June–mid-Sept., daily 9 AM–midnight; mid-Sept.–May, weekdays 10–6, Sat. 10–10, Sun. 10–7; closed during inclement weather.*

❹ More than 75 years of movie magic are immortalized at the **Movieland Wax Museum,** which holds several hundred wax sculptures of Hollywood's greatest stars, including Michael Jackson, John Wayne, Marilyn Monroe, Geena Davis, George Burns, and Bruce and Brandon Lee. Figures are displayed in a maze of realistic sets from movies such as *Gone with the Wind, Star Trek, The Wizard of Oz,* and *Home Alone.* You can buy a combination ticket for $16.90 that also allows you admission to the so-so Ripley's Believe It or Not, across the street. ⊠ *7711 Beach Blvd., between La Palma and Orangethorpe Aves.,* ☎ *714/ 522–1155.* ⊠ *$12.95.* ☉ *Daily 9–7.*

Dining and Lodging

$ ✗ **Mrs. Knott's Chicken Dinner Restaurant.** Cornelia Knott began serving her famous fried-chicken dinners and boysenberry pies in 1934 on her wedding china. Knott's Berry Farm, the amusement park, was started to keep the hungry customers occupied. The restaurant, at the park's entrance, still serves crispy fried chicken, along with tangy coleslaw and Mrs. Knott's signature chilled cherry-rhubarb compote. It's open for breakfast, lunch, and dinner. Expect long lines on weekends. ⊠ *Knott's Berry Farm, 8039 Beach Blvd.,* ☎ *714/220–5080. AE, D, DC, MC, V. No lunch Sun.*

$$ ▥ **Buena Park Hotel and Convention Center.** Rooms have a modern, muted feel, with light-color oak furniture and earth-tone fabrics. The hotel, which is within easy walking distance of Knott's Berry Farm, provides complimentary shuttle service to Disneyland. Ask about Family Value Vacation packages, which include admission to one of the parks.

✉ 7675 Crescent Ave., 90620, ☎ 714/995–1111 or 800/854–8792, FAX 714/828–8590. 314 rooms, 36 suites. 2 restaurants, bar, pool, concierge floor. AE, D, DC, MC, V.

Nightlife

For $36 per person, the **Medieval Times Dinner and Tournament** (✉ 7662 Beach Blvd., ☎ 714/521–4740 or 800/899–6600) brings back the days of yore, with medieval games, fighting, and jousting. Standard chicken-and-ribs dinners with plenty of sides are served just as they were in the Middle Ages: with no utensils.

Wild Bill's Wild West Extravaganza (✉ 7600 Beach Blvd., ☎ 714/522–6414), a two-hour action-packed Old West show ($33 per person), features foot-stomping musical numbers, cancan dancers, trick-rope artists, and sing-alongs. An all-you-can-eat chicken-and-ribs dinner is served by a chosen "grub-server" guest at each multigroup table during the show.

Fullerton

8 mi east of Buena Park, Hwy. 91.

Fullerton is an educational center in Orange County, with Cal State Fullerton, Southwestern University of Law, and two other houses of higher learning. It's also an old railroading and citrus-processing town with a shop-lined, brick walking street running through its center.

Dining

$$$ ✗ **The Cellar.** Choosing a vintage to pair with the your *sole de Douvres amandine* (classic pan-fried Dover sole with slivered almonds) or *côte de veau grillée d'Auge* (veal chop with apples, walnuts, and calvados) might be a challenge. This stone-walled underground French restaurant has one of the finest wine collections in the West, featuring more than 1,200 vintages from 15 countries. ✉ 305 N. Harbor Blvd., ☎ 714/525–5682. AE, D, DC, MC, V. Closed Sun.–Mon. No lunch.

$$–$$$ ✗ **Mulberry Street Ristorante.** Resembling a turn-of-the-century New
★ York Italian–style eatery, Mulberry Street is a favorite among North Orange County hipsters. All the pasta is homemade, and the menu also includes chicken, veal, and several daily fish specials. ✉ 114 W. Wilshire Ave., ☎ 714/525–1056. AE, D, DC, MC, V. No lunch Sun..

$–$$$ ✗ **Angelo's & Vinci's Cafe Ristorante.** Families with kids love this boisterous Italian café, where huge portions of Sicilian-style pizza and pasta are served in circus surroundings. You can't miss the giant knights in shining armor, tableaux of Italian street scenes, an altar with old family photos and cherubs from Sicily, and a pair of aerialist puppets and a tightrope walker overhead. ✉ 550 N. Harbor Blvd., ☎ 714/879–4022. AE, MC, V.

Yorba Linda, La Habra, and Brea

7–12 mi north of Anaheim, Hwy. 57.

Clustered together just north of Anaheim, Yorba Linda, La Habra, and Brea are quiet, suburban towns with plenty of parks, shopping centers, and cinemas. Yorba Linda's main claim to fame is the **Richard Nixon Presidential Library and Birthplace,** final resting place of the 37th president and his wife, Pat. Exhibits illustrate the checkered career of Nixon, the only president forced to resign from office. Visitors can listen to the so-called smoking-gun tape from the Watergate days, among other recorded material. Life-size sculptures of world leaders, gifts Nixon received from international heads of state, and a large graffiti-covered section of the Berlin Wall are on display. In contrast to some of the high-tech displays here are Pat Nixon's tranquil rose garden and the small farmhouse where Richard Nixon was born in 1913. ⊠ *18001 Yorba Linda Blvd., at Imperial Hwy., Yorba Linda,* ☎ *714/993–3393.* ⊡ *$5.95.* ⊙ *Mon.–Sat. 10–5, Sun. 11–5.*

❻ The **Children's Museum at La Habra** is housed in a 1923-vintage Union Pacific railroad depot, with old railroad cars resting nearby. Children can climb behind the wheel of Buster the Bus, a retired transit bus; "dig up" bones in the huge Dinosaur Dig sandbox; or pretend they're early settlers fishing, camping, and exploring caves. ⊠ *301 S. Euclid St., at E. Lambert Rd., La Habra,* ☎ *562/905–9793.* ⊡ *$4.* ⊙ *Mon.–Sat. 10–5, Sun. 1–5.*

Dining

$$$–$$$$ ✕ **La Vie en Rose.** It's worth the detour to Brea to sample the stylishly
   ★   presented traditional French cuisine served in this reproduction Norman farmhouse, complete with a large turret. There's seafood, lamb, veal, and for dessert, a silky crème brûlée and a Grand Marnier soufflée. ⊠ *240 S. State College Blvd. (across from Brea mall),* ☎ *714/529–8333. AE, DC, MC, V. Closed Sun.*

Garden Grove and Orange

South of Anaheim, I–5 to Hwy. 22.

Around the intersection of Glassell Street and Chapman Avenue is Orange Plaza (or Orange Circle, as locals call it), the heart of **Old Towne Orange.** One of the few historic towns in Orange County, this area takes great pride in its many California Craftsman–style cottages; Christmas is a particularly lovely time to visit, when all the cottages are festooned with decorations. If the town looks familiar to you, perhaps it's because this was where "That Thing You Do" was filmed. In

❼ Garden Grove the main attraction is the **Crystal Cathedral,** the domain of television evangelist Robert Schuller. Designed by architect Philip Johnson, the sparkling glass structure resembles a four-pointed star, with more than 10,000 panes of glass covering a weblike steel truss to form translucent walls. Two annual pageants, "The Glory of Christmas" and "The Glory of Easter," feature live animals, flying angels, and other special effects. ⊠ *12141 Lewis St. (take I-5 to Chapman Ave. W), Garden Grove,* ☎ *714/971–4013.* ⊡ *Donation requested.* ⊙ *Guided tours Mon.–Sat. 9–3:30; call for schedule.*

OFF THE   **LITTLE SAIGON** –With about 115,000 residents, Little Saigon is the
BEATEN PATH   largest Vietnamese community outside Vietnam. The neighborhood is between Garden Grove and Fountain Valley in the city of Westminster, but the heart of the action is around Brookhurst and Bolsa streets, where colorful Little Saigon Plaza tempts shoppers with jewelry and gift shops, Asian herbalists, and restaurants. ⊠ *Bolsa St. between Bushard and Magnolia Sts.*

Dining and Lodging

$$–$$$$ ✕ **La Brasserie.** It doesn't look like a typical brasserie, but the varied French cuisine befits the name over the door. The specialty here is veal chops. There's also an inviting bar-lounge. ⊠ *202 S. Main St., Orange,* ☎ *714/978–6161. AE, DC, MC, V. Closed Sun. No lunch Sat.*

$$–$$$ ✕ **P.J.'s Abbey.** Locals like to walk from their charming bungalow residences in historic Old Towne to this former abbey to enjoy American favorites such as pork tenderloin in cherry-walnut sauce with garlic-

mashed potatoes. ⊠ *182 S. Orange St., Orange,* ☎ *714/771–8556. AE, MC, V*

$$$ ⬚ **Doubletree Hotel Anaheim.** This contemporary 20-story hotel has a dramatic lobby of marble and granite, with waterfalls cascading down the walls. The hotel is near The City shopping center, Anaheim Stadium, and the Anaheim Convention Center. ⊠ *100 The City Dr., Orange, 92868,* ☎ *714/634–4500 or 800/222–8733,* 𝔽𝔸𝕏 *714/978– 3839. 394 rooms, 19 suites. 2 restaurants, bar, pool, 2 tennis courts, health club, concierge floor. AE, D, DC, MC, V.*

Santa Ana

12 mi south of Anaheim, I–5 to Hwy. 55.

⊛ ❽ The main attraction in Santa Ana, the county seat, is the **Bowers Museum of Cultural Art.** Permanent exhibits include sculpture, costumes, and artifacts from Oceania; sculpture from west and central Africa; Pacific Northwest wood carvings; dazzling beadwork of the Plains cultures; California basketry; and still-life paintings. The 11,000-square-ft **Bowers Kidseum,** adjacent to the main facility, has interactive exhibits geared toward kids ages 6–12, in addition to classes, storytelling, and arts and crafts workshops. ⊠ *2002 N. Main St., off I-5,* ☎ *714/567– 3600.* 🎟 *$6.* ☉ *Tues.–Sun. 10–4, Thurs. 10–9.*

Dining

$$$–$$$$ ✕ **Gustaf Anders.** At this cool, Scandinavian restaurant, you'll find top-
★ notch grilled gravlax, and a wonderful fillet of beef prepared with Stilton cheese, a red-wine sauce, and creamed morel mushrooms. Next door is the more casual, less expensive Gustaf Anders' Back Pocket, with equally excellent food. Don't miss the flatbreads, parsley salad, and Swedish beef casserole. *South Coast Plaza Village, 1651 Sunflower Ave.,* ☎ *714/ 668–1737. AE, DC, MC, V. No lunch Sun. at Back Pocket.*

$$$–$$$$ ✕ **Morton's of Chicago.** Luscious onion bread and huge portions of prime-aged steaks make this the place to indulge your cravings. The wood paneling and soft lighting are just what you'd expect of a fine steak house. ⊠ *South Coast Plaza Village, 1661 Sunflower Ave.,* ☎ *714/444–4834. AE, DC, MC, V. No lunch. Valet parking.*

$–$$ ✕ **National Sports Grill.** Here you can grab a burger, watch the game, and play a round of pool. There's pasta, chicken, and more on the menu; the bar has domestic and imported beer on tap. ⊠ *101 Sand Pointe,* ☎ *714/979–0900. AE, D, DC, MC, V.*

Irvine

6 mi south of Santa Ana, Hwy. 55 to I–405; 12 mi south of Anaheim, I-5.

Love it or hate it, Irvine is undeniably a suburban utopia, with its tree-lined streets, manicured lawns, and child-filled parks. Ranked in several national surveys as America's safest city, the master-planned community has top-notch schools, a university and a community college, dozens of shopping centers, and a network of well-lit walking and biking paths for the town's active residents.

❾ Some of the California impressionist paintings on display at the small **Irvine Museum** depict the California landscape in the days before freeways and housing developments. The paintings, which are displayed on the 12th floor of the circular, marble-and-glass Tower 17 building, were assembled by Joan Irvine Smith, granddaughter of James Irvine, who once owned one-quarter of what is now Orange County. ⊠ *18881 Von Karman Ave., at Martin St.,* ☎ *949/476–2565.* ⊡ *Free.* ⊙ *Tues.–Sat. 11–5.*

⑩ The **University of California at Irvine,** best known for its biological sciences, was established on 1,000 acres of rolling ranch land donated by the Irvine family in the mid-1950s. The campus contains more than 11,000 trees from all over the world. The **Art Gallery at UC Irvine** (☎ 949/824–6610) sponsors exhibitions of student and professional art. It's free and open from mid-September through mid-June, Monday through Saturday from noon to 5. ⊠ *I–405 to Jamboree Rd., west to Campus Dr. S.*

⑪ The mind-boggling 32-acre **Entertainment Center at Irvine Spectrum** contains a huge, 21-theater cinema complex (with a six-story IMAX 3-D theater), lively restaurants and cafés, and an outdoor shopping arcade. Other highlights include Sega City's virtual-reality arcade and an Out-Takes digital photo studio. ⊠ *Exit Irvine Center Dr. at intersection of I–405, I–5, and Hwy. 133,* ☎ *949/450–4900 for film listings.*

⑫ **Wild Rivers Water Park** has more than 40 rides and attractions, including a wave pool, a few daring slides, a river inner-tube ride, and several cafés and shops. ⊠ *8800 Irvine Center Dr., off I–405,* ☎ *949/768–9453.* ⊡ *$19.95.* ⊙ *Mid-May–Sept.; call for hrs.*

Dining and Lodging

$$$–$$$$ ✕ **Bistango.** A sleek, high-style, art-filled bistro, Bistango serves first-rate American cuisine with a European flair: salads, seafood pasta, Mediterranean pizzas, and grilled ahi tuna. Beautiful people come to savor the food, listen to live jazz, and mingle with their well-dressed peers. ⊠ *19100 Von Karman Ave.,* ☎ *949/752–5222. Reservations essential. AE, D, DC, MC, V. Valet parking.*

$$–$$$ ✕ **Prego.** Reminiscent of a Tuscan villa, this is a much larger version
★ of the Beverly Hills Prego, with soft lighting, golden walls, and an outdoor patio. Try the spit-roasted meats and chicken, charcoal-grilled fresh fish, or pizzas from the oak-burning oven. California and Italian wines are reasonably priced. ⊠ *18420 Von Karman Ave.,* ☎ *949/553–1333. AE, DC, MC, V. No lunch weekends. Valet parking.*

$–$$$ ✕ **Il Fornaio.** Two weeks a month, regional dishes from Tuscany or Puglia supplement the regular fare—duck lasagna, rotisserie chicken, pizza, succulent grilled eggplant with goat cheese—at this elegant Italian chain eatery. It's packed at lunch with stylish businesspeople. ⊠ *18051 Von Karman Ave.,* ☎ *949/261–1444. AE, D, DC, MC, V. No lunch weekends. Valet parking.*

$–$$$ ✕ **Sam Woo.** From fresh- and saltwater tanks comes seafood cooked to order at this formal Chinese restaurant. Whole fish is presented tableside. Service is gracious and the setting peaceful. ⊠ *15333 Culver Dr., Suite 720,* ☎ *949/262–0688. AE, MC, V.*

$–$$ ✕ **Kitima Thai Cuisine.** Tucked away on the ground floor of an office building, Orange County's best Thai restaurant is a favorite with the business-lunch crowd. The names may be gimmicky—"rock-and-roll shrimp salad," "Rambo chicken" (sautéed with green chiles and sweet basil), "Four Musketeers" (shrimp with asparagus, mushrooms, and spinach)—but fresh ingredients are used in every dish. ⊠ *2010 Main St., Suite 170,* ☎ *949/261–2929. AE, D, DC, MC, V. Closed Sun.*

$$$–$$$$ ▥ **Atrium Hotel.** Across the street from John Wayne Airport and near most area offices, this garden-style hotel caters to business travelers. Rooms have large work areas, coffeemakers, two phones, and private

balconies overlooking either the pool or gardens. ✉ *18700 MacArthur Blvd., 92612,* ☎ *949/833–2770 or 800/854–3012,* FAX *949/757–1228. 211 rooms. Restaurant, bar, pool, health club, car rental. AE, D, DC, MC, V.*

$$$–$$$$ 🏨 **Irvine Marriott.** Towering over Koll Business Center, the Marriott is convenient for business travelers. Despite its size, the hotel has an intimate feel, due in part to the convivial lobby with love seats and evening entertainment (usually a jazz pianist). Weekend discounts and packages are usually available, and there's a courtesy van to the South Coast Plaza mall and the airport. ✉ *18000 Von Karman Ave., 92715,* ☎ *949/553–0100 or 800/228–9290,* FAX *949/261–7059. 484 rooms, 8 suites. 2 restaurants, sports bar, sushi bar, indoor-outdoor pool, hot tub, 4 tennis courts, health club, concierge floors, business services, airport shuttle. AE, D, DC, MC, V.*

$$$ 🏨 **Hyatt Regency Irvine.** The modern rooms here have coffeemakers, irons, and hair dryers. Special golf packages at nearby Tustin Ranch and Pelican Hills are available, and a complimentary shuttle runs to local shopping centers. Rates are lower on weekends. ✉ *17900 Jamboree Rd., 92714,* ☎ *949/975–1234 or 800/233–1234,* FAX *949/852–1574. 516 rooms, 20 suites. 2 restaurants, 2 bars, pool, 4 tennis courts, health club, bicycles, concierge, business services. AE, D, DC, MC, V.*

Nightlife

Irvine Improv (✉ 4255 Campus Dr., ☎ 949/854–5455) is a comedy club that's open from Wednesday through Sunday nights. The **Irvine Meadows Amphitheater** (✉ 8808 Irvine Center Dr., ☎ 949/855–4515 or 949/855–6111), a 15,000-seat open-air venue, presents musical events from May through October. **Metropolis** (✉ 4255 Campus Dr., ☎ 949/725–0300) has five pool tables, a sushi bar, a restaurant, entertainment, two large dance floors, and theme nights throughout the week.

Costa Mesa

6 mi northeast of Irvine, I–405 to Bristol St.

Though it's probably best known for its top-notch shopping mall, Costa Mesa is also the performing-arts hub of Orange County, and a local business center. A steadily increasing number of modern office buildings, theater and movie houses, and new restaurants are making the town more hip and more crowded all the time.

★ ⓲ Costa Mesa's most famous landmark, **South Coast Plaza** is an immense retail, entertainment, and dining complex consisting of two enclosed shopping areas—Jewel Court and Crystal Court—and an open-air collection of boutiques at South Coast Village. The Plaza rivals Rodeo Drive in its number of top international designers' shops—Gucci, Armani, Versace, and Prada, to name just a few—along with standard upscale shops such as J. Crew, Ralph Lauren, Calvin Klein, Liz Claiborne, and F.A.O. Schwarz. A free shuttle transports the Plaza's 20 million annual visitors between sections. ✉ *3333 S. Bristol St., off I–405,* ☎ *714/435–2000.* ☉ *Weekdays 10–9, Sat. 10–7, Sun. 11–6:30.*

The **Orange County Performing Arts Center** (✉ 600 Town Center Dr., east of Bristol St., ☎ 714/556–2787) contains a 3,000-seat facility for opera, ballet, symphony, and musicals. Richard Lippold's enormous "Firebird," a triangular-shape sculpture of polished metal surfaces that resembles a bird taking flight, extends outward from the glass-enclosed lobby. Within walking distance of the center is the **California Scenario** (✉ 611 Anton Blvd.), a 1½-acre sculpture garden designed by Isamu Noguchi.

Dining and Lodging

$$–$$$ ✕ **Diva.** If you're seeing a show at the South Coast Repertory Theater
★ or the Performing Arts Center, Diva is a perfect place to stop for dinner. Entrées such as salmon with wilted greens and blackberry vinegar
or grilled veal chops with hazelnut butter are heart-warmingly good,
and the dessert soufflés are renowned. ⊠ *600 Anton Blvd.,* ☎ *714/
754–0600. AE, D, DC, MC, V. No lunch weekends.*

$$–$$$ ✕ **Habana Restaurant and Bar.** With rustic candelabras and murals
in a candlelit former industrial space, Habana blends an Old World
flavor with a hip '90s flair. The Cuban and Caribbean specialties are
as flavorful as the setting is cool: Try the *ropa vieja* (shredded beef) or
the plantain-crusted chicken. Chocolate lovers can't miss the Café
Cubano—chocolate mousse topped with chocolate whipped cream
and rum sauce. ⊠ *2930 Bristol St.,* ☎ *714/556–0176. AE, D, DC,
MC, V.*

$–$$$ ✕ **Bangkok IV.** Despite its shopping-mall location—it occupies the
★ third floor of the Crystal Court, an enclosed shopping area within the
South Coast Plaza—Bangkok IV has a dramatic, white-and-black in-
terior, with striking flower arrangements on every table. The *pla dung,*
steamed catfish with a chili-garlic-lemongrass sauce, is exceptional. Or
try the *kai pudd keng,* succulent ginger chicken with mushrooms and
garlic. ⊠ *Across from South Coast Plaza, 3333 Bear St.,* ☎ *714/540–
7661. AE, D, DC, MC, V.*

$–$$ ✕ **Memphis Soul Café and Bar.** The gumbo is the best in the county,
★ bar none. The turkey sandwich with pesto is addicting, and the pork
chops are a work of art. The retro setting—it used to be a dive bar—
and Southern-influenced menu have made this one of the area's most
worthwhile (and affordable) eateries. ⊠ *2920 Bristol St.,* ☎ *714/
432–7685. AE, DC, MC, V.*

$$$–$$$$ 🏨 **Westin South Coast Plaza.** This downtown high-rise adjoins the South
Coast complex, making it convenient for shoppers and businesspeo-
ple. ⊠ *686 Anton Blvd., 92626,* ☎ *714/540–2500 or 800/228–3000,*
FAX *714/662–6695. 373 rooms, 17 suites. Restaurant, lobby lounge,
pool, 2 tennis courts, shuffleboard. AE, D, DC, MC, V.*

$$$–$$$$ 🏨 **Country Side Inn and Suites.** The Queen Anne–style rooms have a
vaguely European feel. In addition to a full breakfast, the reasonable
room rates include evening cocktails and hors d'oeuvres. ⊠ *325 Bris-
tol St., 92626,* ☎ *714/549–0300 or 800/322–9992,* FAX *714/662–0828.
150 rooms, 150 suites. Restaurant, bar, 2 pools, 2 hot tubs, exercise
room, business center. Full breakfast. AE, D, DC, MC, V.*

$$–$$$ 🏨 **Doubletree Hotel.** Near John Wayne Airport, this modern, spacious
hotel has an atrium lobby with glass elevators. Usually there's live music
Saturday night in the dance club. ⊠ *3050 Bristol St., 92626,* ☎ *714/
540–7000,* FAX *714/540–9176. 474 rooms, 10 suites. 2 restaurants,
lounge, lobby lounge, pool, beauty salon, hot tub, health club. AE, D,
DC, MC, V.*

Nightlife and the Arts

Orange County Performing Arts Center (⊠ 600 Town Center Dr., ☎
714/556–2787) presents major touring companies, among them the
New York City Opera, the American Ballet Theater, and the Los An-
geles Philharmonic Orchestra, along with musicals and theater pro-
ductions. Free, guided backstage tours are conducted Mondays,
Wednesdays, and Saturdays at 10:30 AM.

South Coast Repertory Theater (⊠ 655 Town Center Dr., ☎ 714/957–
4033) is a Tony award–winning theater presenting new and traditional
works on two stages.

Outdoor Activities and Sports

Costa Mesa Country Club (⊠ 1701 Golf Course Dr., ☎ 714/540–7500) has a pro shop, a driving range, and two 18-hole courses (par 70 and 72). Greens fees range from $16.50 to $26; optional cart-rental is $22. Reservations are a must.

THE COAST

Running along the Orange County coastline is the scenic Pacific Coast Highway (Highway 1, known locally as PCH); it's well worth the effort to take this route instead of the freeways. Wherever you pull over on PCH, a public beach is only steps away.

Huntington Beach

25 mi west of Anaheim, Hwy. 57 South to Hwy. 22 West to I–405.

Once a sleepy residential town with little more than a string of rugged surf shops, Huntington Beach has transformed itself into a shining resort area. The town's appeal arises from its broad white-sand beaches and often towering waves, as well as a pier, a large shopping pavilion on Main Street, and the luxurious Waterfront Hilton resort. In 1996 the family-oriented town was ranked as America's eighth-safest city. Another draw: The U.S. Open professional surf competition takes place here every August.

⑭ **Huntington Pier** stretches 1,800 ft out to sea, well past the powerful waves that made Huntington Beach America's "Surf City." At the end of the pier sits **Ruby's** (☎ 714/969–7829), part of a California chain of '40s-style eateries. The **Pierside Pavilion,** across Pacific Coast Highway from the pier, contains shops, restaurants, bars with live music,
⑮ and a theater complex. Just up Main Street, the **International Surfing Museum** (⊠ 411 Olive Ave., ☎ 714/960–3483), open from Wednesday through Sunday between noon and 5 (⊡ $2), pays tribute to the sport's greats in a Surfing Hall of Fame, with an impressive collection of surfboards and related memorabilia.

Huntington City Beach stretches for 3 mi from the pier area. The beach is most crowded around the pier; amateur and professional surfers brave the waves daily on its north side. Continuing north, **Huntington State Beach** (☎ 714/536–1454) parallels Pacific Coast Highway. On the state and city beaches there are changing rooms, concessions, lifeguards (except in winter), and ample parking; the state beach also has barbecue pits and RV campsites. At the northern section of the city, **Bolsa Chica State Beach** (☎ 714/846–3460) has barbecue pits and is usually less crowded than its southern neighbors.

★ ⑯ **Bolsa Chica Ecological Reserve** beckons wildlife-lovers and bird-watchers with an 880-acre salt marsh that is home to 315 species of birds, including great blue herons, snowy and great egrets, and common loons. Throughout the reserve are trails for hiking, bird-watching, and jogging. Free guided tours depart from the visitor center the first Saturday of each month at 9 AM. ⊠ *Entrance at Warner Ave. and PCH, opposite Bolsa Chica State Beach,* ☎ *714/897–7003.* ⊡ *Free parking.* ☉ *Daily dawn–sunset.*

Dining and Lodging

$–$$$ ✕ **Baci.** Romantic or kitschy, depending on your style, Baci nevertheless serves dependable Italian food. Among the best dishes are carpaccio with shrimp, tortellini soup, and cannoli for dessert. ⊠ *18748 Beach Blvd.,* ☎ *714/965–1194. AE, D, DC, MC, V.*

$–$$ ✕ **Louise's Trattoria.** The local branch of this Italian chain is just across the street from the Huntington Beach pier. The chicken marsala and fettucine with sun-dried tomatoes in a chardonnay-cream sauce hit the spot, especially after a day at the beach. ⊠ *300 PCH,* ☎ *714/960–0996. AE, D, DC, MC, V.*

$ ✕ **Alice's Breakfast in the Park.** Consider starting your day at this wooden brunch house tucked among Huntington Park's eucalyptus trees near Huntington Lake. There's seating on the outdoor patio, from which children can feed the ducks, and a small, indoor dining room with flowers and antiques. Be sure to try Alice's "outrageous cinnamon roll," freshly baked breads, and homemade muffins. ⊠ *6622 Lakeview, off Edwards St.,* ☎ *714/848–0690. No credit cards. No dinner.*

$ ✕ **Wahoo's Fish Taco.** Mahimahi- and wahoo-filled tacos are the specialty of this casual restaurant, part of a national chain capitalizing on the trend towards healthful fast food. Surf stickers cover the walls. ⊠ *120 Main St.,* ☎ *714/536–2050. MC, V.*

$$$–$$$$ ▥ **Waterfront Hilton.** Rising 12 stories above the surf, this Mediterranean-style resort occupies 8½ mi of white-sand beach. All guest rooms have private lanais, many with panoramic ocean views. With 19,000 sq ft of meeting space, the Hilton is also a prime conference facility. ⊠ *21100 PCH, 92648,* ☎ *714/960–7873 or 800/822–7873,* ☎ *714/960–2642. 258 rooms, 32 suites. 2 restaurants, bar, pool, hot tub, 2 tennis courts, exercise room, children's programs (ages 5–12; summer only), concierge floor. AE, DC, MC, V.*

Outdoor Activities and Sports

BICYCLING

Team Bicycle Rentals (⊠ 8464 Indianapolis Ave., ☎ 714/969–5480) rents touring and other bicycles.

TENNIS

Edison Community Center (⊠ 21377 Magnolia Ave., ☎ 714/960–8870) and the **Murdy Community Center** (⊠ 7000 Norma Dr., ☎ 714/960–8895) both have four courts available on a first-come, first-served basis in the daytime. Both accept reservations for play after 5 PM and charge $2 an hour.

Shopping

In search of authentic beach clothes or a new surfboard? Head to the pier, where hard-core surf shops like **Jack's** (⊠ 101 Main St., ☎ 714/536–4516) and **Huntington Beach Surf and Sport** (⊠ 300 PCH, at Main St, ☎ 714/841–4000) carry the latest styles. Or try the **Huntington Beach Mall** (⊠ Beach Blvd., off I–405, ☎ 714/897–2533).

Newport Beach

6 mi south of Huntington Beach, Hwy. 1.

Newport Beach has two distinct personalities. It's best known for its island-dotted yacht harbor and wealthy residents (Newport is said to have the highest number of Mercedes-Benzes per capita of any city in the world). And then there's inland Newport Beach, just southwest of John Wayne Airport, a business and commercial hub with a shopping center and a clutch of high-rise office buildings and hotels.

★ ⑰ **Newport Harbor,** which shelters nearly 10,000 small boats, will seduce even those who don't own a yacht. Exploring the charming avenues and surrounding alleys can be great fun. To see Newport Harbor from the water, take a one-hour gondola cruise operated by the Gondola Company of Newport (⊠ 3400 Via Oporto, Suite 102B, ☎ 949/675–1212). It costs $60 for two.

Within Newport Harbor are eight small islands, including Balboa and Lido. The houses lining the shore may seem modest, but this is some of the most expensive real estate in the world. Several grassy areas on Lido Isle have views of Newport Harbor but, evidence of the upper-crust Orange County mind-set, each is marked "Private Community Park."

Newport Pier, which juts out into the ocean near 20th Street, is the heart of Newport's beach community. On the pier you can go fishing or grab a burger and shake at **Ruby's** (☎ 949/675–7829). Street parking is difficult here, so grab the first space you find and be prepared to walk. A stroll along West Ocean Front reveals much of the town's character. On weekday mornings, head for the beach near the pier, where you're likely to encounter the dory fishermen hawking their predawn catches, as they've done for generations. On weekends the walk is alive with kids of all ages on Rollerblades, skateboards, and bikes dodging pedestrians and whizzing past fast-food joints, swimsuit shops, and seedy bars.

Newport's best beaches are on **Balboa Peninsula,** whose many jetties ⑱ create good swimming areas. The **Balboa Pavilion,** on the bay side of the Balboa Peninsula, was built in 1905 as a bath- and boathouse. Today it houses a restaurant and shops and is a departure point for harbor and whale-watching cruises. Look for it on Main Street, off Balboa Boulevard. Adjacent to the pavilion is the three-car ferry that connects the peninsula to Balboa Island. Several blocks surrounding the pavilion contain restaurants, beachside shops, and the small **Fun Zone**—a local hangout with a Ferris wheel, video games, rides, and arcades.

⑲ The **Orange County Museum of Art** has an esteemed collection of abstract expressionist paintings and cutting-edge contemporary works by California artists. ⊠ *850 San Clemente Dr.,* ☎ *949/759–1122.* ⊠ *$5.* ☉ *Tues.–Sun. 11–5.*

Dining and Lodging

$$$–$$$$ ✕ **Aubergine.** The husband-and-wife team who run this restaurant (he
★ mans the kitchen and she handles the dining room) have set new standards for fine cuisine in Orange County. The six-course prix fixe menu is surprisingly affordable; you can also order à la carte. Classic French dishes are prepared with a modern flair, using only the freshest ingredients. ⊠ *508 29th St.,* ☎ *949/723–4150. Reservations essential. AE, MC, V. Closed Sun.–Mon. No lunch.*

$$$–$$$$ ✕ **Pascal.** You'll think you're in St-Tropez when you step inside this
★ bright and cheerful bistro in a shopping center. And, after one taste of Pascal Olhat's light Provençale cuisine, the best in Orange County, you'll *swear* you're in the south of France. Try the sea bass with thyme, rack of lamb, and lemon tart. ⊠ *1000 N. Bristol St.,* ☎ *949/752–0107. AE, DC, V. Closed Sun. No dinner Mon.*

$$$–$$$$ ✕ **The Ritz.** Indeed, this is one of the ritziest restaurants in southern California, complete with black leather booths, etched-glass mirrors, and polished brass trim. Don't pass up the "carousel" appetizer—a lavish spread of cured gravlax, prawns, Dungeness crab legs, Maine lobster tails, goose liver pâté, fillet of smoked trout, Parma prosciutto, filet mignon tartare, and marinated herring, all served on a lazy Susan. ⊠ *880 Newport Center Dr.,* ☎ *949/720–1800. Reservations essential. AE, DC, MC, V. No lunch weekends.*

$$–$$$$ ✕ **Twin Palms.** Pasta, chicken, pizza, fish specials, and salads are all on the creative menu in this intriguing, spacious, tentlike restaurant, a sister property to the original Twin Palms in Pasadena. There's live music nightly (usually jazz or blues), plus dance music Saturday after

10. ⊠ *630 Newport Center Dr.,* ☎ *949/721–8288. AE, DC, MC, V. Valet parking.*

$–$$ ✕ **P. F. Chang's China Bistro.** The tasty Cal-Chinese food at this trendy chain restaurant includes Mongolian spicy beef and Chang's chicken, stir-fried in a sweet-and-spicy Szechuan sauce. Almost every table has an ocean view, but many diners are too busy people-watching to notice. Food can also be ordered at the lively bar. ⊠ *Newport Fashion Island, 1145 Newport Center Dr.,* ☎ *949/759–9007. Reservations not accepted. AE, MC, V.*

$–$$ ✕ **Crab Cooker.** People line up at this shanty for fresh, mesquite-grilled fish served on paper plates at rock-bottom prices. The seafood skewers, clam chowder, crusty rounds of French bread, and coleslaw are all top-notch. ⊠ *2200 Newport Blvd.,* ☎ *949/673–0100. Reservations not accepted. No credit cards.*

$–$$ ✕ **El Torito Grill.** You'll find southwestern and south-of-the-border
★   specialties here: The just-baked tortillas with fresh salsa and the blackened chicken with pasta are good choices. The bar serves hand-shaken margaritas and 80 brands of tequila. ⊠ *Fashion Island, 951 Newport Center Dr.,* ☎ *949/640–2875. AE, D, DC, MC, V.*

$$$$ ▦ **Four Seasons Hotel.** A suitably stylish hotel in an ultrachic neigh-
★   borhood (it's across the street from the Fashion Island mall), the 20-story Four Seasons caters to luxury seekers by offering weekend golf packages (in conjunction with the nearby Pelican Hill golf course), fitness weekend packages, and the use of extensive fitness facilities. Guest rooms have spectacular views, private bars, and original artwork on the walls. Kids are given special treatment: balloons, cookies and milk, game books, and more. ⊠ *690 Newport Center Dr., 92660,* ☎ *949/759–0808 or 800/332–3442,* ℻ *949/759–0568. 285 rooms. 2 restaurants, bar, pool, beauty salon, massage, sauna, steam room, 2 tennis courts, health club, mountain bikes, concierge, business services. AE, D, DC, MC, V.*

$$$$ ▦ **Sutton Place Hotel.** An eye-catching ziggurat design is the trademark of this ultramodern hotel in Koll Center. Despite its modern exterior, the inside remains traditional with beige and burgundy accents. Many of the spacious rooms have canopy beds. ⊠ *4500 MacArthur Blvd., 92660,* ☎ *949/476–2001 or 800/243–4141,* ℻ *949/476–0153. 435 rooms. 2 restaurants, 2 bars, in-room modem lines, minibars, refrigerators, pool, spa, 2 tennis courts, health club, basketball, bike rentals, concierge, business services, airport shuttle. AE, D, DC, MC, V.*

$$$–$$$$ ▦ **Newport Beach Marriott Hotel and Tennis Club.** A largely foreign clientele patronizes this hotel overlooking Newport Harbor. A distinctive fountain surrounded by a plant-filled atrium is the first thing you'll see inside. Rooms are in one of two towers; all have balconies or patios that look out onto lush gardens or the Pacific. ⊠ *900 Newport Center Dr., 92660,* ☎ *949/640–4000 or 800/228–9290,* ℻ *949/640–5055. 570 rooms, 8 suites. Restaurant, bar, 2 pools, sauna, 8 tennis courts, health club, concierge, business services. AE, D, DC, MC, V.*

$$–$$$ ▦ **Sheraton Newport Beach.** Bamboo trees and palms in the lobby add to the tropical feel of this hotel 5 mi from the beach. Vibrant teals, mauves, and peaches make up the guest-room color scheme. The hotel is convenient to John Wayne Airport. ⊠ *4545 MacArthur Blvd., 92660,* ☎ *949/833–0570 or 800/325-3535,* ℻ *949/833–3927. 329 rooms, 4 suites. Restaurant, bar, pool, 2 tennis courts, exercise room. AE, D, DC, MC, V.*

Nightlife

The **Cannery** (⊠ 3010 Lafayette Ave., ☎ 949/675–5777) is a packed seaside restaurant and bar with karaoke and live entertainment. The house drink, a Purple Hooter, is a deadly mix of vodka, Chambord, and pineapple juice over ice. The **Studio Cafe** (✉ 100 Main St., Balboa Peninsula, ☎ 949/675–7760), locally famous for its potent blue drinks, has blues and jazz musicians nightly. **Tibbie's Music Hall** (✉ 4647 MacArthur Blvd., ☎ 949/252–0834) is a small dinner theater that's open weekends only. (You can also come only for the show).

Outdoor Activities and Sports

BOAT RENTAL

You can rent sailboats ($25 an hour), small motorboats ($30 an hour), and ocean boats ($65–$80 an hour) at **Balboa Boat Rentals** (✉ 510 E. Edgewater Ave., ☎ 949/673–7200). You must have a driver's license, and some knowledge of boating is helpful; rented boats are not allowed out of the bay.

BOAT TOURS

A fun way to take in the scenery of Newport's harbor is on the two-hour **Cannery Restaurant weekend brunch cruise** (✉ 3010 Lafayette Ave., ☎ 949/675–5777). Cruises cost $31, and depart at 10 AM and 1:30 PM. **Catalina Passenger Service** (✉ 400 Main St., ☎ 949/673–5245) at the Balboa Pavilion operates sightseeing tours ($6 to $8), fishing excursions ($33), and, during the winter, whale-watching cruises ($14). **Hornblower Dining Yachts** (✉ 2431 W. Coast Hwy., ☎ 949/646–0155) books 2½-hour Saturday dinner cruises with dancing for $56.95; Sunday brunch cruises are $39.45. Reservations are required.

CAMPING

Newport Dunes Resort (✉ 1131 Back Bay Dr., ☎ 949/729–3863) has RV and tent spaces, picnic facilities, rest rooms with outdoor showers, boat rentals, and a place to launch boats. The resort is surrounded by Newport Bay, a large ecological reserve for ducks, geese, and other wildlife.

GOLF

Newport Beach Golf Course (✉ 3100 Irvine Ave., ☎ 949/852–8681), an 18-hole, par-59 course, is lighted for nighttime play. Greens fees range from $14 to $17; hand carts rent for $2. Reservations are required one week in advance.

Pelican Hill Golf Club (✉ 22651 Pelican Hill Rd. S, ☎ 949/640–0238) has two 18-hole courses (par 70 and 71). Greens fees range from $135 to $195 and include the mandatory cart.

RUNNING

The **Beach Trail** runs along the coast from Huntington Beach to Newport. Paths throughout **Newport Back Bay** wrap around a marshy area inhabited by lizards, squirrels, rabbits, and waterfowl.

SPORTFISHING

In addition to a complete tackle shop, **Davey's Locker** (✉ Balboa Pavilion, 400 Main St., ☎ 949/673–1434) operates sportfishing trips starting at $25, as well as private charters and whalewatching trips.

SURFING

The River Jetties in northern Newport are good for beginners. The Wedge, farther south, is famous for its steep, punishing shore break.

TENNIS

Call the **recreation department** (☎ 949/644–3151) for information about use the city's 26 public courts, where play is free and first-come, first-served. You must reserve the courts at the **Newport Beach Marriott Hotel and Tennis Club** (✉ 900 Newport Center Dr., ☎ 949/640–4000) for $25 per hour.

Shopping

Resplendent with Mediterranean tiles and dramatic arches, the ritzy outdoor **Fashion Island** complex has suitably upscale boutiques and major department stores, including Bloomingdale's, Robinsons-May, Neiman-Marcus, and Macy's. ⊠ *Newport Center Dr., between Jamboree and MacArthur Blvds., off PCH,* ☎ *949/721–2022.*

Corona del Mar

2 mi south of Newport Beach, Hwy. 1.

A small jewel on the Pacific Coast, Corona del Mar (known by locals as "CDM") has exceptional beaches that some say resemble those in northern California. **Corona del Mar Beach** (☎ 949/644–3044) is actually made up of two beaches, Little Corona and Big Corona, separated by a cliff. Facilities include fire pits, volleyball courts, food stands, rest rooms, and parking. Two colorful reefs (and the fact that it's off-limits to boats) make Corona del Mar great for snorkeling.

Midway between Corona del Mar and Laguna, on the inland side of Pacific Coast Highway, **Crystal Cove State Park** (☎ 949/494–3539) is a hidden treasure: a 3½-mi stretch of unspoiled beach with some of the best tidepooling in southern California. Here you can see starfish, crabs, and other sea life on the rocks. The park's 2,400 acres of backcountry are ideal for hiking, horseback riding, and mountain biking. Docents lead nature walks on weekend mornings. Parking costs $6 per car.

The town of Corona del Mar stretches only a few blocks along Pacific Coast Highway, but some of the fanciest stores in the county line the route.

㉑ Sherman Library and Gardens, a botanical garden and library specializing in the history of the Pacific Southwest, provides a diversion from sun and sand. You can wander among cactus gardens, rose gardens, a wheelchair-height touch-and-smell garden, and a tropical conservatory. ⊠ *2647 PCH,* ☎ *949/673–2261.* ⊡ *$3, free Mon.* ☉ *Daily 10:30–4.*

Dining

$$–$$$$ ✕ **The Bungalow.** Specializing in prime steaks and seafood, this Craftsman-style restaurant is known for its lobster with wild rice. The younger local moneyed set packs the place. ⊠ *2441 E. Coast Hwy.,* ☎ *949/673–6585. AE, MC, V. No lunch.*

$–$$$ ✕ **Bandera.** Pork cutlets, barbecued salmon, and New Orleans–style jambalaya are a few of the American regional specials you'll find at this popular, wood-paneled eatery. ⊠ *3201 E. Coast Hwy.,* ☎ *949/ 673–3524. Reservations not accepted. AE, DC, MC, V. No lunch.*

$ ✕ **Ruby's.** One of several branches of a home-grown chain of '40s-style diners serves Ruby's trademark burgers—widely regarded as the best in Orange County—along with "frings," a combination of onion rings and fries, and of course, thick shakes. Vegetarian tacos on whole-wheat tortillas aim to satisfy health-conscious eaters. ⊠ *2305 E. Coast Hwy.,* ☎ *949/673–7820. AE, D, DC, MC, V. No dinner.*

Laguna Beach

★ *10 mi south of Newport Beach on Hwy. 1; 60 mi south of Los Angeles, I–5 south to Hwy. 133 to Laguna Canyon Rd.*

The wealthy artist colony of Laguna Beach has been compared with New York City's SoHo, although its location is decidedly more picturesque. Traditionally a haven of conservative wealth, the town attracted the beat, hip, and far-out during the 1950s and '60s (along with what has grown to be Orange County's most visible gay community). The two camps coexist in relative harmony, with Art prevailing in the congested village, and Wealth entrenched in the surrounding canyons and hills. A 1993 fire, which destroyed more than 300 homes in the hillsides surrounding Laguna Beach, miraculously left the village untouched.

A statue commemorates Eiler Larsen, Laguna's town greeter, an old Dane who for years stood at the edge of town saying hello and goodbye to visitors. From time to time a man who calls himself Number One Archer assumes the role of greeter, waving to tourists from the corner of Pacific Coast Highway and Forest Avenue.

The town's main street, Pacific Coast Highway, is referred to as either South Coast or North Coast Highway, depending on the address. All along the highway and side streets such as Forest or Ocean avenues, you'll find dozens of eclectic fine-art and crafts galleries, clothing boutiques, and jewelry shops.

At the **Pageant of the Masters** (☎ 949/494–1145 or 800/487–3378), Laguna's most impressive event and part of the city's annual Festival of Arts, live models and carefully orchestrated backgrounds are arranged in striking mimicry of classical and contemporary paintings. The festival usually takes place in July and August.

㉑ The **Laguna Art Museum** displays American art, with an emphasis on California artists and works. Special exhibits change quarterly. ⌧ *307 Cliff Dr.,* ☎ *949/494–6531.* ⌧ *$5.* ☉ *Tues.–Sun. 11–5.*

Laguna Beach's **Main Beach Park,** at the end of Broadway at South Coast Highway, has sand volleyball, two half-basketball courts, children's play equipment, picnic areas, rest rooms, showers, and street parking. The colorful crowd ranges from authentic hippies to beach volleyball champs to celebrities such as Bette Midler, who has a home in Laguna.

Aliso Beach County Park (⌧ 31131 S. Coast Hwy., ☎ 949/661–7013) in south Laguna is a recreation area with a fishing pier, a playground, fire pits, parking, food stands, and rest rooms.

Woods Cove, off South Coast Highway at Diamond Street, is especially quiet during the week. Big rock formations hide lurking crabs. As you climb the steps to leave, you can see an English-style mansion that was once the home of Bette Davis.

Dining and Lodging

$$$–$$$$ ✕ **Five Feet.** Others have mimicked this restaurant's innovative blend
★ of Chinese and French cooking styles, but Five Feet remains the leader of the pack. Among the standout dishes: cheese wontons with raspberry coulis, fish in a garlic black-bean sauce, and rabbit with foie gras and wild mushrooms. The setting is pure Laguna: exposed ceiling, open kitchen, high noise level, and brick walls hung with works by local artists. ⌧ *328 Glenneyre St.,* ☎ *949/497–4955. AE, D, DC, MC, V. No lunch.*

$$$ ✕ **Sorrento Grille.** High ceilings and two walls of floor-to-ceiling windows create an illusion of space at this narrow restaurant on a quiet side street downtown. Mesquite steaks, seafood, and pastas predominate on the contemporary menu. ⌧ *370 Glenneyre St.,* ☎ *949/494–8686. AE, DC, MC, V. No lunch.*

$$–$$$ ✕ **Ti Amo.** A romantic setting and creative Mediterranean cuisine have earned this place acclaim. Try the seared tuna with a sesame-seed crust or farfalle with smoked chicken and creamy bell-pepper sauce. All the nooks and crannies are charming, candlelit, and private, but to max-

imize romance, request a table in the enclosed garden in back. ⊠ *31727 S. Coast Hwy.,* ☎ *949/499–5350. AE, D, DC, MC, V. No lunch.*

$$–$$$ ✕ **Odessa.** Sweet-potato gnocchi with salmon, potato-crusted catfish, and grilled lobster are on the Southern U.S.–influenced French menu. In the romantically dim-lit space, you may not notice the celebrities at the next table—or the stylish crowd heading upstairs to the nightclub. ⊠ *680 S. Coast Hwy.,* ☎ *949/376–8792. Reservations essential. AE, D, DC, MC, V. No lunch. Valet parking.*

$–$$ ✕ **Tortilla Flats.** This hacienda-style restaurant with a fireplace has a wide selection of Mexican tequilas and beers, and a quiet upstairs bar. Sunday brunch is a lively affair. ⊠ *1740 S. Coast Hwy.,* ☎ *949/494–6588. AE, MC, V.*

$ ✕ **Café Zinc.** Laguna Beach cognoscenti gather at the tiny counter and plant–filled patio of this vegetarian breakfast-and-lunch café. Oatmeal is sprinkled with berries, poached eggs are dusted with herbs, and the orange juice is fresh-squeezed. For lunch, try a sampler plate, with various salads like spicy Thai pasta, and asparagus salad with orange peel and capers; or one of the gourmet pizzettes. ⊠ *350 Ocean Ave.,* ☎ *949/494–6302. No credit cards. No dinner.*

$$$$ ▦ **Surf and Sand Hotel.** Laguna's largest hotel is right on the beach. Rooms have an appropriately beachlike feel, with soft sand colors, bleached-wood shutters, and private balconies. ⊠ *1555 S. Coast Hwy., 92651,* ☎ *949/497–4477 or 800/524–8621,* ℻ *949/494–2897. 145 rooms, 19 suites. Restaurant, bar, health club, pool, beach, concierge. AE, D, DC, MC, V.*

$$$$ ▦ **Inn at Laguna Beach.** On a bluff overlooking the ocean, the inn has
★   a Mediterranean feel, with terra-cotta tiles and exotic flowers all over the grounds. Most guest rooms have views; those on the coastal level border Laguna's oceanfront cliffs. The inn is close to Main Beach, yet far enough away to feel secluded. ⊠ *211 N. Coast Hwy., 92651,* ☎ *949/497–9722 or 800/544–4479,* ℻ *949/497–9972. 70 rooms. In-room VCRs, minibars, refrigerators, pool. AE, D, DC, MC, V.*

$$–$$$$ ▦ **Eiler's Inn.** A light-filled courtyard with a fountain is the focal point
★   of this quaint, European-style bed-and-breakfast. Every room is unique, but all are full of antiques and travelers' journals for you to fill in. Afternoon wine and cheese is served in the courtyard or in the cozy reading room, where you'll find the inn's only TV and phone. Breakfast usually includes scrumptious homemade breads; the owner used to be a pastry chef, and she still has the knack. A sundeck in back has an ocean view. ⊠ *741 S. Coast Hwy., 92651,* ☎ *949/494–3004,* ℻ *949/497–2215. 12 rooms. Full breakfast. AE, D, MC, V.*

$$–$$$$ ▦ **Hotel Laguna.** The oldest hotel in Laguna (opened in 1890) has manicured gardens, a private beach, and an ideal location downtown. Four rooms have canopy beds and reproduction Victorian furnishings. Others have whitewashed furniture and pastel bedspreads and curtains (none has air-conditioning). Complimentary wine and cheese are served every afternoon. ⊠ *425 S. Coast Hwy., 92651,* ☎ *949/494–1151 or 800/524–2927,* ℻ *949/497–2163. 63 rooms. 2 restaurants, bar, beach. Continental breakfast. AE, D, DC, MC, V.*

$–$$$$ ▦ **Coast Inn.** Gay men and some lesbians have been staying at the Coast Inn for more than three decades. Some rooms are standard motel-style; others are larger, with private decks and fireplaces. ⊠ *1401 S. Coast Hwy.,* ☎ *949/494–7588 or 800/653–2697,* ℻ *949/494–1735. 23 rooms. Restaurant, bar. AE, D, DC, MC, V.*

Nightlife

The **Boom Boom Room** (⊠ Coast Inn, 1401 S. Coast Hwy., ☎ 949/494–7588) is Laguna Beach's most popular gay club. The **Sandpiper**

(✉ 1183 S. Coast Hwy., ☎ 949/494–4694), a hole-in-the-wall dancing joint, attracts an eclectic crowd. Laguna's **White House** (✉ 340 S. Coast Hwy., ☎ 949/494–8088), a chic club on the main strip, has nightly entertainment and dancing.

Outdoor Activities and Sports

BICYCLING

Mountain bikes can be rented at **Rainbow Bicycles** (✉ 485 N. Coast Hwy., ☎ 949/494–5806).

GOLF

Aliso Creek Golf Course (✉ 31106 S. Coast Hwy., ☎ 949/499–1919) is a scenic nine-hole facility with a putting green. Greens fees range from $15 to $22; carts (optional) cost between $2 and $8. Reservations are taken up to a week in advance.

TENNIS

Six metered courts can be found at **Laguna Beach High School.** Two courts are available at the **Irvine Bowl.** Six courts are available at **Alta Laguna Park** on a first-come, first-served basis. **Moulton Meadows** has two lighted courts. For more information, call the **City of Laguna Beach Recreation Department** (☎ 949/497–0716).

WATER SPORTS

Because its entire beach area is a marine preserve, Laguna Beach has great snorkeling. Scuba divers head to the Marine Life Refuge area, which runs from Seal Rock to Diver's Cove. You can rent surfboards and bodyboards at **Hobie Sports** (✉ 294 Forest Ave., ☎ 949/497–3304).

Shopping

Forest and Ocean avenues are full of art galleries and fine jewelry and clothing boutiques. **Georgeo's Art Glass and Jewelry** (✉ 269 Forest Ave., ☎ 949/497–0907) has a large selection of etched-glass bowls, vases, and fine jewelry. **Marcus Animation Gallery** (✉ 220 Forest Ave., ☎ 949/494–8102) displays 3-D multimedia art and animation from Disney and Warner Bros. The **Art Center Gallery** (✉ 266 Forest Ave., ☎ 949/376–7596) exhibits the works of local artists.

Dana Point

10 mi south of Laguna Beach, Hwy. 1.

Dana Point's claim to fame is its small-boat marina tucked into a dramatic natural harbor and surrounded by high bluffs. In late February, a whale festival features concerts, films, sports competitions, and a weekend street fair. **Dana Point Harbor** was first described more than 100 years ago by its namesake Richard Henry Dana in his book *Two Years Before the Mast.* At the marina are docks for small boats, marine-oriented shops, and some restaurants.

Inside Dana Point Harbor, **Swim Beach** has a fishing pier, barbecues, food stands, parking, rest rooms, and showers. At the south end of Dana Point, **Doheny State Park** (☎ 949/496–6171) is one of southern California's top surfing destinations. Here you'll also find an interpretive center devoted to the wildlife of the Doheny Marine Refuge, as well as food stands and shops, picnic facilities, and a pier for fishing. Camping is permitted, though there are no hookups.

🖐 ㉒ Two indoor tanks at the **Orange County Marine Institute** contain touchable sea creatures, as well as the complete skeleton of a gray whale. Anchored near the institute is *The Pilgrim,* a full-size replica of the square-rigged vessel on which Richard Henry Dana sailed. You can tour the boat Sunday from 10 to 2:30. Weekend cruises are also available. You can arrange to go whale-watching from January through March, or to explore regional tide pools year-round. ⊠ *24200 Dana Point Harbor Dr.,* ☏ *949/496–2274.* ☜ *Donation requested.* ☉ *Daily 10–4:30.*

Dining and Lodging

$–$$$ ✗ **Luciana's.** This intimate Italian restaurant is a real find, especially for couples seeking a romantic evening. Dining rooms are small, dressed with crisp white linens and warmed by fireplaces. Try the linguine with clams, prawns, calamari, and green-lip mussels in a light tomato sauce; grilled cured pork chops in a fennel-herb marinade; or veal medallions with haricot verts and oven-dried tomatoes. ⊠ *24312 Del Prado Ave.,* ☏ *949/661–6500. AE, DC, MC, V. No lunch.*

$ ✗ **Proud Mary's.** On a terrace overlooking the fishing boats and pleasure craft in Dana Point Harbor, Proud Mary's serves the best burgers and sandwiches in southern Orange County. Steaks, chicken, and other American standards are served at dinnertime, and you can order breakfast all day. ⊠ *34689 Golden Lantern,* ☏ *949/493–5853. AE, D, MC, V. No dinner.*

$$$$ ✗🏨 **Ritz-Carlton, Laguna Niguel.** An unrivaled setting on the edge of
★ the Pacific combined with the hallmark Ritz-Carlton service have earned this grand hotel worldwide recognition. An imposing marble-columned entryway is surrounded by landscaped grounds; the overall impression is that of a Mediterranean country villa. Rooms have marble bathrooms and private balconies with ocean or pool views. Tea is served afternoons in the library. In the formal Dining Room men must wear jackets), you can choose courses from chef Yvon Goetz's French-Mediterranean prix-fixe menu; the price depends on the number of courses. Foie gras with baby leeks in a truffle vinaigrette makes an outstanding precursor to monkfish medallions with pearl onions or roasted duck breast. Subdued lighting, crystal chandeliers, and original paintings on the walls add to the dining experience. The Dining Room is open for dinner only; reservations are essential. ⊠ *1 Ritz-Carlton Dr., 92629,* ☏ *949/240–2000 or 800/241–3333,* 𝖥𝖠𝖷 *949/240–0829. 332 rooms, 31 suites. 3 restaurants, lobby lounge, 2 pools, beauty salon, massage, 4 tennis courts, health club, concierge. AE, D, DC, MC, V.*

$$$–$$$$ 🏨 **Blue Lantern Inn.** Combining New England–style architecture with
★ a southern California setting, this white clapboard B&B rests on a bluff, overlooking the harbor and ocean. A fire warms the intimate living area, where guests are invited to enjoy complimentary afternoon snacks and play backgammon. The French country–style guest rooms also have fireplaces, as well as soda-filled refrigerators and whirlpool tubs. The top-floor tower suite has a 180° ocean view. ⊠ *34343 St. of the Blue Lantern, 92629,* ☏ *949/661–1304,* 𝖥𝖠𝖷 *949/496–1483. 29 rooms. Exercise room, concierge. AE, DC, MC, V. Full breakfast.*

$$$–$$$$ 🏨 **Marriott's Laguna Cliffs Resort.** Formerly known as the Dana Point Resort, this white-washed hillside hotel looks straight out of Cape Cod, except that its views are of the Pacific, not the Atlantic. On Sunday evenings in summer, the Capistrano Valley Symphony performs on the resort's landscaped grounds. ⊠ *25135 Park Lantern, 92629,* ☏ *949/661–5000 or 800/533–9748,* 𝖥𝖠𝖷 *949/661–5358. 332 rooms, 18 suites. Restaurant, bar, lobby lounge, 2 pools, 2 outdoor hot tubs, basketball, croquet, health club, volleyball. AE, D, DC, MC, V.*

Outdoor Activities and Sports

Rental stands for surfboards, Windsurfers, small powerboats, and sailboats can be found near most of the piers. **Embarcadero Marina** (⊠ *34512 Embarcadero Pl.,* ☏ *949/496–6177*) has powerboats and sailboats for rent near the launching ramp at Dana Point Harbor. **Hobie Sports** (✉ 24825 Del Prado, ☎ 949/496–2366) rents surfboards and Boogie boards. **Dana Wharf Sportfishing** (✉ 34675 Golden Lantern St., ☎ 949/496–5794) runs charters and weekend parasailing trips, and whale-watching excursions (from early December to late March).

San Juan Capistrano

5 mi north of Dana Point, Hwy. 74; 60 mi north of San Diego, I–5.

San Juan Capistrano is best known for its mission and for the swallows that migrate here each year from their winter haven in Argentina. The arrival of the birds on St. Joseph's Day, March 19, launches a week of festivities. After summering in the arches of the old stone church, the swallows head home on St. John's Day, October 23.

If you arrive by train, you will be dropped off across from the Mission at the San Juan Capistrano depot. With its appealing brick café and preserved Santa Fe cars, the depot retains much of the magic of early American railroads. If driving, park near Ortega and Camino Capistrano, the city's main streets, which are lined with colorful restaurants and boutiques.

★ ㉓ **Mission San Juan Capistrano,** founded in 1776 by Father Junípero Serra, was the major Roman Catholic outpost between Los Angeles and San Diego. Though the original Great Stone Church is permanently supported by scaffolding, many of the mission's adobe buildings have been preserved to illustrate mission life, with exhibits of an olive millstone, tallow ovens, tanning vats, metalworking furnaces, and padres' living quarters. The bougainvillea-covered Serra Chapel is believed to be the oldest building standing in California. Mass takes place at 7 AM daily. ✉ *Camino Capistrano and Ortega Hwy.,* ☎ *949/248–2049.* 🎫 *$4.* ☉ *Daily 8:30–5.*

㉔ Near Mission San Juan Capistrano is the **San Juan Capistrano Library,** a postmodern structure erected in 1983. Architect Michael Graves combined a classical design with the style of the mission to striking effect. Its courtyard has secluded places for reading. ✉ *31495 El Camino Real,* ☎ *949/493–1752.* ☉ *Mon.–Thurs. 10–9, Fri.–Sat. 10–5.*

Dining

$$–$$$ ✕ **L'Hirondelle.** Roast duck, rabbit, and many Belgian dishes are on
★ the menu at this French and Belgian restaurant. You can dine inside or out on the patio. ✉ *31631 Camino Capistrano,* ☎ *949/661–0425. AE, MC, DC, D, V. Closed Mon. No lunch Tues.*

$–$$$ ✕ **Cedar Creek Inn.** Equally suitable for family meals and romantic get-
★ away dinners, the inn has a children's menu as well as a secluded outdoor patio with a roaring fireplace for couples dining alone. The contemporary American menu features crowd-pleasers like an ahi burger, rack of lamb, and herb-crusted halibut. ✉ *26860 Ortega Hwy.,* ☎ *949/240–2229. AE, DC, MC, V.*

$–$$ ✕ **El Adobe.** This historic, early Mission–style eatery serves enormous portions of mildly seasoned Mexican food. Mariachi bands play Friday and Saturday nights and during Sunday brunch. ✉ *31891 Camino Capistrano,* ☎ *949/830–8620. AE, D, DC, MC, V.*

Nightlife

Coach House (✉ 33157 Camino Capistrano, ☎ 949/496–8930), a roomy, casual club with long tables and a dark wood bar, draws crowds of varying ages for entertainment from hip, new bands to mellow acoustic guitar to comedy acts.

OFF THE
BEATEN PATH

SAN CLEMENTE – Ten miles south of Dana Point on Pacific Coast Highway, San Clemente has 20 sq mi of prime bicycling terrain. Camp Pendleton, the country's largest Marine Corps base, welcomes cyclists to use some of its roads—just don't be surprised to see a troop helicopter taking off right beside you. Surfers favor San Clemente State Beach (☎ 949/492–3156), which also has camping facilities, RV hookups, and fire rings. San Onofre State Beach, just south of San Clemente, is another surfing destination. Below the bluffs are 3½ mi of sandy beach, where you can swim, fish, and watch wildlife.

ORANGE COUNTY A TO Z

Arriving and Departing

By Bus

The **Los Angeles MTA** ☎ 213/626-4455 has limited service to Orange County. From downtown, Bus 460 goes to Knott's Berry Farm and Disneyland. **Greyhound** (☎ 714/999–1256) serves Anaheim and Santa Ana.

By Car

The San Diego Freeway (I–405) and the Santa Ana Freeway (I–5) run north and south through Orange County. South of Laguna I–405 merges into I–5 (which is called the San Diego Freeway south from this point). Avoid these freeways during rush hours (6–9 AM and 3:30–6 PM), when they can back up for miles.

By Plane

The county's main facility is **John Wayne Airport Orange County** (✉ MacArthur Blvd. at I–405, ☎ 949/252–5252, in Santa Ana. It is served by Alaska, America West, American, Continental, Delta, Northwest, Southwest, TWA, United, and several commuter airlines. ☞ Air Travel *in* the Gold Guide for airline phone numbers.

Los Angeles International Airport, known as LAX, is only 35 mi west of Anaheim. **Ontario International Airport** is just northwest of Riverside, 30 mi north of Anaheim. **Long Beach Airport** is about 20 minutes by bus from Anaheim. See the Gold Guide for more information.

BETWEEN THE AIRPORTS AND HOTELS

If you're driving from John Wayne to downtown Anaheim, take Highway 55 North to the Golden State Freeway (I–5) North, and exit at Katella Avenue. To get to downtown L.A., take the San Diego Freeway (I–405) to the Santa Monica Freeway (I–10) East to the Harbor Freeway (I–110) North; to Beverly Hills, take the San Diego Freeway North to Santa Monica Boulevard.

Airport Bus (☎ 800/772–5299), a shuttle service, carries passengers from John Wayne and LAX to Anaheim and Buena Park. The fare from John Wayne to Anaheim is $10, from LAX to Anaheim $14.

Prime Time Airport Shuttle (☎ 800/262–7433) provides door-to-door service from Orange County hotels to LAX and the San Pedro cruise terminal. The fare is $37 per person, plus $9 for each additional family member, from Anaheim hotels to LAX.

SuperShuttle (☎ 714/517–6600) provides 24-hour door-to-door service from all the airports to all points in Orange County. The fare to the Disneyland area is $10 per person from John Wayne, $34 from Ontario, $13 from LAX, and $33 from Long Beach Airport.

BY TRAIN

Amtrak (☎ 800/872–7245) makes several daily stops in Orange County: at Fullerton, Anaheim, Santa Ana, Irvine, San Juan Capistrano, and San Clemente.

Metrolink (☎ 714/808–5465) is a weekday commuter train that runs to and from Los Angeles and Orange County, starting as far south as San Clemente and stopping in San Juan Capistrano, Irvine, Santa Ana, Orange, and Anaheim.

Getting Around

By Bus
The **Orange County Transportation Authority** (OCTA, ☎ 714/636–7433) will take you virtually anywhere in the county, but it will take time; OCTA buses go from Knott's Berry Farm and Disneyland to Huntington and Newport beaches. Bus 1 travels along the coast; there is also an express bus to Los Angeles.

By Car
Highways 55 and 91 head west to the ocean and east into the mountains: Take Highway 91 to Garden Grove and inland points (Buena Park, Anaheim). Highway 55 leads to Newport Beach. Pacific Coast Highway (Highway 1) allows easy access to beach communities and is the most scenic route.

Contacts and Resources

Emergencies
Ambulance (☎ 911). **Fire** (☎ 911). **Police** (☎ 911).

Anaheim Memorial Hospital (✉ 1111 W. La Palma Ave., ☎ 714/774–1450). **Western Medical Center** (✉ 1025 S. Anaheim Blvd., Anaheim, ☎ 714/533–6220). **Hoag Memorial Presbyterian Hospital** (✉ 301 Newport Blvd., Newport Beach, ☎ 949/645–8600). **South Coast Medical Center** (✉ 31872 PCH, Laguna Beach, ☎ 949/499–1311). **Children's Hospital of Orange County** (✉ 455 S. Main St., Orange, ☎ 714/997-3000).

Guided Tours
Pacific Coast Gray Line Tours (☎ 714/978–8855) provides guided tours from Orange County hotels to Disneyland, Knott's Berry Farm, Universal Studios Hollywood, Six Flags Magic Mountain, and the San Diego Zoo.

Visitor Information
Anaheim-Orange County Visitor and Convention Bureau (✉ Anaheim Convention Center, 800 W. Katella Ave., 92802, ☎ 714/999–8999). **Huntington Beach Conference and Visitors Bureau** (✉ 101 Main St., Suite 2A, 92648, ☎ 714/969–3492). **Laguna Beach Visitors Bureau and Chamber of Commerce** (✉ 252 Broadway, 92652, ☎ 949/494–1018). **Newport Beach Conference and Visitors Bureau** (✉ 3300 W. Coast Hwy., 92663, ☎ 800/942–6278). **San Juan Capistrano Chamber of Commerce and Visitors Center** (✉ 31931 Camino Capistrano, Suite D, 92675, ☎ 949/493–4700). **Southern California Golf Association** (☎ 818/980–3630). **Southern California Public Links Golf Association** (☎ 714/994–4747).

10 Portraits of Los Angeles

Beneath Mulholland

It's Back to the Future for L.A.

Books and Videos

BENEATH MULHOLLAND

IT IS A DRIVE and a highway, running east-west, the supreme vantage point for the entirety of Los Angeles and the San Fernando Valley. You can stand up there and feel like Christ—or the Devil. Mulholland Drive allows both roles.

Like any road, it has an A and a B that it connects. But Mulholland is more concerned with being up there than with destination. Few travel its length, except as explorers; and as it makes that winding automobile journey it is several different roads and moods, going from Shampoo to Shane. Mulholland is a phenomenon of Los Angeles, both an idealized spectacle and a place from which to survey the classic city of visibility. Even as you drive, the panorama turns into a model for grace and dread.

Imagine Marilyn Monroe, 50 mi long, lying on her side, half-buried on a ridge of crumbling rock, the crest of the Santa Monica Mountains, with chaparral, flowers, and snakes writhing over her body, and mists, smog, or dreams gathering in every curve. You'd need a certain height to recognize that intricate course as a body. But that's Mulholland, and you can drive it whenever you've got an hour and a half to spare, pursuing the ridge between Cahuenga and the Pacific. It's about as long as an old movie, and as full of scents and half-grasped fears and splendors as Marilyn's drowsy state.

Play with that fancy. Her toes twitch at the Hollywood Freeway, vaguely disturbed by the furious traffic of gnats. From the knob of her ankle you can look down on the Hollywood Bowl, turn east to the HOLLYWOOD sign or see downtown skyscrapers looming in the stream like guns in a Turkish bath. As the legs become thighs, Mulholland enters its richest stretch, full of designer security systems for houses hiding from the road, of sprinklers hissing at the bougainvillea and the blinding roses, of glamourous real estate, the Mulholland where young giants of the city live, some of them with views north and south, of San Fernando's pimento suburbia and the gray daytime swell of L.A., which at night goes MTV in black fur and diamond lights. At the most precious, privileged part of the body, where the thighs widen and foliage starts, you can find the secret mansion of Warren Beatty, high on its own escarpment, guarded by trees and Bauhaus bars.

There are those who think of only this Mulholland, who would not go beyond the low belt that is the San Diego Freeway. But there's much more to find. A little west of the freeway, Mulholland becomes a dirt road for nearly 8 mi, as far as Topanga Canyon Boulevard. In a minute of driving, you give up the serene sway from one curve to another for a violent, jolting surface and roadside weeds so dusty their short season of green looks like the color of dollars.

This must be the belly of the beast, grumbling at what is has eaten. There are no houses or telephones, none of the firehouses from the wealthy, worried section. If you broke down, you would be stranded. To the north you can see the sharkskin surface of the Encino Reservoir, but to the south there are only empty concertina folds of hillside where hawks spin in the mauve and gold dust of sunset. You could lose a Live Aid concert down in Topanga State Park. How much easier for a few desperate people to lurk there. The dirt road section of Mulholland is a place for paranoia—eerily empty on weekdays at noon, a bikers' track on weekends and a place for furtive love and dealing. You sometimes come upon a parked care with talk too delicate to approach. And there are mattresses dying in the brush where who knows what trysts were enjoyed, or how long ago.

Just as you think you are lost, the hardtop resumes and you slide into a little patch of community before the last long section—the ribs, the breasts, the shoulders, and throat. This rolling countryside contains a distant dewdrop green golf course; a ranch where stunts are filmed; riding trails; the homes of solitaries, artists, and eccentrics; a mock Alpine section; a trashy trailer park; the three satellite dishes of a Jewish recreation center; hillsides burnt black by the latest fires; and, at last, the highest number on Mulholland, 35375, a camp for blind children, which is set among eucalyptus trees. Then there's the sea. A beach named after actor Leo Carrillo, sidekick to the Cisco Kid, and platinum surf like Marilyn's hair in her last pictures.

Some say the road was built for that journey, so that the sweaty poor of Bunker Hill and Fairfax secretaries could get to the sea for relief. There are faster ways now, of course, on the freeways of Santa Monica Boulevard. And even in 1923–24, when Mulholland was built, the road was more a gesture of triumph and philosophy than a means of transport.

That's why it was named after William Mulholland (1855–1935), the superintendent of the L.A. Water Department, who designed and presided over the scheme that sucked water from the Owens Valley, 250 mi away, to make Los Angeles fertile, flush-friendly, and be-pooled. No water tanks need more pumping than those on Mulholland, and the well-watered thighs still bloom in William's honor. Mulholland is regarded now as a robber baron and an ecological rapist: this is the "bless me for I have sinned" the Angeleno murmurs whenever he enters the shower or drops into the copper sulphate pools that fill every navel and armpit along Mulholland. In other words, no one is sending the water back to the parched and desolate Owens Valley. They're keeping it, along with the casual guilt.

"There it is—take it," is what Mulholland is supposed to have said, of the water and the brutal advantage of clout. Mulholland Drive still lives on that advice, just as Hollywood taught us to cherish scoundrels. The road is like a location in a film, chosen and dressed for its magnificent vantage and for the juxtaposition of inane civilization and a dangerous wilderness. This is where the desert touches Gucci and Mercedes, where pet chihuahuas can be eaten by coyotes. Mulholland has buildings that could topple into the canyons: the John Lautner Chemosphere stands on one concrete stem, and there is a tennis court on stilts. It has rich homes that might be descended on at night by anarchists, murderers, or nightmare Apaches. There is even a Manson Avenue that runs off Mulholland: you have to wonder whether it was scripted tribute or magical impromptu.

Mulholland is a pinup and an idea: it has Brancusis in some groomed gardens, and beer bottles shattered from target practice a few miles farther on. Its function is to embody that contrast: it is a highway made for narcissism and envy, an example of privilege, luxury, and airy superiority that whispers, "Look at me—take me, if you can." The road, the drive, the highway all thrill to the way man has commanded natural power and beauty here and turned them into a property or a story. That HOLLYWOOD at the eastern end, letters 50 feet high, is a title, a caption: it's there to tell us the landscape is a kept woman as well as collapsing topography. And the road is called Mulholland Drive so that you know you should be wary of anyone on foot.

— David Thomson

IT'S BACK TO THE FUTURE FOR L.A.

WE STEPPED INTO the elevator at the L.A. International Airport's central building, the one that looks like a spaceship with legs, and pressed the button for Encounters restaurant. Pulsating space-age music—wild synthesizer riffs with a strong backbeat—throbbed from speakers overhead. It sounded like music to leave the galaxy by, and when the doors opened again it seemed we actually had. Picture a handful of sci-fi movies tossed together and arranged at random, and you get an idea of what the place looked like: Designed by Disney Imagineering, it's a riot of free-form stainless steel modules, sinuous bar counters with bright, gemlike blobs suspended in clear primordial ooze, and a white plastic reception stand that looked capable of wrapping itself around the hostess and taking a bite.

Through panoramic windows we gazed out at real life going on outside as planes from all over the world landed, taxied, and stood waiting for passengers and cargo. How appropriate that this restaurant inside the gateway to the City of Angels should look like a set from *The Jetsons*. L.A. has always had a knack for reaching back to historic ideas of the future in its tireless quest to remake its own image. From the silent film *Metropolis* to *Blade Runner* to the *Alien* movies, Hollywood has predicted the fate of everything from technology to fashion, sometimes with uncanny accuracy. Miscues are easy to fix: If one image doesn't turn out as planned, the dream machine simply cranks out another.

The future has always been an L.A. specialty. About the time Walt Disney was planning Disneyland in the nearby Orange County city of Anaheim and science-fiction films were pouring out of Hollywood, mid-'50s L.A. was replacing its wartime airplane-production economy with postwar aeronautics. Engineers, scientists, and other futurists developed the systems that eventually linked the entire region, from roadways to telephone lines to early cyberlinks.

"It's back to the future for L.A." Sam Hall Kaplan, an urban-affairs commentator who has studied trends and social issues in the city for decades. Ranging over 34,000 sq mi, with a population larger than that of 47 states in the United States, the five-county L.A. area "has become again a number of villages, scattered but not fragmented, thanks to connections built between them." Many of those connections travel along fiberoptic cable—nearly a million citizens telecommute.

The stage was set early on for L.A.'s lightning-speed growth. By the 1960s, as tourists were pouring into California in ever-increasing numbers, movie studios realized the potential for a lucrative amusement-park business. At Universal Studios Hollywood, what started in 1963 as a short tour that included a single stunt and a peek at a film set has grown into a full-fledged theme park with what is widely considered the best ride simulator in the world—appropriately named Back to the Future and based on the movie. The visceral experience of flying through the air as objects of the past whiz by may well sum up the essence of L.A. Meanwhile Disneyland unveiled its new Tomorrowland in 1998, a vision of the future as seen through the eyes of Jules Verne and other futurists of yesterday. Tomorrowland's Rocket Rods thrill ride, which travels on the tracks of the park's former monorail, is the fastest and longest ride in Disneyland's history. (A second Disney park, California Adventure, is scheduled to open nearby in 2001, with Hollywood- and Yosemite-themed rides.)

But regardless of theme-park attractions, the original Tomorrowland is L.A. itself. Taking a page from the book of Proteus, the Greek god who could change form at will, residents have a knack for remaking their town and themselves. There are more plastic surgeons per capita in Los Angeles than any other city in the world. At a prominent Westside hotel, an entire floor is set aside discreetly for people recovering from plastic surgery, from eye lifts to tummy tucks. At the megapopular fitness club Crunch!—just off Sunset in the new Virgin complex—the latest exercise fad, a Sunday-only affair, illustrates what happens when the quest for meaning collides with the pursuit of a perfect body: At "Gospel Aerobics," live singers belt out spirituals like "The Saints Go Marching In" while the faithful do their daily penance for yesterday's double latte.

As L.A. spins toward the end of the century, the present culture doesn't look much like the one portrayed in the films of the future. Sandy Potter of Directives West, a local company that predicts fashion trends, suggests that 2000 and beyond will not look at all like what was predicted in the sci-fi films of the 1950s, at least in what we wear. Potter and her partner haunt hot shops and clubs to find that instead of hard-edged, minimalist space uniforms, softness, comfort, and femininity are in. A response to today's hectic lifestyle? Yes, partly—but it's also what they're wearing on the TV shows of the moment. Says Potter, "*Melrose Place, Beverly Hills 90210,* and MTV can change fashion in a nanosecond." Even technology plays a role, as evidenced by Gothic touches—dark, cloak-like clothing and heavy, chain-style jewelry—cropping up in couture, a nod to Dungeon and Dragons–style video games.

Across town, a different kind of change is happening. The Jet Propulsion Laboratory (JPL) in Pasadena has reinvented itself so thoroughly that it no longer has anything to do with jet propulsion. The facility's job these days is to launch unmanned spacecraft and develop robotics. Hardly immune from the influence of sci-fi movies and TV series, JPL has even named its New Millennium project Deep Space 1, a nod to the TV series *Deep Space Nine,* according to physicist Dr. Marc Rayman. The media connection carries over in other ways, too: The term "ion propulsion" first appeared on a *Star Trek* episode before it was even possible in real life, says Rayman's colleague, John Watson. Now, years later, the technology has progressed and JPL is using xenon ion propulsion on its Deep Space 1 project to Mars and beyond, the first time this type of energy source has ever been tested.

During the 20th century, the world viewed Los Angeles as the prototypical city of the future in part because of its jagged sprawl. Freeways reshaped the city as the automobile erased former boundaries. The car will always be the defining icon of L.A., a point the Petersen Automobile Museum makes clear, but Los Angeles is now refashioning itself as a landscape knit together by public transportation: the blue, green, and red subway lines. Soon the Metro will even reach Los Angeles International Airport.

Even though tourism has increased in Los Angeles, L.A. refuses to rest on its showbiz laurels. As the millennium approaches, its imagemakers are forging a new identity for the city: that of an art and culture capital. Residents hope that as the world's eye gazes on the spectacular new Getty Museum complex in Brentwood, it will wander also to some of its other 50-plus major museums, and to its hundreds of theaters and performance spaces.

Intent on becoming the arts powerhouse of the next millennium, L.A. continues to trumpet its cutting-edge contemporary concepts and technology. Signs of its cultural bloom have sprung up all over the county. At a downtown artist colony in the former Pabst brewery, 400 artists live, paint, sculpt, and create.

For those who think of L.A. primarily as the land of the permanent tan and endless beaches, the local retort is: "A beach with a ballet is a better beach!" Will L.A. become the Paris of the next thousand years? Stranger things have happened. Stand back: L.A. is reinventing itself once again.

—Judith Babcock Wylie

Judith Babcock Wylie is a travel writer who lives in Santa Cruz, California, and writes in a cabin overlooking the ocean. She is a contributing editor for Honeymoon *magazine and editor of* Travelers' Tales, Love and Romance, *an anthology of essays about romance on the road.*

BOOKS AND VIDEOS

Books

Los Angeles: The Enormous Village, 1781–1981, by John D. Weaver, and *Los Angeles: Biography of a City,* by John and LaRee Caughey, will give you a fine background in how it came to be the city it is today. The unique social and cultural life of the whole southern California area is explored in *Southern California: An Island on the Land,* by Carey McWilliams.

David Thomson muses on Hollywood and its ghosts in the essay anthology *Mulholland Drive.* *Stars Screaming,* the first novel by John Kaye, explores the seamier side of the "new" Hollywood of the late 1960s and early '70s.

City of Nets: A Portrait of Hollywood in the '40s, by Otto Friedrich, is a social and cultural history of Hollywood's golden age. Mike Davis's *City of Quartz* discusses the social history of Los Angeles as both a utopia and dystopia.

One of the most outstanding features of Los Angeles is its architecture. *Los Angeles: The Architecture of Four Ecologies,* by Reyner Banham, relates the physical environment to the architecture. *Architecture in Los Angeles: A Compleat Guide,* by David Gebhard and Robert Winter, is exactly what the title promises and is very useful.

Many novels have been written with Los Angeles as the setting. One of the very best, Nathanael West's *Day of the Locust,* was first published in 1939, but still rings true. Budd Schulberg's *What Makes Sammy Run?,* Evelyn Waugh's *The Loved One,* and Joan Didion's *Play It As It Lays* are unforgettable. Other novels that give a sense of contemporary life in Los Angeles are *Sex and Rage,* by Eve Babitz, and *Less Than Zero,* by Bret Easton Ellis. Raymond Chandler and Ross Macdonald have written many suspense novels with a Los Angeles background. Some of Chandler's titles include *Farewell My Lovely, The Big Sleep,* and *The Long Goodbye.*

Get Shorty, by Elmore Leonard, is an amusing tale about a Miami loan shark in Tinseltown. Another entertaining read is *Los Angeles Without a Map,* by Richard Rayner.

Compass American Guides' *Hollywood* is a photo-filled guidebook with a history of L.A. as seen through the movies.

Videos and TV

Los Angeles appears in countless films and television shows as Anywhere, U.S.A., but it stars as itself each year in a handful of productions, some of which analyze the city's hold on the country's imagination. *What Price Hollywood?* (1932) was one of the first sound films to explore cinematic stardom—it was remade, three times, as *A Star Is Born* (1937, 1954, 1976). The price young actresses will pay to make it to the big time has been the subject of numerous pictures, among them the goofy *Hollywood Boulevard* (1977), whose producer bet Roger Corman, the impresario of the low-budget New World production company, that he could whip up a movie for less than any of Corman's other films. (He succeeded: The movie cost $80,000 to make.) *Hollywood Cavalcade* (1939), the story of an aging producer, provides a glimpse into the silent era. For a look at the lighter side of moviemaking's golden age, check out *Hollywood Canteen* (1944), which depicts Tinseltown doing its part during World War II.

The ups and downs of stardom are the subject of director Billy Wilder's *Sunset Boulevard* (1950), in which Gloria Swanson plays a faded film star, and the Gene Kelly musical *Singing in the Rain* (1952). The era of *Sunset Boulevard* seems innocent when compared to the shenanigans highlighted in the film version of the novel *Play It As It Lays* (1972), in which a failed actress reflects on a life gone awry. Director John Schlesinger's brilliant film version of the *The Day of the Locust* (1975), starring Donald Sutherland, is perhaps the most scathing analysis of the movie business ever shot. Robert Altman's *The Player* (1992), in which a movie producer commits murder, shows how little has changed in Tinseltown, the proliferation of cellular telephones and other high-tech accoutrements of deal-making notwith-standing.

Roman Polanski's *Chinatown* (1974), arguably one of the best American films ever made, is a fictional account of the wheeling and dealing that helped make L.A. what it is today. Some of the same themes are explored in Curtis Hanson's *L.A. Confidential* (1997). Another mood piece in which Los Angeles plays itself is *The Big Sleep* (1946), the Howard Hawks adaptation of Raymond Chandler's novel. Hal Ashby's *Shampoo* (1975), starring Warren Beatty as a libidinous hairdresser, blithely skewers the mores of 1970s L.A. *Fast Times at Ridgemont High* (1982) and *Valley Girl* (1983) do the same for the 1980s; *Romy and Michelle's High School Reunion* (1997) carries the theme into the 1990s.

INDEX

WHEVER YOU TRAVEL, *H*ELP IS NEVER FAR AWAY.

From planning your trip to providing travel assistance along the way, American Express® Travel Service Offices are always there to help you do more.

Los Angeles

American Express Travel Service
The Omni Center
901 West 7th Street
213/627-4800

American Express Travel Service
8493 West 3rd Street
At La Cienega Blvd.
310/659-1682

Wide World Tours, Inc. (R)
11777 San Vincente Blvd.
310/207-5570

Travel

http://www.americanexpress.com/travel

American Express Travel Service Offices are located throughout California. For the office nearest you, call 1-800-AXP-3429.